O'NEILL'S SCENIC IMAGES

O'NEILL'S
SCENIC
IMAGES

BY TIMO TIUSANEN

PRINCETON UNIVERSITY PRESS

PRINCETON, NEW JERSEY 1968

Printed in the United States of America
by Princeton University Press, Princeton, New Jersey

This book has been composed in Times Roman type.

To Ritva, my wife

in memory of those long hot summers

PREFACE

If Finland had not kept paying back her debts to the United States between the two world wars, this book would probably not exist. A program of cultural exchange financed by those payments made it possible for me to spend the academic year 1963-64 at Yale University on an ASLA (Amerikan Suomen lainan apuraha, or Grant from America's Loan to Finland) scholarship. This book is the result of that year's research.

I am thus indebted to the ASLA program itself and to those who encouraged me to apply for it and helped me to get it by their recommendations: Dr. Kaarlo Marjanen, Professors Arvi Kivimaa, Oiva Ketonen, Ole Reuter, and Irma Rantavaara. Miss Rantavaara, my teacher and superior colleague at the University of Helsinki, has helped me greatly with her valuable criticism at various stages of the work. I am grateful to Professor Tauno F. Mustanoja for his remarks on an early version of the manuscript, and to Suomen Kulttuurirahasto (The Finnish Cultural Foundation) and Emil Aaltosen Säätiö (Emil Aaltonen's Foundation) for the grants which made it possible for me to complete my project in Finland.

The late John Gassner, a fine scholar and a generous man, was my academic advisor at Yale. He was the first to read portions of an early version of the manuscript, and to encourage me to go on. Professor Alois M. Nagler conducted a lecture and seminar class at Yale based on a scenic approach to drama, from which I learned a great deal. All in all, I found the atmosphere at Yale favorable for my work. (Apparently there have been so many foreign students at Yale that their idiosyncracies are accepted with tolerance.) Mr. and Mrs. John A. Sword, Mrs. Hilma Penttinen, and Mr.

and Mrs. Oliver Penttinen helped to make my stay in New Haven a pleasant one.

It has been a pleasure to cooperate with Princeton University Press. I am especially grateful to Miss R. Miriam Brokaw and Miss Lalor Cadley for their constructive criticism of my work, for the sympathy shown to my special situation, and for their dedication, care, and skill in preparing and printing the manuscript. Miss Cadley has done a superb job of editing the text and helping me to collect the photographs and sketches published herein.

My thanks are due to Mrs. Carlotta Monterey O'Neill for her generous permission to quote from three of O'Neill's unpublished manuscripts and to reprint three stage settings drawn by O'Neill. These sketches, as well as a copy of *Now I Ask You* and a portrait of the playwright published here, belong to the O'Neill Collection in the Collection of American Literature, Yale University Library. Dr. Donald Gallup, Curator of the Collection, has been very sympathetic and helpful.

The Plays of Eugene O'Neill I-III, The Iceman Cometh, and *A Moon for the Misbegotten* are quoted by permission of Random House, Inc.; *O'Neill*, by Arthur and Barbara Gelb, by permission of Harper & Row, Inc.; and Robert Brustein's *The Theatre of Revolt* (Atlantic-Little, Brown) by permission of Little, Brown and Co.

Miss Rauha Riihinen, Mr. Kaarlo Lausti, the staffs of the HYY Library and the Helsinki University Library, Mrs. Ritva Heikkilä, and Messrs. Veikko Sorsakivi, Ahmed Riza, Simo Tavaste, and Veli Sandell have helped me in various ways; I am grateful to them and to Mr. Reima Kekäläinen, who checked my quotations and worked on the index. The index was completed with the assistance of Miss Liisa Byckling.

This book is dedicated to my wife—in gratitude for her patience and encouragement during the past five years.

Helsinki, on the 5th of August, 1968
Timo Tiusanen

CONTENTS

CONTENTS

ILLUSTRATIONS

1. *All God's Chillun Got Wings.* Ella and Jim (Anni Hämäläinen and Kalle Kirjavainen) leaving the church in the scenic image of Act I. The play was directed by Eino Salmelainen in the Tampereen Teatteri, Tampere, in 1932.

2. *Mourning Becomes Electra.* Christine (Pauline Brunius) sitting above Lavinia (Kerstin Nylander) and Ezra (Axel Slangus) on the steps of the Mannon house. The play was performed in the Swedish Theatre of Helsinki in 1934 under the direction of Gerda Wrede.

3. Profile of the young O'Neill. Reprinted by permission of Dr. Donald Gallup, Curator of the Collection of American Literature at Yale University.

4. *More Stately Mansions.* O'Neill's own sketch of the façade of the Harford mansion.

5. Sketch by O'Neill of the sitting room in Sara's house, *More Stately Mansions*, Act I, Scene iii.

6. O'Neill's sketch for the parlor of the Harford mansion, Act II, Scene iii.

7. *More Stately Mansions.* Deborah (Ingrid Bergman) and Sara (Colleen Dewhurst) trying to devour Simon (Arthur Hill), in the New York production directed by José Quintero at the Broadhurst Theater during the fall season of 1967. Reprinted by permission of Tony Esparza.

8. *The Iceman Cometh.* Hickey (Sasu Haapanen) at the moment of his final self-revelation. The photograph was taken at a 1958 production, directed by Matti Kassila, at the People's Theatre—Workers' Theatre of Helsinki.

9. A drunken chorus of roomers, from the same production. Photographs by Pentti Unho.

10. *Long Day's Journey Into Night.* Mary (Kirsti Ortola) and Edmund (Ismo Kallio) in the People's Theatre—Workers' Theatre (and the Helsinki City Theatre) production, directed by Timo Tiusanen in 1965.

11. The Tyrone family falling apart—Risto Mäkelä, Kirsti Ortola, Ismo Kallio and Hannes Häyrinen. Photographs by Pentti Auer.

12. *A Touch of the Poet.* Major Cornelius Melody (Tauno Palo), having abandoned his social pretensions, is ministered to by Nora (Ruth Snellman), Sara (Leena Häkinen), and Cregan (Jalmari Rinne). The play was directed by Edvin Laine in the Finnish National Theatre in 1961.

13. *A Moon for the Misbegotten.* Josie (Salome Jens) and Jamie (Mitchell Ryan), virgin and son in the moonlight, from the 1967 production, directed by Theodore Mann at the Circle in the Square Theatre in New York. Photograph by Max Waldman.

ABBREVIATIONS

The Ancient Mariner (adaptation by O'Neill)	AM
Hughie	H
The Iceman Cometh	IC
Long Day's Journey Into Night	LDJ
Lost Plays of Eugene O'Neill	LP
A Moon for the Misbegotten	AMM
More Stately Mansions	MSM
The Plays of Eugene O'Neill I-III	P I-III
Thirst And Other One Act Plays	THIRST
A Touch of the Poet	TP
Bread and Butter	BREAD
Now I Ask You	NOW
Shell Shock	SS

Page numbers are given immediately after the abbreviation; for example (P II 37) is to be read *The Plays of Eugene O'Neill*, volume II, page 37). The last three plays in the list are unpublished; they exist as manuscripts in the Library of Congress. There is a copy of *Now I Ask You* in the Beinecke Rare Book and Manuscript Library at Yale University.

O'NEILL'S SCENIC IMAGES

INTRODUCTION

SCENIC APPROACH TO DRAMA

How should one read drama? If we try to judge a dramatist's art, what should be included among our criteria? Most basically, what is the text of a play? "Is it the published version which gathers dust on library shelves or is it the live, palpitating something that comes into being as a result of the collaborative efforts of a number of creative artists?"[1] These are some of the problems facing anyone who tries to probe the relations between a playwright and his medium.

The most obvious difference between drama as a written text and drama as performed before an audience is the presence or absence of the stage. The word "stage" here includes functional aspects, most conspicuously the participation of actors and the setting. They are an active element in every production; yet they are not entirely absent even from the written text. Visualization is extremely important when reading a play, even more so, in fact, than when reading poetry. It happens primarily in terms of the stage, especially if we have a large selection of scenic memories at our disposal. In this sense, the stage is, or should be, ever present in our imagination as readers[2]—as it has been in the playwright's mind.

Nor is the idea of the stage anything extraneous. "The acting possibilities are *in* the play rather than outside it for anybody who knows how to look for them in texts for the theatre,"[3] John Gassner writes about *Mourning Becomes Elec-*

---

[1] Oscar Cargill, N. Bryllion Fagin, William J. Fisher (eds.), *O'Neill and His Plays*, p. 11. The introduction is attributed to Fagin in the index of the volume, p. 523.

[2] E. E. Stoll claims that "every dramatist" expects the critics to put him "on the stage of their imaginations" (*Shakespeare and Other Masters* [1940], p. 358).

[3] John Gassner, *The Theatre in Our Times*, p. 264.

tra. All the scenic qualities are there, waiting for the critic or the stage director to realize them. The idea of the stage can be more or less vivid, more or less activated in the reader's mind. It is probably most alert right at the beginning of the reading, when it is essential to receive at least a vague picture of the setting and of the outer appearance of the characters. It is certainly active in the mind of the director as he plans his interpretation.

A basic assumption in this study is the presence of the idea of the stage in all actable drama, particularly in every play written by Eugene O'Neill. It is there, concealed "on library shelves"; it "comes into being" as a result of the individual creative work devoted to it by artists of the theatre. Not even the German-born "Lesedrama" or closet drama denies the validity of this general conclusion: a "Lesedrama" is simply a play written and read with a vague idea of the stage. Consequently, all drama can be approached from the scenic viewpoint.

Seeing the presence of the stage in drama is certainly nothing new. In this study we shall be dealing primarily with four of the six "essential parts" of drama mentioned by Aristotle in his *Poetics*: (I) plot or structure, as it is influenced by the use of scenic means of expression; (III) diction, mainly in its capacity as a language of the stage; (V) "the Lyrical or Musical element provided by the Chorus"; and (VI) "the Spectacular."[4] Modifications were necessary in Parts I and III; only Parts V and VI, in order and probably also in importance for Aristotle, deal with scenic elements squarely, rather than by way of implication. It is to be concluded that Aristotle was not particularly interested in a scenic approach; moreover, he says of the element of the spectacle that it "concerns the property-man rather than the poet."[5]

This viewpoint, accepted by the most authoritative of dramatic critics, has certainly had its effect on generations of scholars; perhaps it still has. Theatre history has slowly

[4] F. L. Lucas, *Tragedy*, p. 79.
[5] *Ibid.*, pp. 29, 183.

emerged as an independent branch of study; Alois M. Nagler mentions the year 1901 as a turning point in the German approach to drama.[6] A neighboring field, to be called the scenic approach to drama, has become prominent only recently, though there were foreshadowing lines of thought in the dramatic criticism of earlier centuries. Artur Kutscher calls Lessing "the forefather of our 'Theaterwissenschaft,' "[7] and shows how Lichtenberg, Tieck, A. W. Schlegel, and representatives of "the young Germany" foreshadowed this new approach. He mentions Max Herrmann, Carl Weitbrecht, Robert Petsch, and Oskar Eberle as important figures in our century.[8]

Shakespeare has doubtless attracted the best critical minds in the English-speaking world, among them experts in the theatre. It is possible to say that Dr. Johnson's well-known statement in the preface of his Shakespeare edition, in which he dispenses with the rigorous application of the "three unities," is based on a scenic approach, on the experience of the spectators. This was an exception rather than the rule, however; and the picture of Shakespeare's relation to his stage has been blurred by subsequent theatrical traditions and by other interests in the minds of critics. A reaction against one-sidedly literary interpretations of Shakespeare came in the 1920's and 1930's, following important studies in theatre history by Sir E. K. Chambers.

Harley Granville-Barker defined the text of a play as "a score waiting performance"[9] and applied an actor's viewpoint to Shakespeare in a consistent and fruitful way, paying due attention to visual and sound effects.[10] In 1922 Levin L. Schücking concentrated on studying Shakespeare's char-

---

[6] Alois M. Nagler, *A Source Book in Theatrical History*, p. xxi.

[7] Artur Kutscher, *Stilkunde des Theaters* (1936), p. 176. All translations from texts originally published in German, French, Swedish, or Finnish (see Bibliography) are my own.

[8] *Ibid.*, pp. 177-79, 190-97.

[9] Harley Granville-Barker, *Prefaces to Shakespeare*, I, 1958 (1927), p. 5.

[10] *Ibid.*, I, pp. 11, 25-27, 448; II, 289 *et passim*. About the visual aspects, see I, 384, 407-08. Cf. Y. M. Biese, *Aspects of Expression I*, pp. 9-12, where a philologist pays some attention to the expressive possibilities of actors.

acters, as A. C. Bradley had done in 1904. He sought psychological inconsistencies and found in them evidence of "almost childish primitiveness."[11] Yet he also emphasized Shakespeare's close contact with Elizabethan and Jacobean audiences,[12] and this led him to an appreciation of the baroque contrasts and theatrical effectiveness in the plays.[13] In the 1940's, he was ready to enter a Renaissance playhouse and give a vivid description of the theatrical effects employed there: he had been converted to a true scenic approach.[14] J. Dover Wilson had made a similar journey in imagination in 1932.[15]

A firm stand against the dangers of psychologism is taken by E. E. Stoll, who insists that Shakespeare's characters are not to be interpreted as if they were real people. A playwright's starting point is a striking situation; his primary concern is to create "an illusion whereby the spirit of man shall be moved."[16] Wolfgang H. Clemen combines his main interest in verbal images with a consciousness of the presence of the stage[17]—as a contrast to the statistical methods employed by Caroline Spurgeon. The enthusiasm aroused by her study was shared by Una Ellis-Fermor in 1937, but given up later on; in her *Jacobean Drama* Ellis-Fermor connects the plays with the contemporary stage traditions.[18] In a recent study on Shakespeare's Roman plays,

[11] Levin L. Schücking, *Character Problems in Shakespeare's Plays* (1922), p. 66. Cf. pp. 26-27, 51, 119. A. C. Bradley, *Shakespearian Tragedy* (1904), p. xiii.

[12] *Ibid.*, pp. 19, 25.

[13] Schücking, *The Meaning of Hamlet* (1935), pp. 2-3, 72.

[14] Schücking, *Shakespeare und der Tragödienstil seiner Zeit* (1947), pp. 11-12; *Essays* (1948), pp. 277-78.

[15] J. Dover Wilson, *The Essential Shakespeare* (1932), pp. 30-31.

[16] Stoll, *Art and Artifice in Shakespeare* (1933), p. 168. Cf. *ibid.*, pp. 2, 19, 21-22, 48, 105, 120-21, 139, 162.

[17] Wolfgang H. Clemen, *The Development of Shakespeare's Imagery* (1936), pp. 3, 57, 219.

[18] Una Ellis-Fermor, *Some Recent Research in Shakespeare's Imagery* (1937), p. 38. Cf. a BBC broadcast by her in 1949; in it "the investigation of imagery" is judged as fruitful "only in so far as the dramatic function of the images is kept unwaveringly before the critic's mind" (*Shakespeare the Dramatist*, pp. 123-24). In *The Jacobean Drama* (1936), see Chapter II, pp. 28-52.

Maurice Charney insists that a dramatist's "imagery should not be separated from its context in the theater," and calls words "only a part of the full imaginative experience of the play."[19] And in Nevill Coghill's study on Shakespeare's professional skills, the scenic approach is central: where Schücking, in an early study, had found "an instinctive, impulsive, and altogether sketchy mode of working,"[20] there Coghill sees "a surpassing intelligence" and "the continual exercise of craftsmanlike understanding."[21] What has been growing is an understanding of Shakespeare's time and his craft.

The above paragraphs claim to include samples of attitudes rather than a complete summary of the results achieved through scenic approach to Shakespeare. It is noteworthy that the significance of the playwright's medium has also been acknowledged in studies focusing on other aspects of his work: interpretations of character or verbal images are connected with stage situations. Finding a scenic school of thought in the case of Shakespeare, an eagerly scrutinized playwright, should not make us blind to the fact that scenic qualities are less frequently analyzed in books dealing with modern dramatists. Out of 28 book-length studies on Eugene O'Neill, only one concentrates on the theatrical aspect of his plays—and this book, written by a German in the 1930's, has been ignored in America.[22] Critics of modern drama have been accused on several occasions of knowing too little about the workings of the theatre.[23]

There is need for a scenic approach to O'Neill. There is reason to put emphasis on things theatrical, as has been done by those Shakespearean scholars listed above. What is lacking is a theoretical basis for a systematic study.

[19] Maurice Charney, *Shakespeare's Roman Plays* (1961), p. 4.
[20] Schücking, *Character Problems*, p. 199.
[21] Nevill Coghill, *Shakespeare's Professional Skills* (1964), p. x.
[22] Otto Koischwitz, *O'Neill* (1938).
[23] Cf. Gassner, *Theatre at the Crossroads*, p. 111; Charney, p. 2; Cargill *et al.*, p. 12: "Most of these critics [new critics] are but inadequately trained to deal with drama; they are academicians, literary scholars, 'classical' minded; moreover, if they are American, they are likely to have retained some of the suspicion of the theatre the 'best' people in America have always had."

The paradox of every art theory is that it must fulfill two conflicting criteria: first, coherence and clarity; second, elasticity and comprehensiveness. The dilemma is basically similar to that of a democratic government: how to combine firmness of purpose and vision with a respect for the rights of the individual? If the first of these is neglected in a theory of art, the result is confused subjectivism and critical impressionism, neither of which is a valuable constituent in an aesthetic theory. If the latter is neglected, the result is pedantic pigeonholing, where the characteristics of individual works of art are sacrificed to formulas of thought.

Drama, perhaps by its very nature, has invited more rigorous theoreticians than poetry or the novel. Various formulas of critical thought can be traced from Aristotle through Seneca to the Renaissance; other formulas are discernible in Bertolt Brecht and in the theatre of the absurd. In our search for a theory which combines coherence and porousness, we may turn to Ronald Peacock and his study *The Art of Drama*, published in 1957.

Theatrical components are duly considered in Peacock's discussion, and he makes an effort to liberate "the term imagery from its over-narrow connotation, for figures of speech, in English literary criticism."[24] The term is extended to all kinds of art. Peacock is also careful to base his theoretical conclusions on natural phenomena: the interaction of different kinds of images in art corresponds to similar relations outside art. Basic to drama is thus the "inescapable union of dialogue and acting," which forms "a natural intertexture of imagery."[25] Of the highest significance to us is this fact of interaction itself: "One of the marks of finished art is that it is an organic interstructure of differing kinds of imagery."[26] "Interaction," "intertexture," "interstructure": Peacock's favorite among prefixes hints at a dynamic conception of the relations between the various components of a work of art. And so it is: "Central in our conception has

[24] Ronald Peacock, *The Art of Drama* (1957), pp. 1-2.
[25] *Ibid.*, p. 167.
[26] *Ibid.*, p. 43.

8

been the idea of the functioning of images. . . ."[27] Just as central in the case of drama is the functioning of images, which are of the theatre, not of literature: drama "is an art; it is imagery for eye and ear and mind; it shows a characteristic intertexture. . . . It incorporates the visual images of scene and persons, it uses words in dialogue, which may however include many uses of speech, emotive, analytic, declamatory, exclamatory, rhetorical, descriptive, lyrical, musical and so on."[28]

This idea of functional units as essential parts of a work of art is worth remembering. It is one of the visions that guarantees the individuality of analyzed works of art. The interaction need not follow any rigid formulas. After these considerations we are free to see drama as a conglomerate of several different kinds of images, not only verbal ones.

Peacock's aim differs from the purpose of this study. He speaks "a language of generality," because the essence of his inquiry "is not the analysis of particular arts in unique examples but the search for generalizations that account for kinship, unity in variety, overlap, and forms of synthesis."[29] This sentence defines, by way of negation, the purpose of the present study, which is, indeed, to analyze a particular art "in unique examples."

The word "image" is applied more specifically to Eugene O'Neill by Rudolf Stamm. Some of the central scenes in O'Neill's late plays are called "images we cannot easily forget, for they are compact symbols of everything developed in the actions and speeches of O'Neill's characters." The American playwright is in Stamm's opinion "an 'absolute' dramatist, i.e. one who does not merely create speeches . . . but complete situations, visualized as stage events, characters with their unmistakable gait, their gestures, their speeches, and their changing facial expression."[30]

Stamm's statement helps in its own way to justify a scenic

---

[27] *Ibid.*, p. 241.   [28] *Ibid.*, p. 157.   [29] *Ibid.*, p. 3.
[30] Rudolf Stamm, " 'Faithful Realism': Eugene O'Neill and the Problem of Style," *English Studies, 40* (1959), 250.

approach to O'Neill's plays: there is something in them to analyze. Yet the task is far from easy; the object of study certainly becomes more intricate when the interaction of scenic images is added to that of verbal images.[31] Some of the problems arising were formulated by Kutscher more than thirty years ago: "The dramaturgic question is: how far is drama dramatic? What do the words give to the performance? . . . Does the verbal form correspond to the scenic one? . . . It is not at all easy to judge these matters."[32]

We have now come to the point where it is necessary to define three central concepts to be used throughout this study. The idea of the stage, though useful as a starting point, is too vague and general to be of considerable value; the concepts of image and interaction require a systematic framework in order to be fruitful.

The discussion can begin with the supposition that there is in a writer's mind a vision which he seeks to concretize in terms of language. To keep the argument clear, let us imagine the creative process to be more mechanical than it actually is, ignoring such inevitable complications as verbal and other artistic deficiencies, intervening directors or producers, in short, all those factors that prevent a playwright from ever achieving perfect communication. So, in this hypothetical sense, at the beginning there is a vision.

This vision consists of, or can be divided into, several ideas. (The neutral word "idea" is better here than the word "image" which will be reserved for another usage.) A poet transforms his ideas into verbal images, with which he constructs a poem; a novelist turns them into characters, plot,

[31] "I say it is extremely difficult and tiring, when reading a play, to hold it in the mind's eye, and in the mind's ear, with any constancy, as it moves from moment to moment. It asks more concentration than most of us have to remember (for instance) while we are reading, what characters are on the stage, in what costumes and attitudes. The less we can do this, the more we are likely to lose important inflections of meaning" (Coghill, p. xiii).

[32] Kutscher, *Die Elemente des Theaters* (1932), p. 122.

10

action, descriptive passages—and at long last into language. A playwright's achievement depends not only on language, dialogue. For him, there are several other kinds of phenomena involved, all of which are connected with the idea of the stage: setting, properties, costumes, sound and lighting effects, music, groupings, the actor's individual expression, his gestures, movements, make-up, vocal and facial expressions. These are his *scenic means of expression*.

An intriguing point in this connection is the position of dialogue. It is, of course, a central means of expression; but is it scenic? The problem could perhaps be solved by referring to dialogue as a scenic means of expression only insofar as its most conspicuous stage qualities are concerned: rhythm, pace, appropriateness as a part of a character's expression. Yet dialogue is always on the stage, taking part in interaction of all kinds, not only between the actors, but sometimes even with, say, the lighting or sound effects. It seems plausible then to include dialogue among scenic means of expression.

One and the same sentence (or speech) can be taken in several different ways. It can be approached as a verbal entity, with attention to its vocabulary, syntax, verbal images, or other means of verbal expression. Or it can be taken as a scenic means of expression, related to other scenic means. It is in this latter sense that dialogue will be treated in my study. Clemen and Charney believe that verbal images cannot be analyzed without considering the stage situations; conversely, stage situations cannot be analyzed without their dialogue.

A poet or novelist uses verbal means of expression; a playwright, verbal and scenic. The characteristics of verbal images are not discussed in this study, which focuses rather on the creation of scenic images. A scenic image cannot be defined as unequivocally as a verbal image; yet it is something existing, something real. An effort must be made to define it if we want to use the term in anything more than a descriptive sense.

A *scenic image* is a scene (or, more often, part of a scene) in which several scenic means of expression are used to achieve an effect charged with thematic significance.

This definition needs explanation and elaboration. Before going into the basic reasons for presenting it at all, let us deal with some of its details. In the first part of the definition it is implied that in order for a scenic image to be striking it cannot last very long—not for a whole act, for example. The phenomenon can be connected with the fundamental question of rhythm in drama and with a spectator's ability to remain attentive. Rather than giving the scenic image a legitimate length in minutes and seconds, it is sensible to grant it some variable length, some dimension in time. Conceding it the possibility of lasting a whole scene leaves the door open for hectic short scenes, typical of the German and American expressionists. *The Emperor Jones* can be taken as a rapid succession of scenic images.

The cooperation or fusion of several means of expression is presupposed in my definition in order to emphasize the importance of interaction. At the same time, a relation is established to the first basic concept in this study. The theoretical question—why not just one means?—can be answered by referring to the list of scenic means given above. The setting is always present on the stage, and just placing an actor in front of it already leads to the use of several means; a bare-stage production presupposes some kind of lighting, while an open-air production is hardly feasible without a setting. In most cases, of course, the interaction occurs quite naturally.

The last phrase in the definition tries to connect this formal element with the theme or "message" of the play.[33] Irrelevant events are apt to bore rather than impress us as members of the audience. This does not mean that the image

[33] Speaking of Shakespeare's "startling uses of the facts and possibilities of theatre" Coghill finds a similar connection: "They are always vested by Shakespeare with important significances: they are theme-bearers" (p. 16).

must be full of violent outer action, however; Anton Chekhov's plays are made up of quietly intensive images. The theme can be present in a scenic image carried by one or several means: the actors, dialogue, property, setting, sound effects, music.

When trying to justify the existence of the entire concept, it is worth noting first of all that it has grown quite naturally out of the material of this study. The phenomenon referred to has preceded its name. A particular part of a total play or production, furnished with extra significance in a reader's or spectator's mind, is given a distinct name here for the purpose of making analyses possible.[34]

Yet the distinction between scenic images and other elements in a play needs closer consideration. A stage presentation can be seen as a continuous flow of imagery, partly visual, partly auditive. Every moment of stage action is a composite image consisting of a group of characters or a single individual in front of or within a setting, with a fragment of dialogue in the air, together with certain sound and lighting effects. Where, then, should we draw the dividing line between images and "non-images"?

First of all, there is the fourth dimension of time opening up behind the scenic images. What has happened five lines or half an hour or two acts earlier can be brought vividly to the memory of the spectators by means of a scenic image; one of O'Neill's favorite methods was the use of a repetitious sound effect. Or a scenic image may affect a sudden twist in the plot of the play: in a moment charged with tension a character may suddenly be revealed as something quite different from what we thought him to be. A scenic image may also convey an impression of completeness: nothing can be added, all has been said. Or an accepted idea can be revaluated, by having an actor change his attitude toward it. Or we may, in a moment of enlightenment, receive the "message" of

[34] There is every reason to agree with Clemen: "Only one thing really exists: the play as a whole, as a totality. Everything else is simply an aspect which *we* detach from the whole in order to facilitate our investigation and make it feasible" (p. 2).

the play. Or we may recognize ourselves and our own situation in the play: *mea res agitur,* they are talking about me. A scenic image may also have a kind of aftereffect: only when safely at home do we see connections between the scenes and conceive the interaction of separate images. Whichever of these possibilities is realized in a particular scenic image it is always charged with thematic significance. When looking for the scenic images of a play it is thus advisable to trace its themes to a moment of crystallization.

Secondly, locating the scenic images of a play is necessarily dependent on a critic's individual judgment. As members of a theatre audience, we are sensitive to stage action in varying degrees. I have, as a stage director, experienced this many times at performances of plays I have directed. No two groups of people would react to a performance in exactly the same way. Every actor knows that there are "good" and "bad" audiences, and the reasons for this variation are not constant. The quality of the performance, for example, may vary.

I think, however, that the decisive point is a spectator's memory. If he refuses to be impressed by what has happened earlier in the play, when a moment charged with thematic significance comes, it is lost on him, no matter how carefully it has been prepared by the director and the actors. If he reacts with extreme sensitivity to the image, it is because he remembers so well what has happened before, because he is deeply involved in the totality of the performance.[35] It is not an easy task to get the spectators involved in what they see and hear on the stage. That is why a playwright had better charge his images with the help of several effective

[35] Coghill speaks of "a total engagement of the imagination": "It is true that this profound attention cannot be easily or long sustained, but it is the real thing, the thing we should always hope for and perhaps attempt to achieve by conscious effort" (pp. 38-39). A similar description of the influence of scenic images on the spectators is written by Stoll: "identifying themselves with the hero, they live mainly in the moment, notice mainly what the dramatist is actually presenting" (*Shakespeare and Other Masters,* p. 12).

14

scenic means of expression. If he tries too hard, however, he may achieve only melodrama.

What and how many scenic means of expression are to be employed in constructing a scenic image is a problem intimately bound up with the totality of the play and the performance. Without a doubt, scenic images will be found at different places in different productions of the same play, simply because the stage director has used his individual judgment. If I could give you all the criteria needed to distinguish a scenic image from a "non-image," I certainly would. I cannot. There are too many variables, there are too many things depending on our artistic sensibilities. Two words delivered by a great actor may have a more stunning effect than the crescendo of a chorus of fifty. A scenic image may be found where the outer action of a play reaches its high point—or it may mean a thematic "inner" climax.[36]

There is no lack of quotations dismissing the "scientifically" objective method in literary criticism as an impossibility. One of them is formulated by Fagin: "It seems clear once again that criticism can be only relatively objective," because "all creative expression involves a commitment to a point of view, an orientation, and a strategy which, in turn, involves selection, organization, suppression, and stress—in other words, subtle participation as man and writer."[37] The data presented in this study have doubtless undergone a process of selection, organization, suppression, and stress. Whether the resulting subjectivism has led to erroneous conclusions or not is a matter to be decided in each concrete case separately.

As for the term "scenic image," it is noteworthy that Charney makes several suggestions toward a corresponding concept: "I use the word 'presentational' as a convenient term for the large body of images that is not part of the spoken words of the text, but directly presented in the theater. Some synonyms might be 'dramatic metaphor' or

---

[36] Ellis-Fermor is concerned with "an inner level of plot" (*Shakespeare the Dramatist*, p. 98). This concept could perhaps be equated with "a series of scenic images."

[37] Cargill *et al.*, p. 4.

'stage image' (as contrasted with 'verbal' image)."[38] The contrast with the "verbal" image is the same in this study, but preference has been given to the adjective "scenic," as the word "stage" has more concrete overtones here. As to Peacock's terminology, it has not served my purposes to preserve his distinction between "representational images" and "expressive formula-images."[39]

There remains a third, auxiliary concept to be introduced: the scenic unit.

> A *scenic unit* is a specific kind of scenic means
> of expression, characteristic of the playwright in
> question and used by him as an element in con-
> structing scenic images.

The most important distinction here is that not all the scenic means used by a playwright are scenic units, but only those repeated with some regularity. When trying to approach a playwright's world it is significant to notice certain consistent elements that seem to be symptoms of relatively lasting characteristics. Scenic units are signs of artistic continuity, scenic images of variety and fresh creation.

It is, however, especially dangerous to assume that the function of a certain scenic unit will be the same every time.[40] A new means combined with an old unit may give the resulting scenic image a totally renewed flavor. Interaction, the functioning of these units with other kinds of scenic means, is all-important.[41] O'Neill, for example, used masks in very differ-

[38] Charney, pp. 7-8. James H. Clay and Daniel Krempel acknowledge the importance of both a scenic and a literary analysis for a stage director (*The Theatrical Image*, p. 39). Their "image" (p. 26) aims at a synthesis: it is a comprehensive concept dealing with the totality of a stage interpretation. Mine is a vehicle for analysis.

[39] See Peacock, pp. 30-31, 38.

[40] A similar danger is seen by John Henry Raleigh: "It is difficult to say what the sea finally means in O'Neill's plays, for, as in *Moby Dick*, it means everything" (*The Plays of Eugene O'Neill* [1965], p. 22). Raleigh speaks of the *idea* of the sea; yet the same reservation applies to scenic units: they may express different things.

[41] When describing the musical structure of Shakespeare's tragedies, Stoll emphasizes interaction: "He can take the highest notes as well as low, the loudest as well as the soft and tender. And, as in a masterly

ent ways, to serve several different functions in *The Ancient Mariner* and *The Great God Brown*.

It is now time to give some examples. One of O'Neill's favorite ideas is that life is like stumbling in a fog. This idea is realized on the stage by the use of several scenic means of expression. In *Long Day's Journey Into Night*, for example, there are several references to fog in the dialogue, and it is a participant in the action of the play when Jamie Tyrone comes home: "a noise from outside the house" (LDJ 154) is heard, as the fog makes him stumble and fall. Most conspicuously, of course, the presence of the fog is expressed by the foghorn which sounds "at regular intervals" (LDJ 97) throughout Acts III and IV. We can thus see how one and the same idea is conveyed by using several means of expression: dialogue, movement (James Tyrone and Edmund "jump startedly"), sound effects. The foghorn is a scenic unit: a repetitive sound effect. As we shall see, it is employed throughout the O'Neillian canon.

This is what may be said of the idea of "fog" in *Long Day's Journey Into Night* in the present connection. Let us now alter our point of view and look at a scenic image in the same play. James and Edmund Tyrone have a long scene together, covering more than half of Act IV, for which O'Neill has prepared us to concentrate all our attention. First Tyrone tells us about his miserable youth, thus opening up a new perspective on his character. Then we have a scenic image: he tells about the disappointment of his life, his failure as a good actor—and to make his tragedy and tragicomedy complete, he turns off some of the lights. What he has just said about his niggardliness is both confirmed and touched with irony by this action. He cannot help being what he is. Edmund senses both the tragedy and the irony, the foghorn can be heard in the distance, and the lights are dimmed as a fore-

---

orchestral composition, they then seem higher or lower, louder or softer, than they really are. They throw each other into relief—the comic does the tragic; the real, the ideal; the homely or humble, the grand or sublime" (*Art and Artifice*, p. 132). Coghill devotes a whole chapter, called "Juxtaposition of Scenes," to interaction (pp. 61-77).

17

boding sign of Tyrone's approaching death. Everything we learn about James Tyrone during this long day's journey is embodied here. Within a scenic image there is thus interaction between different ideas and fusion between different scenic means of expression; within a whole play there is interaction between several images.[42] A scenic image is not indivisible—or, it is breakable like the atom.

When looking for a scenic image charged both with a sense of completeness and with great thematic significance we can turn to the final moments of the play. It seems inescapable that the foghorn is heard both during James Tyrone's confession and after Mary has come down with her wedding gown, even if the exact timing of this repetitive sound effect is left unspecified by the playwright. As it is, we have a perfect example of a striking and yet outwardly quiet scenic image: the gown; the bottles on the table; dim lighting to suggest night; the foghorn; all of the Tyrones, together and separated; bits of dialogue, mostly reminiscent monologues.

These examples should demonstrate clearly enough that each of the three special concepts is needed. Otherwise, it would not be possible to distinguish between the idea, its expression through certain scenic means and units, and the resulting images, particles of a play. At this point of the argument the terms may seem to schematize the discussion more than they actually do when applied to critical practice; they are only means to an end, not ends in themselves. It is too early to say anything of their potentialities as tools, let alone of their theoretical validity or applicability outside the plays of Eugene O'Neill—though they have been phrased in general terms in the hope that they might have some general relevance.

Not every scenic image will be traced in this study. The concept is a vehicle for critical analysis; it is not worth the

[42] It can be said that Clemen and Schücking have in fact described a few central scenic images and their function in Shakespeare: the abdication scene in *King Richard II* (Clemen, pp. 57-58), or the ghost and council scenes in *Hamlet* (Schücking, *The Meaning of Hamlet*, pp. 2, 72-73, 75-76). The scenes are not, however, divided into several scenic images.

trouble to analyze indifferent plays with its help. A complete scenic analysis of forty-six published and three unpublished plays is a practical impossibility. It is also to be hoped that the dangers of pigeonholing mentioned above can be avoided by a constant emphasis on functional interaction in the plays and within the images, to guarantee their individuality as works of art or particles of them.

The introduction of this trinity of concepts can be closed with a remark that connects it with the practices of the theatre. The critical procedure to be followed in this study is in principle parallel to the procedure followed when a stage presentation is constructed. An analysis is needed before one can build up a synthesis. In our case the synthesis is a critical picture of a playwright's vision, as exact as possible but even at best only an approximation; in the case of the director it is a stage interpretation, another approximation.

While in the mainstream of scenic approach to drama, this study will rely at least partially on the special concepts introduced above. There are, of course, other methods to use when discussing drama in general and O'Neill in particular; it is now time to make an effort toward defining the positions.

There are four main approaches in dramatic criticism, all of them justified: literary, psychological, sociological, and scenic. Every play speaks of something, has a theme. It is written by someone; consequently, it is useful to know as much as possible about him. It has been created in a country, in a certain year, in reaction to its surroundings; in order to know what kind of reaction it is, we should know about the circumstances which prompted it. And it has been written for the stage.

Errors occur at the point where one or several of these aspects have been completely ignored in favor of the basic approach chosen by the critic. A play is not only an abstract statement on the human dilemma; nor a basin full of psychological secretion; nor a letter to the editor; nor an excuse for histrionic pyrotechnics. It is, in a paradoxical way, all of these things and more—it is a work of art. When treating this elusive thing, the best results are achieved if it is discussed not from one but from several points of view.

To speak with a picture: let us think of the critic in front of a circle. It has been said that the only completely adequate description of a work of art is that work itself—the circle *in toto*. According to the rules of the game the critic should try to verbalize the essential features of that elusive circle by covering part of its total area. Let us divide the circle into four sectors of equal size representing the four main approaches mentioned above. A scholar may decide not to choose any particular approach or sector, satisfying himself with just scraping the surface. Or he may choose one method, a kind of wedge through which he can drive toward the center of the circle; if it goes deep enough, it hits the center. The best critic is not satisfied even with this; after reaching the center, he turns around, a full circle, and tries to cover part of all the other sectors as well. In so doing he draws a line which has the form of a keyhole: he has found a key to that work of art. Those looking through that hole have complete freedom to decide whether that wedge ever really hit the center, whether the other sectors were made visible.

The sector directly opposite to mine is the literary approach to drama. I do not bear a grudge against the majority of people crowding toward the center of O'Neill from that direction; as we shall see, this approach has produced many examples of perceptive writing which not only clarify the themes of plays, but also give us glimpses of the scenic sector. In some cases the scenic elements are neglected, mostly for the simple reason that reading a play tends to bring the words into the foreground and suppress the scenic images; this is especially so if the reader is not very familiar with the practices of the theatre.

Evaluations are crucial points where fallacies become apparent. Hickey's final confession in *The Iceman Cometh* is in Signi Falk's opinion "sadly in need of editing," as it lasts, "with few interruptions," "for about twelve pages."[43] Yet in

---

[43] Signi Falk, "Dialogue in the Plays of Eugene O'Neill," *Modern Drama, 3* (1960), 323.

fact it is not necessarily too long at all. The playwright has placed it, with great care, at the climax of the entire play. In the theatre, it does not last for "twelve pages"; it lasts for several exciting minutes. Bits of Hickey's secret are revealed to arouse curiosity, and the "few interruptions" are made by a chorus which is present throughout the scene and gives further emphasis to the speech.[44]

Statements of O'Neill's famous repetitiousness are to be taken with reservation. It is a well-known fact that what looks like unnecessary tautology on a written page may in spoken word prove to be surprisingly effective, as it brings important themes back to our memory. An example is Antony's burial speech in *Julius Caesar*, built mainly on repetitions used ironically and plentifully, like a refrain in a poem. All repetitions cannot be motivated, to be sure, but some of them can. Consequently, statements deploring their existence should be modified and specified. Repetitions are, as a rule, a challenge to the stage director: they are to be handled so as to achieve new variations and extra significance, not monotony.

The time factor creates a further complication not present in the criticism of poetry and the novel. A literary interpreter, having an unlimited amount of time at his disposal and the entire canon of a playwright before him, in addition to letters and previous critical studies, may see connections and trace ideas that have not the slightest chance of being introduced on the stage within three hours of continuous stage traffic. The thin lines of literary themes are apt to drown in the abundance of expression filling the stage—with the setting, with lighting, movements, gestures, groupings, vocal and facial expressions—that is, if the themes are not carried by one or several of these scenic means of expression. It may be perfectly clear for a reader that a passage in Act I, Scene ii is to be connected with a line in Act V, Scene iii, because

---

[44] Coghill writes about the possible results of an insufficient knowledge of things theatrical: "The distortions of the study are mainly due to that lawlessness that can overtake an imagination that has forgotten the nature of the medium in which it is trying to imagine" (p. xii).

the same verbal image occurs in these two contexts[45]—and yet this association can very well remain unseen on the stage. Having discovered the themes of a play, the critic must still judge how far the playwright has succeeded in giving them a realizable scenic form.

A commonly held legend about O'Neill is that his "sense of the theatre" or "theatre instinct" was so fully developed that he never made a mistake.[46] What is there behind these labels? A force of nature, undescribable and unanalyzable? I cannot resign myself to that conclusion. Rather the theatre is another field of art in which artistic intellect and imagination, experience and continuous experimentation have their say. Instead of an instinct working automatically and unerringly, we shall see here groping efforts, errors, and a final synthesis. We shall follow a dramatist's quest.

The word "theatrical" is sometimes used with pejorative overtones.[47] I have chosen to use the word "theatre," its derivatives, and the hopefully more neutral synonym "scenic" in this study without any emotional connotations, either pejorative or appreciative. The theatre is simply a phenomenon to be studied; its name should be taken just as neutrally as the term "word" must be taken by a linguist. Even though a scenic viewpoint has been applied, this is, of course, no reason for being critically blind. No amount of scenic approach will make *Lazarus Laughed* even a mediocre play; it is one of the very worst plays O'Neill ever wrote, mainly because the means used are out of harmony with the theme expressed. This is a conclusion drawn after an analysis of details in a concrete case, not because of a general suspicion toward all things theatrical.

[45] A similar example is given by Stoll (*Shakespeare and Other Masters*, p. 141), while Clemen mentions a "law of the succession of time," immanent in drama (p. 6).

[46] Cf. Edwin A. Engel, *The Haunted Heroes of Eugene O'Neill* (1953), p. 52.

[47] Cf. a statement by Charney, an American: "suspicion of the theatre is a part of our literary tradition, if not of our moral tradition as well" (p. 2). For other examples, see Jordan Y. Miller, *Eugene O'Neill and the American Critic* (1962), p. 32, and Cargill *et al.*, pp. 302-03, a reprinting from *Minority Report* by Bernard De Voto (Boston, 1943).

Realism is the style most readily appreciated in the modern theatre. There are no "gimmicks" in realism, nothing "artificial," nothing to leave an awkward question in a critic's mind. The "stark simplicity" of the play can always be applauded. Yet realism, whatever its merits and limitations, is only one of the major styles in the modern theatre, as Gassner proves in his panoramic *Form and Idea in the Modern Theatre*.[48] A priori opinions with regard to style are especially dangerous in the case of Eugene O'Neill, whose plays cut across several trends in this multi-faceted age of drama. None of the numerous schools of playwriting in our century is taken as an absolute standard in this study. A play influenced by the expressionists may be a bore or a masterpiece, depending on its intrinsic merits.

Some of those who approach O'Neill from the psychological sector are psychoanalytic interpreters. Their argument is based, on the one hand, on the undeniable Freudian echoes in these plays, on the other (at a deeper level), on the tensions between members of the same family, a focal theme in almost every play by O'Neill. Moreover, since he wrote in the heyday of the Freudian boom, there are intriguing connections to the history of ideas. This is where the psychoanalytic and sociological approaches meet.

W. David Sievers goes so far as to call O'Neill's drama "schizophrenic" and "the period of the twenties in American drama," the "Psychoanalytic Era."[49] With this epithet, a limit is already imposed on psychoanalytical drama in one respect, and, as a sequitur, on the corresponding school in criticism.[50] Both are closer to the twenties than to the sixties.

[48] Gassner, *Form and Idea in the Modern Theatre, passim*, especially Part II, pp. 77-130.

[49] W. David Sievers, *Freud on Broadway* (1955), pp. 52, 65.

[50] The results of several scholars are summarized by Arthur H. Nethercot in a lengthy article "The Psychoanalyzing of Eugene O'Neill," *Modern Drama, 3*, 3-4 (Dec. 1960, Feb. 1961). The article tells of a kind of stalemate situation: there is no way of knowing for sure to how large an extent O'Neill was influenced by Jung or Freud.

Half a century has banalized Freud:[51] themes of incest, the prevalence of sexuality, complexes and theories of the origin of neurosis have lost their stunning effect. They belong now to *Gemeingüter*, to public domain, in- and outside art. History has played against Freudianism; and literature has not been slow in looking for new ways out. Social drama, in the case of Brecht, Dürrenmatt, and Arden, and poetic tragicomedy, in the case of Beckett, Ionesco, and Pinter, have offered new alternatives.

It is certainly true that psychoanalysis is helpful in clarifying some of O'Neill's interwar plays. The weakness of this approach is its self-sufficiency; the solutions proposed are rarely related to the other sectors. Its followers profess to know the "real," which is rarely the apparent, theme of a play.[52] This theme can be found out only through their guidance, regardless of whether the scenic means carry it or not. In principle, psychoanalysis tends to simplify two basic relations: that between a work of art and the receiver on one hand, and that between the work and the *artifex* on the other. Hamlet loved his mother; therefore . . . O'Neill hated his father. . . . These are hardly sufficient reasons for a play such as *Hamlet*, which has thrilled audiences for four hundred years, or, respectively, for anyone to write *Long Day's Journey Into Night*. No amount of references to the importance of subconscious experiences can change the fact that causal relations are more complex than that.[53]

[51] It is interesting to note that Freud himself makes an important distinction: "It must be answered to the layman, who perhaps expects too much of the [psycho-]analysis, that it does not throw any light on two problems that probably interest him most of all. The analysis cannot say anything to explain the artistic talent, nor is it possible for the analysis to reveal the means with which an artist works, his artistic technique" (*Selbstdarstellung, Gesammelte Werke*, XIV, p. 91).

[52] A war against one-sidedly psychological interpretations has been fought by Stoll, in a persistent way: "What can be discovered (instead of invented) by the critic is not in the matter but the manner, not new truths but new or improved strokes of art" (*Shakespeare and Other Masters*, p. 150). Cf. *Art and Artifice*, pp. 29, 31, 76.

[53] Even so subtle an analysis as *Eugene O'Neill and the Tragic Tension* by Doris V. Falk sometimes emphasizes too heavily the origin of a work of art instead of the work itself. This is certainly

One might summarize, admitting that the results can be partially illuminating: when the theories of psychoanalysis are used to explain art, what is explained by them is not art.

Hunting fallacies is a dangerous sport. Lest this study be accused of a "scenic fallacy" I should like to offer several statements as a defensive maneuver. What has been criticized above is not the literary or the psychological approach as such, but only those cases in which the presence of the stage has been neglected. "An art moves in its own medium,"[54] Coghill writes; it is difficult to approve of evaluations of art formed without a reasonable knowledge of the medium. Yet the medium is not all of art; it is my aim to try to see the other sectors, too. In my definition of a scenic image itself there is a link to the themes of the play—and this connection is preserved throughout the discussion.

Furthermore, as there have already been several thematic studies on Eugene O'Neill it has not been necessary to deal with this part of the problem as comprehensively as might have been advisable in the case of a less-studied playwright. Rather, it has in many cases been possible to select among the presented thematic interpretations the one most strongly supported by scenic evidence, and modify it according to the new aspect, not neglecting connections to contemporary theatre history. It was mentioned as an encouraging sign that the presence of the stage has been acknowledged by some Shakespearean scholars, even if their interest was focused elsewhere; it is perhaps time to head toward a kind of synthesis of different methods, sketched by Clemen in the conclusion of his study.[55]

There have been some fifty years of O'Neill criticism. Barrett H. Clark published the first edition of his pioneering biography forty years ago, and in the last few years O'Neill

---

true of *A Moon for the Misbegotten*; in her discussion (pp. 171-78) Falk finds, easily enough, the neurotic pattern she is looking for; after that her view of the merits of the play is dim, partly because she does not consider its scenic means of expression carefully enough.

[54] Coghill, p. xv.
[55] Clemen, p. 231.

has been the center of eager activity: he has been the subject of several books, along with a great number of shorter studies, not to mention newspaper articles. Included in my bibliography are studies written in five languages; they will be considered as the argument proceeds. Now I shall mention only a few major contributions. *The Haunted Heroes of Eugene O'Neill* by Edwin A. Engel opened the postwar era with a thorough, mainly literary discussion; it was followed by a Neo-Freudian study by Doris V. Falk, a soundly critical short survey by Clifford Leech, and three biographies, written by Arthur and Barbara Gelb, Doris Alexander, and Croswell Bowen. Especially noteworthy is Otto Koischwitz's scenic study, published in Berlin in 1938, in which he touches on some essential problems in O'Neill's use of the stage. Impressions left by major productions of O'Neill since the 1920's provide the background for several short studies by John Gassner. *The Plays of Eugene O'Neill* by John Henry Raleigh is a remarkable achievement, published after the body of my study had been written; it is rich in new observations, wide in its interests, and connects O'Neill in a convincing way to American civilization.[56]

The viewpoint of this study being what it is, one has full reason to wonder whether it would not be obligatory to have first seen a play produced before presenting any theories of its scenic images. A sensible requirement, but not very easily fulfilled—least of all in the United States where revivals, even in the case of the only native playwright to win the Nobel Prize, are the exception rather than the rule. In order to have seen the major plays of Eugene O'Neill in original or

[56] Barrett H. Clark, *Eugene O'Neill: The Man and His Plays* (1926), Edwin A. Engel, *The Haunted Heroes of Eugene O'Neill* (1953), Doris V. Falk, *Eugene O'Neill and the Tragic Tension* (1958), Clifford Leech, *Eugene O'Neill* (1963), Arthur and Barbara Gelb, *O'Neill* (1960), Doris Alexander, *The Tempering of Eugene O'Neill* (1962), Croswell Bowen, *The Curse of the Misbegotten* (1959), Otto Koischwitz, *O'Neill* (1938), John Gassner, *Eugene O'Neill* (1965), and other volumes, John Henry Raleigh, *The Plays of Eugene O'Neill* (1965). *Die Erlösungsthematik bei Eugene O'Neill* (1968) by Knut Dorn includes new observations about the theme of redemption in O'Neill and about the structure of his late plays.

major productions one should have been born in America not later than circa 1905 and have lived on and off Broadway ever since. Instead of forging my passport and birth certificate I have done as well as I could without the privilege of membership in the audience of most of these plays. (I have, however, seen several revivals in Finland and two in America.)[57] I have relied mainly on the idea of the stage in my mind, and on a close reading of the texts. If all problems are not solved, several are at least stated; for this is how the unknown zone between a modern playwright and the stage is seen in this study: as problematic and intriguing.

[57] The productions I saw in the United States during the winter season of 1963-64 were of *Marco Millions* by the Repertory Company of Lincoln Center and of *A Touch of the Poet*, a student performance at the Yale Drama School. At least the following plays have been produced in professional theatres in Finland since 1956, either in Finnish or Swedish: *'Anna Christie,' The Emperor Jones, All God's Chillun Got Wings, Ah Wilderness!, The Iceman Cometh, Hughie, A Moon for the Misbegotten, A Touch of the Poet* (three productions), *Long Day's Journey Into Night* (four). I was responsible for directing *Long Day's Journey* when it was given in Finnish for the first time. *Ile, The Rope,* and *Where the Cross Is Made* have long been popular among amateur companies.

PART ONE

REALISM MIXED WITH

MELODRAMA

". . . I want to be an artist or nothing . . ."

O'Neill to Professor Baker, July 16, 1914. Published in *George Pierce Baker and the American Theatre* [Cambridge: Harvard University Press, 1954]. Cargill *et al.*, p. 20.

❧ 1 ❧

THE MAN AND HIS BACKGROUND

With the emergence of Eugene O'Neill the American drama
entered the international scene. Allardyce Nicoll, John Gassner, and Alan S. Downer, three historians of the drama,
are careful in cataloguing late nineteenth-century and early
twentieth-century forerunners; and they are just as careful in
treating playwrights like James A. Herne, Clyde Fitch, William Vaughan Moody, or Edward Shelton only as forerunners.[1] O'Neill was the first American measured with the
"yardstick of world drama"[2] by Gassner, following a passage
in which he concluded that "although a popular kind of
theatre flourished mightily, the American drama remained
feeble until after the World War. Even the kindest critics
must concede its decided inferiority to European plays."[3]

O'Neill did not, however, emerge by himself. Theatre is a
collective art; no playwright can grow in a vacuum. There
was, luckily for both O'Neill and the young American drama,
a growing interest in theatre as an art, not just as an enter-
tainment. The Provincetown Players, a group that might be
called "O'Neill's men," was one of many groups formed
about this time in different parts of the country. In New
York, it was preceded by the Washington Square Players,
followed by the Theatre Guild, "the longest-lived 'art theatre'
in America"[4] and the patron of most O'Neill world premieres
in the late twenties, thirties, and forties.

[1] Allardyce Nicoll, *World Drama* (1949), pp. 763-65, Alan S.
Downer, *Fifty Years of American Drama* (1951), pp. 40-41; cf.
Downer, "The Revolt from Broadway," in *A Time of Harvest*, Robert
E. Spiller (ed.), pp. 43-44.

[2] Gassner, *Masters of the Drama*, p. 637n.

[3] *Ibid.*, p. 631; cf. Gassner's introduction to *O'Neill* (1964), an
anthology of essays edited by him, p. 2.

[4] *Masters of the Drama*, p. 639. Hans Galinsky has compared the
Provincetown Players with late nineteenth-century "free stages" in
France, Germany, and England ("Eugene O'Neill: Die Wendung des
modernen amerikanischen Theaters zur Tragödie," *Die neueren
Sprachen*, 1953, 238).

31

Kenneth Macgowan, a critic, and Robert Edmund Jones, a scene designer, cooperated with O'Neill as directors of the Provincetown Playhouse in 1923-26. It is noteworthy that all three felt both before and after the year 1920 that the American theatre was lagging behind and looked to Europe for their models. If we try to see the postwar European stage through their eyes, we shall see first of all the great background figures of Ibsen and Strindberg,[5] surrounded by a group of followers, then the vigorous and controversial Shaw, a handful of German expressionists, and a few symbolists. Stage lighting was developing rapidly; new vistas were being opened up by pioneers like Appia and Craig. Reinhardt, the great magician, aroused admiration with his stagecraft. Richard Wagner, with his dream of *das Gesamtkunstwerk*, was not far behind in time.

America experienced these new movements in rapid succession: stylistic layers got confused; realism and naturalism were not given their due ripening time when new antirealistic ideas crossed the ocean.[6] Non-expert American audiences might well have gotten the impression that Ibsen and Strindberg were contemporaries of O'Neill, and the expressionists, Ibsen's younger brothers. Belasco's surface realism and romantic melodramas were replaced by serious social realism and expressionistic departures from it.

In this crisscrossing of ideas and impulses Eugene O'Neill probably looked more original than he actually was. He was prompt in confessing his debt to Strindberg,[7] less so to the German expressionists. What is, however, of greater impor-

[5] Several reasons for O'Neill's early and lasting popularity in Sweden are given by Karl Ragnar Gierow in his *Introduktioner till Eugene O'Neills dramatik* (1958), pp. 10-11. Stage directors Olof Molander, Per Lindberg, and Alf Sjöberg and the actors shared the enthusiasm shown by Martin Lamm, a scholar of the drama. They were used to doing Strindberg, O'Neill's master. We might add that there are Swedish and other Scandinavian characters in O'Neill's early plays; Anna Christie was played by Greta Garbo in the film.

[6] Gassner, *O'Neill*, p. 3: "O'Neill brought to a head a belated naturalistic trend in the American drama."

[7] Cargill *et al.*, pp. 108-09: a reprinting of O'Neill's statement in the Provincetown playbill for *The Spook Sonata*, Jan. 3, 1924.

tance than these more or less controversial influences is the existence of a lively and encouraging climate. For the first time, and with good reason, there was a general consensus that something important was happening in American drama. That is why the man who had given the finest promise, who was exciting and prolific, was given a freer hand to experiment than anyone before him, and perhaps ever since.

Only against this background of stylistic mixture and a spirit favorable to artistic enterprise can we understand the abrupt transformations which occurred during O'Neill's early career. He had hardly established himself as the pioneer of realism in America when he abandoned it for expressionism and even traditional romanticism (*The Fountain*). No wonder he was suspected of taking a short cut to the melodramas of the preceding decades.[8]

This is, however, to jump into the second part of my study; right now it is enough to know that at the outset O'Neill had his roots in the tradition of melodrama, while his conscious models were in Europe.[9] From the viewpoint of scenic expression the models mentioned above are more important than the undeniably strong Nietzschean undercurrent in O'Neill's philosophy.[10] And for our introductory picture, that of a young man dedicated to serious drama, confronting an empty stage, it is worth noticing, by way of prognosis, that there was to come in the twenties and thirties "a veritable

[8] Raleigh has shown in detail the influence of a particular melodrama, *The Count of Monte Cristo*, on O'Neill (*The Plays of Eugene O'Neill*, pp. 179-94; cf. "Eugene O'Neill and the Escape from the Château d'If," in Gassner, *O'Neill*, pp. 7-22). Helmut M. Braem has remarked that O'Neill had seen only melodramas when he started to write himself (*Eugene O'Neill* [1965], p. 32).

[9] Downer ("Revolt from Broadway," pp. 45-46), Braem (p. 41), Raleigh (pp. 242-85), and Koischwitz (pp. 15-16) tend to stress the importance of O'Neill's affinities with American culture, while Margret Dietrich connects him with European traditions (*Das moderne Drama* [1961], p. 227), and Robert Brustein with "a cosmopolitan movement" (*The Theatre of Revolt*, p. 10).

[10] E.g. Koischwitz, p. 41, Alexander, *The Tempering of Eugene O'Neill*, pp. 106, 261; Cyrus Day, "*Amor Fati*," *Modern Drama, 3* (1960), 297. As a rule, it is my aim to follow theatrical influences and connections rather than literary or sociological ones.

galaxy,"[11] and that he had a greater share in this transformation than anyone else. He certainly had two personal characteristics demanded by the role: integrity and a determination bordering on stubbornness.

Jordan Y. Miller had some justification in 1962 for calling Eugene O'Neill "one of the most inaccessible and unknown American literary artists ever to achieve international recognition."[12] Today, however, after three carefully documented biographies and several special studies have been published, this definition is hardly acceptable. Though isolated from the public in his later years, O'Neill spent most of his youth in the midst of an outspoken Bohemian minority. And recent efforts have uncovered a great many documents and reminiscences even from his years of seclusion. Gradually a complete picture of the man is emerging.

Two of O'Neill's basic characteristics bear direct relevance to his use of scenic means of expression: his obsessive inclinations, referred to above as stubbornness; and a paradoxical tension between love and hate. He certainly was, as Edwin A. Engel puts it, "obsessed by obsessions."[13] *Ile*, *Where the Cross Is Made* (and naturally *Gold*), *Diff'rent*, *Strange Interlude*, and *A Touch of the Poet* are plays in which the obsession of the central character is given emphatic thematic significance. Thirty years after the time in which he placed the events and twenty years after the death of the last member of his family he was still haunted by the memories of his childhood and adolescence—so much so that he reproduced them almost exactly for one of his last and best

[11] Gassner, *Masters of the Drama*, p. 662; cf. Nicoll, pp. 766-67. Eric Bentley came with strict demands (*The Dramatic Event* [1954], pp. 270-71), and did not find them fulfilled; the importance of the twenties has been restated by Downer ("Revolt from Broadway," p. 53).

[12] Jordan Y. Miller, *Eugene O'Neill and the American Critic*, p. 9.

[13] Engel, *The Haunted Heroes*, p. 221. Hans Daiber has referred to works by Ibsen, William James, Freud, and Pirandello, and concluded that the power of delusions was a common theme in literature: it was "in the air" ("Der Tragiker der neuen Welt," *Neue Deutsche Hefte*, 8 [1961], p. 21).

34

plays. Once he had allowed an idea to enter through the thick, protective wall into the inner spheres of his personality, it had a pervading effect on his work—not just once, or on only one level, but continually and on several levels. The idea of eternal recurrence, for example, not only provided the consoling solution in a few of his plays; it also gave him the prototype of play structure, the circle. Masks are not only pieces of property, but also concepts mentioned throughout the O'Neill canon in stage directions and in dialogue; they seem to demonstrate a dominant vision of human nature.

Paradoxically, this restless experimenter was inclined to use certain means of expression over and over again in different variations and combinations because they apparently corresponded to some deeply personal needs. The whole concept of scenic units can be connected with this feature: playwrights who are more versatile and less stubborn than Eugene O'Neill are probably less open to an approach using this concept.[14]

Ambivalent love-hate relations are, of course, more relevant in thematic than in scenic analyses. Yet this feature is so pervasive that certain phenomena cannot be explained without referring to this paradoxical tension, so deeply rooted in O'Neill's creative work. Fog not only leads astray, it also conceals; moonlight is ghastly and beautiful. *The Iceman Cometh* is a difficult play to interpret, on any level; one possible key to its thematic or structural solutions seems to be that "pipe-dreams" are not only condemned but just as furiously loved. Tensions of this kind, psychological in origin, artistic in effect, have long been acknowledged by critics.[15]

These two general ideas, taken from the psychological approach, will remain with us as we follow a dramatist's quest

[14] Koischwitz, calling O'Neill a theatricalist above all, has already seen his inclination to repeat certain means of expression: "Behind the curtain . . . he has a couple of properties and settings, built again and again, his 'favourite motifs' " (p. 12).

[15] E.g. Sophus K. Winther, *Eugene O'Neill* (1934), p. 12: "He is complex, intricate, a divided personality, a man at war with himself." Lauri Viljanen has described *Mourning Becomes Electra* in similar terms (*Taisteleva humanismi*, pp. 470-71). The theme of love-hate in O'Neill's life is followed by the Gelbs, e.g. pp. 4, 9, 369, 849.

through thirty years of playwriting. They will not, let us hope, lead us into sheer speculation as they did Richard Dana Skinner, who read the plays directly as confessions, as reflections of "the inner development in his own soul of the universal poet's quest."[16] Rather, it is sensible to agree with Leech: "We do need to know the conditions of his life, so that we can see where memory has overburdened his work, why dissatisfaction is here or there provoked, but we need to see that work impersonally and dispassionately."[17] Among these conditions of his life there are the adventures of a famous actor's son on the sea, on the stage, and as a bum; they are for everyone to read in the plays and biographies.

The field of this study consists of 46 printed plays: 20 one-acters, 26 full-length plays. This sounds unequivocal enough; yet there are bibliographical complications. An "Alphabetical Check List of Plays," published by Cargill *et consortes*,[18] lists 75 plays, out of which 64 were actually written; 11 remained mere names and 49 have been preserved. It remains to be seen whether those three early plays, which are original in subject matter and have been registered at the Library of Congress, will ever be published. With Mrs. Carlotta Monterey O'Neill's generous permission, these plays are discussed in the third chapter of this study. In addition, there are sketches, letters, notebooks, and personal papers in the O'Neill Collection at Yale waiting for the required twenty-five years after the playwright's death to elapse.[19] For a list of the plays, see Appendix A, pp. 349-50.

[16] Richard Dana Skinner, *Eugene O'Neill: A Poet's Quest* (1935), p. 35.

[17] Leech, p. 2.

[18] Cargill *et al.*, pp. 479-82.

[19] Notebooks and other personal papers are not available for scholars; different manuscript versions of several plays are. Until now, copies of these have not been sent abroad. In his answer to my inquiry Dr. Donald Gallup, curator of the O'Neill Collection at Yale, said that he might get permission to send a copy of the original manuscript of *The Iceman Cometh* to me, but not of all four versions of that play. As the manuscript is not easily legible, and as no comparisons could be based on one version only, I gave up the idea of studying it. From the point of view of scenic expression what matters is, most of all, the final version.

Among the numerous plays destroyed by O'Neill himself there were, most notably, 6 drafted plays of the planned cycle of 11 chronicle dramas entitled "A Tale of Possessors Self-Dispossessed." One of the "Cycle" plays, *A Touch of the Poet*, was finished by the playwright himself, and produced and published after his death; another, *More Stately Mansions*, has been shortened by Karl Ragnar Gierow from the author's partly revised text, and was produced in 1962 by the Royal Dramatic Theatre in Stockholm and edited as a book version in English by Donald Gallup. It was produced in New York in 1967-68 under the direction of José Quintero.

If we start to worry about the details of bibliography or correct chronological order in the case of a playwright, matters become complicated by the fact that there are three possible bases for a chronology: the dates of composition, of first stage production, and of first edition. In O'Neill's case, the exact dates of composition cannot be defined because it was his habit to revise his texts continually. Production and publication sequences do not always agree, some plays were printed beforehand, some afterwards, and these two versions of his plays do not necessarily coincide: "a number of his published plays were greatly rewritten versions of the produced ones."[20] Moreover, there are several discrepancies between the stage history and the (approximate) order of composition; a case in point is *Long Day's Journey Into Night*, which was written before its sequel *A Moon for the Misbegotten* but not produced until ten years later.

For an O'Neill scholar chronology is a servant, not a master. It has thus seemed permissible to deal with it somewhat freely, grouping under the same heading plays written over a period of several years which show a common trend. O'Neill did not proceed in any definite direction, continuously and without digressions: rather, there were several growing points, left at peace for a while, then returned to. It is thus possible to gather his less important plays around some particularly striking scenic means of expression while dedicat-

[20] The Gelbs, p. 651.

ing full-scale analysis to the central ones. On the other hand, following the development of certain means of expression all through the canon, each in its own chapter, would have led to an over-schematized structure; it is the interaction of different means that builds up the play and makes it an individual whole.

The generally acknowledged unevenness of O'Neill's total output is a further justification for not analyzing every play in depth. Joseph Wood Krutch contends that "the work of no other important contemporary has been more uneven."[21] O'Neill's self-criticism is just as uneven: the Gelbs give many examples of wild fluctuation and conclude that, like many fellow-artists, he was usually convinced only of the greatness of the work he was currently doing.[22] If unreliable in this respect, he wrote more accurately about his method of creating. The following passage may serve as a kind of motto for what follows, for the variety and stylistic mixture in Eugene O'Neill's plays—and as a reminder that he wrote with the idea of the stage in his mind:

I always let the subject matter mould itself into its own particular form and I find it does this without my ever wasting thought upon it. I start out with the idea that there are no rules or precedent in the game except what the play chooses to make for itself—but not forgetting that it is to be played in a theatre—("theatre" meaning my notion of what a modern theatre should be capable of instead of merely what it is). I usually feel instinctively a sort of rhythm of acts or scenes and obey it hit or miss.[23]

The passage is from a letter to Kenneth Macgowan, another American interested in "what a modern theatre should be capable of."

[21] Joseph Wood Krutch, *The American Drama Since 1918* (1957), p. 78. O'Neill's constant fluctuation "between monumental achievement and abysmal failure" is also mentioned by Jordan Y. Miller in his introduction to *Playwright's Progress: O'Neill and the Critics* (1965).
[22] The Gelbs, p. 376.
[23] *Ibid.*, p. 469.

2

APPRENTICESHIP I

EXERCISES IN CONSTRUCTING

A SCENIC IMAGE

When viewing the early works of an author in retrospect, it is most fruitful to see in these often deficient achievements the origins of themes and technical solutions later employed to full advantage. The main purpose of this chapter is to follow Eugene O'Neill's groping efforts to gain mastery over the central scenic means of expression, setting, dialogue, sound effects, music, lighting, and the individual expression of the actors. A chronological order is followed; the less important plays are scarcely mentioned. Three unpublished manuscripts and all full-length plays worth more than a passing reference are discussed in later chapters. A few scenic images, more characteristic and powerful than the rest, are analyzed to show how O'Neill used his newly won competence to make his scenic means function together. They occur in what might be called his "fate plays" and form a direct line of development in his scenic thinking. And they occur in one-act plays: O'Neill started his career with exercises in constructing just one scenic image.

Careful stage directions are a common feature all through the O'Neill canon, so we might just as well deal with them right now.[1] Their language is not polished, and they are full of clichés: the word "dully" is repeated in almost every play. Yet the directions serve their purpose and give testimony to

[1] Raleigh calls O'Neill's stage directions "accurate, convincing, and suggestive," and sees in them a line of development toward "programmatic and systematic concreteness" (*The Plays of Eugene O'Neill*, pp. 211-12), while Biese speaks of "a running commentary," and remarks that they "may have been at least partly instrumental in the evolution of the silent monologue" in *Strange Interlude* (*Aspects of Expression I*, p. 22).

the fact that the idea of the stage was actively and continuously present in O'Neill's mind during the process of writing. Along with an enjoyment in expressing his feeling about life went an interest in the structure of the play and in "the theater itself, into which it was all going. He was happy in that, and sure of it too—very sure. He wrote the descriptions of the scenes as he came to them with as much creative absorption as when he wrote the dialogue."[2]

The other side of the coin is that this procedure was a guarantee to this obstinate artist that his vision would also be realized on the stage—or was it a guarantee? "It never failed to infuriate him that despite his knowledge of actor craft and the pains he always took to forestall an actor's personal interpretation of a role by spelling out every important gesture, look and vocal nuance, he could still not get the effect he wanted."[3]

Here we are, in the middle of a tempestuous love-hate affair—with the theatre. With a possessive love for the stage, O'Neill wrote down those minute directions; and with hatred he saw the independence of the resulting works of art in the hands of the directors and actors. This paradox explains, at least partially, the contrasting reactions to the stage directions themselves. The playwright Virgil Geddes does not approve of them: "His plays are written with strong dictations to the actor and stage directions which invite antagonism more than they spur imagination."[4] Yet they have been appreciated by others, who sense the love and care which motivated them: even if "his written instructions about characters turning pale or sweating . . . seem pointless and impossible to project, they are actually important road signs for the intelligent actor, and many of O'Neill's actors have expressed gratitude for them."[5] Seeing them as "road signs" rather than absolute laws is the most sensible approach, for directors as well as actors. Critics, too, have reason to be grateful for them, because they

[2] Agnes Boulton, *Part of a Long Story*, pp. 112-13.
[3] The Gelbs, *O'Neill*, p. 590.
[4] Virgil Geddes, *The Melodramadness of Eugene O'Neill* (1934), pp. 8-9.
[5] The Gelbs, p. 325.

help to clarify our picture of the dramatist's vision. And they are available from the very first plays, poor as these are: the stage had been among the universities of Eugene O'Neill's youth.

O'Neill's first play was probably *A Wife for a Life* (written in 1913), though he sometimes gave that honor to *The Web*, calling the former a vaudeville sketch in his mind.[6] In *A Wife* we can register the first—and fumbling—use of the monologue, which was to develop into one of O'Neill's major assets. In fact, there are three monologues on eleven pages, one of them with a variation: Jack speaks "dreamily, absorbed in his own thoughts" (LP 151). He is not the last character to do so in an O'Neill play.

In *The Web* (1913) the theme of fate is mentioned bluntly in the stage directions: "Rose seems in a trance. . . . She seems to be aware of something in the room which none of the others can see—perhaps the personification of the ironic life force that has crushed her" (THIRST 69). She tries to speak to it, and is misunderstood by a policeman. The idea is not properly conveyed to the audience.

Though hidden in a stage direction, this key passage has been noticed by several critics.[7] O'Neill arrived at basically tragic situations when following his natural inclinations, when trying to give a scenic form to his experiences on the seas and on the shore. If he had come to these situations more theoretically, he might have written structurally orthodox, full-length tragedies; instead, he wrote one-act plays, in which the theme of fate is crystallized in just one scenic image, constructed to make the audiences share O'Neill's awareness of an ironic life force.

[6] Cf. Cargill *et al., O'Neill and His Plays*, p. 482, and the Gelbs, pp. 134, 231-33.

[7] Isaac Goldberg sees in the phrase "ironic life-force" a symptom of Shaw's influence (Cargill *et al.*, p. 236, a reprinting from *The Drama in Transition*, Cincinnati: Stewart Kidd, 1922). Joseph Wood Krutch remarks in a comparison with Maxwell Anderson that O'Neill found "his subject before he realized that it was a traditional, tragic subject (*"Modernism" in Modern Drama* [1953], p. 120).

It is certainly O'Neill's intention to make his characters, readers, and audiences experience vivid sensations from *Thirst* (1913-14): "The heat is terrific. Writhing, fantastic heat-waves rise from the white deck of the raft. Here and there on the still surface of the sea the fins of sharks may be seen slowly cutting the surface of the water in lazy circles" (THIRST 7). On the raft, under this fateful sun that is like "a great angry eye of God" (THIRST 43),[8] there are two whites in miserable rags and a West Indian sailor. Variations of monologue are employed: "the Gentleman" speaks out in spite of "the Dancer," who later becomes insane and dies after a long soliloquy. The theme of superstition, foreshadowing *The Emperor Jones*, is carried by a monotonous song hummed by the sailor. Lighting, setting, and pantomime are fused in a violent climax, in a scenic image.

The dancer's solo number, preparing the way for the climax, is in fact the only sequence in which the themes are properly concretized in terms of the stage. Elsewhere, the situation is left undeveloped, the dialogue is jerky, and the life force, expressed by using the blazing sun, is immovable. The characters keep talking mainly because the playwright wants to; the main subject of discussion, the short past which they share, includes both melodramatic and commonplace events. O'Neill does not rely on his ability to make his scenic image speak for itself; instead, he compels his characters to speak and gesture grotesquely. The description of the dance is remarkable, both because it can be called a picture of the awkward, mechanical quality of the entire play, and because a certain scenic unit, the automaton effect, occurs in it for the first time: "She is like some ghastly marionette, jerked by invisible wires. She dances faster and faster. Her arms and legs fly grotesquely around as if beyond control" (THIRST 40). The end of the play reveals O'Neill's eye for the irony of fate.

[8] Raleigh has observed that O'Neill's late plays "take place on, or begin on, excessively hot days," and sees in this feature a suggestion of "a secular, naturalistic version of hell" (pp. 204-06). *Fog, Thirst, Beyond the Horizon, Strange Interlude*, and *The Hairy Ape* are mentioned as further examples.

A valuable necklace, now completely worthless, "lies glittering in the blazing sunshine" (THIRST 43).

There is an effort to dramatize the theme of fate with the aid of the setting, lighting and action, in *Thirst*—as there is in *Fog* (1913-14), another play which opens just after a shipwreck. "The life-boat of a passenger steamer is drifting helplessly off the Grand Banks of Newfoundland. A dense fog lies heavily upon the still sea. There is no wind. . . . A menacing silence, like the genius of the fog, broods over everything" (THIRST 108). There are more layers of meaning in this play than in the preceding ones. The constellation of characters which it contains was favored by O'Neill later on: a poet and a businessman are contrasted, in order to drive home a social point. Even if the former is idealized, the latter satirized, the characters belong more closely together than those in *Thirst*, who are thrown on the same raft merely by chance. Furthermore, the tone is calmer here and the dialogue more natural. Lighting effects and ironic twists are, again, among the interesting facets. The final scenic image has a mystifying flavor: the shipwrecked are saved, fate is defeated, because a child's cry is heard through the fog—and yet the child on the boat has been dead for a day and night.

When dealing with *Fog*, Doris V. Falk says that the action of the play takes place in "the same fog of ignorance and fear which surrounds [O'Neill's] characters in later plays, even as late as *Long Day's Journey Into Night*. Through this fog sails the *S. S. Glencairn* in *Bound East for Cardiff*, written also in 1914."[9] This is an oversimplification; the same idea or even the same scenic unit need not necessarily mean the same thing in different scenic contexts (here it is almost inevitable to create a neologism: constage). Ideas may interact; fog has, no doubt, more subtle overtones in later plays than here. The ambivalent tension between fear and joy of life is introduced as early as in *'Anna Christie'*, while

[9] Doris V. Falk, *Eugene O'Neill and the Tragic Tension*, pp. 19-20. Cf. Raleigh, pp. 23-25, where the different functions in different plays are considered.

the dying Yank transforms the fog into a symbol of death in *Bound East for Cardiff*. We might say that it represents fate in *Fog*: it both leads astray and is constantly and gracelessly present, in the "menacing silence" where "there is no wind." This time, fate is defeated.

Warnings, a two-act play dealing with the sea, is a mixture of naturalism and melodrama. Fate here is dumb, not blind; pathos is achieved. Even more insignificant is *Recklessness*, an elementary melodrama on the same lines with O'Neill's first full-length play, *Servitude* (all three, 1913-14). After *Now I Ask You*, a play existing only as a manuscript, O'Neill luckily stepped out of the middle- or upper-class living room —to return successfully as late as in *Strange Interlude*, masterfully in *Long Day's Journey Into Night*. Some efforts in between were hardly successes, in any sense.

The next step forward is *Abortion* (1913-14), another fate play. Its milieu is "a large eastern university" (LP 11), its hero, Jack Townsend, has had an affair with a girl of low birth, now dead after an abortion. The playlet certainly has its flaws: its ideas are puerile, its characterization is conventional. Yet the carefully prepared climax has a powerful, ironic tinge, as several means of expression fuse together to form a scenic image: lighting, music, and song, furnished by the approaching parade of college students, the whole dormitory atmosphere present in the setting. This, and not *The Emperor Jones*, as is commonly assumed, is the first play in which O'Neill makes use of a repetitive sound effect with an increase in intensity—and does so in a purposeful way: "From this point to the end these sounds are continuous, the band only being silenced to permit the giving of the cheer, and as the action progresses they become more and more distinct" (LP 30). Lighting, too, is given attention: "The glare of the red fire glows dully on the window shades." And then, as "the first part of the cheer booms out," Jack Townsend, the baseball hero so magnificently celebrated, shoots himself, and "the report is drowned by the cheering. . . . The band strikes up: 'For He's A Jolly Good Fellow.' The students commence to sing" (LP 33-34).

A crude and over-obvious point? Perhaps; yet not without merit in its effectiveness and thematic significance. Fate, here a "benevolent" symbol to all those social forces which led Jack to disaster, comes marching closer and closer, inevitably and ironically; the guilty hero is helpless. The only way out is in violence, self-destruction.

Bound East for Cardiff (1914) is an important play for several reasons. It is a logical continuation of O'Neill's previous fate plays: he is now applying what he learned from past experiments with more confidence and less contrivance than ever before. Two scenic units, monologue and repetitive sound effect, are used to deepen the characterization and to intensify the atmosphere peculiar to the play. *Bound East* was also the first of his works to be produced; it encouraged the Provincetown Players to give the young playwright an opportunity to experiment freely; it ranks high among O'Neill's one-act plays; and it has received more critical attention than any of its predecessors. Basically it is a simple play, set in the seamen's forecastle on board the *S. S. Glencairn*, which was later to give her name to a quartet of short plays. One of the seamen, Yank, is dying as a result of an accident, in the process exerting a soothing effect on his shipmates. One of them, Driscoll, has remained in the forecastle to keep Yank company, and his consoling, nostalgic speeches form a background for Yank's monologue. Outside, the night is foggy: "At regular intervals of a minute or so the blast of the steamer's whistle can be heard above all the other sounds" (P I 477).

Koischwitz sees in this setting an arrangement typical of O'Neill. The stage is divided into fore- and backstage areas: the whistle, a "sound coulisse," is used to remind the audience of the space outside the walls of the forecastle; the rhythmic snoring of sleeping seamen forms a sound coulisse in the foreground.[10] Another facet in the setting is the claustrophobic closeness of the room: "An irregular-shaped com-

[10] Koischwitz, *O'Neill*, pp. 104-05. About "Geräuschkulissen," see p. 73.

partment, the sides of which almost meet at the far end to form a triangle" (P I 477).

Within the walls of the forecastle, O'Neill begins, as Kenneth Macgowan puts it, "to work on the problem of getting out upon the stage more of a man's inner consciousness than a man would ordinarily bare to his fellows. O'Neill did the trick by throwing his chief character into the fever of death."[11] Previously when O'Neill used monologues, the characters to whom he gave them had little inner consciousness to reveal; here he has created an interesting individual, with experiences on the sea (among them a shipwreck—reminiscent of *Fog* and *Thirst*). Death and life are contrasted in a barren yet expressive language, supported by the setting, by the acting, and by the whistle: "This sailor life ain't much to cry about leavin'—just one ship after another, hard work, small pay, and bum grub; and when we git into port, just a drunk endin' up in a fight, and all your money gone, and then ship away again" (P I 486).

Toward the end, Yank discloses his life-long dream of life on a farm far from the sea. Eugene M. Waith comments: "It is an unexpected revelation of his character and by its intimacy it brings Driscoll closer to him than ever before." The action of the play is thus to be seen as "the characteristic movement of an O'Neill play—a movement toward discovery or revelation or both—a kind of unmasking."[12] The mask is removed in the scenic image of the play.

This is the place to make a distinction within the concept of monologue. Yank's revealing speech is not addressed to the audience, as in the aside technique of the "well-made play." Nor is it a fragment of ordinary dialogue, spoken only to his fellow-actors. One might call it a *modified monologue*, spoken in spite of another character, out of inner compulsion, not in reaction to a previous speech, nor aside, as an

[11] Cargill *et al.*, p. 450: a reprinting of Kenneth Macgowan's article "The O'Neill Soliloquy," first published in the *Theatre Guild Magazine* (Feb. 1929).

[12] Eugene M. Waith, "Eugene O'Neill: an Exercise in Unmasking," *Educational Theatre Journal, 13* (1960), 185. The article is republished in Gassner (ed.), *O'Neill*, pp. 29-41.

interpolation of the playwright.[13] It is a specific kind of dialogue employed by O'Neill continually and with several variations, and can be considered one of his scenic units according to the definition given above (p. 16). A notable example of a modified monologue is the "thought-asides" technique of *Strange Interlude*. O'Neill was perhaps encouraged to use them by the model found in the "well-made plays." Yet he quickly turned his borrowed technique to his own purposes.

The steamer's whistles, a repetitive sound effect, is also a scenic unit worth noticing. It has been connected with several precedents by Isaac Goldberg, who finds evidence of O'Neill's "fondness for aural effects" in Rose's coughing in *The Web*, in "the whining of the wireless in *Warnings*, the steamer whistles and the dripping water of the icebergs in *Fog*; there are, in *The Web* itself, the falling raindrops."[14] In *Abortion*, the sound effect was both repetitive and increasing in intensity, foreshadowing *The Emperor Jones*.

Bound East for Cardiff is a unicellular play; it contains just one scenic image, which receives very little elaboration from the outer action. Its components are the dying Yank, the shipmates, the forecastle, the whistle. Yank's whole life is present in this image. Since the elements are rare, each of them is emphatic. The whistle is called by Engel "the audible symbol of the lonely sea, of the oppressive fog, of approaching death"[15]—an appropriate characterization. The oppressive setting, again a prototype of similar solutions later on, is both

---

[13] Coghill quotes a passage from *Elizabethan Acting* by B. L. Joseph (Oxford, 1951): the dialogue is divided into four different types, according to the persons addressed. Coghill himself distinguishes seven functions given to soliloquies: "Comedy, Exposition, Comment, Prediction, Meditation, Prayer and Personal Epiphany" (*Shakespeare's Professional Skills*, pp. 131, 137). Neither of these classifications suits my purposes: what is called a "modified monologue" is a "Personal Epiphany" spoken while there are other characters present. Whether these other characters hear or not, a decisive point in Joseph's system, has no bearing; in the focus, there is the *speaker* and his obsession. Raleigh (p. 184) sees the "Fechter version" of *The Count of Monte Cristo*, rather than Elizabethan drama, as the source of O'Neill's soliloquies.

[14] Cargill *et al.*, p. 235.

[15] Engel, *The Haunted Heroes*, p. 14.

expressive and easily manageable on the stage; the settings of *Thirst* or *Fog* were less successful in the latter respect. As a whole, O'Neill is firmly in control of his scenic means of expression here. He knows how to use them in constructing a striking scenic image.

Tragic irony is again present at the very end of the play— as it had been shortly before, when the voice of the lookout cut across Yank's first thought of his impending death with the cry: "Aaall's welll" (P I 482). One of Yank's last wishes is that he might die on a clear night: "Why should it be a rotten night like this with that damned whistle blowin' and people snorin' all round? I wish the stars was out, and the moon, too; I c'd lie out on deck and look at them, and it'd make it easier to go—somehow" (P I 489). Yet it is not until just after his death that O'Neill lifts the fog. Although Yank does not live long enough to get his wish fulfilled, we, as spectators, do see his fate against the perspective of a star-lit sky. We are allowed to see both sides of the matter, the tragic and the ironical, and to appreciate both the warmth and clear-sightedness shown by O'Neill in a way typical of his last phase.[16]

The most remarkable feature in *Bound East for Cardiff* is its bare realism, a violent contrast to the melodramas all around. A sailor dies, without heroism; just as his life has been banal and insignificant, so is his death. Yet the play in stating these simple things is neither banal nor insignificant. The life of a human being, drawing close to its end, is weighed—as it was to be weighed in the great modified monologue of James Tyrone, the actor, at the end of *Long Day's Journey Into Night.*

Nature furnished the opening night of *Bound East for Cardiff* with an appropriate setting: a dense fog surrounded the Wharf Theatre. And a new playwright was born, in alliance with the Provincetown group, whose strong man George

---

[16] Both are evaluated by Koischwitz in his analysis of the play; he also pays attention to the contrast between "the miserable closeness" of the forecastle and the wideness of the starlit sky (pp. 104-06).

Cram ("Jig") Cook played the leading role.[17] If this event did not put an end to O'Neill's restless "*Wanderjahre*," it gave him a firmer purpose, together with a theatre and an audience. In just a few years he was to be called the leading American playwright.

The remaining one-act plays of this early phase are all of lesser interest. They are exercises of one kind or another, and, though their scenic means of expression may include foreshadowing features, they are not important enough to warrant close analysis; a scenic image is described in just one case. These playlets are fateful melodramas rather than fate plays.

The Sniper (1914-15), a pacifist piece dealing with the effects of World War I on a Belgian village, includes two scenic units: an introductory pantomime, which is typical not only of O'Neill but also of the "well-made play," and the setting, of which more need be said. "The rear wall has two enormous breaches made by the shells of the artillery. . . . Through the breaches . . . a dark green vista of rolling fields can be seen. Where they meet the horizon they are already shimmering in the golden dust of the sunset" (LP 52). What is present here is not only an ironical contrast in the setting, but also an important theme—the feeling of alienation. Nature is beautiful, man's creations are ugly; here not only ugly but also senselessly destroyed by man himself. It is a theme that was to occupy O'Neill's mind long afterwards, in *The Hairy Ape,* in *Desire Under the Elms,* and in *A Moon for the Misbegotten,* in which he conveys variations of it through similar contrasts in the settings. We may see the beginnings of O'Neill's skeleton setting here: "No trace of the doorway to the road remains. The larger breach in the rear wall is used as exit and entrance" (LP 52). The idea of a disharmonious relation between man and nature is expressed here through a

[17] Cargill *et al.*, pp. 30-31, a reprinting from *The Road to the Temple* by Susan Glaspell (New York, 1927).

specific kind of setting, through a scenic unit: a destitute house in contrast to the smiling fields.

Before Breakfast (1916) offers another example of O'Neill's early interest in soliloquies, and it has been compared with *Den starkare* (The Stronger) by Strindberg, O'Neill's acknowledged master. The only person visible on the stage is a youngish married woman, who is starting her day, with little interest in anything, in a shabby combined kitchen and living room. Instead of writing a monologue fluctuating paradoxically from one state of mind to another, as O'Neill might have done in his mature years, or as Cocteau and Beckett have done, he presents a continuous outburst of accusations—well-founded, no doubt. The audience never sees the husband; after being given a glimpse of a sensitive hand, they hear a crashing noise as his body hits the floor, and learn that he has cut his throat.

In his special study, "Strindberg and O'Neill," Frederic Fleisher deals with the problems of influence and finds in this case "little similarity in themes," some in structure. "In both these plays the silent figure is used as a sort of mirror for the other character's disturbed mind."[18] Since Strindberg's play was translated and produced in America in 1913, it is possible that O'Neill was familiar with it. It is worth noticing, however, that the play represents a phase in Strindberg's development when he was strongly influenced by Nietzsche, O'Neill's master par excellence—and yet the thematic parallels are negligible.[19] Be that as it may, this technical solution was to remain with O'Neill a long time; as late as in *A Touch of the Poet* he used Nora and Sara, mother and daughter, as mirrors of one another, in a memorable scene of intertwined monologues.

In 1916-17, after the success of *Bound East for Cardiff*, O'Neill wrote three more plays dealing with the *S. S. Glencairn* and her crew. All four were produced together in 1924,

[18] Frederic Fleisher, "Strindberg and O'Neill," *Symposium*, *10* (1956), 85-86.

[19] *Before Breakfast* is also connected with Strindberg by Viljanen who sees Nietzsche's influence in *Ile* (*Taisteleva humanismi*, p. 454).

under the name of the ship. *The Moon of the Caribbees* comes closest to the level of its predecessor. The emphasis is strongly on the atmosphere, evoked by lighting, songs, and action: the Caribbean moon is full, and a Negro chant drifts broodingly over the water, "faint and far-off, like the mood of the moonlight made audible" (P I 474). The last phrase gives a picture of the fusion of the scenic means of expression in this playlet by employing synesthesia.

In the focus of the play there is Smitty, a drunkard and an ex-gentleman, who has a confidant, a listener to his monologue, modified as in the case of Yank. In the background there is O'Neill's first group and chorus scene; it was not to be his last. The central weakness of the play is that the melancholy atmosphere and Smitty belong too harmoniously together. Yank and fog do not; they are contrasted, and a miracle is needed to relieve the tension. We may see in Smitty the prototype of later O'Neill heroes, as Engel does,[20] and conclude that his self-pity cannot be as readily approved as Yank's, who was after all face to face with death.

Three short plays can be called germs for full-length ones. *The Rope* (1918), which was to grow into *Desire Under the Elms*, has a structural pattern that was to become O'Neill's favorite: the circle. The play both begins and ends with a pantomime of Mary, a retarded child. It also belongs to that phase in O'Neill's development when he began to make his precise descriptions of characters carry his themes. Conventional elements, inherited from the prevalent theatrical tradition, were replaced by more personal, individualized features. In the description of Luke Bentley, an early sketch for Jamie Tyrone, we meet the paradoxical conflict between opposite characteristics, so typical of O'Neill's later heroes: "What his face lacks in intelligence is partly forgiven for his good-natured, half-foolish grin, his hearty laugh, his curly dark hair, a certain devil-may-care recklessness and irresponsible youth

[20] Engel, p. 12; his evaluation of the play is sound. The two other members of the *S.S. Glencairn* cycle are *In the Zone* and *The Long Voyage Home*. The cycle as a full-length play is discussed by R. Dilworth Rust ("The Unity of O'Neill's *S.S. Glencairn*," *American Literature, 37*, 280-90).

in voice and gesture. But his mouth is weak and character-less; his brown eyes are large but shifty and acquisitive" (P I 587). The words "but" and "yet" in emphatic positions are repeated over and over again in these descriptions. There is an ironically pointed end in *The Dreamy Kid* also—and there is again an affinity with a longer play, *The Emperor Jones.*

Throughout these years O'Neill was on his way toward full-length plays, a fact which can be seen in these pairs of plays. He apparently felt that completing a one-act play did not empty the potentialities of his material, not at least if crossed with new elements. This is overt in the case of *Where the Cross Is Made*, a one-act play employed, with some re-markable changes, as the last act in *Gold*, a four-act melodrama. O'Neill called *Where the Cross Is Made* "an amusing experiment in treating the audience as insane."[21] Captain Bartlett, a prisoner of delusions, sees three crew members of his lost ship flow into the room. The scenic image is constructed with the help of lighting and sound effects: "The sound of the wind and sea suddenly ceases and there is a heavy silence. A dense green glow floods slowly in rhythmic waves like a liquid into the room—as of great depths of the sea faintly penetrated by light" (P I 570). A repetitive sound effect, a conglomerate of the wind and "an insistent monotone of thundering surf, muffled and far-off" (P I 555), is here not intensified but cut off, to achieve a climactic effect.[22] When the ghosts have gone, with their light-ing, the sounds return.

O'Neill was to employ apparitions, with greater skill if not with lesser thrill, in *The Emperor Jones*, and in a less remark-able way in *The Fountain* and *The Ancient Mariner.* Still later the ghosts were transferred to the minds of his protago-nists and were expressed by details in the setting and by ref-

[21] Isaac Goldberg, *The Theatre of George Jean Nathan* (1926), p. 150, a reprinting of a letter from O'Neill to Nathan, June 20, 1920.

[22] Koischwitz has noticed that "muffled" is a word often repeated in O'Neill's descriptions of sound effects; in a similar way, light is dimmed "by shades, window curtains and walls of fog, furnishing O'Neill's settings with a peculiar, charmful atmosphere" (p. 74).

erences in the dialogue. When used within a short play and concretized on the stage, they leave a markedly romantic impression, reminiscent of E.T.A. Hoffman or of American horror melodramas, so popular in the latter half of the nineteenth century. These latter plays are perhaps as good a guess for O'Neill's source as Shakespeare, suggested by the Gelbs.[23] This kind of scenic image is not easily realized on the stage, and, if executed, it probably is not worth the trouble. It was abandoned in *Gold.*

The setting of *Where the Cross Is Made,* an imitation of a captain's cabin on board a vessel, helps to evoke the intended atmosphere. So does the over-all lighting. Moonlight, a scenic unit, serves a function different from that in *The Moon of the Caribbees*: it is ghastly, not beautiful. In *A Moon for the Misbegotten* these two connotations were fused: the atmosphere created by this lighting is both ghastly and beautiful, in a grotesque way.[24]

In his use of the stage, young O'Neill was surprisingly sure in some respects. He rarely fumbled with sound effects or descriptions of the outer appearance and behavior of his characters. He had a special gift for evoking poetic moods with the help of music and sound effects, and an absolute ear for the expressive tones of the human voice—if the language spoken included elements of slang.[25] In the stage directions for the actors he was both willing and able to take great responsibilities: his eye was as sharp as his ear. A kind of bravura performance is *Before Breakfast,* in which O'Neill gave a precise description of the entire action of his heroine, practically the only character seen by the audience. He was

[23] The Gelbs, p. 381.
[24] When comparing O'Neill with nineteenth-century American novelists, Raleigh speaks of "Hawthorne's scenes in the spiritualizing moonlight" (p. 243), while "*Ile, Diff'rent, Gold* and *Where the Cross Is Made* all have as their center the Ahab-figure," a New England sea captain with a drive to possess something (p. 52).
[25] Raleigh (p. 219) calls the *S. S. Glencairn* cycle "a Melvillean 'melting pot,'" where there is a "medley of dialects." O'Neill's use of the dialects is certainly to be judged from the point of view of its dramatic merits.

not afraid of using dance or pantomime, and had a special fondness for what has been called an automaton effect. In these fields, O'Neill was a master from the very beginning.

Setting and lighting were equally tempting areas to O'Neill, not as easily conquered as the craft of acting or aural effects. His earliest plays take place on the sea or shore, mostly in sordid surroundings. From neutral and inexpressive settings (*The Web, Recklessness*), he quickly graduated to plays like *Abortion* and *Bound East for Cardiff*, in which the milieu was an integral part of the play. Claustrophobic or disharmonious settings (*The Dreamy Kid, The Sniper*), moonlight (*A Moon of the Caribbees, Where the Cross Is Made*), and blazing sunshine (*Thirst, Gold*) were among his favorite scenic units.

The success or failure of a play does not, of course, depend on its scenic means of expression alone. Characters in plays like *A Wife for a Life* or *Recklessness* are hopeless clichés, not to be helped by any amount of scenic imagination. Young O'Neill was, remarkably enough, more naïve and inexperienced in drawing a character than in his use of the stage. He understood the actions and appearances even of flat characters of the conventional stage; he read the faces more closely than the minds. He had not yet solved the problem of how to penetrate beyond personal ways of sitting or laughing into personal ways of thinking and feeling. When he tried to characterize upper-class people and capture their idioms, he was particularly inept. Yet he had a special device growing somewhere in the back of his mind: modified monologues were to prove a great asset in making the speakers interesting, three-dimensional human beings.

Effective scenic images presuppose the coordination of several kinds of scenic means of expression. In an amazingly short time, during his first two years of playwriting, O'Neill learned the importance of fusing his means together. An idea mentioned in a stage direction of *The Web* (1913) was turned into a fully conceived play, *Bound East for Cardiff* (1914). In between, there were several partly successful efforts to write a fate play with an effective scenic form. The scenic images of these interim plays deserve more attention than the plays themselves. Young O'Neill is more personal than ever in his fate plays: he is a would-be tragedian. Later on he was to become a master of tragic irony.

In addition to the theme of fate, several other subjects were treated for the first time, with inconclusive results. O'Neill's characters suffer from delusions or "pipe-dreams" (*Where the Cross Is Made, Ile*); they are self-pitying outsiders (*The Moon of the Caribbees, In the Zone*), haunted, guilt-ridden heroes (*Abortion, The Dreamy Kid*), or country people with strong desires (*The Rope*). These themes are ambitious; to be fully developed, they demand more time than just one act.

O'Neill was too enterprising a playwright to keep repeating what he had already done. He had written a faultless one-act play, *Bound East for Cardiff*, a successful exercise in creating a piece with just one scenic image. He was anxious to try more intricate forms in which several scenic images could interact. And he was bound to fail, for a while. *Servitude* and *Gold*, two early efforts in the longer form, really deserve little attention. It was a necessary task, however, in order to enlarge the scope of the plays—and the scope, intellectual, emotional, and scenic, was to grow during the coming quarter of a century, until O'Neill ended his career with a cycle of eleven plays in his mind. His best achievement was not reached without growing pains, without failures all the more embarrassing in that they were failures on a grand scale.

When following O'Neill's development we cannot yet bid adieu to melodramatic elements. Like so many artists in the years of their apprenticeship, he had to work his way up through layers of conventions. Out of these, the structural pattern imposed by the "well-made play" was more suffocating to his individuality than the violent stage effects of melodrama, which corresponded to his rebellious state of mind.

The prevailing melodramatics in these early plays leave a more innocent impression than the commercially calculating hollowness of Scribe or Sardou. The sins of violence are committed in the name of truth and with a pathos sympathetic in its youthfulness.

3

APPRENTICESHIP II

THREE LOST PLAYS REFOUND

Three early plays considered "destroyed" by Eugene O'Neill do exist—in addition to those published in *Lost Plays*. None of them is of great merit, yet all of them are interesting and contribute to making our picture of O'Neill's development more complete. They were written during a four-year period belonging to O'Neill's apprenticeship: *Bread and Butter* was registered at the Library of Congress on May 2, 1914, *Now I Ask You* in 1917, and *Shell Shock* on August 5, 1918.[1] Since none of these plays have been discussed in any previous study, they are considered here from several viewpoints.

It is possible that *Bread and Butter* is O'Neill's earliest full-length play; another candidate for this position is *Servitude*, also completed in 1914.[2] *Bread and Butter* moves in two surroundings O'Neill knew by experience: a small town in Connecticut and a studio apartment in New York. The action centers around John Brown, the son of a hardware merchant in Bridgetown. Like Dion Anthony in *The Great God Brown*, he wants to become a painter, and compels his unwilling father to let him have a try in an art school. John is engaged to Maud, the daughter of another local merchant.

---

[1] In a letter dated November 27, 1964, the Copyright Office of the Library of Congress gives the dates of *Bread and Butter* and *Shell Shock*, and reports that copies of the following plays were not found: *Exorcism, Atrocity, Belshazzar, The Dear Doctor, The G.A.M., Honor Among the Bradleys, Till We Meet,* and *The Trumpets.* There is a copy of *Now I Ask You* in the O'Neill Collection at the Yale University Library. The page numbers mentioned in this study are based on numbers given when that play was copied for Yale, on the playwright's pagination (*Shell Shock*), or on numbers given by me (*Bread and Butter*).

[2] The Gelbs (*O'Neill*, p. 261) take *Bread and Butter* to be earlier.

57

The conflict in his mind between art and love is resolved in favor of Maud, which leads him to quick disaster.

There are satirical elements in the description of the first stage picture in the play. The Brown sitting room is "papered a dull blurred crimson. This monotony of color is at well-regulated intervals monotonously relieved by pretentiously stupid paintings of the 'Cattle-at-the-Stream,' 'Sunrise-on-the-Lake' variety. These daubs are imprisoned in ornate gilt frames" (BREAD 3). It is not John's intention to add a few more exhibits of cattle or sunrises to this collection; he prefers nudes, much to the consternation of his family.

The conventional, Philistine attitudes prevailing in Bridgetown, Connecticut, materialize in Edward Jr., John's elder brother, who is dressed "exactly as a small-town alderman should be" (BREAD 3) and who later becomes mayor. He is John's rival, and O'Neill really exploits this theme by allowing him to go on courting Maud even in Act IV, after she has been unhappily married to John for two years. Edward is a hypocrite and, as such, is in direct contrast to the freely bohemian kind of life led by John and his artist friends.

Harry Brown is the Jamie Tyrone of the family, "a bit of a sport, given to beer drinking, poker parties and kelly pool" (BREAD 5), and biting in his remarks. The Browns are quite a family: there is also a spinsterish daughter Mary, and Bessie, a beauty. Mrs. Brown does not dare to speak much, while her husband inevitably reminds one of James O'Neill: he is "a tall, lean old man with a self-satisfied smile forever on his thin lips" (BREAD 3). "Remember your father was a working man and a farm hand, and all the education he's got beyond grammar school he picked up along the way" (BREAD 4), he lectures to one of his sons. Their weekly allowances are small, and the hardware merchant does not, of course, see any money in painting. Maud's father Richard Steele, who does see money in art—at least in the commercial branch of it—finally persuades him to give John a chance. When a year and a half have elapsed and John has not shown any inclination to start creating cover pictures for ladies' magazines, John's father loses his patience and leaves

John to his own devises: "Starve awhile, and see how much bread and butter this high art will bring you! No more coming to me for money, do you understand?" (BREAD 30).

In Act III John is still living in the New York studio which he shares with two art students and a would-be writer turned journalist. In their apartment there is, of course, "a profusion of paintings of all sizes and subjects" (BREAD 19). John has taken a job on the docks—"day after day of monotonous drudgery—life nothing but a panorama of sugar bags!" (BREAD 33). The days of hilarious small adventures are over. The decisive turning point is reached when Maud comes to fetch her hero from "this wicked old city" (BREAD 40). John hates the idea of returning to Bridgetown as "a self-confessed failure" (BREAD 42), but Maud is triumphant: "We're just going to be so happy, aren't we, dear?" (BREAD 44).

They are not. After two years John has confessed his failure; he does not take any interest in his work at his father-in-law's, he drinks in the club and at home, according to the town rumors he even meets girls of low reputation. The misery of the marriage is contrasted with the happiness of John's sister Bessie who married "Babe" Carter, another student, now about to make his reputation as an artist. Yet Maud refuses to give John a divorce; she is afraid of the scandal, she was brought up to consider marriage as sacred, and she wants to take revenge on John. Her wildly melodramatic outburst ends with an "Oooohh!" John "clutches her by the throat," yet controls himself and runs upstairs. There is a "muffled report of a revolver" (BREAD 60-61).

There can be no doubt that the play is basically autobiographical. John is another alter ego for O'Neill, "an altogether different type" from the other members of the Brown family: "a finer, more sensitive organization . . . graceful in his flannel clothes of unmistakable college cut. . . . His hair . . . is black, as are his abnormally large dreamer's eyes, deep-set and far apart in the oval of his face . . . his nose straight and thin with the nostrils of the enthusiast" (BREAD 9). John's situation in the play is similar to O'Neill's at the time

59

the play was written. Eugene was living in New London, quarreling with his father, convalescing from tuberculosis, and writing his first plays, full of contempt for the commercial theatre. He was hardly approved of by the pillars of that society: his escapades to the sea and his unsuccessful first marriage, which dissolved in October 1912, were known well enough.

Several other characters in the play are also modeled on real people. O'Neill stayed with the Rippin family during the winter season 1913-14; the first names of Mrs. Rippin were Helen Maude.[3] She gave only her names to two characters in the play: Helene and Maud. O'Neill's characterization of Maud is strikingly similar to the descriptions the Gelbs have given of two girls in O'Neill's life: Kathleen Jenkins, his first wife; and Maibelle Scott, a New London girl rather innocently courted by O'Neill in 1912-14.[4] It is as if O'Neill had asked himself this question when starting to write *Bread and Butter*: what follows if I decide to marry one of these nice girls and try to live with her? Nothing good, was his answer.

O'Neill and Maibelle Scott met for the first time at the wedding of a girl named Bessie Young; John's sister Bessie seems to be drawn according to Emily Rippin, while another

[3] The Gelbs, p. 240.

[4] This is Maud Steele: "a remarkably pretty girl of twenty with great blue eyes, golden brown hair, and small delicate features. . . . Her rather kittenish manner and the continual pout of her small red mouth indicate the spoiled child even before one hears the note of petulance in her soft, all-too-sweet voice" (BREAD 16). Kathleen Jenkins, O'Neill's first wife, was twenty years old when they met: "an extremely pretty, vivacious girl . . . a little spoiled and a little bored. . . . She had big blue eyes, her fair hair was piled high on her head, and her carriage was a graceful imitation of the Grecian bend" (the Gelbs, p. 131). And this is Maibelle Scott: "tall and slender, with long, lightbrown hair, large blue eyes, a peaches-and-cream complexion, enchanting dimples, and a soft, appealing voice" (the Gelbs, p. 206).
I think both Kathleen and Maibelle may have sat as O'Neill's models for Maud. He felt tricked into marriage by Kathleen. He tried to educate Maibelle (the Gelbs, pp. 209-10); John is anxious to make Maud understand. Maibelle is called "intelligent, sensitive, surprisingly free of small-town prejudices and self-confident enough to trust her own judgment" (the Gelbs, p. 208); against all warnings, Maud wants to marry John.

of the Rippin girls, Jessica, may have served as the model for John's sister, Mary Brown.[5] In 1908, O'Neill lived in New York in a studio apartment with Edward Keefe and George Bellows, two art students; Keefe was from New London, and had been one of O'Neill's friends there—along with Arthur McGinley, a journalist. It is not impossible that these three figure in the background of *Bread and Butter*.[6] The McGinley family has been associated with *Ah, Wilderness!*[7]— which leads our thoughts to the fact that both Richard Steele, Maud's father, and David McComber, Muriel's father in *Ah, Wilderness!* are dry goods merchants, while Maibelle Scott was the daughter of a captain who ran a general store.[8]

After these considerations, we may try to place *Bread and Butter* in the O'Neill canon. The love story that was recollected in tranquillity in *Ah, Wilderness!*, over a distance of twenty years, was taken in deadly earnest in 1914. Satirical elements were emphasized in *The First Man*, a description of the small town written in 1921; in 1932, all is sunshine.

[5] Bessie Brown is "small, plump, with a mass of wavy black hair and great hazel eyes, a red, pouting, laughing mouth, glowing complexion and small restless hands and feet . . . quite adorable" (BREAD 8). Emily Rippin, another victim of O'Neill's educational zeal, though more along sisterly lines, was "the shortest member of the Rippin family; a brunette, with hazel eyes, a rosebud mouth and a seductively full figure" (the Gelbs, p. 247). When Emily's married brother was somewhat concerned about her relations with O'Neill, he was called by the playwright "Mr. Platitude" (the Gelbs, p. 248)—exactly as Edward Brown is called by John (BREAD 43). Jessica Rippin was "working at a school in Philadelphia"; in 1914, she was 27, and "somewhat contemptuous of what she considered his [O'Neill's] parasitical existence" (the Gelbs, p. 246). Mary Brown, definitely an unsympathetic character, is a schoolteacher of 28.

[6] The similarities are less remarkable than in the case of the female characters. Ed Keefe was "tall, dark, good-looking"; George Bellows was a graduate of Ohio State University (the Gelbs, p. 124). "Babe" Carter is from somewhere in the West, "a broad-shouldered giant with a mop of blond hair and a feeble attempt at a blond mustache" (BREAD 19). Art McGinley was "tall and lanky" (the Gelbs, p. 89); Steve Harrington, another student of art in the play, is "a tall slender fellow" (BREAD 19). Perhaps O'Neill mixed the appearances: McGinley, a long-time friend and drinking companion, does not at all resemble Ted Nelson, the journalist.

[7] The Gelbs, pp. 81-87.

[8] The Gelbs, p. 206. Cf. Dorn, *Erlösungsthematik*, p. 92n.

On the other hand, there are a few expressions mindful of the city slang employed in *The Iceman Cometh,* and Ted Nelson once develops ideas close to the philosophy of his colleague Jimmy Tomorrow in the same play (BREAD 32). Remarkable idioms are "a hair of the dog" (BREAD 38), the name of an unfinished play belonging to the Harford cycle, and "before breakfast" (BREAD 53), used at the end of the play. In *Before Breakfast,* Mrs. Rowland closes her outburst of accusations with a refusal to give her husband a divorce; obviously suffering from the aftereffects of the previous night's drinking, he commits suicide in the bathroom. In the fourth act of *Bread and Butter,* John comes down in "a faded bath-robe and bedroom slippers" (BREAD 50), and his hands are shaky. When reading this stage direction, one cannot help remembering O'Neill's last years; the shaking of hands is a bad omen in the tragedy of his life.

O'Neill's view of marriage in this play can certainly be called Strindbergian. "We're two corpses chained together," he once makes John exclaim (BREAD 56). In John's demand for the freedom to develop his artistic talents, there is an echo from Ibsen; speaking to his father about Bessie, John comes close to the curtain lines of *A Doll's House:* "She must be true to herself. Her duty to herself stands before her duty to you" (BREAD 25).

Bread and Butter is a hero-centered play. John is admired by his city friends, among them his teacher in the art school: "Never in my long experience as teacher have I met a young man who gave finer promise of becoming a great artist. . . . He has the soul, he has everything" (BREAD 23). This was, of course, something O'Neill, writing his very first plays, would have heard with the greatest pleasure. In his palette there were as yet no middle hues: the Browns & Co. are either black or white. The strain of writing a long play seems to have been considerable for him: his characters tend to speak only obvious things; some of the secondary characters appear only once; passages of comedy are heavygoing and solemn; and the main reason for melodrama is Maud's sudden transformation from a loving bride into a monster. Her obstinate refusal to give John a divorce is used to contrive the play toward John's suicide. O'Neill knew Kathleen and Maibelle as girls—he did not know them as wives. What he imagined was a fear-fulfillment.

As to the scenic means of expression employed, there is not much to say. The satirical and realistic elements in the settings are fairly conventional,[9] and the play is mainly a series of discussions, among them a modified monologue in which John confesses the truth about his marriage to Bessie. Three years later O'Neill was to write another "lost" play in which the truth about marriage was quite the contrary.

Now I Ask You is a rather surprising piece: a full-length comedy, with elements of parody in it. Technically, it is much smoother than *Bread and Butter*. It was finished in 1917, apparently just after the two last *Glencairn* plays, more or less simultaneously with *Ile* and the short story version of *The Hairy Ape*, but before *The Dreamy Kid*, *The Rope*, *Where the Cross Is Made*, and *Beyond the Horizon*, all of which were written in a more serious vein. It is O'Neill's second comedy, preceded only by *The Movie Man*, a crude farce written in 1914, published in 1950.

As far as the surroundings are concerned, *Now I Ask You* follows the same line as *Servitude* and *Recklessness*: we are again brought into a middle-class home. The prologue, the epilogue, and two of the three acts take place in the library of a young married couple in the suburbs of New York.[10] Mrs. Lucy Drayton is shown in a state of nervous tension in the

[9] It is to Raleigh's credit that *Bread and Butter*, unknown to him, is a play about the contrast between city and country, a theme which he discusses in *The Plays of Eugene O'Neill*, pp. 25-33. Furthermore, the two decisive acts (I and III) and *Shell Shock* take place on hot days (cf. Raleigh, p. 204).

[10] There is a common element in both the Drayton and John Brown homes: each has two modern paintings. "The only jarring note is supplied by two incredible paintings in the Synchromist manner which are hung in conspicuous places" (Now 34). "In startling incongruity with the general commonplace aspect of the room are two paintings in the Impressionist style" (BREAD 47). In the older play, the paintings are approved of; in the later, they are ridiculed.

prologue; her husband looks for her, then leaves the house by car together with another woman. Lucy takes out a revolver, the car door slams, "a wild look of determination comes into Lucy's face and she snatches the revolver from the table. The noise of the motor increases in volume. The curtain starts to fall. The car outside starts. Closing her eyes tightly, Lucy lifts the revolver to her temple. The curtain hides her from view. As it touches the stage, there is the sound of the shot" (Now 4).

A highly improbable opening for a comedy, is it not? In fact, this is a play in which O'Neill gives a horse laugh not only to his own inclination to violent, melodramatic solutions, but also to several of his acknowledged masters. Nietzsche, Ibsen, and Strindberg are quoted derisively;[11] the practicability of Nora's solution in *A Doll's House* is tested by making it the basis of behavior for Lucy, a healthy American girl who has read too many Russian novels and Scandinavian plays—and who is most definitely not married to Torvald Helmer.[12] Tom Drayton and Lucy's understanding mother

[11] In fact, a passage quoted seriously from Ibsen in *Bread and Butter* is now parodied: "My highest duty is toward myself, and my ego demands freedom, wide horizons to develop in" (Now 23; cf. p. 62 above). *Servitude*, another play about marriage, includes a quotation from Ibsen with serious intentions. "Logos in Pan, Pan in Logos!" (LP 136) is from *Emperor and Galilean* where the tension between mental and bodily love is a central issue. Egil Törnqvist mentions Shaw's *Quintessence of Ibsenism* as O'Neill's probable source for this quotation ("Ibsen and O'Neill: A Study in Influence," *Scandinavian Studies, 37,* 219). He concludes that "the Ibsen impact is most noticeable in the early and late plays" (p. 234).

Raleigh (p. 230) speaks of the plentiful quotations used in *Long Day's Journey*, and remarks that O'Neill had done so before, in *The First Man*, in a less convincing way. This kind of experimentation was indeed started early.

[12] Lucy Drayton has some resemblance to Agnes Boulton, O'Neill's second wife. Lucy is "slender, dark, beautiful, with large eyes . . . a healthy complexion subdued by powder to a proper prison pallor, a vigorous, lithe body which frets restlessly beneath the restriction of studied, artificial movements" (Now 20). "Agnes had a pale, bony face and large, gray-blue eyes. Her hair was light brown. . . . Unsure of herself and rather shy, she often seemed even younger and more ingenuous than she was. Uncertain about where she was going, she assumed an air of breezy bohemianism" (the Gelbs, p. 364). Lucy assumed an air of Ibsenism.

Mrs. Ashleigh emerge victorious, of course: this is shown in the epilogue, which is a continuation of the prologue. Lucy did not, after all, shoot herself. A tire of the car had exploded.

O'Neill's most courageous structural solution in *Now I Ask You* was to start with the logical end of his situation, to repeat the prologue at the end of Act III, and then close everything with a scene from a horror farce. Otherwise, the play consists of conventional elements which are clearly recognizable: the characterization of Tom and Mr. Ashleigh is schematic; the plot clicks too well, and the audience should guess during Act II, if not before, what the playwright is about to do. Lucy and Tom are contrasted with a freely bohemian couple, Gabriel, a poet, and Leo(nora), an artist. Out of the entire cast, Leo is the most living and charming creation: a beatnik model 1917, sketched with gusto and obvious delight. She is possibly a recreation of Helene in *Bread and Butter*.[13] Her disarming way of opening a discussion is employed as the title of the play.

It is impossible to ignore the fact that O'Neill was living in Greenwich Village and Provincetown when writing this play—or that he had recently met his second wife, Agnes Boulton. Marriage is not such a bad invention after all, he seems to imply; and he is not unwilling to laugh at his fellow-bohemians. Nor is it unreasonable to find elements of self-irony and self-parody in the play. Gabriel, who is continuously begging for the admiration of his lady readers, is ridiculed, and the end of the play sounds like a parody of *Recklessness*. In that melodrama the jealous husband sends his rival, the chauffeur, to his death, after which the wife shoots herself. Another possibility is that Gabriel is intended as a parody of the young poet Marchbanks in Shaw's *Candida*.[14]

[13] Leonora, an idealized character, resembles Louise Bryant, the triangle Leo—Gabriel—Tony is a variation of a paradoxical constellation in O'Neill's life: Louise—O'Neill—John Reed (the Gelbs, pp. 311-12, 331). Leo and Gabriel conceal that they are married (Now 84); they practice monogamy "somewhat sheepishly" (the Gelbs, p. 324).

[14] *Candida* is quoted by Richard in *Ah, Wilderness!* (P II 216)—as remarked by Raleigh (pp. 82-83).

A scenic unit, a repetitive sound effect which increases in intensity, is used in the prologue of *Now I Ask You*—as it was in *Abortion*. Both the noise of the car and the approaching parade are natural in their surroundings. It is even more interesting to see how fluctuation between two roles is a major source of comedy in the case of Lucy, in a way typical of much later plays by O'Neill. When Lucy poses as the melancholy heroine of books she has read she quotes from O'Neill's favorites: "Strindberg's daughter of Indra discovered the truth. Life is horrible, is it not?" In the next moment she may fall from her life-weary role: "(Abandoning her pose for an unguarded moment—with real, girlish pleasure) A painting? From Leo? How charming of her" (Now 21).

From a critic's point of view it is annoying not to have known what kinds of experiments were going on in O'Neill's unpublished plays. If *Now I Ask You* had been known in the twenties and thirties, the satirical elements in *Marco Millions* or the relaxed family comedy of *Ah, Wilderness!* would not have been so surprising. Apparently, among the paradoxes immanent in O'Neill, there was an ability to laugh at his own tensest problems, at his most burning questions. *Exorcism*, a one-act play produced in 1920 yet definitely lost to us, was a farce about his attempted suicide. Astonished by this inclination we can share Leo's curtain line, though not its spelling error: "General Gabbler's pistol! Fancy that, Hedda!" (Now 98). Fancy O'Neill parodying his fellow tragedians! This is the most important new feature that emerges from this play, which is neither highly individual nor excessively clumsy. O'Neill's real talent can hardly be seen in it.

In two unknown plays, marriage was viewed as a war or a game; in the third, war is a game at long last won by a man. Women, let alone marriage, are not even mentioned. *Shell Shock* was written in Provincetown during the summer of 1918, together with two other short plays, *The Dreamy Kid* and *Where the Cross Is Made*.[15] Again, O'Neill is skill-

---

[15] The Gelbs, p. 381.

ful in evoking an atmosphere. The scene is a university club in New York: "It is the middle of the afternoon of a hot day in September, 1918. Through the open windows, the white curtains of which hang motionless, unstirred by the faintest breeze, a sultry vapor of dust-clogged sunlight can be seen steaming over the hot asphalt [MS: ashpalt]. Here, in the grill, it is cool. The drowsy humming of an electric fan on the left wall lulls to inertness" (SS 1). Against this peaceful, yet tense background O'Neill places three officers.

Two of them are recovering from their wounds, physical and psychological, the third is a Medical Corps officer. Herbert Roylston, Lieutenant, opens the play by describing to Doctor Robert Wayne how he had been saved by his friend and idol Jack Arnold. He had been lying between the lines, half unconscious, for three days and nights: "Finally I came to in the dark. I heard someone screaming—damn horribly! I listened and discovered that *I* was doing it—screaming at the top of my lungs" (SS 5)—and then Jack came and carried him to safety. Roylston has hardly left the stage, when Jack Arnold appears. Though we have been told that he "has the nerves of an ox" (SS 7), he is now suffering from the consequences of a nervous breakdown, a shell shock: "His dark eyes have a strained expression of uncertain expectancy as if he were constantly holding himself in check while he waited for a mine to explode. His hands tremble a little. He has a queer mannerism of continually raising the fore and middle fingers of his right hand to his lips as though he were smoking an invisible cigarette" (SS 9-10). Here we have the patient and his symptom; and Wayne is ready to play the doctor. He has, in fact, been assigned to the job, with little more preparation than a hurried note from the doctor who had taken care of Jack in France: "Watch Arnold—cigarettes" (SS 8).

O'Neill goes on describing in minute detail the movements of Jack's nervous hands. "With a detached air, as if he were unconscious of what he is doing, he puts out the cigarette from which he has hardly taken more than a few puffs, and carefully puts the butt into a pocket of his uniform" (SS 11).

67

While doing it, he sees Wayne's probing eyes and reacts aggressively against being revealed. He knows of his obsessive actions, yet is a slave to them: "(Forgetful of the full boxes on the table he calls to the waiter roughly) . . . A box of cigarettes" (SS 13). Jack's second symptom is a dread of silence.

After a few reminders from the sympathetic Wayne about his cigarette obsession, Jack's inner compulsion has grown so tense that he elicits his first confession, in the form of a modified monologue worth quoting at length:

> Just that—*the* silence. It hits you when you're sent back home after you've been in the lines for a long time—say a year or more without a holiday . . . A holiday! A rest period! Rest! Good God! . . . Understand that I'm only speaking from my own experience and my feelings may have no general significance. But I believe they have. I've seen them verified in the faces of those men who come back to the trenches after a leave at home—their expression of genuine happiness at being back—Why, man, they look relieved, freed from slavery! (*He pauses for a moment, reflecting—then continues intensely*) You've been hearing the rumble and crash of the big guns, the rat-a-pet riveting of the machine-guns, the crack of rifles, the whine of bullets, the roar of bursting shells. Everything whirls in a constant feverish movement around you; the earth trembles and quakes beneath your feet; even the darkness is only an intermittent phenomenon [MS: phenomena] snatching greedily at the earth between the wane of one star shell and the bursting brilliance of the next; even the night is goaded into insomnia by the everlasting fireworks. Nothing is fixed or certain. The next moment of your life never attains to the stability of even a probable occurrence. It hits you with the speed of a bullet, passes through you, is gone. (*He pauses*) And then you come out into the old peaceful world you once knew—for a rest—and it seems as if you [were] buried in the tomb of a pyramid erected before the stars were born. Time has died of old age; and the

silence like the old Chinese water torture, drops leadenly drop by drop—on your brain—and then you think—you have to think—about the things you ought to forget (SS 14-15).

"Nothing is fixed or certain." In this significant passage O'Neill takes a firm grip on one of his most profound experiences, that of chaos, of utter insecurity. The helplessness of the individual in the midst of unstable human relations is a basic principle underlying the structure of *Long Day's Journey Into Night*; here a similar feeling is expressed directly, in terms of a lyrical outburst. What is to Yank in *The Hairy Ape* an experience of not belonging, of being lost in a hostile yet outwardly peaceful world, is here explained in terms of a psychic wound caused by the war; Yank began his wanderings after a moment in the stokehole which hit him "with the speed of a bullet." O'Neill is a tragedian, a dramatist of disharmony; he has experienced a moment of primordial fear, of "*Ur-Erschütterung.*"

O'Neill's play may have been based on what was written in newspapers or magazines about the "silence," the shell shocks experienced in France during World War I. However, this is not as important as the fact that O'Neill, as a tragedian, was constantly searching for dramatic equivalents for his basic experience of insecurity—and that he found one here. He has also been able to give Jack Arnold's moments of metaphysical anxiety an adequate verbal form, in a language that is rhythmic and auditive, written to be spoken—in short, in a dramatist's language. He has, most definitely, *heard* the war, and given it a hearable artistic form. Dialogue is the prevailing element. In a couple of years O'Neill was to turn similar experiences into strings of scenic images.

It is possible to connect the passage still more firmly with the time when it was written. Downer calls O'Neill's plays "important and revolutionary because for the first time in the American theatre they reflect the postwar world, the world in which most certainties—moral, ethical, and to an extent legal—had given way to uncertainties. . . . All actions had to be freshly examined, all positions freshly argued, all characters and situations freshly analyzed, in the attempt to establish new values, and new certainties for the 1920's."[16] The moral problem here freshly argued is the contemporary question of heroism. To O'Neill, heroism is nothing straightforward or easily explained.

The quoted passage may strike us as the core of *Shell Shock*. Yet it is only one of a series of revelations: as in O'Neill's later plays, *The Iceman Cometh* or *A Moon for the Misbegotten*, there is a story behind the story, there comes a confession after the confession. When Wayne mentions the name of Roylston, Jack is visibly shaken. He starts reminiscing about those terrible days when his company, cut off from the others, waited for the enemy to counterattack. They had to stand insomnia, fear, darkness, the shrieks of their wounded friends, the smell and touch of corpses, the noises —and the lack of cigarettes. A cigarette "would have been heaven" (SS 19); it became the symbol of their entire misery. Like a refrain in a poem, their longing is repeated, with variations, in Jack's speech which brings us close to the second rhythmic climax of the playlet. The company is eventually joined by the other troops—but they do not get any cigarettes: "There'd been a delay, a mistake, something" (SS 19). Jack cursed, he got wild, he went mad—and he went out after Roylston. The thing he "ought to forget," yet could not, was this: he knew Roylston had cigarettes, and must have saved his friend only in order to get them. Otherwise, why save Roylston? Everybody thought he was dead.

It is time for exorcism: the scream. Wayne remembers that Roylston had screamed and he is able to convince Jack: "Yes—there was screaming—driving you mad . . . Yes— and then—God!—one voice—when all the others were silent for a second—like this (He throws his head back and screams as if in horrible pain)" (SS 20). The symptoms meet one another—silence, cigarettes, the scream—the situation is reenacted and all feelings of guilt are exorcised. The ten-

---

[16] Downer, "The Revolt from Broadway," in *A Time of Harvest*, Spiller (ed.), p. 47.

sions are even turned into laughter, when Roylston returns to the stage for a happy reunion and offers Jack a cigarette: "Not on your life! Never another! A pipe for me [MS: mine] for the rest of my life!" (SS 21).

Shell Shock is another fate play, turned into a psychological thriller. As such, it has been banalized by later plays with similar ambitions. And by earlier ones: there was Susan Glaspell and her *Suppressed Desires*, a Freudian farce which was part of the opening bill of the Provincetown group in 1915. The desire suppressed by Jack is his compulsion to confess: he was taken to be a hero, and he could not admit what he thought was his real reason for saving Roylston. He needed, for his modified monologue, an attentive and sympathetic listener; he needed Wayne. With Wayne's help, the mine was unloaded.

Basically a modified monologue, this short play of twenty-one pages has other interesting features as well. Repetitions of phrases and actions are used in a clever and purposeful way, and the rhythmic whole is firmly controlled. In one of his lines Jack foreshadows the painful repetitions of *The Emperor Jones*: during the hours of anxious waiting one of the soldiers kept singing "some idiotic nonsense . . . over and over again—till it drove you nearly mad to listen to him" (SS 17). Both Wayne and the dumb figure of the waiter are used to reflect the reactions the playwright expects from his audience. All significant action in the play belongs to the past —a characteristic technique in some of O'Neill's last work. In 1918, he was already capable of writing a short play based on memories. The beginnings of the play can be seen in *The Sniper*, which also dealt with World War I; its central theme was finally amalgamated into *Mourning Becomes Electra*, where Orin is a war hero who explains his bravery only as a result of craziness. Like Jack, he ran right across the lines (P II 95). His illusion, however, is not exorcised.

O'Neill apparently considered names of characters once invented too good to be wasted. In *Abortion*, there is a college hero named Jack Townsend; here we have a war (and college) hero named Jack Arnold. In *Strange Interlude*

71

the war hero is Gordon Shaw; the girl who marries Gordon Evans, his namesake, is Madeline Arnold. In *Servitude* there are Alice and David Roylston, here Herbert Roylston. And in *Bread and Butter* we meet all the Browns; in *The Great God Brown*, William A. Brown, architect. Other elements from these plays also emerge in O'Neill's later works, in *Before Breakfast*, in *Ah, Wilderness!* and in *Mourning Becomes Electra*.

Taken as a whole, these three lost and found plays tend to stress the importance of the Provincetown group for O'Neill. Only with their assistance was he able to make his real break with the theatrical traditions of prewar America and Europe, not least in his use of the expressive possibilities of the stage. *Bread and Butter* was both started and finished before O'Neill became a member of the group, *Now I Ask You* only started; for some reason he did not submit *Shell Shock* for production.[17] In these cases O'Neill relied on the dialogue. He wrote Ibsenesque discussion plays. The most interesting of these three pieces is *Shell Shock*; both *The Dreamy Kid* and *Where the Cross Is Made*, written during the same summer, are of lesser worth. It is a pity *Shell Shock* was not produced. We at least, seeing it against the background of the entire canon, know that it came from the horse's mouth.

[17] The Gelbs, pp. 280, 345, 381.

4

APPRENTICESHIP III

PASSING THE HORIZON

Beyond the Horizon brought to its author his first Pulitzer
Prize and sent him on his way to national and international
fame. On his eastbound voyage, he passed the nearest horizon. In spite of these circumstances associated with the play,
it is most appropriate to deal with this rural tragedy as a representative of O'Neill's apprenticeship. It is, no doubt, "an
immature work,"[1] "over-grown . . . overpraised . . . too often
unnecessarily violent and direct in action and speech."[2]
Like a prism, it seems to focus several lines of development
followed earlier: there is need for a summarizing discussion
on the distance traveled.

Symptoms of overgrowth can be seen in the way the setting is utilized in *Beyond the Horizon*. After having written
so many unicellular plays, O'Neill enjoyed being able to fill
several cells with different settings. Yet it is no easy task to
control several interacting scenic images. In his eagerness
O'Neill realized his theme of dreaming in a crude manner,
placing one of his scenes in each act outdoors, the other within the walls of his farmhouse. The pattern is not quite regular
(the outdoor scenes are Act I, Scene i; II, ii; and III, ii);
yet there were so many scene changes that Alexander Woocl-
cott had reason to suspect O'Neill of remoteness from the
theatre in a lengthy review of the play.[3]

[1] Gassner, *Masters of the Drama*, p. 649.
[2] Clark, *Eugene O'Neill*, pp. 65, 67.
[3] "Certainly it was a quite impractical playwright who split each
of his three acts into two scenes. . . . It was natural enough for him
to want to show the high-road of Robert Mayo's dreams, inevitable
that he should itch to place one scene on the hilltop, with its almost
protagonistic vista of the distant sea. But no essential purpose is
served by these exteriors" (Cargill *et al., O'Neill and His Plays*, p.
137; Alexander Woollcott's review was originally published in the
New York Times, Feb. 8, 1920).

O'Neill explained his intentions in an interview. "One scene is out of doors, showing the horizon, suggesting the man's desire and dream. The other is indoors, the horizon gone, suggesting what has come between him and his dreams. In that way I tried to get rhythm, the alternation of longing and of loss. Probably very few people who saw the play knew that this was definitely planned to produce the effect."[4] Woollcott was among those who knew; his review shows that he had understood the function of the scene changes. When the play is read with a knowledge that thematically significant changes in the setting have been common in the modern theatre for several decades, the procedure adopted here leaves an impression of clumsiness.[5] The possibilities of receiving the effect only unconsciously seem negligible.

Yet it probably was, if not altogether new, at least rare in the American theatre before the twenties. Popular melodramas were usually set in upper-class surroundings, regardless of the specific themes of the play or the conditions among the majority of the audience. It took some courage to depart from this cliché and use such "low" backgrounds as seamen's forecastles and farmhouses. O'Neill did not do so in order to shock his middle-class spectators, but because the characters in his plays demanded surroundings of this kind.

O'Neill was not satisfied only with enlarging the sphere of acceptable social backgrounds, however. He employed three types of settings in rapid succession: from indifferent and inexpressive stage pictures (*Recklessness*), he proceeded through realism (*Bread and Butter*) into a kind of symbolic realism (*Beyond the Horizon*). A reasonable way of distinguishing between the last two is to speak of a setting as realistic when it is free to reflect different social strata, and as symbolic when it concretizes an aspect of the more specific theme

[4] The Gelbs, *O'Neill*, pp. 411-12.

[5] Both Koischwitz and Raleigh see in sharp contrasts something typical of O'Neill's early phase. Koischwitz says that O'Neill prefers "the gross and antithetic," such as glaring sunshine and dark shadows (*O'Neill*, p. 67); cf. Raleigh, *The Plays of Eugene O'Neill*, p. 174: "The impulse toward contrast tends to be more obsessive in the earlier plays and is often schematic, as in *Beyond the Horizon* or *All God's Chillun Got Wings*."

of the play. Symbolic realism meant to O'Neill a step toward becoming conscious of the expressive possibilities implicit in the setting.

This development of O'Neill's reflected a progress throughout the American theatre. Downer speaks of "surface realism," and sees a sign of maturing in plays where "important subjects or ideas" were taken realistically.[6] An effort to give form to his realistic idea about seamen's life made O'Neill step into the forecastle of the *S. S. Glencairn*.

Downer has paid attention to the beginnings of O'Neill's symbolic realism, too. The settings in *Beyond the Horizon* certainly "make explicit something about the inner conflict which is O'Neill's principal concern in the play," and some details in the interior symbolize "the change which the action of the play has brought about in particular characters."[7] It is even possible to speak of a deterministic function assigned to the setting: the characters are dependent on their surroundings. So it goes, in the stage directions: "The room has changed, not so much in its outward appearance as in its general atmosphere. Little significant details give evidence of carelessness, of inefficiency, of an industry gone to seed" (P III 112). One act or five years later the room "presents an appearance of decay, of dissolution" (P III 144). Robert Mayo's wife Ruth in II, ii is "dressed in white" (P III 135); in III, i she wears a "dress of deep mourning. She has aged horribly" (P III 144). Changes like these are a regular feature in the later technique of O'Neill (witness plays like *Diff'rent* and *More Stately Mansions*).

If the American critics were looking for a native Ibsen in Eugene O'Neill, they seemed to have found what they wanted. Yet, in that same year of 1920, when *Beyond the Horizon* (written 1917-18) was produced, another O'Neill play was also presented for the first time: *The Emperor Jones*, with its wholesale expressionism. When searching for

---

[6] Downer, "The Revolt from Broadway," in Spiller's *A Time of Harvest*, p. 44. Cf. Nicoll, *World Drama*, p. 764.

[7] Downer, *Fifty Years of American Drama*, p. 43. A similar observation is made by Koischwitz, p. 71.

an example of how stylistic layers conceived in the European theatre got mixed up in America, how the different artistic movements of several decades were telescoped into a few hectic years, this is as good a piece of evidence as any.

Woollcott's review might have given O'Neill an impetus toward the skeleton setting employed in *Desire Under the Elms*. When pondering the farm surroundings used in that play, O'Neill may well have remembered what happened to *Beyond the Horizon*, and how his professional pride was hurt. Here he had another play demanding the same kind of schedule of changes between exterior and interior settings. What if the changes were again handled awkwardly and the outer landscapes realized carelessly? In this situation, perhaps also through recalling the earlier solution in *The Sniper* and some settings utilized by other playwrights, he created a setting in which the conflict between man and nature was included in one and the same stage construction. It was also to be present in every single scenic image in the play. Instead of separating the conflicting elements and using them in alternating settings in alternating scenic images, he concealed the tension between two contrasting parts of the farmhouse setting. The result was both more suggestive and more practical than in *Beyond the Horizon*.

If the overall execution of the scenery is crude rather than refined in *Beyond the Horizon*, there is one minor feature which tells of expert knowledge of the theatre. In the first scene the "road runs diagonally from the left, forward, to the right rear" (P III 81); in *The Hairy Ape* the row of cells in the prison scene extends "diagonally from right front to left rear" (P III 239). These two descriptions are not different by chance; it is a fact that the natural movement of the eye (at least among nations reading from left to right) follows this direction, even when we are sitting in a theatre audience —a fact utilized, of course, by stage directors. And here by a playwright: the road in *Beyond the Horizon* "takes" the eye with it toward the distant hills, as the theme of the play demands; while the row of cells "stops" the eyes—as it should in a prison.

76

This is another of O'Neill's plays with a circular structure; there is a melodramatic use of a sound effect; and a thematic parallel is drawn by placing Ruth's mother in a wheelchair— she is another prisoner of circumstances. The elder brother Andrew is moved back and forth according to the wishes of the playwright.[8] Of greater significance than these details is the patterning of time, connected by Leech with the symbolic setting. The play proceeds from spring to fall and from sunset to sunrise: "the change in the season suggests a movement from growth to decline; the change in the time of day works conversely. It is evident from this that O'Neill, as in the best of his later plays, combines the realistic and symbolic modes."[9]

The final scenic image of the play is given a lift by the sunrise lighting. Robert has a vision shortly before his death, outside the deterministic interior setting of the play: "Don't you see I'm happy at last—free—free!—freed from the farm —free to wander on and on—eternally!" (P III 167). A fact not mentioned previously is that O'Neill, with his expert knowledge of tuberculosis, must have been aware that its victims, especially in advanced stages, have an inclination to see queer, often happy visions. Robert Mayo is dying of consumption when he utters these exultant words; they are written to add a poetic and even clinically motivated dimension to his fate.[10] Robert Mayo dies as he lived, as a dreamer.

[8] ". . . the plot is propelled by the periodic returns of the travelers. The characters are arranged in schematic fashion" (Raleigh, p. 174).

[9] Leech, *Eugene O'Neill*, pp. 20-21. Koischwitz goes somewhat further in his interpretation of the symbolism: between youth and death, between spring and fall, there is "the high point of life: the summer" (p. 91). Raleigh sees in the alternation of day and night "the great natural metaphor for the principle of polarity"—"hence the high incidence of sunsets and sunrises in O'Neill's plays" (p. 17).

[10] To me, Doris V. Falk misses the point of the scene because of her effort to experience the play through Aristotelian and Christian terminology: "His [Robert's] death brings with it an implicit resurrection in the form of his exultant insights; but the truth of the resurrection is negated by the final scene. What appeared to be a tragic affirmation of man's nobility in the face of inevitable suffering turns out to be a study in frustration, where weak and foolish people waste their lives" (*Eugene O'Neill and the Tragic Tension*, p. 42).

The end is a matter of logic, not of religion; of physiology, not of metaphysics. The tone is of tragic irony, not of affirmation.

The development of one of O'Neill's central scenic units, the monologue, requires a few supplementary notes. Under the influence of European realism, and before his expressionistic phase, O'Neill was careful to preserve the illusion of the fourth wall. Yet he felt an urge to reveal the inner states of mind of his characters.[11] He solved this dilemma by creating a variation of the monologue that was somewhere in between the orthodox asides of the "well-made play" and ordinary realistic dialogue. Ibsen has soliloquies arising out of inner compulsion in *A Doll's House*, motivated as credible manifestations "of the disturbed mental state of a character."[12] In O'Neill the characters have an inclination to fall into modified monologues even when they are not particularly disturbed; Smitty, for example, is only melancholy and reminiscent in *The Moon of the Caribbees*. The wall of reticence to be broken through by the compulsion is of variable thickness, and this results in different variations of the modified monologue. Yank speaks of his dream only shortly before his death, Jack Arnold tries to suppress his eagerness to confess, while John Brown breaks through the barriers of middle-class decency, held in honor by the American stage tradition: "What rot! Why should I lie and keep up this pretence to you?" (BREAD 56). In *Bound East for Cardiff* and

---

Carpenter calls it the weakness of the play that Robert's character, the nature of his dream "and—most of all—the attitude of the author toward this dream seem to vacillate" (*Eugene O'Neill*, p. 88). I cannot see any vacillation.

[11] "Nothing is more certain than that soliloquy is the most intimate and potent of all the instruments of discourse in theatre; it is of perennial power in a medium that has ranged from heaven to hell and can explore the internal as well as the external world" (Coghill, *Shakespeare's Professional Skills*, pp. 130-31). It was to be an exceptionally potent instrument in the hands of O'Neill: "More than most creative writers, O'Neill concerned himself with the inner thoughts and feelings of his protagonists and of himself" (Carpenter, p. 47).

[12] Gassner, *Form and Idea in the Modern Theatre*, p. 31.

Shell Shock the structural emphasis is strongly on a modified monologue—as it was to be in all the plays of O'Neill's last phase.[13]

The whole phenomenon is an outgrowth of the monologue proper. Yet we cannot fully comprehend the emergence of O'Neill's late style, with its long reminiscent speeches cut into pieces by stage directions, if we do not see the other element responsible for it. The habit of writing stage directions even within individual speeches was fairly well-established at the end of O'Neill's apprenticeship. The playwright was especially anxious to dictate to his actors how to voice their climactic speeches, often expressed in an emotional and fragmentary language.[14] In *Beyond the Horizon* we find as many as six definitions of tone, facial expression, gestures, or movements within a single speech. A shorter example is from a speech by Andrew: "(*sulkily*) . . . (*Suddenly overcome with anger and grief; with rising intensity*) . . . (*Tears of rage starting to his eyes—hoarsely*) . . ." (P III 107). Even if no stage director would take all of these directions literally, they are important as indications of the playwright's vision and technique. In this phase they still lead to monotony; there are no sudden, paradoxical twists of tone within the speeches, as we remember from *Before Breakfast* and can see from the above example.

The late O'Neill style of dialogue writing can be understood only as a conglomerate of two tendencies. One led to monologues, the other to stage directions within the speeches. O'Neill was able to satisfy fully his need for indulging in monologues, proper or modified, only after he had learned to make them fluctuate paradoxically between different, even opposite, states of mind; and he was able to make certain that the fluctuations were understood and followed by the actors only by using stage directions within the speeches, a

[13] Cf. Coghill on Shakespeare: "In the works of his maturity, soliloquies are only placed at points of structural necessity and are carefully prepared for, often several scenes in advance" (p. 142).

[14] Braem has paid attention to the frequent dissonances in O'Neill's dialogue (*Eugene O'Neill*, p. 52).

practice first employed in the climactic, "nonfluctuating" speeches of ordinary dialogue. Seeing the interaction between the stage directions and the dialogue, seeing how the way of writing monologues is dependent on the intervening hints, we can understand the importance of these stage directions, even if they are never heard by the audience. And there is no doubt that the use of monologues as a means of expressing states of mind was a problem which intrigued O'Neill all through his playwriting career, from *A Wife for a Life*, if you will, to the unfinished *More Stately Mansions*.

Remembering how many of the scenic means of expression typical of O'Neill were tentatively applied during these early years of playwriting, there is reason to correct a fairly general inexactitude, phrased by Clark, perhaps the first critic to draw this conclusion: "O'Neill seems . . . to have been driven by some inner necessity to devise a whole new set of tools every time he planned a new work, as though its implications and its physical shape could not be fitted into any mould he had already used."[15] The combination of tools may have been new every time, but there were old units in it; the mould may have had its individual shape, but some of its corners had been explored before.

Eugene O'Neill did not emerge ready-made from the head of Thespis; every technical device, every means of expression in his mature plays has a prehistory of efforts, failures, and new adaptations, a prehistory written by an obstinate artistic experimentation. He may have shocked the contemporary critics and audiences by seemingly unexpected novelties in the twenties and thirties—and yet each of these corresponds to some urge of expression, directed into similar or

---

[15] Clark, p. 82. The statement is echoed, e.g., by Richard Hayes, in his "Eugene O'Neill: The Tragic in Exile" (*O'Neill*, Gassner [ed.], p. 55). Koischwitz, having not read the last plays, does not evaluate the freshness of new adaptation highly enough; it is true that "O'Neill used his effective means already in his earliest plays" (p. 99), yet they were seldom used in a masterful way. It can also be said that the themes with which O'Neill's scenic images are charged in his early plays are lacking in significance.

slightly different channels before. In other words, his scenic images, individual and fresh as they are, can be seen in the perspective furnished by his previous experiments, during the time of his apprenticeship and later.

5

EARLY REALISM

FROM *THE STRAW* TO *THE FIRST MAN*

Eugene O'Neill did not spare himself in the years shortly before and after his first success with a full-length play. In fact, 1918 to 1921 was his most hectic creative period: he wrote no less than nine full-length and eight one-act plays during these four years. They were not all independent in their subject (*Chris Christophersen*, produced in 1920, is an earlier version of *'Anna Christie'*; *Where the Cross Is Made* was utilized as a part of *Gold*), nor did all satisfy even their author (four one-act pieces were withdrawn from publication). Yet the output is still formidable. A clear sign of O'Neill's growing importance is that all of the remaining thirteen plays (and *Exorcism*, lost to us) were produced by early March 1922.

The results of this period were not only uneven in quality, but also stylistically mixed. Four plays are a direct continuation of O'Neill's apprenticeship and can be dealt with under the general heading "Realism Mixed with Melodrama"; what they show is mainly an increasing control over the full-length form, in details and in total structure. Characterization did not fill up *Beyond the Horizon*—the play was repetitious and drawn-out. These faults do not markedly disturb *The Straw*, the first and in many respects the best member of this group.

The settings in four out of five scenes in *The Straw* follow safely the footpath of realism. A few symbolic touches are added in the forest scene (II, ii) which is the only one placed outside the box-set formula. It is also thematically important, the second among three consecutive emotional climaxes: here Eileen Carmody confesses her love to Stephen Murray, a would-be author about to leave the tuberculosis sanatorium where they have met.

The scene is placed, appropriately enough, at a cross-road:[1] "At the junction of the two roads there is a signpost, its arms pointing toward the right and the left, rear." The atmosphere, charged with ill omens, is evoked by using two scenic units, the moonlight and the forest. The lighting helps to further dramatize the setting: "A full moon, riding high overhead, throws the roads into white shadowless relief and masses the woods into walls of compact blackness" (P III 383). The moonlight is fused with the idea of the forest as something dark and threatening—an idea fully developed in *The Emperor Jones.*

Eileen is the focus of attention during the first moments of this scene: she stands "front center," and "her face shows white and clear in the bright moonlight as she stares with anxious expectancy up the road to the left. . . . She has shrunk instinctively as far away as she can from the mysterious darkness which rises at the road's sides like an imprisoning wall." (P III 383). Eileen's tension is temporarily relieved by the arrival of Stephen. A love scene outwardly reminiscent of the nightly meeting of Richard and Muriel in *Ah, Wilderness!* can begin; here it is love with fear and with ironic overtones, for Stephen does not share the attachment felt by the girl.

The signpost, an immobile part of the setting, is brought vividly to the attention of the audience in two key phases of this scene. In the central scenic image of the play Eileen is about to leave the stage, without confessing her love, "but, as she passes the signpost, she suddenly stops and turns to look again at Murray. . . . A great shuddering sob shatters her pent-up emotions" (P III 389)—and she returns for the confession. At the very end of the scene the signpost is utilized again, now in connection with Stephen's movements: "(*He starts to run after her but stops by the signpost and stamps on the ground furiously, his fists clenched in impotent*

[1] To Koischwitz the signpost is a symbol of "the last crossroads of life" (*O'Neill*, pp. 70-71).

rage at himself and at Fate.) Christ!" (P III 392). The curtain falls.

The setting, here clearly combined with the action of a scene, certainly adds to its emotional impact. It hardly leads to melodramatics. The signpost is only one of the elements in the setting: the forest, emphasized by an appropriate lighting arrangement, plays an equally important role. The symbols are employed in an Ibsen-like manner, without breaking the boundaries of realism dominant in the play. Blending realism and theatricalism does not, of course, destroy a play; on the contrary, it is common in the modern theatre, as has been emphatically stated by Gassner, who also sees in it the possibility of an interesting synthesis.[2] Yet we can see from this scene that when writing *The Straw* O'Neill was still one step short of expressionism—a step he was to take the following year with *The Emperor Jones*. Luckily so—for *The Straw*. Full-scale expressionism would hardly have been appropriate in this forest scene where the reality and truthfulness of the emotions are a central issue; nor would it, in all probability, have done any good to a play so strongly bound to realistic surrounding for its effect.

The encounter in the forest is carefully prepared for in the preceding scene. What happens in II, i in the assembly room of the sanatorium is present in the scenic image of the forest scene. When constructing this series of three interacting scenic images O'Neill moved in the dimension of time more smoothly than in *Beyond the Horizon*. Throughout II, i, Eileen is in a state of confused, conflicting emotions; this fits into the line of development sketched above of O'Neill's technique in writing dialogue. While the patients are weighed, to determine their rate of recovery, Eileen fluctuates between joy, because Stephen has a good chance of being released, and fear that this will happen. The tension arises quite naturally out of the situation, which is a part of both O'Neill's milieu description and of Eileen's personal dilemma. The crowd is cleverly utilized to build up tension toward Stephen's

[2] Gassner, *Form and Idea in the Modern Theatre, passim*, e.g. pp. 13, 133, 175-90, 210-24.

turn at the scales, the scenic image of this scene. And when Eileen is weighed and found to have lost weight, this is an omen of the tragic ending of the whole play.

Confusion, the simultaneous presence of conflicting impulses, is one of the most typical states of mind in the characters of the maturing O'Neill. The opposites are getting closer to one another, the paradoxes within a speech are about to be conceived. Murray speaks both "remorsefully" and "irritably" (P III 371) in one and the same utterance; Eileen makes "a pitiful effort at a smile" (P III 382). The ironical contrast between Eileen's feelings and Stephen's blindness to them is developed through a series of minor revelations—to the audience. So much has been written of O'Neill's inadequacies of language, often with good reason, that it should be observed how well he manages with Eileen, even in the love confession, a passage requiring extreme delicacy. The short phrases and the panting rhythm make it an example of a language fit for the stage; supported by the milieu this should make a constituent in a memorable scenic image.[3]

The end of the play is left slightly open, though there should be little doubt of the hopelessness of hope, grasped too late. Eileen's revelation is the last scenic image of the play.[4] These sentiments are counterbalanced by a few touches of comedy in Stephen's relations with the nurses, and by a strong undercurrent of irony. It is even too strong in the case of Eileen's family, pictured as a group of cartoon characters —as also happens in *The First Man*, another play belonging

[3] Raleigh calls Eileen's lines "perfectly commonplace " (*The Plays of Eugene O'Neill*, p. 129), yet gives credit to the power of the passage, due to its context in the action of the play. What matters still more is the scenic context.

[4] Robert A. Parker has written appreciatingly about this moment of revelation. He sees O'Neill's "thrilling point" in Eileen's decision to live: with it "his heroine lives, lives intensely, triumphantly, if only for a few days or a few moments" (Miller, *The Playwright's Progress*, p. 30: originally published in *The Independent* and *The Weekly Review*, 107, Dec. 3, 1921). As in the case of Robert Mayo, there is an ironic overtone, for the vision can be interpreted as a result of Eileen's tuberculosis.

to this quartet. This, rather than sentimentality, is the weak spot, especially in the beginning before the interacting scenic images gather significance in the three decisive twists of the plot, and before the watertight realism is mixed with symbolic overtones in the forest scene. Not overgrown in scope, not one of O'Neill's major achievements, this sympathetic play really "needs no condescension."[5]

O'Neill turned his vision into real people in *The Straw*, except when creating his gallery of two-dimensional family portraits. It is not as easy to separate the sheep from the goats in the case of *'Anna Christie'*. The hollowness of characterization was remarked upon early;[6] yet the play was received with enthusiasm,[7] and to a generation of theatre- and moviegoers it apparently meant more than can be seen from a mere reading of the script.[8]

The three central characters consist of both melodramatic and truthful elements: the former are most conspicuous in Mat Burke, an Irish stoker, the latter in Chris Christopherson, captain of a coal barge. Anna, his daughter, is in between.[9] To American audiences it may have been a daring move to show a prostitute with a golden heart on the stage; European theatre and literary traditions were familiar with this figure through Dumas *fils* and Dostoevski.

'Anna Christie' is doubtless both more ambitious and more melodramatic than its predecessor; the crucial point is how the idea of fog is expressed. At the beginning of Act II the

[5] Leech, *Eugene O'Neill*, p. 28.

[6] Cargill *et al.*, pp. 152-54: a reprinting of Francis Hackett's review on *'Anna Christie,'* originally published in *The New Republic*, Nov. 30, 1921.

[7] A review by Kenneth Macgowan stresses the importance of the original production: "The playwright, the producer, and player met last night in one of those moments of accomplishment which make dramatic history" (Miller, p. 27; originally published in the *New York Globe and Commercial Advertiser*, Nov. 3, 1921).

[8] See the estimates, on the whole favorable, in Carpenter, *Eugene O'Neill*, pp. 93-96, and Gassner, *Eugene O'Neill*, p. 13.

[9] Raleigh calls Mat Burke's language "transparently stagey" (p. 221), and places Anna partly in "the Franco-Dostoevskian tradition," partly in O'Neill's American realism (pp. 119-20).

coal barge of "the old Swede" Chris Christopherson is at anchor, at night: "Dense fog shrouds the barge on all sides, and she floats motionless in a calm. . . . The doleful tolling of bells, on Long Point, on ships at anchor breaks the silence at regular intervals" (P III 25). This might be a deck scene onboard the *S. S. Glencairn*, with Yank dying in the cabin. Yet a new attitude toward the fog is introduced on the following page by Anna, brought up on a farm, "started wrong" by one of her cousins, and now convalescing from her experiences in a brothel: "And now—this fog—Gee, I wouldn't have missed it for nothing . . . I love it! . . . It makes me feel clean—out here—'s if I'd taken a bath . . ." (P III 26). Mat Burke enters the barge out of this fog, and the triangle between father, daughter, and a hopeful son-in-law is formed.

Obviously the function of the fog is not as simple as in the earlier plays, where it was utilized as a symbol of fate or death. Yet this fateful meaning is frequently implied when Chris curses "dat ole davil, sea" and the fog, "vorst one of her dirty tricks" (P III 26). These outbursts are placed into the most emphatic structural positions, at the end of three of the four acts. This is not the last time O'Neill employs words as if they were sound effects: repeating a few phrases, used as a leitmotif.[10]

The ambiguity is further sharpened by a passage early in the play. Chris not only hates the sea, he also loves it, as he is made to confess in a mellow state of mind brought on by Anna's arrival and his eagerness to get her to settle down on the barge: "You don't know how nice it's on barge, Anna. Tug come and ve gat towed out on voyage—yust water all round, and sun, and fresh air, and good grub for make you strong, healthy gel. You see many tangs you don't see before. You gat moonlight at night, maybe; see steamer pass; see schooner make sail—see everytang dat's pooty" (P III 23). Here we have an early version of O'Neill's lyrical confession of love for the sea, more fully developed in *The Hairy*

[10] Raleigh connects "dat ole davil, sea" with a universal inclination to repeat one's own phrases and to believe in a kind of protective magic in words (p. 176).

Ape and *Long Day's Journey Into Night*—and we get it from the mouth of Chris, who sees in "dat ole davil" his archenemy.

A kind of resolution is given by Mat Burke in one of the speeches in which he expresses his contempt for Chris: "The sea's the only life for a man with guts in him isn't afraid of his own shadow! . . . 'Twas yourself knew it once, and you a bo'sun for years" (P III 48). Chris is a fugitive from his wife, from his duties as a father, and from the sea, another object of his love. Is he simply a man who fears what he loves, is a major theme in the play a fear-love relation to life, carried also by Mat's superstition and overcome by Anna's courage?

This is a possible interpretation; yet it should not make us blind to the fact that the theme is not skillfully dealt with by O'Neill. Here we have perhaps the first example of his inclination to overburden his symbols, to give them several, even conflicting connotations, and to rely too readily on the communicative power of subtle overtones—an inclination let loose in his mask plays, most notably in *The Great God Brown*. The sea is quite a lot of things, mostly huge and vague; it is fate—and life; it is feared and loved; it cleans and helps Anna to be reborn; it gives her Mat and a questionable happiness. It is not very probable that the kind of puzzle play practiced above, connecting far-off passages to achieve a picture of a vital theme, will succeed, if we are looking at a production of the play.

The Gelbs have found obvious parallels between Anna's speech on the barge and a letter written to O'Neill's friend Terry Carlin by his girlfriend Marie.[11] Anna's exultation is not in keeping with the gloomy, fateful function given to the sea;[12] this is one of the reasons for ambiguity. We should not fail to notice here the very O'Neillian theme of obsessive

---

[11] The Gelbs, *O'Neill*, pp. 290-91.

[12] Travis Bogard has followed O'Neill's steps through the remaining three versions of the play—*Chris Christophersen, The Ole Davil*, and the final script—in an excellent short study entitled "*Anna Christie*: Her Fall and Rise," first published in Gassner (ed.), *O'Neill*, pp. 62-71.

family fate, introduced as it was in *Gold* and *Where the Cross Is Made*: generations of sea-faring Christophersons have preceded Chris and Anna.

This is not the first time it has been observed that there is something rotten in this play dealing with the Swedes.[13] In *'Anna Christie'* O'Neill was face to face with a situation where he was unable to control an intricate form with a large number of interacting ideas and scenic images. In *The Straw* he succeeded in constructing a string of three interacting images; in *'Anna Christie'* he lost his grip. After successfully creating a fateful atmosphere with the help of several scenic means of expression early in the play, O'Neill came to rely too heavily on melodramatic action and dialogue. These means, when employed later (the whistles of the steamers in Act IV), were not strong enough to carry the full implications of the theme of fate, confused as the play was by other issues. Insistent repetition of a phrase or two was not the correct solution.

'Anna Christie' is obtuse; *Diff'rent*, another play completed in 1920, is overschematic and obviously melodramatic in its violent conclusion. The setting in Act I represents that kind of photographic, detailed realism which O'Neill himself was to denounce a few years later:[14] "The room is small and low-ceilinged. Everything has an aspect of scrupulous neatness. . . . Several enlarged photos of strained, stern-looking people in uncomfortable poses are hung on the walls. . . . Stiff, white curtains are at all the windows." So were the ancestors of the Mannon house to watch over their descendants, in another story of sexual repression in New England; here the forefathers see Emma Crosby, "a slender girl of twenty" with "absent-minded romantic dreaminess" about her eyes, but with a heavy mouth and chin, "full of a self-willed stubbornness" (P II 493-94). This paradox is respon-

[13] Joseph T. Shipley calls Mat "too much the man," "too little the symbol" (*The Art of Eugene O'Neill* [1928], p. 18). Cf. Engel, p. 44, and Koischwitz, p. 110.

[14] Cargill *et al.*, pp. 108-09: O'Neill on Strindberg in the Provincetown playbill.

sible for the action of the first act: Emma, under the delusion that her bridegroom Caleb Williams must be something "diff'rent," repudiates him because of an incident of impurity on a far-away island.

After thirty years, the ancestors are gone: ". . . the scene is the same but not the same. The room has a grotesque aspect of old age turned flighty and masquerading as the most empty-headed youth. There is an obstreperous newness about everything. Orange curtains are at the windows . . ." (P II 519). Several references are made to this change in the dialogue, and a jazz band record is played. Not satisfied with these means of expression O'Neill brought the setting frankly into the action in the last scenic image of the play. Emma, now a withered old maid of fifty, dressed too youthfully, lets Caleb's greedy nephew Benny court her and causes Caleb's suicide—after which she has her revelation, too late: "Emma sits straight and stiff in her chair for a while, staring before her with waxy eyes. Then she gets to her feet and goes from window to window taking down all the curtains with quick mechanical movements. She throws them on a pile in the middle of the floor. She lifts down the framed pictures from the walls and piles them on the curtains. . . ." But the wheel of time does not turn back thirty years; all the playwright can do is to employ the automaton effect in the last stage direction of the play, too. Emma "moves like a sleepwalker" (P II 548-49) to her own suicide.

The elements of *Diff'rent* are bare; it is thus interesting to see how heavily O'Neill was willing to emphasize the role played by the setting. This is, in a marked way, a characteristic of his "milieu-determined" plays, such as *All God's Chillun Got Wings* and *Mourning Becomes Electra*, which were influenced by expressionism. The setting belongs pronouncedly to Emma: she is a product of New England; the men around are, to employ an early title for *Bound East for Cardiff*, "children of the sea." It is the parlor itself, with the portraits on the walls, with the Bible on the table, with the joyless furniture, that makes Emma "a Puritan maiden." She is more pronouncedly this than the "daughter of a seafaring family."[15]

Yet O'Neill overdid the number and broad-mindedness of his secondary characters; he needed a contrast to Emma and in his eagerness to make Emma look strong he gave too much strength to her counterweights. Something similar had happened in *Ile*, an earlier play on monomania. *Diff'rent* is a play of clear and sharp contrasts: in the interval between the two acts, in Emma's transformation, in the degree to which she deviates from her rough relatives, in the melodramatic roguishness of Benny as contrasted with Caleb, a constant suitor for thirty years. In fact, the contrasts are too sharp to suit the realistic style chosen by the playwright.

There is also a homogeneous group of secondary characters in *The First Man*: but here they are not made to represent a viewpoint sympathetic to the playwright. They are a dismal crowd of gossiping, narrow-minded, jealous small-towners, whose scenes are unfortunately the prevailing element in the play.[16]

There is little to be said of *The First Man*: it is surely "one of O'Neill's most dismal misses," with its "mechanical awkwardness."[17] Passing attention may be paid to the living room setting, a scenic unit analyzed in Appendix B (pp. 351-57) of this study; to the melodramatic use of childbed moans and cries throughout Act III; and to a modified monologue, employed as Martha Jayson tells of the experience that made her want a child. As a rule, the behavior of the characters in this play consists of that queer mixture of hysterical gestures and conventionality met only in full-blown melodramas.

---

[15] Engel, p. 32.

[16] Koischwitz (p. 140) compares the satiric treatment of the Jaysons with the caricatures drawn in *Frühlings Erwachen*. There is, however, a model that was closer to O'Neill than Wedekind: his own *Bread and Butter*. Both it and *The First Man* take place in Bridgetown, Connecticut; in both, there is a family, largely unsympathetic. In the earlier play, the hero was called John and had a brother Edward, his father's namesake; this time, John Sr. and Jr. are the heads of the dynasty, while Edward Bigelow is Curtis' closest friend.

[17] The Gelbs, p. 466. Cf. Leech, pp. 28-29.

If *The First Man* (1921) is compared with *The Straw* (1918-19), there is little doubt that the line of development has been running downhill. In fact, O'Neill's expressionism, starting with *The Emperor Jones* in 1920, was disturbing his realism. If he was one step short of full-scale stylization in the forest scene of *The Straw*, he had crossed the border when writing *Diff'rent*: hence the violent contrasts within a style not fit for them. And hence the final impression left by *The First Man*: it is as if the realistic formula were cracking in the playwright's hands, as if the boiling emotions of his characters were to lead to an explosion any moment.[18]

Realism was a dead end to O'Neill in 1921, a growing point not sprouting anymore. He had completed his first phase in the surroundings which he knew by experience and which were thus easily turned into realistic milieus on the stage. In his next phase, begun before this was finished, the emphasis was to shift from realism to symbolism. The playwright was to use the surroundings more imaginatively, relying more confidently on the suggestiveness of scenic elements even outside the settings. Sound and lighting effects, eagerly grasped even up to this point, were to gain additional independence and importance. Scenic images were to have more sharply cut edges.

Structurally and thematically, three out of these four plays deal with the problem of an individual in a crowd. *'Anna Christie'*, with its triangle of characters and its theme of fate, is an exception. Unfortunate for the artistic success of these plays is that the crowds receive mainly scorn from O'Neill, and the scenes dealing with them, often in emphatic positions, are consequently either dull or monotonously sardonic. Having, on the other hand, an urge to reveal the inner states of mind of his heroes, he was to find a temporary solution in two plays that might be called modified monologues in their entirety. Still later, when he had the form of the full-length

[18] In 1921 Parker wrote about O'Neill: "O'Neill sometimes has so much to convey that his vehicle of expression creaks and groans under the load" (Miller, p. 29).

play and the interaction of scenic images more safely under control, he was able to focus on one or two characters not counteracted by a whole group of homogeneous secondary figures. This was perhaps the beginning of his distinctly symbolic characters: instead of resorting to a crowd he began to create representative individuals, concepts turned into characters.

And, seeing this quartet as an outgrowth of the preceding period of apprenticeship, we may conclude the first part of this study by remarking that enough errors and awkwardness have been found to repudiate the legend of O'Neill's unerring "theatre instinct." Instead, we might speak of a young playwright who is inclined to use over- rather than understatements, and who is more talented in employing several kinds of scenic means of expression than in writing faultless, effortless literary prose.[19] When at its best, his language in these early plays is speakable and actable everyday prose tinctured with slang; at its worst, as in *The First Man*, it is clearly derivative and full of clichés.[20] There are fewer out-worn elements in his scenic means of expression than in his language; yet one can clearly see those two spheres of theatrical expression in which he felt at home: the traditions of melodrama and of realism.

By 1921 Eugene O'Neill had, in fact, already explored these two possibilities of the stage, first in one-act, then in full-length plays—and he was to go on exploring them. Yet the realistic and melodramatic components found in the remaining plays are connected not only with one another, but with a third element, to be called most safely and also some-

[19] In the words of Gassner, O'Neill was "disproportionately effective on the stage and disappointing in print" (Gassner [ed.], *O'Neill*, p. 4).

[20] ". . . when he was trying to project deep emotions in conventional, educated, normative English, he very often fell back right into the rhetorical patterns of the Fechter version [of *The Count of Monte Cristo*], which consists of stringing together in a fragmentary manner a series of fairly neutral and abstract nouns and/or adjectives and indicating their desired intensity by repeated exclamation points" (Raleigh, in *O'Neill*, Gassner [ed.], p. 18).

what loosely "experimental."[21] At first, the departures from realism have a pronouncedly expressionistic flavor. With these departures, the outer harbors of the then-known American drama are left behind, and the real exploration can begin.[22] It will bring results requiring a more careful analysis of the scenic images and their interaction than any of the plays discussed so far.

[21] Downer sees in experimentalism something typical not only of O'Neill but of the entire American theatre in those years ("The Revolt from Broadway," in *A Time of Harvest*, Spiller [ed.], p. 47).

[22] What Coghill says of the works of Shakespeare applies also to O'Neill: "Their endless originality and variation is not haphazard but experimental. Like other great artists, Shakespeare was continually exploring and extending his medium" (*Shakespeare's Professional Skills*, p. xi).

PART TWO

EXPLORING THE STAGE

"To be called a 'sordid realist' one day, a 'grim, pessimistic Naturalist' the next, a 'lying Moral Romanticist' the next, etc. is quite perplexing. . . . So I'm really longing to explain and try and convince some sympathetic ear that I've tried to make myself a melting pot for all these methods, seeing some virtues for my ends in each of them, and thereby, if there is enough real fire in me, boil down to my own technique."

O'Neill to Professor Arthur Hobson Quinn in an undated letter published in 1927 in *A History of American Drama*, II, 199.

6

FUSION OF THE MEANS

THE EMPEROR JONES

It is difficult to construct a coherent picture of expressionism, or, in fact, of any movement, in the theatre. Paintings, poems, films, plays survive and are ready to be analyzed—but theatre productions vanish. This general disadvantage, overcome to some extent by utilizing literary and pictorial documents, is especially injurious in the case of expressionism, for two reasons. This movement did not lay foundations to any continuous tradition as did realism; its results were assimilated into the prevailing styles. An approximation of Ibsen's realistic style can be seen in modern presentations which are not nearly so rare as productions of expressionistic plays. Secondly, this style in playwriting operated in the closest association with the practices of the stage, then in a state of artistic expansion: stylized settings, experimental lighting arrangements, stage movement approaching dance, and choral mass scenes were part and parcel of the style. The emphasis was on the productions, not on the preserved texts.[1]

Further complications are caused by social and national factors. Extreme expressionism was a product of postwar Germany, with its broken social order, with its unrest and militant humanism;[2] the roots of the style, closely associated with a new view of the world, were in Wedekind and Strindberg. Elsewhere, the movement gained some foothold in the

---

[1] Siegfried Melchinger speaks about revolutionary production and acting techniques during the second phase of German expressionism (1914-18): the actors were before the curtain, in the glaring light of projectors, and they followed the emphatically sharp acting style started by Wedekind (*Drama zwischen Shaw und Brecht* [1961], p. 128). Otto Mann has called expressionism the first modern movement to create plays that could be given "only on a stylized stage" (*Expressionismus*, Hermann Friedmann and Otto Mann [eds.] [1956], p. 232).

[2] Cf. Otto Mann, *Geschichte des deutschen Dramas* (1960), p. 556.

Soviet Union, in France, Italy, and America, practically none in England. As a result, there are several schools of nationally modified expressionism, even called by different names.[3] Expressionism certainly includes plays of a large stylistic variety.

Consequently, most definitions of expressionism are presented without excessive self-confidence. In fact, expressionism is usually defined in negative terms, as a departure from realism, as "anti-naturalism." A key word is "distortion," and a key figure is Strindberg; the two plays taken as models in a great many countries are *Ett drömspel* (A Dream Play) and *Till Damaskus* (To Damascus, sometimes translated as The Road to D). Louis Broussard writes when introducing expressionism in his *American Drama*:

> Strindberg abandoned the photography of realism, the dramatic sequence of events, for a stream of consciousness in terms of stage symbols whereby the surface of life becomes disjointed, scattered, as in a dream, to suggest the inner reality which lies beneath that surface. Not concerned with externals, the dramatist explores the idea, the source of conduct, until reality becomes a subconsciousness and character mere abstraction. Scenes are often brief; they sometimes succeed one another without time sequence; they have neither order nor unity and they suggest, as they alternate between reality and fantasy, between objective action and analysis, the disorderly, disconnected features of a psychoanalysis.[4]

The passage has certain overtones which make it appropriate as a definition of the American version of expressionism

---

[3] Melchinger makes an effort to reserve the term exclusively for German drama: *The Emperor Jones* and *The Hairy Ape* were only described as expressionistic in America (pp. 17, 332-33). A contemporary critic of O'Neill's is cautious in using the term: *The Hairy Ape* "might almost be called an expressionistic tragi-comedy" (Miller, *Playwright's Progress*, p. 33: a review by Walter Prichard Eaton, first published in *The Freeman, 5*, Apr. 26, 1922).

[4] Louis Broussard, *American Drama* (1962), p. 5. The dreamlike quality of expressionistic works of art is also emphasized by Walter H. Sokel, in his *Der literarische Expressionismus* (1959), pp. 42, 52.

rather than of this style in toto. It is phrased more in terms of the individual than in terms of society; in fact, Broussard goes on to say on the same page that Hauptmann, Kaiser, Toller, and Čapek added to this basic Strindbergian expressionism "social and economic issues."

This is a crucial point in trying to find the correct context for Eugene O'Neill's contributions in this field of experimentation. It is advisable to call two of his plays, *The Emperor Jones* and *The Hairy Ape*, expressionistic and to state that there are expressionistic elements in a group of others, most notably in *Welded*, *All God's Chillun Got Wings* and *The Great God Brown*. O'Neill himself was ready to confess Strindberg's influence but denied having received any stimuli from the Germans:[5] "The point is that *The Hairy Ape* is a direct descendant of *Jones*, written long before I had ever heard of Expressionism, and its form needs no explanation but this."[6]

Yet in an interview O'Neill made a remark which could

[5] "Continental Influences on Eugene O'Neill's Expressionistic Dramas," is a short study by Clara Blackburn, published in *American Literature, 13* (1941), 109-33. Blackburn states that the productions of German expressionistic plays in America came too late to have an influence on O'Neill, yet acknowledges that reading Strindberg and the Germans may account for certain similarities. *The Emperor Jones* is "a good illustration of *Ausstrahlungen des Ichs* (radiations of the ego)" (p. 114), typical of expressionism in general, while *From Morn to Midnight* by Georg Kaiser also describes a type character, turned almost to a primitive, and *To Damascus*, basically a dramatic monologue, has a circle structure as *The Emperor Jones* has. Blackburn concludes that "O'Neill's indebtedness to Continental expressionistic dramas and dramatists, especially Strindberg, is greater than has generally been recognized" (p. 133). The case is restated by Mardi Valgemae, who also presents new observations ("O'Neill and German Expressionism," *Modern Drama, 10*, 111-23).

Gierow mentions *Samum*, a short play by Strindberg which utilizes an "oriental suggestion," as a possible impetus for *The Emperor Jones*—which is, however, in Gierow's opinion a better play (*Introduktioner till Eugene O'Neills dramatik*, p. 13). *Samum* was produced in Chicago and New York in 1911. Brustein thinks of O'Neill's expressionism and messianism as "borrowed, ill-fitting robes," and the European drama as "an untapped mine of material," O'Neill being "the first dramatist to exploit it" (*The Theatre of Revolt*, pp. 324-25).

[6] Clark, *Eugene O'Neill*, p. 83.

99

lead to a different conclusion: "The real contribution of the expressionist has been in the dynamic qualities of his plays. They express something in modern life better than did the old plays. I have something of this method in *The Hairy Ape*." In the same interview O'Neill makes an important distinction: "Expressionism denies the value of characterization. . . . I personally do not believe that an idea can be readily put over to an audience except through characters . . . the character Yank remains a man and everyone recognizes him as such."[7]

To O'Neill (and, incidentally, to the whole American drama) characterization was an area so recently conquered by artistic experimentation that it was impossible to give it up altogether. The presence of identifiable human beings in American expressionistic drama is also observed by Broussard.[8] O'Neill had his realistic plays behind him; he did not start as an expressionist, as the German leaders of the movement did. Moreover, he had his very real experiences as a seaman; there was Driscoll, a friend of O'Neill's, as a model for Yank, while Jones is a man in a concrete situation and with a past (we certainly learn to know him better than, say, Sonja Irene L. in *Masse-Mensch* by Ernst Toller). O'Neill was saved from the over-abstractness of the Germans[9]—though not from accusations to this effect. He did not write self-centered plays; he wrote hero-centered ones.[10] He had already written his "*Sturm und Drang*" or Storm and Stress play—*Bread and Butter*. And his first expressionistic hero,

[7] Cargill *et al.*, p. 111: from an interview originally published in the *New York Herald Tribune*, March 16, 1924.

[8] Broussard, pp. 7, 14-15.

[9] "The combination of missionary zeal and formal abstraction proved to be an artistically weakening factor to a great many expressionists" (Sokel, p. 34).

[10] Sokel speaks of "Ich-Dramen" (p. 30), Mann of plays that were "lyrical outbursts of the poet, with the help of dramatic heroes" (Friedmann and Mann, p. 216). Nicoll tries to deny the subjective and romantic starting point of the expressionists; to him, they almost "belong to a modern classicism," characterized by mass scenes, stylization, and typification (*World Drama*, pp. 795-96). His formula is too narrow: the devices of his "classicism" were used in modern "Sturm und Drang" plays (p. 802).

Jones, was not an idealized figure;[11] rather, he had affinities with the guilty haunted heroes of O'Neill's earlier plays.

Both O'Neill and the German expressionists rebelled against objective realism, which they felt to be a limitation on their freedom; and they rebelled under the flag of Nietzscheism.[12] Yet under the influence of the recently initiated American realism, O'Neill was closer to Strindberg's "psycho-expressionism" than to its German variant, to be called "socio-expressionism"—especially in *The Emperor Jones*, written in all probability with greater independence than its more consciously patterned descendant, *The Hairy Ape*.

After these distinctions it is possible to see how far the passage quoted from Broussard can be applied to *The Emperor Jones*. Stream of consciousness is expressed in "terms of stage symbols"; inner reality is suggested in dream-like fashion; the scenes are brief; they alternate between reality and fantasy; stage reality becomes subconsciousness; and sources of conduct are explored. Yet the hero does not become a mere abstraction; *The Emperor Jones* belongs to that sect of expressionism, sometimes called "monodrama," where the distortion is motivated "by a character's state of mind,"[13] and where that character is still a human being. Furthermore, there is a certain unity and order: the time proceeds—backwards, and the fear of the hero grows all the time.

It has been necessary to describe the expressionistic background of *The Emperor Jones* in order to show both O'Neill's

[11] A central idea in German expressionism was the victory of pure humanity over non-human powers: "The expressionistic writer . . . did not want to demonstrate a tragic but a philanthropic idea in his play" (Mann in Friedmann and Mann, p. 223). A battle against inhuman powers is, in fact, conducted by Yank—a losing battle; the play cannot be called educational. "Bildungsdrama" is a term used by Mann (*Geschichte des deutschen Dramas*, p. 562).

[12] Sokel has remarked that the "declamatory and pseudo-biblical Nietzsche" from *Thus Spake Zarathustra* was the prophet of the naïve expressionists, rather than "the brilliant aphorist of *Jenseits von Gut und Böse*" (p. 30). *Thus Spake Zarathustra*, O'Neill writes, "has influenced me more than any book I've ever read" (the Gelbs, *O'Neill*, p. 121).

[13] Gassner, *Form and Idea in the Modern Theatre*, p. 121.

models and his independence. The picture will change in O'Neill's favor when we start to analyze the play, marked clearly by his personal style.[14]

The play consists of a realistic exposition scene, a rapid series of six scenic images, all expressionistically shaped, and a return to realism: a familiar circular structure. Scene i is already charged with ill omens; it is set in the palace of the "Emperor" Jones, a colored ex-convict who has been ruthlessly robbing his subjects, "common bush niggers," "on an island in the West Indies as yet not self-determined by White Marines" (P III 172). The palace is now empty; this is the first suggestion of a threat against Jones. The second is an opening pantomime in which a Negro woman tries to sneak from the palace and meets Smithers, a white trader and Jones's fellow robber. After the Emperor appears, two sound effects show that something is amiss: just after Jones enters, he rings the bell—and nobody comes; and then, toward the end of the scene, his real trouble begins when "from the distant hills comes the faint, steady thump of a tom-tom, low and vibrating. It starts at a rate exactly corresponding to normal pulse beat—72 to the minute—and continues at a gradually accelerating rate from this point uninterruptedly to the very end of the play" (P III 184).

This is the play's central scenic means of expression, its skeleton—or its pulse. At this point there are no symbolic overtones; the tom-tom is simply a sign that the Emperor's subjects have deserted him and gathered on the hills, "gettin' their courage worked up b'fore they starts after you" (P III 184), as Smithers explains to Jones. The victim is still fully garnished in his uniform of self-importance: "He is a tall, powerfully-built, full-blooded Negro of middle age. His features are typically negroid, yet there is something decidedly distinctive about his face—an underlying strength of will, a hardy, self-reliant confidence in himself that inspires respect.

---

[14] The Gelbs have probed some of the sources of *The Emperor Jones*, apart from artistic models: O'Neill's own experiences while prospecting for gold in a tropical forest, combined with scattered reading and discussing a decade later, started his imagination working (pp. 135, 438-39).

102

. . . He wears a light blue uniform coat, sprayed with brass buttons, heavy gold chevrons on his shoulders, gold braid on the collar, cuffs, etc" (P III 175). The palace setting, with its pillars and its throne "painted a dazzling, eye-smiting scarlet" (P III 173), interacts with the costume: Jones is, apparently, a man of stature.[15]

And he has taken the necessary precautions in case of a revolt. He has created a myth that only a silver bullet can kill him; he has sent the robbed fortune to safety; all he needs to do is to cross a plain and a forest to reach a waiting ship. If anything should go wrong, he has six bullets in his revolver; the last is made of silver—for himself. All of these details are important, even for the form of the play: there are six forest scenes to come, and the silver bullet is used in the last of these.

The pendulum swing between self-assurance and fear is a central mental movement in the play. The fluctuation in the dialogue begins right in the first scene, where Smithers speaks to Jones "in a manner half-afraid and half-defiant" (P III 176), and the tom-tom makes Jones look apprehensive. O'Neill has also been careful to tell us so much of his hero's past that we can easily place the ghosts of the forests into their correct contexts. There is Jeff, killed by Jones while he was a Pullman porter; there are the fellow convicts and a guard, even he a victim of the Emperor. These details are told as hearsay, as legends surrounding a great man.

The visions of Scenes iii and iv are thus explained beforehand; after them the playwright was able to rely on the imagination of his audience. There is not, in fact, any abundance of distortion in this play; the non-realistic elements are based on the assumption that the audience will share Jones's visions and his fear of the ghosts of his past. The way for them is further prepared by using phantom creatures called "Little Formless Fears." They enter the stage from the forest, from

[15] Törnqvist associates the name "Brutus" both with its dictionary sense ("stupid, irrational") and, agreeing with Lionel Trilling, with Caesar's murderer ("Personal Nomenclature in the Plays of Eugene O'Neill," *Modern Drama, 8,* 366).

103

a nightmare—and from the world of expressionism. Contrasts in lighting and setting help to evoke the intended atmosphere. In Scene i "the sunlight still blazes yellowly" (P III 173); now "the forest is a wall of darkness dividing the world." And the wind blows, as if it came from another play of nightmare and delusions—from *Where the Cross Is Made*: "A somber monotone of wind lost in the leaves moans in the air" (P III 187).

Jones is alone; his fluctuating monologue, which will last six scenes, has begun: "Cheer up, nigger, de worst is yet to come. . . . What you gittin' fidgety about? (*But he sits down and begins to lace up his shoes in great haste, all the time muttering reassuringly*) . . ." (P III 188). Confident after having used his first bullet he enters the forest built of terrors —and of scenic units. The rays of the moon, "drifting through the canopy of leaves, make a barely perceptible, suffused, eerie glow" (P III 190); "a wide dirt road runs diagonally from right, front, to left, rear" (P III 192)—as the arresting row of cells does in *The Hairy Ape*; Jeff plays dice again, "picking them up, shaking them, casting them out with the regular, rigid, mechanical movements of an automaton" (P III 191). As the play progresses, as Jones is stripped of his self-assuring costume, the ghosts are brought closer and closer to him, until he is made to participate in their action—and the automaton effect, utilized in scene after scene, is transferred to the description of Jones: "The expression of his face is fixed and stony, his eyes have an obsessed glare, he moves with a strange deliberation like a sleep-walker or one in a trance" (P III 200).

Jones's throne with its scarlet color had fitted well with his light blue uniform garnished with gold; now there is mainly green and darkness, out of harmony with his outfit. This scale of colors gives rise to an interesting question: what about the playwright's knowledge of optics? It is possible that O'Neill knew the physical qualities of light well enough to choose light blue for Jones, a color that remains visible on a relatively dark stage where green trees are turned into a menacing darkness.

104

The ghosts are mostly silent, so that the tom-tom, beating all the time more wildly, and the reports can be heard. The bullets are used by Jones to expel the spirits; as if to avoid overschematization, O'Neill makes his hero use two bullets in a particular scene and lets him escape once without resorting to the weapon. The latter happens in the scene with the Negro slaves, which may imply that Jones did not need to shoot because he belongs to their company. Another exception from a rigid patterning is a change in the "correct" time sequence: Jones goes further back in time, but the murder of the white guard, a recent but ominous crime, is presented after the scene with Jeff.[16]

Having dealt with Jones's individual past, O'Neill jumped into racial memory in his quest for more and more horrible climaxes. Scene v pictures a group of Southern planters in an auction, about to sell Jones; the next glimpse transforms a claustrophobic forest setting into an interior of a slave ship. Parts of the scenery are moved even during the scenes: the walls of the forest fold in when Jones fires his revolver.

The tom-tom, the prevailing sound effect, compels the "low, melancholy murmur" of the slaves under its command (P III 199). The Emperor joins his blood brethren in their chorus of despair: in his retrogressive flight he has now reached the level of "bush niggers." Having only the breech cloth of his imperial uniform left, he is ready to walk into an African scene, charged with superstitious fear.

The remaining step from pantomime to dance is taken in this scene, in which a witch doctor performs an incantation. Jones is to be sacrificed to the crocodile god, present on the stage in his own person. To get rid of the charm Jones is compelled to fire his last bullet, the silver one, while the tom-tom reaches its mad climax. There is a report as early as Scene ii, an imagined murder in Scene iii; as more and more terrors were demanded by the structure of the play, O'Neill went all the way down to the Congo. After that, there is only a return to realism: the rebels have spent all night moulding silver bullets, Jones is promptly killed at the end of his circle

[16] Leech remarks on this (*Eugene O'Neill*, p. 39).

in the forest,[17] and Smithers has an opportunity to close the play with an admiring remark. Jones has met the death he chose for himself.

Quite a lot has been written about *The Emperor Jones*; yet its most conspicuous stylistic feature has hardly been emphasized strongly enough. It is not the tom-tom, striking as this repetitious sound effect is; it is not the presence of the visions as such. It is the fusion of the scenic means employed; it is the interaction of the scenic images. The above quotations from the play show the abundance of imaginatively used scenic means of expression within the space of thirty-odd pages or about an hour and a half of acting time. *The Emperor Jones* is a play written for two actors, a revolver, a tom-tom, a lighting apparatus, a cast of dancers, and several movable pieces of forest scenery.

The means are fused in several of the above passages. Moonlight and forest setting together create a ghastly atmosphere; scenes of pantomime are played against this background; the fluctuating monologue shows how Jones is stripped of his self-assurance along with his uniform; the tom-tom controls the chorus of the slaves. As for the interaction of scenic images, part of an important aspect is clearly seen by Engel who speaks of "a remarkable concentration of dramatic power" achieved "by means of several unifying effects." The time is just one night; the place is mostly the forest; the reports, the tom-tom, and the character of the play as a "monodrama" bind the action together.[18]

The phenomenon counterbalancing concentration should also be given its name: there are explosive elements in *The Emperor Jones*. Compression is usually a virtue in drama; so is movement. A combination of these virtues ranks even

---

[17] Raleigh has connected *The Emperor Jones* with O'Neill's inclination to follow the cycle of day and night. It happens here "quite explicitly": "afternoon (confidence)" is followed by "night (terror, disintegration, retrogression), dawn (retribution)" (*The Plays of Eugene O'Neill*, p. 19).

[18] Engel, *The Haunted Heroes*, pp. 52-53.

106

higher: movement within a limited space, strong dynamics.[19] Or, to use a familiar terminology: interaction within and between the scenic images. Day and night, light blue and dark green, hope and fear, past and present, reality and nightmare, guilt and certain human stature, realism and expressionism, are among the dynamic, interacting elements of this play— all kept together by a central tension.[20] In fact, there are more contrasts within the images than between them; the six forest scenes form a series of as many climaxes, all working toward the same direction, and not relieved by any interludes— exactly as the tom-tom beats continuously, mercilessly. The images form a series of synonyms, not of antitheses.

By combining this with a knowledge of O'Neill's recent starting point, his crisp one-acters, we might draw a picture of *The Emperor Jones* as a structural whole. The scenic images work cumulatively,[21] not in clear-cut contrasts as in *Diff'rent*. *The Emperor Jones* is essentially still a unicellular play—or a special kind of multicellular play in which the scenes are, as it were, minor cells within a similar major one. The presence of Jones and the tom-tom create a strong sense of continuity. The constellation of elements has definite similarities in each of the six forest scenes; if an emphasis is put on stylistic differences, the realistic scenes can also be seen as separate cells, as outgrowths at both ends of the play.

Somewhat surprising variants are achieved when O'Neill jumps into racial memory. It is indeed noteworthy how boldly he creates movement in the dimension of time, and how strong is the sensuous appeal of the memories utilized[22]—

[19] Stoll has spoken of the great stage effect of *Oedipus Tyrannus* and *Othello*, arising "out of a peremptory compression and a violent contrast" (*Shakespeare and Other Masters*, p. 213).

[20] Carpenter catalogues a slightly different set of contrasts: "the eternal conflict of good and evil, of sunlight and moonlight, of civilization and savagery, of the clearing and 'The Great Forest' " (*Eugene O'Neill*, p. 92).

[21] According to Gassner, there are "cumulative excitations" in *The Emperor Jones*; the play is an "amplification of the one-act form in eight short scenes" (*Masters of the Drama*, p. 652).

[22] Biese says that the dumbshows make "a much more direct appeal

before the flash back technique so eagerly employed by film directors banalized the procedure. A central means in this exploration of memories, those of the individual and those of the race, and its effect on the audience is described by Goldberg, an expert in O'Neill's use of sound effects: "The tom-tom is part and parcel of the psychological action; at first it is the call to war; then it merges into the Emperor Jones's vision of the slaves rolling to its beat; finally it becomes his own throbbing, feverish temples, and all the while it is our heart beating more and more rapidly as we follow his fate."[23]

There comes a point, however, where one must take a critical distance from *The Emperor Jones*. The play is manifestly written under the influence of C. G. Jung—and of a more general current of thought, to be called fallacy toward primitivism.[24] The great background figure is, of course, Freud; the field to be considered in this connection covers a large area of post-Freudian literature and the theatre. In general terms, the fallacy consists of a belief that if the origin of a phenomenon was probed, then all one needed to do was to give this explanation—and there it was, the phenomenon itself.

The effect of this philosophy on O'Neill's use of masks as a stage device will be discussed later on. Now it is enough to state that at least to those of O'Neill's contemporaries who were familiar with the Jungian philosophy, the scenes operating with racial memories were probably profound mystical illuminations of the nature of things as they once were—and as they still are. Today, when the words "mystic" or "poetic"

---

to the imagination of the spectators than could have been achieved by using any kind of orthodox dramatic technique" (*Aspects of Expression I*, p. 63).

[23] Cargill *et al.*, p. 240: from *The Drama of Transition* (Stewart Kidd Co., 1922).

[24] Michael Anderson speaks about "a movement in the twentieth century towards an interest in primitive modes of thought and their lingering survival in myths and ceremonies," and connects it with *The Golden Bough*, Jane Harrison, Gilbert Murray, and F. M. Cornford ("Dionysus and the Cultured Policeman," *Tulane Drama Review*, 11, 4 [Summer 1967], p. 99).

seem to be more or less constant epithets in descriptions of the Jungian psychology,[25] the scenes have not retained these overtones. On the other hand, their existence does not disturb us—they can be taken simply as flights of poetic fancy, as added dimensions to Jones's fate. The witch doctor and the crocodile in Scene vii are, however, somewhat puerile elements, especially when used as a climax—not because Jung has fared somewhat badly in the intellectual stock exchange since the twenties, but because a totally different breed of literature has thrived so mightily: there has been a flood of jungle books and films, most of which are furnished with those two figures.

In our picture of *The Emperor Jones* the emphasis is on the importance of fusion and interaction. We can say that the play fulfills, *mutatis mutandis*, Peacock's definition of a painting as "a unified image-pattern": "all the elements of the scene are adjusted and assimilated to each other within one predominant visual purpose."[26] Instead of "elements of the scene," we have means of scenic expression; instead of a visual purpose, a theatrical one.

It is possible now to dismiss a few critical opinions which do not take the function of particular means of expression into consideration. Ever since Clark mentioned a previous use of the tom-tom in Austin Strong's melodrama *The Drums of Oude* in 1906,[27] it has been convenient to call the device "little more than a gimmick, and not even a new gimmick."[28] Although easy, it is hardly recommendable to loosen a specific detail of expression from its proper context and call it downright imitation; the results may be even absurd. The verb "to be" is certainly a cliché; how is it possible that Shakespeare uses it so plentifully in that monologue of some reputation, "to be or not to be"? The function of words, sound

[25] Cf. Doris V. Falk, *The Tragic Tension*, p. 6.
[26] Peacock, *The Art of Drama*, p. 11.
[27] Clark, p. 72.
[28] Bamber Gascoigne, *Twentieth-Century Drama*, p. 111. Cf. Miller, *Playwright's Progress*, p. 104: "Eugene O'Neill and the Highbrow Melodrama," by H. G. Kemelman.

effects, settings, any particles of expression, is all-important,[29] and, consequently, to be considered when passing judgments on art. The manifold functions of the tom-tom create in *The Emperor Jones* a fresh and powerful artistic experience, notwithstanding a previous usage.

Signi Falk complains that O'Neill "forgot or ignored the distinctive idiom and speech of the Negro" in *The Emperor Jones*, and goes on about *The Hairy Ape*: "Speeches like this make good theater because of their vitality and strength but are not particularly noteworthy as dramatic literature."[30] Considering the play as an artistic whole one has to ask: who would expect, in the middle of an exuberance of expression, to hear "distinctive idioms" from Jones?[31] His speech reflects the staccato rhythm of the play, until all the words we need are a few ejaculations, adequate against their proper background. From the standpoint taken in this study it is not purposeful to make any distinction between the "theatre" and "dramatic literature."

An error of another kind is to read O'Neill's expressionistic plays too narrowly through the theory of orthodox German expressionism, seeing in their heroes only ciphers.[32] It is hardly feasible to imagine audiences not getting emotionally involved with Jones and Yank, two figures so powerfully characterized. Both of these monologue plays are constructed to have an emotional impact, developed by the continuous presence of the hero on the stage and by a wide variety of scenic means employed.

These means are fused; and, what is of equal importance,

[29] "The questions with which I have armed myself have mostly been in terms of function, of bare dramatic analysis. . . . What is the use or point of this act, scene, speech, movement, gesture and so forth?" (Coghill, *Shakespeare's Professional Skills*, p. xii).

[30] Signi Falk, "Dialogue in the Plays of Eugene O'Neill," p. 317.

[31] "But what audience will examine them as they flash by?" Granville-Barker asks about the inconsistent definitions of time in *Romeo and Juliet* (*Prefaces to Shakespeare*, II, p. 302).

[32] "But Jones and Yank are purely symbolic figures, moulded entirely by the social pressures of past and present. . . . *The Emperor Jones* and *The Hairy Ape* end in the deaths of the central figures, but we are not emotionally involved with them, or intended to be" (Leech, pp. 36-37).

they are employed in harmony with the theme of the play. It would be absurd to think that the only criterion when evaluating drama would be an abundance of expression, that the greatest sum of means used yields the greatest work of art, automatically. The arithmetic of art does not work as simply as that; if it did, O'Neill's incomparable masterpiece would be *Lazarus Laughed*, where all possible tricks are employed. The means must be used in harmony with the theme, in harmony with the style chosen by the playwright, and in harmony with the author's personal qualities.

Within all of these areas there are possibilities for variation. In the same playwright's realistic plays the theme may be more or less forceful, requiring a corresponding scale of means. Similarly, in his expressionistic plays the theme may require more or less drastic means, more or less hectic rhythms; as a rule, the means needed are more violent than in realistic plays. And we may appreciate Chekhov's quiet and poetical qualities with quite as good a reason as we appreciate O'Neill, even if the latter is, by his very nature and by his cultural climate, more inclined to use striking, powerful means of expression—provided that these are used harmoniously with the theme and style of the play, as they are in *The Emperor Jones*, this study of atavistic fear.

On the other hand, what makes poor plays is in several cases a friction between and within these three dimensions. The theme of Dionysian joy of life did not fit well with the gloomy view of life characteristic of O'Neill, and the means employing the whole orchestra of theatrical expression were sadly in disharmony with the mystical message of *Lazarus Laughed*. In *Diff'rent* the realistic style chosen was not appropriate for the violent conflicts exposed. As a contrast, *The Emperor Jones* is a meeting place for an individual, highly talented playwright, who had just passed his period of apprenticeship, and an artistic movement, still fresh and full of potentialities. These stylistic resources were turned to their best advantage by O'Neill, who was able to utilize with distinction several means of expression, several scenic units, which he knew through previous experience. This is, in fact, an answer to the problem of artistic independence: a maturing artist met something in his age that started him reverberating—and created a work that was soon to arouse an echo everywhere.[33]

[33] What happened is aptly summed up by Daiber. O'Neill transformed what he took from Europe, and had an influence on the European drama: the giving partner started to receive ("Der Tragiker der neuen Welt," p. 34).

7

BRIEF ENCOUNTER

THE HAIRY APE

O'Neill called *The Hairy Ape* "a direct descendant" of *The Emperor Jones*. The plays were finished in 1921 and 1920 respectively; there is a complication, however, for the later work was first written as a short story in 1917 and turned into a play "in three weeks."[1] It is to be argued that there were elements in Yank's story which O'Neill was unable to transform into a dramatic form—in his 1917 phase of development.[2] Four years later he was able to do so; *The Emperor Jones* came in between, and so did reading *Vom Morgen bis Mitternacht* by Georg Kaiser.[3] As far as the form of the play is concerned, as far as we are dealing with the development of O'Neill's scenic thinking, *The Hairy Ape* belongs definitely to the year 1921.

It is an eagerly disputed question whether Yank is a man or a cipher.[4] The closest we can come to a solution is to say

[1] Cargill *et al., O'Neill and His Plays*, p. 481.

[2] Doris V. Falk reasons that "the short-story version must have been almost complete as an outline of the play's theme and action" (*Eugene O'Neill and the Tragic Tension*, p. 10), and discusses the play as if it had been finished in 1917. Additional causes for preferring 1921 to 1917 are: everything said about the short story is bound to be only hypothetical, as the version is not preserved, and we have O'Neill's own words about the significance of transformation, in a letter to Kenneth Macgowan. The play "has changed and developed immensely in the doing" (the Gelbs, *O'Neill*, p. 490).

[3] Clark, *Eugene O'Neill*, p. 83.

[4] Yank has been called a symbol, not a man, by H. G. Kemelman ("Eugene O'Neill and the Highbrow Melodrama," in Miller, *Playwright's Progress*, p. 104), and by Robert E. Spiller (*The Third Dimension*, p. 167). The original production awoke "a profound pity" in Walter Prichard Eaton who also approved of the stylistic mixture employed (Miller, pp. 33-35). To Margaret Gump, Yank "remains very human to the end in his tragic search for his place on earth" ("From Ape to Man and from Man to Ape," *Kentucky Foreign*

that *The Hairy Ape* apparently developed in the direction of expressionism, yet never reached full-fledged German style. Its position is somewhere between the expressionism of *The Emperor Jones* and that of playwrights like Toller or Kaiser: realistic and stylized elements are mixed, and there is still quite a lot of emphasis on characterization—but also on social ingredients. To O'Neill, the play seemed to run "the whole gamut from extreme naturalism to extreme expressionism—with more of the latter than the former."[5]

The Hairy Ape lacks the long realistic opening scene of *The Emperor Jones*; instead, its first and fourth scenes are described by Gassner as typical examples of expressionism: "the individual was likely to be placed in a truncated scene usually deprived of the padding of 'manners' and small talk customary in cup-and-saucer living room scenes. Only the *dramatic moment* was allowed to matter. This moment was given to the spectator without the familiar preparatory detail of nineteenth-century realism; frequently, it was hurled at him like a missile. In some plays the individual was submerged in the automatism of a milling and shrieking chorus."[6] These dramatic moments were often powerful scenic images with clear-cut edges.

The first missile in the play consists of twenty-nine short lines, mostly ejaculations of a word or two; they are assigned, without specification, to "voices." In that short space O'Neill succeeds in giving us a picture of three typical elements in the life of the stokers: drinking, telling stories about women, and fighting. Collective stage action is present, by way of implication, in these barren sentences. Then the focus is transferred from the chorus to the individual, to Yank, who "seems broader, fiercer, more truculent, more powerful, more sure of himself than the rest. . . . He represents to them a self-expression, the very last word in what they are, their most highly developed individual" (P III 208).

Language Quarterly, 4, 1957, 183). Both Koischwitz (*O'Neill*, p. 114) and Blackburn ("Continental Influences," p. 117) emphasize that Yank is more clearly typified than Jones—a reasonable standpoint.

[5] The Gelbs, p. 490.

[6] Gassner, *Form and Idea in the Modern Theatre*, p. 120.

With this description O'Neill connects himself with expressionism: his hero is a representative of a group of people. He also says that the "treatment of this scene, or any other scene in the play, should by no means be naturalistic," and wants the group of stokers to be stylized toward uniformity: "All the civilized white races are represented, but except for the slight differentiation in color of hair, skin, eyes, all these men are alike" (P III 207). The character of this group as an unspecified mass is preserved throughout the play, by letting the speeches remain assigned only to "voices"; the roles are later inherited by groups of churchgoers, of prisoners—and, at long last, of apes. There are no red herrings in *The Hairy Ape*; the focus is on a girl and three stokers. The rest of the actors are not granted an opportunity to create three-dimensional character portraits—not at least by O'Neill.

The contrast between an individual and a group is established in a much more effective way than, say, in *The First Man*. It is developed all through the play. Another central idea is the setting, reminiscent of a cage; its roots are in *Bound East for Cardiff* and in the claustrophobic forest scene with the slave ship in *The Emperor Jones*: "The effect sought after is a cramped space in the bowels of a ship, imprisoned by white steel." In this setting, with its suggestiveness typical of the expressionists, the "shouting, cursing, laughing, singing" of the stokers, resembling Neanderthal Man, is given "a sort of unity, a meaning—the bewildered, furious, baffled defiance of a beast in a cage" (P III 207).

Yank is perfectly in harmony with his primitive surroundings. He takes pride in his work; the passengers on board are "just baggage. Who makes dis old tub run? Ain't it us guys? Well den, we belong, don't we? We belong and dey don't. Dat's all" (P III 212). O'Neill uses different stylistic layers in this play, building out of these a kind of collage—consisting of dialogue used in interaction with other scenic means of expression.[7] Paddy, an old Irish stoker, is given in between

[7] ". . . O'Neill builds up the dialogue and the action in this play by a pattern arrangement because he is striving for a certain emotional

an opportunity of voicing a lyrical outburst, a confession of love to the sea. It is Yank, however, who gives the prevalent note: "Yuh're all wrong. Wanter know what I t'ink? Yuh ain't no good for no one. Yuh're de bunk. Yuh ain't got no noive, get me? Yuh're yellow, dat's what. Yellow, dat's you" (P III 212). This is how he refutes Long, a socialist agitator.

The passages are strikingly different from Paddy's long, sweepingly rhythmical sentences in his pantheistic speech, reminiscent of Strindberg's expressionistic plays. Yank's utterances proceed in small circles, as it were, repeating the same sentence structure or the same phrase at short intervals. He speaks as if through a wall of language difficulties; every so often he has to go back, to gather more speed with the help of a phrase which has already burst wondrously out of his mouth. Yank is an inarticulate character, and his way of speaking is entirely appropriate for him—a sign of O'Neill's remarkable control over language.[8]

A new patch of color is added to this collage called *The Hairy Ape* in Scene ii: a throng of dirty firemen in a narrow forecastle, talking, singing, fighting; and now two passengers in a section of the promenade deck.[9] "The impression to be conveyed by this scene is one of the beautiful, vivid life of the sea all about—sunshine on the deck in a great flood, the fresh sea wind blowing across it" (P III 218). This is a setting in which Paddy might feel at home—Paddy with his longing for the bygone days of sailing vessels—Paddy, a kind of foreshadowing picture of the hairy ape in his old age: "His face is extremely monkey-like with all the sad, patient pathos of that animal in his small eyes" (P III 210). Yet the two figures sitting in their deck chairs are as sadly incongruous

effect rather than for verisimilitude in speech and in action. . . . Some of O'Neill's best lyric poetry is found in the first scene of this play" (Blackburn, p. 118).

[8] Braem attributes part of Yank's tragedy to his inability to articulate his longing for a brighter world (*Eugene O'Neill*, p. 50).

[9] Alexander Woollcott finds "the greatest visible contrast in social and physical circumstances" in the first two scenes of *The Hairy Ape* (Miller, p. 31: a reprinting from the *New York Times*, March 10, 1922).

as Paddy was down in the forecastle. Bitterly ironical contrasts like this are characteristic of this "comedy of ancient and modern times."

The discussion of Mildred Douglas and her aunt adds a third kind of language to the company of those two employed in Scene i. Mildred, a social worker and daughter of the president of Nazareth Steel, speaks artificially, as she should according to O'Neill's vision; yet the effect is achieved in an over-obvious way. After a few pages of teasing discussion the latter part of the dual exposition is finished: Mildred and Yank are ready for their brief encounter in the stokehole.

Scene iii is without a doubt the core of *The Hairy Ape*. Two lines carefully drawn in the preparatory scenes converge; two totally different worlds clash in the central scenic image of the play. Before Mildred descends into the stokehole to satisfy her curiosity, the atmosphere there is heightened by fusing several scenic means of expression: lighting, noises, collective action. The over-all lighting is specified as dim, as it is also in Scenes vi and viii; presumably not even the forecastle is brightly lighted.[10] Against this background of dimness the special effect employed gathers extra significance: "A line of men, stripped to the waist, is before the furnace doors. . . . They use the shovels to throw open the . . . doors. Then from these fiery round holes in the black a flood of terrific light and heat pours full upon the men who are outlined in silhouette in the crouching, inhuman attitudes of chained gorillas" (P III 222-23). There is thus an effort to carry the theme of "the hairy ape" even collectively, by this line of "Neanderthal Men."

Action and sound effects are entwined to achieve a powerful, coordinated impression. The men handle "their shovels as if they were part of their bodies, with a strange, awkward, swinging rhythm. . . . There is a tumult of noise—the brazen clang of the furnace doors as they are flung open or slammed shut, the grating, teeth-gritting grind of steel against steel, of

[10] Sokel has called the lights an important actor in expressionistic plays (*Der Literarische Expressionismus*, p. 56).

117

crunching coal. This clash of sounds stuns one's ears with its rending dissonance. But there is order in it, rhythm, a mechanical regulated recurrence, a tempo. And rising above all, making the air hum with the quiver of liberated energy, the roar of leaping flames in the furnaces, the monotonous throbbing beat of the engines" (P III 223).

This is the modern hell where Yank is so proudly working as a self-appointed leader of his fellow stokers.[11] Though the scene leaves an impression of originality, it is possible to draw certain connections, on the one hand to Strindberg, on the other to the literature and films of the twenties.[12] The dangers of mechanization in the machine age are emphasized in plays by Elmer Rice, Kaiser, Toller, or Čapek, in the film *Modern Times* by Charles Chaplin.

In *The Hairy Ape* the danger is not caused by the machines themselves, but by an extraneous intruder who scatters Yank's primitive pride. He becomes conscious of his own position; this is his original sin. As in *The Emperor Jones*, O'Neill took pains to give his hero a kind of stature, later tragically demolished. Yank is not only a personification of his profession; in Scene i O'Neill allows him a moment of exultant identification with his surroundings: "I'm de ting in coal dat makes it boin; I'm steam and oil for de engines; I'm de ting in noise dat makes yuh hear it . . . And I'm steel—steel—steel! I'm de muscles in steel, de punch behind it!"

[11] Raleigh connects the mechanical features with Paddy's lyrical speech: "Thus the sea really has two great contrasting rhythms, the 'natural' movements and sounds of the sea and of sailing vessels, and the 'mechanical' movements and sounds of steam vessels and other modern man-made devices. . . . Even in relaxation these men are not men but machines" (*The Plays of Eugene O'Neill*, p. 22).

[12] Blackburn refers to *Die Koralle* by Kaiser where a contrast between the rich and poor is developed in a similar way. Especially marked are the affinities between the coal-heavers scene in Strindberg's *A Dream Play* and O'Neill's forecastle and stokehole scenes, while Indra's daughter and Mildred, daughter of a big businessman, both enter a lower world ("Continental Influences," pp. 118-20). Robert J. Andreach draws a parallel to Dante and concludes that Mildred foreshadows O'Neill's late masterpieces: she is "the female with good intentions . . . who awakens the male to . . . despairing truth" ("O'Neill's Use of Dante in *The Fountain* and *The Hairy Ape*," *Modern Drama, 10*, 56).

(P III 216). In these fragments Yank identifies himself with every significant detail in the setting of Scene iii; in a couple of ejaculations he enlarges the field of his ego even outside the stokehole.

In *The Emperor Jones* O'Neill needed seven scenes to strip his hero bare; now he is trying to do the same in a single scenic image. From the above description we can see that he succeeded in making the scene an impressive one. When Mildred and Yank see one another it is not just a meeting by chance but a focal scenic image emphasized by the presence of a whole arsenal of scenic means of expression. The encounter is further accentuated by its element of surprise: Yank is furiously cursing the whistle of the engineer when Mildred enters, dressed in white, a dramatic contrast to the smoky surroundings.[13] In the middle of his outburst Yank senses something behind him and "whirls defensively with a snarling, murderous growl, crouching to spring, his lips drawn back over his teeth, his small eyes gleaming ferociously. He sees Mildred, like a white apparition in the full light from the open furnace doors. He glares into her eyes, turned to stone" (P III 225).

That is how Yank experienced the brief encounter. This is Mildred's side of it: ". . . during his speech she has listened, paralyzed with horror, terror, her whole personality crushed, beaten in, collapsed, by the terrific impact of this unknown, abysmal brutality, naked and shameless" (P III 225). She faints and is brought away. "An iron door clangs shut. Rage and bewildered fury rush back on Yank. He feels himself insulted in some unknown fashion in the very heart of his pride. He roars 'God damn yuh!' and hurls his shovel . . . at the door which has just closed. It hits the steel bulkhead with a clang and falls clattering on the steel floor." And the final note is supplied by a familiar sound, giving rhythm and continuity to the life in the stokehole. Only this time it has an

---

[13] The contrasts catalogued by Raleigh are mainly human: "woman vs. man; white vs. black; top-dog vs. bottom-dog; frayed nerves vs. brute power; the slight vs. the muscular; civilization vs. the jungle" (pp. 125-26).

ironical effect: "From overhead the whistle sounds again in a long, angry, insistent command" (P III 226).

Up to this point, the setting of each scene has been a direct opposite of the preceding one. In Scene iv, which is a return to the forecastle, Yank himself furnishes the contrast. In Scene i he "belonged"; now he does not. Hurt "in the very heart of his pride" he sits, unwashed, "in the exact attitude of Rodin's 'The Thinker'" (P III 226). A new variation of the relation between the individual and the group is developed in this scene: Yank has always been the chorus leader; now the stokers are all against him.

The few words uttered by the chorus members have, repeatedly, "a brazen, metallic quality as if their throats were phonograph horns" (P III 229). A connection with the preceding scene is drawn by Dorothy J. Kaucher, who says that O'Neill emphasizes "further the relentless spirit of steel" by using "the clang of furnace doors, the clattering of Yank's shovel on a steel bulkhead, the whistle overhead and staccato voices."[14] At the moment of self-glorification in Scene i all the stokers had pounded with their fists against the steel bunks: "There is a deafening metallic roar . . ." (P III 216). Now the voice of metal is turned against Yank: the time of exultant identification with steel is over.

It is clear that O'Neill uses the chorus and the sound effects in order to bring closer to us the feeling of alienation experienced by his inarticulate hero. Furthermore, the dialogue in Scene iv is intended mainly to explain, lengthen, and rationalize the decisive moment included in the previous scene. This elaboration is necessary, since a remarkable part of the emotional impact has until now been given only in stage directions. Hopefully, the audience has experienced all of it, as a result of the skill of the director and the actors. But the latter part of the play needs a stronger motivation, for a new line of development, which will last until the end of the play, is begun in this scene. Cut away from his natural surroundings, Yank begins his search for revenge and a renewed sense

[14] Dorothy J. Kaucher, *Modern Dramatic Structure* (1928), p. 131.

of belonging. His fluctuating monologue, which is to comprise a large part of the remaining four scenes, has begun: he speaks now "furiously," now "with his old confident bravado"—and "again bewilderedly" (P III 231).

Let loose in society Yank is followed by Long. Scene v, as far as the action of the secondary characters is concerned, is the most clearly expressionistic sequence in the entire play.[15] The group of churchgoers Yank and Long meet on Fifth Avenue gives the impression of uniformity and automatism:[16] "A procession of gaudy marionettes, yet with something of the relentless horror of Frankensteins in their detached, mechanical unawareness" (P III 236). If O'Neill had not already used the automaton effect in *Thirst*, its origin could easily be traced to expressionism: now it is to be argued that the outside influence only made him transfer a scenic unit from a single character to a group.

The function of this group, made more homogeneous by identical clothes and voices, is to demonstrate that a stoker is not even seen by the well-to-do. Though Yank deliberately lurches into them, he is barely noticed until he commits a "crime"—by preventing a gentleman from catching the bus. This means mixing up with other people's business, and Yank is promptly arrested. Society is not interested in feelings of "belonging" or "not belonging" or other personal matters—as long as they do not lead to manifest social action.

There are conflicting elements in the setting. It is "a fine Sunday morning. A general atmosphere of clean, well-tidied,

[15] Peter Szondi has written about a paradox immanent in German expressionism: extreme subjectivism leads to a situation in which all heroes are more or less alike. What is revealed is not a character, but a milieu seen through this character—in many cases, a big city (*Theorie des modernen Dramas* [1959], pp. 38-39, 90-91). O'Neill is more profoundly involved in the development of his hero than in Yank's surroundings. Again, we can see that O'Neill's expressionism is of a special kind: he is satisfied with just a glimpse of the big city, expressionistically distorted.

[16] In a purely expressionistic play, only the hero is real: "what is shown as his surroundings on the stage, is only pictures arising from his inner world" (Mann, in Friedmann and Mann, p. 227). This is the *raison d'être* for the churchgoers. Cf. Blackburn, p. 117.

wide street; a flood of mellow, tempered sunshine; gentle, genteel breezes." The incongruous element is included again, as in the deck scene. Diamonds and furs are displayed in two show windows, creating the general effect of "a background of magnificence cheapened and made grotesque by commercialism" (P III 233). If Yank does not belong, neither do Mildred & Co.

For a while, Yank believes that he has found a harbor, a community. This happens in the prison, another expressionistic setting: "The cells extend back diagonally from right front to left rear. They do not stop, but disappear in the dark background as if they ran on, numberless, into infinity" (P III 239). The diagonal arrangement of the cells has been discussed before; it is also worth noticing how a parallel to the stokehole scene is achieved by a similar lighting effect, one electric bulb; Scene iii pictured a prison, too.[17] The necessary chorus consists of fellow prisoners, and its function is ironic, as it was in the previous scenes. Yank refutes social or religious solutions to his problem: "VOICES (*scornfully*): Hurrah for de Fort' of July! Pass de hat! Liberty! Justice! Honor! Opportunity!" (P III 243).

A fourth stylistic layer is added to the dialogue when a senator is quoted from a newspaper. The writer scorns the first American labor union, the I.W.W., so spitefully that a new hope arises in the slow mind of Yank: perhaps these "anarchists" will revenge for him and other outsiders. He joins the union, and for the first time since Scene iii he seems to belong. It is not long before he realizes his gross misunderstanding. He is promptly ousted from the locale as a provocator when he starts preaching his idea of a violent revenge. This time O'Neill provides a silent chorus: eight or ten men are needed to overpower Yank. The scene is placed partly in, partly outdoors. When sitting outside the locale, again in the position of Rodin's "The Thinker," Yank comes as close to self-understanding as anywhere in the play: "Dis ting's

[17] Blackburn (p. 117) associates still further: "The procession of gaudy marionettes on Fifth Avenue is also a cage against the bars of which he beats in vain."

in your inside, but it ain't your belly. Feedin' your face—
sinkers and coffee—dat don't touch it. It's way down—at de
bottom. Yuh can't grab it, and yuh can't stop it. It moves,
and everything moves. It stops and de whole woild stops . . .
Steel was me, and I owned de woild. Now I ain't steel, and
de woild owns me" (P III 250). Using the verbal image of
steel Yank sees himself as a victim of spiritual, or if the word
is too fine, mental dissatisfaction with the machine age. His
longing is not to be satisfied with material goods alone.[18]
This conclusion foreshadows in an engaging way the attitudes of a whole group of later Finnish novelists, all interested in describing the life of the working man: Toivo Pek-
kanen, Olavi Siippainen, Lauri Viita, and Väinö Linna, to
mention only the most prominent representatives of this
tradition.

Yank is close to his grotesque death, anticipated by a fateful moonlight in Scene vii. In the final episode at the zoo there
are again many shadows, little light. Paddy's choice—that
is, the possibility of reconciliation and of a mildly rebellious
position in the stokehole—has been refuted by Yank beforehand; it is refuted again in this final scene. The gorilla that
gives Yank a murderous hug also belongs to this world of
ours, as Yank tells him, complaining at the same time of his
own fate, which has not been relieved by Paddy's pantheism:
"I ain't on oith and I ain't in heaven, get me? I'm in de mid-

---

[18] O'Neill's starting point is social, yet his unrest has other causes,
too: "it would be completely wrong to interpret 'The Hairy Ape'
mainly as a social drama, an attack on social injustice," Gump writes
in her comparative study. In the cage she sees "a symbol of a much
more general oppression and bewilderment, that metaphysical anguish
which Kafka's heroes experience" ("From Ape to Man and from
Man to Ape," pp. 182-83). "The modern dramatist is essentially a
metaphysical rebel, not a practical revolutionary . . . his art is the
expression of a spiritual condition" (Brustein, *Theatre of Revolt*, pp.
8-9). Cf. Charles I. Glicksberg, *The Tragic Vision in Twentieth-
Century Literature* (1963), pp. 83-84. Marden J. Clark has written a
perceptive analysis of Yank's development ("Tragic Effect in *The
Hairy Ape*," *Modern Drama, 10*, 372-82). He sees Yank as a brute
who "moves toward becoming a man" (p. 372), asking "the profoundest questions and defining the profoundest of human dilemmas"
(p. 381) at the end of the play.

dle tryin' to separate 'em, takin' all de woist punches from bot' of 'em" (P III 253). And the play is closed as it was opened, by a chorus, after which O'Neill was not able to resist the whim of including a comment on the action of the play in his last stage direction:[19] "The monkeys set up a chattering, whimpering wail. And, perhaps, the Hairy Ape at last belongs" (P III 254).

Contrasts within the images were a striking stylistic feature in *The Emperor Jones*. It is fruitful to start a discussion of *The Hairy Ape* as a structural whole by stating the importance of contrasts between the images. On the most obvious level, these tensions are achieved by using a wide range of variations in the lighting and settings.[20] The bright outdoor scenes (ii and v) are placed between dimmer interiors, while the two final scenes, even if wholly or partly outdoors, belong to the dimmer end of the scale, with their moonlight and twilight. Of equal significance is the narrowness of the ship interiors; rows of cages going on ad infinitum, without consolation, do not disrupt this formula of settings.

Winifred L. Dusenbury speaks of clearly drawn borders between the milieus—and between the individuals: "The characters in the respective settings are as obviously contrasted, so that the effect is startling, when a character from either level is placed in the inappropriate setting."[21] The voltage of social tension is highest when Mildred visits the stokehole, and Yank Fifth Avenue. Yet there is, in fact, an incongruous element in each of the eight scenes: Paddy in the forecastle, Mildred both on the deck and in the stokehole,

---

[19] Shaw indulged in a similar whim in the last stage direction of *Candida*: "But they do not know the secret in the poet's heart" (*Plays Pleasant* [1955], p. 160). *Candida* was written in 1894.

[20] Being familiar with *The Emperor Jones* and *The Hairy Ape*, Alfred Kerr calls O'Neill above all "a creator of pictures" (*Die Welt im Drama* [1964], pp. 210-14: a reprinting from *Berliner Tagblatt*, 1924). This is not foreign to expressionism as a whole; according to Sokel (p. 54), "expressionism substitutes immediate visual presentation for intellectual analysis." Cf. Gassner, *Eugene O'Neill*, p. 20.

[21] Winifred L. Dusenbury, *The Theme of Loneliness in Modern American Drama* (1960), p. 126.

Yank wherever he turns, after the crushing moment in Scene iii. Contrasts between the images extend their influence over scene lines and help to form new images full of inner tensions. The theme of "not belonging" is carried by several scenic means of expression, as well as by Yank's monologue.

Even if this is true, we have now found the weak spot of *The Hairy Ape*. After having surrounded his inarticulate hero with striking means of expression in the three early scenes of the play, O'Neill chose to face the difficulty of achieving a further climax mainly through Yank's monologue. In this dilemma he came closer to writing genuine poetry than perhaps anywhere else in the whole canon, a fact recognized by several critics—and denied by others.[22] It is probable that O'Neill's later failures to write dialogue on the level of his scenic imagination have colored some critical estimations of the merits of the dialogue in *The Hairy Ape*.

Yet this does not entirely save the play. After broad brush strokes in the early scenes, the line of development carried mainly by Yank's monologue, however distinguished in its own rough way, seems rather thin. Trying to see the play as a figure we might speak of the letter Y lying prone; the strongest point is that at which the two expository lines meet. The emphasis in the play is, in other words, too strongly on the focal scenic image of Scene iii; it is possible to imagine audiences sitting spellbound up to Scene iv and then starting to look forward to an appropriately powerful climax—which never comes, in spite of the marionettes on Fifth Avenue, in spite of the cages and the gorilla. The themes of the play are clarified rather than developed throughout the latter half.[23]

[22] Edmund Wilson, whose attitude toward O'Neill's language is otherwise sharply critical, had an opportunity of seeing *The Hairy Ape*, and afterwards was ready to agree with Eaton that O'Neill wrote slang like "a kind of wild organ music" (Miller, p. 34). Wilson goes on: "The scenes in which the non-illiterate characters talk are as clumsy and dead as ever, but the greater part of the play, in which Yank . . . discourses, has a mouth-filling rhythmical eloquence very rare in naturalistic drama" (Cargill *et al.*, p. 465: a reprinting from *Vanity Fair*, Nov. 1922).

[23] Wilson, *ibid.*, appreciates the merits of the "monodramatic" latter

Perceiving the central weakness in *The Hairy Ape* should not make us blind to its merits. In addition to those mentioned above, it is more intricate in its structure, more ambitious in its social commitment than its predecessor. The emotional experience offered by this sinewy, bitterly ironic play is hardly as overpowering as that of *The Emperor Jones*, with its cumulative structure, yet there are elements of greatness in the stoker's tragedy. Several ideas are controlled throughout the action, in a much more distinguished way than in *'Anna Christie'*, another piece of intricate interrelations. Among these effective and thematically important ideas, there is the contrast between the individual and the group, employed as a chorus in the background in a manner parallel to the handling of apparitions in *The Emperor Jones*. There is the vision of industrial working and living surroundings as oppressive cages, likewise developed through a series of expressive scenic images. The atmosphere of every scene is evoked with a skill familiar to us ever since *Bound East for Cardiff*. And there is the idea of mixing different stylistic layers to achieve the effect of a collage.[24]

Instead of having caused disastrous consequences this procedure has led to remarkable achievements, much to the surprise of stylistic purists. Gassner is explicit in his approval of "an amalgamation of two or more different styles of composition in the very same play": "the result, far from disturbing us, usually gains our approbation."[25] O'Neill utilized here what Gassner calls "the duality of theatre," the ability of the

---

half, yet remarks: "I am not sure that Mr. O'Neill always gives enough dramatic emphasis to his most important ideas. The significance of these last scenes of *The Hairy Ape* was not thrown into relief on the stage." Hugo von Hofmannsthal has presented a similar reservation (Cargill *et al.*, p. 255: originally published in *The Freeman*, March 21, 1923).

[24] Eaton uses, interestingly enough, the word "fusion" when characterizing *The Hairy Ape*: "no such fusion of dialogue and scenery, of the intellectual, the emotional, the spiritual, and the pictorial, into a single thing which is only to be described by the word *theatrical*, has ever before been accomplished by an American playwright" (Miller, p. 35).

[25] Gassner, *Form and Idea in the Modern Theatre*, pp. 12-13.

126

spectators and actors to glide from full participation in stage action to consciousness of the theatre.[26]

Part of the dynamism O'Neill appreciated in expressionism came from this stylistic flexibility. How the collage succeeds on the stage depends decisively on the performances of the stage director and the actors. At long last it is their responsibility to make the outbursts of Yank and Paddy, respectively clumsy and high-flown on the written page, sound effective in their stage surroundings. And it depends on their share in the creative process whether Yank can be taken as a character or a cipher; there are certainly elements of characterization in this role, which were evidently utilized with great skill in the first production of the play.

The Hairy Ape is the second and last of O'Neill's plays which can be called expressionistic with full reason. There are later works which contain elements of this style; but O'Neill did not go further along the road chosen in *The Emperor Jones*, continued in *The Hairy Ape*.[27] This is, in a way, a pity. Expressionism, with its reliance on sharp contrasts and violent effects, corresponded to some deep layers in O'Neill's artistic temperament, evidenced by the freshness of scenic imagery in these two plays and by the prevalent harmony between themes and means. In *The Hairy Ape* the amount of scenic units remained low; in *The Emperor Jones* familiar details of expression were combined with one another and with new elements in a fresh and striking way, a practice which the new style, with its many unexplored regions, encouraged. Furthermore, the subjectivism prevalent in expressionism was in agreement with O'Neill's interest in modified monologues. It was natural for him to write monodramas.

[26] *Ibid.*, pp. 210, 224.

[27] Robert F. Whitman sees progress in *The Hairy Ape*: "The expressionistic techniques are on the whole better integrated than in the earlier play, for the disassociation, the inner conflict, and the futile reversion to a more primitive orientation are all suggested by the action and setting without recourse to interpolated 'visions'" ("O'Neill's Search for a 'Language of the Theatre,'" *The Quarterly Journal of Speech*, *46* [1960], 159; there is a reprinting in Gassner [ed.], *O'Neill*, pp. 142-64).

Presumably O'Neill felt after *The Hairy Ape* that he had written his definitive expressionistic play. Be that as it may, this short phase had produced two plays not easily forgotten.[28] They have an equal right to be counted among his major achievements[29]—and they broke holes in the fourth wall, to be utilized later on.

[28] In his final estimate Mann says that expressionism caused a sensational revolution, yet paid for this by being a transitory phenomenon. O'Neill's contributions do not belong to the most outdated ones; they certainly broke off with realism and grew right from the middle of contemporary life, two features appreciated by Mann (Friedmann and Mann, pp. 233-35).

[29] Per Lindberg calls *The Emperor Jones* and *The Hairy Ape* "the best plays in expressionistic style" (*Kring ridån*, 1932, p. 286).

8

PAGEANTS THROUGH HISTORY

THE FOUNTAIN, MARCO MILLIONS,

LAZARUS LAUGHED

No throng of influential background figures are evident behind *The Emperor Jones* and *The Hairy Ape*: only Strindberg and the German expressionists. As a contrast, we shall
meet a motley crowd when discussing the three plays grouped
here under a common heading: Nietzsche (directly and via
Strindberg) and the authoress of a theosophic book called
Light on the Path, James G. Frazer and C. G. Jung, "Jig"
Cook and Kenneth Macgowan, Robert Edmond Jones and
Max Reinhardt—not to mention historical and biblical figures
like Juan Ponce de Leon, Marco Polo, and Lazarus. In
fact, these plays are a meeting place for various literary
and theatrical influences—which is a polite way of saying
that their artistic weight is slight. After realism and expressionism, O'Neill entered a centrifugal period in his effort
to enlarge the scope of his plays. Three pageants through
history are among the fruits of this orientation.

The word "centrifugal" is used, first of all, as a reference
to the outer form of these plays. *The Fountain* has eleven
scenes, *Marco Millions* thirteen (including a prologue and
an epilogue), *Lazarus Laughed* eight. The distances traveled
are formidable, both in time and in geography: the two
earliest plays cover more than twenty years and two con-
tinents; *Lazarus Laughed* is "compressed" within the space
of a few months, but travels half a circle around the Medi-
terranean. So much the worse, these plays are loose and their
energy has a hysterical flavor.

Paying less attention to the purely literary influences, we
will concentrate instead on those movements in the theatre

which were at least partly responsible for this regressive development. A key figure is Kenneth Macgowan, critic and co-director of the Provincetown group in its later years; the Gelbs called him "O'Neill's closest friend over the longest period of time."[1] Together with O'Neill and Robert Edmond Jones, he led the Provincetown Playhouse in New York in 1923-26, or during and shortly after those very years when these plays were being created. One of them was produced by the triumvirate in spite of its limited resources. And we know that Macgowan was O'Neill's confidant when the earliest play in the group, *The Fountain*, was being written: he was kept busy by O'Neill "with suggestions for background reading"[2]—after the playwright had perused *The Golden Bough* by James G. Frazer.

This happened in 1921, in the same year when Macgowan published his book *The Theatre of Tomorrow*. It covers movements of renewal in stagecraft, in theatre architecture, and in drama. As a mirror of Macgowan's ideas of the theatre this volume is of importance to us. The first impression is of a somewhat vague enthusiasm: despite the book's promising title, Macgowan had greater difficulty in prophesying what the theatre of tomorrow would be like than in denouncing the deficiencies of the American stage as it was. He took a firm stand against realism, saying of modern European theatre that "its one definite limit cuts it off from the theatre of photographic realism."[3] He admired German theatre architecture and stage mechanics, which made rapid scene changes possible, and looked for new playwrights who could bring drama to the level already achieved in the theatre, thanks to the efforts of directors and scene designers. This is the point where his influence on O'Neill begins: it became a task of honor to O'Neill, with his recently won international reputation, to give America plays of the imaginative theatre —to give it pageant plays.

Macgowan's favorite adjective is "spiritual," always pro-

[1] The Gelbs, *O'Neill*, p. 710.
[2] *Ibid.*, p. 469.
[3] Kenneth Macgowan, *The Theatre of Tomorrow* (1921), p. 19.

nounced with the deepest respect. The modern playwright, giving up realism, "will strive to free himself from the necessity of creating actuality in order to suggest the spiritual. He will seek for purer form. He will strive for clearer emotion. He will seek the expression of the spiritual by the most direct means."[4] This vaguely phrased passage (what do "purer form" or "clearer emotion" mean?) may have led O'Neill, among other things, to the spiritual (or spiritualistic) apparitions in *The Fountain*, a play without actuality yet with romantically blurred emotions. And this borders on O'Neill's expressionism: the surroundings of *The Hairy Ape* were distorted in order to make them *more* actual—to Yank and to the audience. Instead of actuality, it was time to offer history; instead of crushing reality, the poetry of the far-away and of pure spirit. Using an easy generalization, Macgowan finds his favorite spice even in technical devices, *an sich*: ". . . there is always a spiritual quality in light, even when it is only illumination."[5]

There is only a short step from here to the idea of the theatre as a temple, drama as a pagan religion—and psychoanalysis as its catechism. This is how Macgowan proceeds in the climactic concluding pages of his book, heading full speed toward the drama of tomorrow—and toward the fallacy of primitivism: we have forgotten the Greek spirit, "the eternal identity of you and me with the vast and unmanageable forces which have played through every atom of life since the beginning. Psychoanalysis . . . has done more than any one factor to make us recover the sense of our unity with the dumb, mysterious processes of nature. We know now through science what the Greeks and all primitive peoples knew through instinct. The task is to apply it to art and, in our case, to the drama." If this task had been fulfilled, a new drama would have been born, "nearer perhaps to the Greek than to any other in spirit, yet wholly new in mechanism and method, mysteriously beautiful and visionary."[6]

Psychology was not to Macgowan or O'Neill a branch of

[4] *Ibid.*, p. 109.   [5] *Ibid.*, p. 47.   [6] *Ibid.*, p. 264.

science, proceeding cautiously through a series of empirical experiments and statistical analyses of the resulting data. It was something "big" and sweeping, an answer to man's metaphysical dilemma, a cult, a ritual, a short cut to universal significance. In this idea lies a key to O'Neill's "behind-life," mystical plays, to his "super-naturalism."[7] Psychoanalysis, this patent medicine prescribed by a critic to a playwright, was even powerful enough to make romanticism acceptable again: "The romantic play, with modern psychological understanding of character added, will be a better thing than the romantic play of a hundred years ago."[8] It is doubtful whether *The Fountain* is "a better thing" than *The Count of Monte Cristo*; what is doubtless is that it is romantic.[9]

Prophesying the form of his imaginative, visionary Greek-Freudian drama Macgowan promises all this and heaven too: "Wherever the dramatist of tomorrow may find his form . . . it will be a form that has room in it not alone for action, music, dance, color, line and movement, but also for the magnificent prose that you find in the speech of the greatest and the simplest of our people."[10] If Macgowan was to be disappointed in O'Neill's ability to write "magnificent prose"[11] (Yank's way of speaking hardly fulfilled his heart's wishes), he received, as a consolation, lots of other ingredients. Two details of his vision of the theatre—the drama of the collective "group-being" and the use of masks—will be discussed to their best advantage in connection with certain plays markedly influenced by these ideas.

It is not purposeful to make of Macgowan the villain of this group of O'Neill's plays—at least not the only villain. In

---

[7] Cargill *et al., O'Neill and His Plays*, pp. 108-09: the terms are used by O'Neill himself in his Provincetown playbill on Strindberg.

[8] Macgowan, p. 262.

[9] Connections between Fechter's (and James O'Neill's) stage adaptation of *The Count of Monte Cristo* and *The Fountain* are also drawn by Raleigh (*The Plays of Eugene O'Neill*, p. 185), and by Brustein (*The Theatre of Revolt*, p. 334).

[10] Macgowan, p. 247.

[11] "Only great dramatic poetry, which O'Neill was never to write, could have fulfilled his intentions," Gassner writes about *The Fountain* (*Eugene O'Neill*, p. 16).

all fairness to him it must be said that his attitude toward several proponents of renewal was not blindly uncritical: he did warn of the dangers of mere pictorialism, and his critical remarks are not, as a rule, as badly outdated as his enthusiasm. Apparently he even had some doubts as to whether O'Neill was the best playwright to deal with the legend of the Fountain of Youth, for he sent his friend a "somewhat awed query"[12] about the outline of the play.

Kenneth Macgowan was a typical prophet, bound to his time. He reflected and developed ideas which were close to his personal way of thinking and were also found in the Western theatre early in this century. He belongs to a line of development begun by the neo-romanticists and the symbolists, playwrights like Rostand and Maeterlinck. Arriving late in America, coinciding with a revolution in stagecraft, another in psychology, and meeting a national stage where realism was barely rooted, this movement produced a few plays with an archaic rather than a progressive flavor. It needed, of course, O'Neill's willing cooperation; and it did confirm his native inclination toward mysticism, encouraged by an early acquaintance with Nietzsche, later with *Light on the Path*, a book written by Mabel Colling, a "member of the London Lodge of the Theosophical Society."[13] Religious overtones were also appreciated by "Jig" Cook, a fellow worker whose association with O'Neill was ended in 1922, however, when two of these plays were not yet begun. And it needed the cooperation of Robert Edmond Jones, an important, creative scene designer, who directed *The Fountain* and by his very talent encouraged experiments toward elaborate, anti-realistic settings.[14]

[12] The Gelbs, p. 469.

[13] Doris Alexander, "Eugene O'Neill and *Light on the Path*," *Modern Drama, 3* (1960), 261.

[14] Gilbert W. Gabriel calls the opening night "an evening of poor rewards": *The Fountain* was "played almost wretchedly, and affording little consolation other than Mr. Robert Edmond Jones's handsome return to romantic designs for his setting and costumes" (Miller, *Playwright's Progress*, p. 15: originally published in the *New York Sun*, Dec. 11, 1925).

The Fountain was completed in 1922; *Marco Millions* was written in 1923-25, *Lazarus Laughed* in 1925-26. Even though O'Neill had several other projects under preparation at the same time, and even though these years mark the phase of his career when he began to devote more time to each new play, it is obvious that he felt more than usually entangled with these plays. None of them was finished in three weeks.

O'Neill's creative efforts were not well rewarded. *The Fountain*, to begin with it, leaves a singularly adolescent impression. Diluted pantheism, refuted by Yank in *The Hairy Ape*, is now very conspicuously the message of the play. The fountain, the central emblem, is present on the stage in Scenes i, iii, vi, ix, x, and xi; in addition, three scenic units are employed in the settings. The Gelbs have gathered a neat piece of statistics on the sea settings in O'Neill: thirteen of his plays were placed either partially or entirely on board ships, in addition to six plays dealing with the influence of the sea on people.[15] The ship here pictured is commanded by no less a person than Columbus. Two of the setting arrangements date back to *Beyond the Horizon* and *The Emperor Jones*: a forest running diagonally from right front to left rear; and a scene depicting a small clearing in the middle of the forest.

Juan Ponce de Leon, a proud Spanish nobleman, enters the forest and sees there a series of apparitions—another remnant from *The Emperor Jones*. Before that, he has refuted the love of a woman, sailed west for the greater glory of the Spanish crown, served as the Governor of Puerto Rico, and is now looking for the Fountain of Eternal Youth —inspired by Beatriz, the beautiful daughter of the woman he rejected. Don Juan is another O'Neill hero with a marked inner conflict, "a romantic dreamer governed by the ambitious thinker in him" (P I 377). Romantic dreams drive him into the forest; ambitions are demonstrated when he single-handedly crushes a middle-sized revolution—"With quick

[15] The Gelbs, p. 157.

thrusts and cuts of his sword he kills or wounds four of the foremost, who drop to the ground" (P I 424); when he does his thinking is a riddle.[16] O'Neill has given him sudden twists of mood that sound like unintentional self-parodies: "Dog! I will burn that scorn from your eyes! (*The Indian stares at the hot iron immovably. Juan lets it fall to the floor with a desperate groan of misery*) Pardon! Forgiveness in Christ's name! It is you who torture me!" (P I 415). No matter how ridiculous Juan's behavior is, "his personality is compelling" (P I 434) as soon as O'Neill so wishes.

The real flood of Macgowanisms begins in Scene x (one of the few merits of the play is that its structural emphasis is in the right place). In this scene, which was certainly a difficult problem even for Robert Edmond Jones, "a strange unearthly light" floods "down upon a spot on the edge of the clearing. . . . Beneath the growing light a form takes shape— a tall woman's figure, like a piece of ancient sculpture, shrouded in long draperies of a blue that is almost black" (P I 438). In this pure spiritual light Juan sees the representatives of four world civilizations, joined to demonstrate their fundamental oneness; they are later shown carrying the emblems of their respective religions—a Chinese poet, a Moorish minstrel, the tortured Indian Nano, and Juan's Dominican friend Luis. Ancient Greece is there, too, represented by the sculpture-like figure of the woman. In his fluctuating monologue, interrupted on the written page by not less than forty-seven guiding stage directions, Juan tries to probe the mystery of these apparitions: "What are you, Fountain? . . . O God, Fountain of Eternity, Thou art the All in One, the One in All—the Eternal Becoming which is Beauty!" (P I 441-42). What all this means, with its plentifully scattered capital letters, is not for the uninitiated to ask; one must only conclude that O'Neill was apparently somewhat tipsy after having swung on the golden bough while

---

[16] "Although the hero is both 'soldier of iron and dreamer,' the conflict of these opposites within his mind never becomes real" (Carpenter, *Eugene O'Neill*, p. 98).

drinking a draught mixed with a few drops of Nietzscheism and of Jungian Freudism from the bowl of anthropological mysticism.[17]

The theme of harmony with nature, with God, with everything, is also carried by a beautiful moonlight and by a quasi-poetical song that is employed as a ritualistic leitmotif. It reaches "an exultant pitch" (P I 449) at the close of the play, blending in harmony with the chant of the monks. Shortly before this, Beatriz has been assigned to Juan's nephew, a clear token of eternal recurrence. "All is within!" (P I 442) Don Juan exclaims; an ejaculation ironically in contrast with the play itself, where so much is outside—scattered in the settings, in the romantic action, in the apparitions, in the mystical background reading. "Beauty resides there and is articulate" (P I 386), he is told; another sentence not in keeping with the play and its sadly inadequate language.[18] Unfortunately, there was more of this to come.

We need not, in fact, part company with several of the phenomena discussed above. *Marco Millions* is partly a direct continuation of *The Fountain*, partly a satire on the American businessman. Engel has connected it with its predecessor for several reasons. This pageant through thirteenth-century Asia shows O'Neill again dedicated "to deal earnestly with religious matters," to depict "the evils of Western civilization as opposed to the virtues of paganism. Apart from the satire the tone . . . is romantic, spiritual, tragic . . . and, as in *The Fountain*, he indulged his taste for voluptuous theatricalism: for pageantry, tableau, multiplicity of elaborate scene, crowds, songs, rhetorical language."[19]

[17] Critical distance is taken e.g. by Raleigh: "*The Fountain* reaches its climax in some rather murky religious symbolism in Scene x . . . when all the discords of his [Juan's] life and time are meant to be dissolved into some misty, rhythmical, transcendental One" (*The Plays of Eugene O'Neill*, pp. 38-39).

[18] The language of *The Fountain* had already been objected to by Stark Young in his review in *The New Republic*, Dec. 30, 1925 (Cargill *et al.*, pp. 172-74).

[19] Engel, *The Haunted Heroes*, pp. 135-36.

In its original form *Marco Millions* was designed as two separate plays, to be presented on two consecutive nights; this is the first symptom of O'Neill's inclination to mammoth projects. Even though the idea was later rejected, it left its mark on the play.[20] Act I could be entitled "Marco's Travels," the rest of the piece, "Kukachin's Love." The prologue was presumably added to bind the two halves together, but serves only to open the action in the wrong key (as was shown by the 1964 revival at the Repertory Theater of Lincoln Center).

The inspiration for the prologue flowed from a fountain well-known to us. The coffin of Princess Kukachin is shown on the stage; she is on her way home, destroyed by her unhappy love for Marco Polo. The entire play, with the exception of the last scene, is a flash back—twenty-three years long. Three merchants are witnesses to a short apparition, achieved again with the help of the "spiritual quality" in light. When the corpse of Kukachin has spoken her message, "a sound of tender laughter, of an intoxicating, supernatural gaiety, comes from her lips and is taken up in chorus in the branches of the tree as if every harp-leaf were laughing in music with her. The laughter recedes heavenward and dies as the halo of light about her face fades and noonday rushes back in a blaze of baking plain" (P II 352). No one has spoken of O'Neill's "theatre instinct" in connection with these special effects. They bring greetings from the laughing Lazarus—or from a common ancestor to all the plays in this group, Nietzsche.

The above fragment hardly seems like an appropriate beginning for a harsh satire on the American businessman. Several other ingredients add to the confusion and help dull the edge of satire. O'Neill continues to preach his ecumenical message and furnishes the prologue with a tree that is sacred to Allah, Buddha, Christ, and Zoroaster. Marco Polo is sent

---

[20] Carpenter has paid attention to the dualism between "broad satire" and "poetic mysticism"; at the end of the play he finds, somewhat surprisingly, "genuine tragic effect" in Kaan's grief. Yet the play is to him "a historical pageant rather than a true drama" (pp. 113-15).

by the Pope to Kublai Kaan to discuss which religion is the best—an unnecessary dispute because O'Neill has a higher knowledge: they are all basically similar. For the enlightenment of his audiences he summarizes Buddhism in three speeches and gives glimpses of uniform rites followed by representatives of four religions: the cast prostrates in four consecutive scenes (I, ii-v). And Kublai Kaan, in his sorrow for the death of his granddaughter, seeks consolation from the priests of four eastern religions (P II 434-35).

All the settings in Act I might be called examples of scenic journalism. The play opens in Venice, and O'Neill got the bright idea of depicting a canal to create local atmosphere. Similar stock details are employed in the scenes which follow: an altar in Acre (as a background for a Papal Legate), a mosque in Persia, a snake-charmer in India, a Mongol ruler in Mongolia. These details struck O'Neill's audiences much more forcefully than they do us, spoiled as we are by films and musical comedies overflowing with local color and lavish decorations. In 1928 when the play was produced for the first time, John Mason Brown called it the "most elaborate of the new American plays, as well as by far the most glamorous."[21]

The use of settings and music is of some importance historically. Admitting that this is our total impression, we can turn to an interesting detail. In three scenes (I, iii-v) during which Marco is turned from a romantic young lover into a soulless traveler and businessman, O'Neill repeated a motionless semi-circle of statists, grouped around a throne: "a mother nursing a baby, two children playing a game, a young girl and a young man in a loving embrace, a middle-aged couple, an aged couple, a coffin. All these Mahometan figures remain motionless." Furthermore, the ruler sitting on the throne has a priest and a soldier, "the two defenders of the State" (P II 364), by his sides. In this scene Marco tries to talk with the figures, later he becomes too hard-boiled to bother with any but the embracing couple.

---

[21] Cargill *et al.*, p. 181: the review was originally published in *Theatre Arts*, March 1928.

The groupings, dressed in different national costumes in each of these three scenes, have apparently never been realized on the stage in their entirety.[22] This static, repetitious arrangement shows that O'Neill was indulging here not only in inflated language, but also in pompous, artificial scenic ideas. Here are the ages of man, neatly gathered in a grouping, there a model of the state; is it not significant? The changes in Marco are adequately represented by a prostitute, similarly figuring in three scenes, thus making the groups even unnecessary. The idea may be traced back to *Till Damaskus* by Strindberg, where in the very last scene a woman with a child and a newly-wed couple are seen passing by, as representatives of man's different ages. The ponderous use of groups and choruses blossomed fully in *Lazarus Laughed*; in *Marco Millions* we have a foretaste.

There is little doubt that *Marco Millions* belongs to that kind of spiritual, imaginative theatre promoted by Macgowan. The name and the idea of Kukachin seems to come from a book called *Masks and Demons*, published by Macgowan in collaboration with Herman Rosse in 1923, the year *Marco Millions* was begun. One of the photographs printed in the book is explained as follows: "Yet this charming little girl with the quizzical smile upon her mask is among the attendants in the First Court of Purgatory. She is one of four servants waiting upon the beneficent Buddhist madonna Kuan-yin, who attends the hellish court doubtless to see that justice is properly tempered. When the Taoist priests act out this scene in their religious and admonitory drama of the afterworld, Kuan-yin sits in the centre at the back with her eight merciful hands and her many other charms displayed against the scenery of the island of P'u-t'o . . ."[23] In 1923, O'Neill was also writing "religious and admonitory drama"; his charming Kukachin speaks from "the afterworld," and

[22] The Gelbs are too concerned about this deletion in the original production; they call the groupings "significant to the play," and conclude that "*Marco Millions* was ahead of its time mechanically" (pp. 645-46).

[23] Kenneth Macgowan and Herman Rosse, *Masks and Demons* (1923), p. 127.

masks, eagerly recommended by Macgowan and Rosse, are employed at the end of *Marco Millions*. There are thus several connecting links between the play and the quoted passage.

Those ingredients of *Marco Millions* that are common to all of the pageant plays have been emphasized up to this point. It is now time to say that, due to its satirical elements, the play is more acceptable than the other two, marred as they are by ponderous quasi-poetry.[24] There are several jokes in *Marco Millions*, mostly of the obvious variant, and a few ideas are turned into stage action. Marco gives a demonstration of the mighty effects of gun powder, which he uses for military purposes; paper money, another Chinese invention, is also attributed to this Western materialist. His gorgeous trappings have a parodical flavor, as does his youthful, energetic, American way of acting as an admiral: "If you look before you leap, you'll decide to sit down. Keep on going ahead and you can't help being right! You're bound to get somewhere!" (P II 406). A meeting between the Kaan and the commanders of his army scores ironical points at the expense of wars in general, holy wars in particular.

The biggest joke of all, Kukachin's love for Marco and her belief in the existence of a soul in the soulless merchant, is a central theme in the latter half of the play. The final meeting of the "lovers" (II, iii) is one of the few scenes where the distant pageant comes close enough to the audience to have an effect of any kind, because of its mixture of comic and serious elements. What is wrong with it is only O'Neill's over-eagerness to exploit the situation by furnishing Kukachin with an excess of feeling. Her love is not expressed through a wall of Oriental reticence;[25] in fact, she comes embarrassingly

---

[24] Leech states that the "satiric scenes at times make their points with considerable liveliness" (*Eugene O'Neill*, p. 66); Gassner speaks of "vivid, if generalized" characterization (*Masters of the Drama*, p. 655). The word "heavy-handed" is used both by Gassner (*Eugene O'Neill*, p. 25), and by Howard Taubman (Miller, p. 174: a reprinting from the *New York Times*, March 1, 1964).

[25] Leech has remarked that Kukachin's predicament is not handled with discretion (p. 69). Cf. Engel, p. 146.

140

close to her counterpart, the bourgeois Venetian Donata.

A misjudgment in self-criticism led O'Neill to assume that the merits of the emerging *Marco Millions* were in its Macgowanisms, not in its satire. Consequently, he both opened and closed the play in a tone of high tragedy—if the whimsical epilogue, with its action spread into the audience and even to the street outside the theatre, is not counted. Tragic elements were misleading in the prologue—which left the spectators wondering whether to laugh or cry—and anticlimactic at the end, with its hollow rituals of mourning. O'Neill never had any talent for epigrammatic sayings, though he scattered pseudo-Eastern wisdom all through *Marco Millions*; and the final scene of mourning serves only to emphasize these platitudes by too strong means of expression: "Chorus (*in an echo of vast sadness*) Death is" (P II 434). In that chorus O'Neill has nine singers and "a troupe of young girls and boys"; they are accompanied by nine musicians (P II 433). Not satisfied with these "low" figures O'Neill was to manifold the number of statists shouting in chorus.

With *Lazarus Laughed*, originally subtitled "A Play for an Imaginative Theatre," the line of development sketched above was followed in absurdum and, finally and fortunately, dropped. As an introductory description we might quote George Jean Nathan, commenting on Max Reinhardt's production of *The Miracle*: "All the elements that go into the life blood of drama are here assembled into a series of aesthetic and emotional climaxes that are humbling in their force and loveliness. The shout of speech, the sweep of pantomime, the sob and march of orchestral music, the ebb and flow of song, the peal of cloister chimes, the brass clash of cymbals, the play of thousand lights, the shuffle and rush of mobs, the rising of scene upon scene amid churning rapids of color, these directed by a master hand are what constitutes this superb psychical pageant, brewed from an ancient and familiar legend and called now 'The Miracle.'" Engel con-

141

nects the passage with O'Neill: it was written in 1924 when *The Miracle* was brought over to the United States—and "about a year before O'Neill appears to have begun work on *Lazarus Laughed*."[26] Furthermore, the Gelbs tell us that O'Neill tried, without success, to interest Reinhardt in *Marco Millions*, after which David Belasco had an option for this play, which he later gave up.[27]

The above description can be transferred to *Lazarus Laughed*, almost as such. Instead of cloister chimes O'Neill has thunder and lightning; and what this "psychical pageant" lacks is, of course, "the life blood of drama." It is replaced by lots of masks and hysterical laughter.[28] For the masks O'Neill gave the following scheme, modified all through the play: "There are seven periods of life shown: Boyhood (or Girlhood), Youth, Young Manhood (or Womanhood), Manhood (or Womanhood), Middle Age, Maturity and Old Age; and each of these periods is represented by seven different masks of general types of character as follows: The Simple, Ignorant; the Happy, Eager; the Self-Tortured, Introspective; the Proud, Self-Reliant; the Servile, Hypocritical; the Revengeful, Cruel; the Sorrowful, Resigned. Thus in each crowd . . . there are forty-nine different combinations of period and type. Each type has a distinct predominant color for its costumes which varies in kind according to its period" (P I 273-74). Further complications to this outgrowth of the immobile groupings in *Marco Millions* are introduced by national characteristics: there are Jewish, Greek, and Roman crowds, and in the crowd of Lazarus' followers (II, i) there are still other nationalities represented—"Egyptian, Syrian, Cappadocian, Lydian, Phrygian, Cilician, Parthian" (P I 306). Whoever was responsible for the masks was certainly kept

[26] Engel, p. 86. The source of the quotation from Nathan is not given.

[27] The Gelbs, pp. 561, 572-73, 599.

[28] Blackburn connects the masks with expressionism. In *Lazarus Laughed*, the "most significant expressionistic characteristics are typification, struggle of opposites, ecstasy, and lyricism" ("Continental Influences," p. 126).

142

busy, and for spectators with acute abilities of observation there were many pleasures available. When seeing a particular mask in a throng of a hundred statists or more they presumably sighed, pleased with the recognition: "That must be a middle-aged Cilician of the self-tortured, introspective kind."

It is indeed difficult to take this scheme seriously. If O'Neill ever strained the expressive possibilities of a particular device too far, this is the case. In "A Dramatist's Notebook" published in 1933, in a decade of political mass movements, he explained that he "was visualizing an effect that, intensified by dramatic lighting, would give an audience visually the sense of the Crowd, not as a random collection of individuals, but as a collective whole, an entity. When the Crowd speaks, I wanted an audience to hear the voice of Crowd mind, Crowd emotion, as one voice of a body composed of, but quite distinct from, its parts."[29] Here O'Neill is clearly echoing Macgowan and Robert Edmond Jones; the former had spoken, in reference to the circus-sized theatre employed by Reinhardt, of the possibility "to reach ever closer to the life-giving vigor of vast audiences, to arouse in such mighty gatherings emotions which sweep in one gigantic swell to the players and are thrown back in still more majestic power to the audience again." Jones, on the other hand, uses the term "group-being," also employed by Percy MacKaye, another American visionary of the theatre: the playwright "may come to understand at last, in an ecstasy of clear seeing, that the radiant heroic beings of which he has dreamed are not supermen, not men at all, not even Übermarionettes, but groups of men—group-beings—and that the hero of his drama is in truth the people."[30] Seeing that the groups and an essential part of this programme are realized in *Lazarus Laughed*, it still passes understanding why O'Neill, in his ecstasy of muddled thinking, had to compete with Jung by creating his pri-

[29] Cargill *et al.*, p. 120: a reprinting of three articles by O'Neill, published in *The American Spectator*, "Memoranda on Masks" in Nov. 1932, "Second Thoughts" in Dec. 1932, and "A Dramatist's Notebook" in Jan. 1933.
[30] Macgowan, pp. 273-74.

vate amateurish typology, and why he furnished his crowds with forty-nine different masks[31]—as if this had turned them into something other than "a random collection of individuals."

In fact, the masks have a shadow of scenic function only when identical masks are given to a certain chorus, and when an effect of accumulation is achieved. So in II, ii, all members of the chorus of Roman senators wear the masks "of the Servile, Hypocritical type of Old Age" (P I 312). Human expression is divided here between three levels: the individuals, the choruses, each with seven members, and the crowds, with forty-nine. Laughter or simple phrases are often voiced first by an individual, then echoed by a chorus, at last also by a crowd. The choruses wear masks double the size of those of the crowd members; secondary characters have half-masks. Lazarus is the only unmasked character.

The idealization of Lazarus, this radiant heroic being, is completed with lighting and make-up.[32] His head is "haloed and his body illumined by a soft radiance as of tiny phosphorescent flames. . . . His face recalls that of a statue of a divinity of Ancient Greece in its general structure and particularly in its quality of detached serenity" (P I 274). O'Neill might have been led to tragic themes in his sea plays more by his natural inclination than by conscious effort—but there is no doubt that he knows what he is doing now: imitating the Greeks. Hence the "choral odes," these slogans written with a more limited vocabulary than the most worn-out hit tunes; hence the dances in the Athenian scene and elsewhere; hence

[31] Raleigh is oversympathetic: "the masks, far from depersonalizing the people of the enormous chorus, individualize them in a peculiarly dramatic fashion" (p. 44). The fashion would be more dramatic, if the crowds and different choruses were played more clearly against one another, and if the scheme were not so complicated.

[32] "But the weakness of *Lazarus Laughed* is that this absolutely perfect hero fails to move us. . . . The tragedy of absolute perfection is not tragic" (Carpenter, p. 72). " . . . *Lazarus Laughed* was intended to praise mysticism; yet to its own thesis it presents two strong counterarguments: first, that Lazarus is an inhuman ideal; second, that his position fails to distinguish good from evil" (Henry F. Pommer, "The Mysticism of Eugene O'Neill," *Modern Drama, 9*, 34).

the setting of II, ii ("In the foreground is the portico of a temple" [P I 312]); and hence Lazarus' entrance into Athens in a chariot ("His countenance now might well be that of the positive masculine Dionysus. . . . Not the coarse, drunken Dionysus, nor the effeminate god, but Dionysus in his middle period" [P I 307]). The pretentiousness of this scene is matched only by the first Roman scene, furnished with "terrific flashes of lightning and crashes of thunder" (P I 318)— apparently in honor of Shakespeare's *Julius Caesar.*

The peak of this series of "aesthetic and emotional climaxes" is achieved as early as in I, ii, where the front and roof of Lazarus' house are filled with three crowds, one dancing, the others fighting; all in all, there is a rushing mob of 158 persons on the stage.[33] After that, the ensuing highlights in this incredible mass spectacle, such as a crucified, almost dead male lion, or the burning of Lazarus (off-stage, for some reason), can hardly surprise anyone. All is, of course, accompanied by appropriate music and sound effects, such as the brass clash of cymbals and the tramp of marching legions. Among familiar scenic units we can notice a moonlight night (II, i); the automaton effect transferred to a chorus, performing a "bestial parody of the dance of the followers" (P I 288); and, more interestingly, a scene of several modified monologues twisted together (P I 350-51).

The most astounding feature of *Lazarus Laughed* is the slightness of its content. At least part of the strong means of expression criticized above might be justified in other contexts; in this case, there is no justification. One might start the general questioning by wondering how it is that the death of several thousands of Lazarus' followers outside the walls of Rome can be taken as a proof for the nonexistence of death. "There is no death!" is an incessant message of Lazarus, "the Laugher" who returned from the other side. Obviously, the phrase can have only a mystical meaning. Putting

---

[33] Cf. Brustein on *Lazarus Laughed*: "its atmosphere is very similar to those silent biblical epics by Cecil B. DeMille, full of frenzied mob scenes and Central Casting Emperors called Tiberius and Caligula" (p. 334).

common sense aside for a while we might proceed by probing some of the sources of this metaphysical idea.

Two recent occurrences of the idea of death in the O'Neill canon form a pair of contrasts: "Death is no more" (*The Fountain*, P I 442); and "Death is" (*Marco Millions*, P II 434). Now O'Neill is once more inclined to think that death does not exist. Lazarus, this strongly positive hero, has been called by Cyrus Day "a Nietzschean superman," who has been assigned "the dual role of savior and tragic hero"; in the same study Day mentions Schopenhauer and Lao-Tze as other influences. The antithesis between man's Apollonian and Dionysian impulses, a central Nietzschean concept, is expressed in *Lazarus Laughed* "by means of the monosyllable 'Yes,' four or five ambiguous slogans and Lazarus' mystical (and mystifying) laughter." O'Neill "never quite succeeds in making his meaning clear," Day states, and goes on to call Lazarus "a static character," not a "recognizable human being," but "a mere mouthpiece—and an inarticulate one at that."[34]

Several central weaknesses of *Lazarus Laughed* are mentioned or implied in these quotations. There is no point in summarizing the plot of the play, for it consists of endless repetitions of the same basic situation: Lazarus converts murderous mobs and murderous individuals to Nietzscheism, all by the force of his irresistible and infectious arias of laughter. O'Neill further enlarges his stature by leaving his antagonists undeveloped. When Tiberius, a gloomy figure foreshadowing the atmosphere of *The Iceman Cometh* in his spite for mankind, asks Lazarus a factual question, the superman evades it by calling "age and time . . . but timidities of thought" (P I 354). If one happens to think that a certain

[34] Cyrus Day, "*Amor Fati*: O'Neill's Lazarus as Superman and Savior," *Modern Drama*, 3 (1960), 303-05. Raleigh calls the play a partial failure, because "the repetiton of simple and abstract words . . . accompanied by repeated exclamation points do not a poem make. Poetry is complex, concrete, and metaphorical, three qualities that were, by and large, denied to O'Neill's invention" (p. 215). As a poet of the theatre, O'Neill was, however, complex, concrete, and metaphorical.

146

amount of timidity is a virtue in a playwright, one gets no answer—nor is the answer given by Miriam, the wife of Lazarus, who "has a much better case than O'Neill allows her to make."[35]

Lazarus is a metaphysical figure, but his counterparts, Tiberius and Caligula, are psychoanalytical case studies. This is the basic fault in O'Neill's dialectics; and his aesthetics fall to pieces when the fundamental incompatibility between Lazarus and the play is observed.[36] As metaphysical ideas, or better still, as pantheistic feelings, the Nietzschean formulation of eternal recurrence and the more general mysticism based on man's fusing with nature may have some validity—but it is impossible to experience pantheism when sitting in the audience and looking at a vast pageant, in which mystical truths are shouted, sung in chorus, discussed, demonstrated by a massacre that should prove the nonexistence of death, and danced by crowds amounting to more than a hundred statists. The philosophical idea of eternal recurrence is hardly demonstrated in the best possible way by bringing thousands to their biological death.[37]

In his centrifugal flight to settings, to masses, to Athens, O'Neill had gone so far that the play no longer had any core.

[35] Leech, p. 71.

[36] Raleigh concludes that *Lazarus Laughed* is, on the printed page, "a play of great interest and force" (p. 47). In the theatre, it is not. Carpenter is rather confused; to him, the play "dramatizes a modern religious idealism that is Christian in origin, Nietzschean in tragic conception, Oriental in mythology, but, perhaps, closest to the spirit of American Transcendentalism" (p. 119). The play also "employed all the experimental techniques which O'Neill had earlier developed to implement his 'theatre of tomorrow' "; yet it "remains essentially a 'closet drama' " (pp. 116-17). If this does not mean admitting O'Neill's failure, what does? Yet Carpenter goes on: "The astonishing fact is that *Lazarus Laughed* should succeed as well as it does in translating this idealistic material into dramatic terms" (p. 119).

[37] "At the climax of the play, as Lazarus is being burned alive— i.e., man, the victim of his own cruelty, inevitably goes to his painful death—Lazarus laughs, i.e., the spirit of man rises above bodily pain and corporeal limitations" (Raleigh, p. 12). This is, apparently, how the scene should be taken. World War II has certainly made us less susceptible to massacres used to drive home an ideological point.

No matter how gigantic the swells of emotions, no matter how radiant the hero, no matter how many "group-beings" are marched through the stage—it all amounts to a bubble. Its surface reflects remnants of Greek tragedy and of nature, beautifully in harmony with man; both images are caused by things outside the bubble itself. The sad task of the onlooker is only to ask how this all came about, how a playwright so obviously in control of the appropriate means of expression in *The Emperor Jones* and *The Hairy Ape* was able to create this coreless monster.

To begin with a simple explanation, O'Neill failed to communicate because he knew too well what he wanted to communicate—a common flaw in works of art with a pronounced "message."[38] Instead of a concrete play O'Neill produced abstract results of thinking. He fell into the pit of abstraction from which he had been saved by his friend Driscoll in the case of *The Hairy Ape*. His way of thinking was not even original: fallacy toward primitivism tempted him to find the easy way out, to recognize as his results the "mysterious age-old processes of nature" "in the behavior of the pagan, the primitive, the child, the crowd."[39]

One of the great dreams by friends of verse drama, in America perhaps even more markedly than in Europe, has been to create something corresponding to Greek tragedy. In a country with a prevalently commercial theatre it has been an exceptionally noble dream: nothing short of the temple has been enough for the idealists, overcompensating their need for an "art theatre." Kenneth Macgowan turns this vision into glowing words in one of the passages quoted above, encouraged as he was by Freud, who never explained this particular dream. The three plays written "for an Imaginative Theatre," and most conspicuously *Lazarus Laughed*, were among O'Neill's earliest attempts to realize this dream.

The problem was solved in a crude manner, by imitating

---

[38] "*Lazarus Laughed* is quite simply propaganda against death" (Daiber, "Der Tragiker der neuen Welt," p. 27).
[39] Engel, p. 75.

the outer form of the model, by borrowing means of expression as such from the Greeks, from Reinhardt. A gap of twenty-three centuries, a long distance in cultural climate, was not to be bridged as easily as this; it is no wonder that the experiments toward a temple theatre were doomed by Eric Mottram as "totally unhistorical."[40] If O'Neill learned anything from this visit in a blind alley, it was a realization that one had to proceed more cautiously—as he later did when writing *Mourning Becomes Electra*, a much more solid work of art than *Lazarus Laughed*, whatever its shortcomings. Besides, he had already achieved a better fusion of modern and ancient elements in *Desire Under the Elms*, to be discussed in the following chapter.

O'Neill's hysterical over-eagerness to affirm the value of life in *Lazarus Laughed* has been motivated by Clark: "Like most converts to a new idea, O'Neill is not content to state, he must reiterate and hammer away until the densest listener understands what he is driving at."[41] Seeing that the idea underlying *Lazarus Laughed* is a positive message of pantheistic harmony we can agree with Janis Klavsons who speaks of O'Neill's "defeated dreamers" with characteristics taken from "down-and-outers personally known to the playwright,"[42] while "the successful ones [like Lazarus] came from books. Failure to O'Neill was observed; success was abstract."[43] Instead of meaningful experiences, O'Neill offers in these plays thin-blooded, derivative aestheticism; instead of going through the long process of assimilating his ideas and means of expression together until both are personal, he relied on quickly digested background reading.

Eugene O'Neill is a dramatist of disharmony. Conse-

[40] Eric Mottram, "Men and Gods: A Study of Eugene O'Neill," *Encore, 10*, 5 (Sept.-Oct. 1963), p. 36.

[41] Clark, *Eugene O'Neill*, pp. 118-19. Cf. Gassner, *The Theatre in Our Times*, p. 255.

[42] Janis Klavsons, "O'Neill's Dreamer: Success and Failure," *Modern Drama, 3* (1960), 269.

[43] *Ibid.*, p. 272. Cf. Raleigh, p. 219: "For O'Neill could not write of what he did not know—harmony, unity, affirmation—but he was eloquent, like a good American, about darkness, meaninglessness, loneliness, and despair. . . ."

149

quently, he is in conflict with himself when he tries to be in harmony with what he gropingly called "All"—with nature, with life. This is why the theme and the scenic means of expression are in such an obvious conflict in *Lazarus Laughed*. The scenic images in all of the three pageants through history speak a language that sounds foreign in O'Neill's own ears.

REMOVABLE WALLS

DESIRE UNDER THE ELMS, DYNAMO

Each of Eugene O'Neill's major plays up to the mid-twenties has a prehistory. Though the early trials were not complete failures, the results were less remarkable than their later descendants. There are three pairs of scripts, with clear thematic parallels within each pair: *The Dreamy Kid* and *The Emperor Jones*; the later-destroyed short story and *The Hairy Ape*; *The Rope* and *Desire Under the Elms*. O'Neill's career seems to be full of rapid twists; yet, paradoxically enough, he was slow in absorbing new ideas, preferring long periods of incubation. In addition to thematic parallels to a one-act play, *Desire Under the Elms* shows the influence of several artistic movements: realism, melodrama, expressionism, and Greek tragedy are all there in the background.

The prevalent element is realism, so much so that Gassner has reason to say that *Desire Under the Elms* "marks the peak" of O'Neill's "relatively naturalistic period"[1]—an evaluation recorded before the posthumous plays were made public. The play, a rustic tragedy of possessiveness and family hatred, depends heavily for its effect on plot, atmosphere, and characterization, on elements that are kept, with important exceptions, within the limits of realism. The plot is marred by a rash, melodramatic solution; an expressive setting and references in the dialogue to supernatural influence from beyond the grave help to evoke the intended atmosphere; and the play deals with fundamental human passions, as Greek tragedy does.

An oft-quoted passage describes the trees in the setting of *Desire Under the Elms*: "Two enormous elms are on each side of the house. They bend their trailing branches down

---

[1] Gassner, *Masters of the Drama*, p. 651.

over the roof. They appear to protect and at the same time subdue. There is a sinister maternity in their aspect, a crushing, jealous absorption." (P I 202). The psychoanalysts see in the elms a symbol of the maternal spirit, and interpret the play in terms of Eben Cabot's struggle between two masks—two conflicting conceptions of his own self—one proud and paternal, the other submissive and maternal.[2]

The interpretation has some validity: the description of the primordial father certainly reminds one of Ephraim Cabot, the vigorous, greedy, God-quoting farmer of seventy-five, who governs his grown-up sons with an iron hand and brings home his third wife at the beginning of the play. The incestuous love affair between Abbie, the determined and sensual bride, and her stepson Eben fits the scheme of the Oedipus complex—and it fits the interpretation given to the setting, confirmed as it is by references in the dialogue to the influence of Eben's "Maw."[3]

Less attention has been paid to certain other aspects in O'Neill's description of the setting; yet these should have as good a chance of being interpreted by the scene designer as the maternal outlook of the elms. "The house is in a good condition," it is said, "but in need of paint. Its walls are sickly grayish, the green of the shutters faded" (P I 202). The contrast between nature and man's creations, a familiar theme, is further emphasized in the first stage direction of the play: "The sky above the roof is suffused with deep colors, the green of the elms glows, but the house is in shadow, seeming pale and washed out by contrast" (P I 203). Furthermore, the stone wall and the wooden gate ordered by O'Neill are fused with the action of the play: the former is a visible symbol of Ephraim's image of God—"God's hard, not easy! God's in the stones!" (P I 237); the latter is frequently uti-

---

[2] Doris V. Falk, *Eugene O'Neill and the Tragic Tension*, p. 94. Cf. Sievers, *Freud on Broadway*, pp. 77, 121.

[3] Edgar F. Racey, Jr. has published a short study, "Myth as Tragic Structure in *Desire Under the Elms*," in which he compares the play with *Hippolytus* by Euripides and finds a myth enacted in the play (Gassner [ed.], *O'Neill*, pp. 57-61: a reprinting from *Modern Drama*, 5, 1 [May 1962], 42-46).

lized as the place where the characters stop to admire the beauty of nature.[4] It gathers symbolic significance from these repetitions, used to heighten the effect of the very last scenic image of the play. Eben and Abbie, both guilty of murder and about to be taken away by the sheriff, "*walk hand in hand to the gate. Eben stops there and points to the sunrise sky*) Sun's a-rizin'. Purty, hain't it?" (P I 269). It is also entirely appropriate that the departing elder brothers carry the gate with them at the end of Part I as their last gesture of defiance. This setting arrangement seems to hint that the Cabot farm is both isolated by Ephraim's lifelong efforts and yet still open to the outer world: there is a hole, for the brothers to walk out, carrying the gate—and for Abbie to bring nature in.

It has been assumed above that O'Neill's failure to fuse inner and outer scenes in *Beyond the Horizon* was one of the reasons that led him to adopt the technique of removable walls in *Desire Under the Elms*. Of greater importance than the origins of this solution, however, are its multiple and well-integrated scenic functions. As Leech notes, O'Neill was not satisfied with "bringing external nature and the domestic interior into permanent juxtaposition"; he also achieves "effective counterpoint at several moments of the play."[5] Leech singles out those two scenic images where the setting, with appropriate walls removed, plays an active part. One of them is at the end of Part III, Scene i, where the grinning neighbors are enjoying themselves in the kitchen in honor of "Ephraim's" child, Abbie and Eben are embracing in the bedroom at the cradle of their son, and Ephraim is outside by the gate, this time in melancholy brooding over the difficulties of "livin' with folks" (P I 253). "The setting emphasises at once the separateness of the figures in the drama, as they are divided by the walls of the house, and their close association with each other and the farm."[6]

[4] Raleigh (*The Plays of Eugene O'Neill*, pp. 31-32) sees in the rocky soil and stone walls a symbol of "back-breaking labor."

[5] Leech, *Eugene O'Neill*, pp. 52-53.

[6] *Ibid.*, p. 53. The same scene is chosen by Stark Young for special

The other scene, somewhat earlier in the play, has given rise to a minor controversy. Both bedrooms are revealed, and Eben and Abbie, having not yet fulfilled their passion, sense the presence of one another through the wall. Eben walks in his room and "Abbie hears him. Her eyes fasten on the intervening wall with concentrated attention. Eben stops and stares. Their hot glances seem to meet through the wall. Unconsciously he stretches out his arms for her and she half arises" (P I 236). Some critics agree with Sophus K. Winther's accusation that O'Neill employed telepathy here, a solution without factual basis.[7] Leech disagrees by calling it "rational enough" that Abbie and Eben are "sensitive to slight sounds of movement": "We see the wall as a barrier about to crumble: it is symbolically right that it should now become paper-thin and transparent; it is, on the naturalistic plane, in accord with everyday experience that the desired person should exercise power through a mere bedroom-wall."[8] Leech is right: this is how the scene works on the stage.

It is possible to elaborate on the analysis of this scenic image. While the pantomime of Eben and Abbie is going on, Ephraim falls into a typical modified monologue: "Then, evidently unable to keep silent about his thoughts, without looking at his wife, he puts out his hand and clutches her knee. She starts violently, looks at him, sees he is not watching her, concentrates again on the wall and pays no attention to what he says" (P I 236). The marks of this familiar scenic unit are here: inner compulsion and the inattentiveness of the intended listener. And there is fluctuation—as far as Ephraim is capable of it. Here he is, tempted as he is by his desire to have another son: "All the time I kept gittin' lonesomer . . . I tuk another wife—Eben's Maw . . . She was purty—but soft. She tried t' be hard. She couldn't. She never

---

praise: it is realistic, yet "written with such poetry and terrible beauty as we rarely see in the theatre" (Miller, *Playwright's Progress*, p. 42: a reprinting from the *New York Times*, Nov. 12, 1924).

[7] Sophus K. Winther, *Eugene O'Neill*, p. 268. Cf. Eric Bentley, *The Playwright as Thinker* (1946), p. 320.

[8] Leech, p. 53. Cf. Koischwitz, *Eugene O'Neill*, p. 88.

knowed me nor nothin'. It was lonesomer 'n hell with her" (P I 237). The image, a fusion of pantomime, setting, and monologue, is charged with central thematic significance: a paradoxical character is revealed, in a scene where his world clashes ironically with Abbie's world, as they were bound to clash.[9]

It is remarkable that one of the climaxes depends on an image devoid of violent action. This is a symptom of O'Neill's general orientation in the phase of *Desire Under the Elms* away from melodrama; his interest is now in revealing the inner worlds of the characters. In this line of experimentation, not immediately rewarded, modified monologues proved to be a major asset. They are employed elsewhere in the play, always in emphatic positions: Part I, Scene iii, ends with Eben's monologue about the village harlot Minnie, preparing the way for his love of Abbie (P I 215); Ephraim finds a reconciliation with his loneliness and with his hard God in a longish speech not directed to anyone on the stage (P I 268); and Eben and Abbie have a scene of intertwined monologues after Abbie has murdered her child, at the point where the ironic tension is at its highest—Eben speaks "going on with his own thoughts," while Abbie is "too absorbed in her own thoughts to listen to him" (P I 260).

The irony is based on the inarticulateness of the characters. If there is a motivation for the murder, it is the failure of Eben and Abbie to communicate. Isolated by the setting in the separate rooms of the farmhouse, the characters are also isolated by their own inability to find a verbal form for their feelings. The only thing the departing elder brothers can say to Eben is "Good-by" (P I 220)—and that only after two awkward silences. Abbie cannot convince Eben of her love for him without killing the child, whom Eben suspects of being only a vehicle for assuring the all-important farm to Abbie.

---

[9] "I have seen few pictures in the theatre so stark as that," Percy Hammond writes about this scene in his otherwise rather peevish review (Cargill *et al.*, p. 171: reprinted from the *New York Herald Tribune*, Nov. 12, 1924).

We are dealing here with a major theme of O'Neill's, emphasized by Raleigh in his short study, "O'Neill's *Long Day's Journey Into Night* and New England Irish-Catholicism." Raleigh speaks of a "national concern with betrayal, the 'Judas-complex' that dominates Irish life and literature."[10] The theme can, in fact, be traced through all the early plays of the O'Neill canon. *Abortion* is based on betrayed love in a straightforward manner; Smitty, the hero of *In the Zone*, is suspected as a traitor; Ruth and Robert are deceived in one another in *Beyond the Horizon*, Maud and John in *Bread and Butter*; Anna's past is a surprise to Mat Burke in *'Anna Christie,'* and so is Caleb's fall of Emma in *Diff'rent.* The Emperor Jones is betrayed by his subjects, Yank by the I.W.W.—to mention only the most conspicuous occurrences of this theme. In *Desire Under the Elms* it has a more prominent position than perhaps ever before—in a closed family circle (another Irish feature mentioned by Raleigh). The theme is carried by turns of the plot and by the inarticulate speech of the characters.

This is a crucial point in our evaluation of *Desire Under the Elms.* Realizing the importance of the theme of betrayal makes it possible for us to explain the rather slight motivation for the murder by assuming that it was too clear to O'Neill that love is always betrayed—he was not concerned with motivating the murder any further.[11] The melodramatic impression is accentuated by the general slowness of the ac-

[10] Raleigh's study was first published in the *Partisan Review, 26* (1959), 573-92; the quotation is from p. 577. It is reprinted in Gassner (ed.), *O'Neill,* pp. 124-41.

[11] Doris M. Alexander writes about Schopenhauer's influence on *Strange Interlude*: "O'Neill, entirely possessed with the Schopenhauerian view of love as most frequently destructive to individual, personal goals, neglected to show in concrete dramatic terms precisely why this is the case; the situation of an unreasoning love was, perhaps, self-evidently destructive for O'Neill" (*American Literature, 25* [1953], 218). This can be applied to *Desire Under the Elms,* too; as the theme of betrayal is important in all of O'Neill, it is possible to connect betrayed love with his personal experiences as well as with a literary influence. The melodramatic rashness of the solution is criticized by Gassner (*Eugene O'Neill,* p. 15), Brustein (*The Theatre of Revolt,* p. 335), and Leech (p. 52).

tion in the play, and by its plentiful repetitions. The elder
brothers mention the idea of leaving the farm in their first
speeches; yet they need a whole act (here called "part") to
get to the road. And Abbie uses "her most seductive tones"
(P I 225) all through her very first meeting with Eben; yet
it takes a whole act until these tones have a final effect, over
the obstacle formed by the ghost of Eben's Maw. Against
this background of a slow-motion picture, as it were, the
sudden decision to kill the child leaves a singular impression of rashness. The fault was not, of course, to be corrected
by giving Abbie another act for pondering it over; it is a symptom of a basic fault, of O'Neill's inclination to direct his plots
toward tragic ends.

The general inarticulateness of the Cabots was not a
strong enough means for conveying the full impact of the
theme of betrayal. Yet the dialogue has been rightfully
praised by several critics. Franz Norbert Mennemeier connects "the abridged, non-grammatic idioms" of the reduced
O'Neillian "Underdog-Sprache" with the creations of several absurdists, such as Adamow, Beckett, and Tardieu.
Similar language is cultivated with a grotesque effect in *The
Hairy Ape, Hughie*, and *A Moon for the Misbegotten*.[12]
Leech speaks of O'Neill's successful journey "to the past
and to a remote farm-land . . . he used characters from whom
words would not come fluently, who would rely on gesture
and truncated utterance to convey their wants and direc-
tives."[13] O'Neill communicates most completely when he
takes the difficulties of verbal communication as one of his
themes, when he does not depend too heavily on the ability
of his characters to make themselves understood by words
alone. Paradoxically, his scenes function on the stage, when
he recognizes his characters as inarticulate.

Pantomime is used quite frequently in *Desire Under the
Elms*. The elder brothers are presented as bound to the
earth, an impression created by their clothes, make-up, and

[12] Franz Norbert Mennemeier, *Das moderne Drama des Auslandes*,
pp. 70-71.
[13] Leech, p. 55.

way of moving: "They clump heavily along in their clumsy thick-soled boots caked with earth" (P I 204). Part II opens with a scene of silent acting, expressing the gradual gliding together of Eben and Abbie; it is followed by a series of speeches in which Abbie goes through her whole scale of love-hate reactions to Eben, ranging from attachment to jealousy, from revengefulness to calculated scheming—she arises in Ephraim the hope of having a son once more (P I 228-35). This comparatively early example of dynamic, paradoxically shifting characterization is, after all, more appropriate within the realistic framework of this play than, say, the corresponding changes in the high-pitched, unintentionally comic behavior of Juan Ponce de Leon or Caligula.

A sudden shift of mood occurs in that scene where the influence of Greek tragedy is most marked. Ephraim's states of mind fluctuate "with drunken suddenness" when he performs a grotesque dance before a chorus of neighbors, whom he calls "a flock o' goats" (P I 249). These Dionysian antics invite one to pay attention to the time scheme of the play: it proceeds from summer to spring, to the time of eternal recurrence.[14] Each of the three parts is concentrated within a short space of time, from afternoon or evening to the following dawn. Perhaps O'Neill called his acts "parts" in memory of the trilogies of Greek tragedy; *Desire Under the Elms*, and not *Mourning Becomes Electra*, might be considered his first trilogy. Yet these ancient echoes are subdued. Greetings from Athens are brought to New England to give the play a subordinate layer of meaning;[15] the play is not taken to Athens, as was the later-completed *Lazarus Laughed*.

Even the sense of doom lingering above the Cabot farm-

---

[14] Cf. Racey, in Gassner (ed.), *O'Neill*, p. 59: "The time is spring, season of awakening and season of ritual."

[15] In a vigorous defense of the play, Joseph Wood Krutch calls it Tragedy, "a play about extraordinarily violent passions" arising "out of man's relation to two irrational forces—belief in the puritan God and a commitment to the land which is as irrational as the commitment to God" (Miller, p. 161: reprinted from *Theatre Arts, 36*, April 1952). This may be true, yet not enough to motivate the child murder.

house is well integrated with the rest of the play.[16] The superstitious fear is concentrated in the parlor, "a grim, repressed room like a tomb in which the family has been interred alive" (P I 241)—or like the Mannon house in O'Neill's later trilogy.[17] The charm of the room is destroyed only by the thought of revenge. The power of the dead, of the past, ceases when Abbie takes the place of Eben's mother and mistress.

So we have returned to our starting point—the setting. No apparitions are needed as in the pageant plays; the setting, together with dialogue, carries even this theme. It is no wonder that O'Neill was careful in his directions, that he was not satisfied with ground plans but also drew four sketches showing the farmhouse with different portions of the front wall removed. In a letter to Kenneth Macgowan he described his purpose: the elms are "characters almost," the setting should guarantee "the flow of life from room to room of the house, the house as character, the acts as smooth developing wholes. . . ."[18]

The idea of the setting as a character shows O'Neill's indebtedness to expressionism, even in this play. Yet, in a paradoxical way, this very device brings *Desire Under the Elms* a long step toward classical concentration. Twelve short scenes, on the average not much longer than the "missiles" in *The Emperor Jones* and *The Hairy Ape*, are made to flow "from room to room." The contrasts between and within scenic images are inherent in the multiple setting itself; the Maw, most conspicuously, is represented by the setting. Her "role" even develops: "the shutters are flung back"

---

[16] Bamber Gascoigne approves of O'Neill's way of using the classics: "he adapted them and made them his own. . . . Eben's mother . . . haunts the play like a figure of ill omen. . . . As with the oracle in Greek tragedy, all that matters is that the characters involved believe it" (*Twentieth-Century Drama*, pp. 91-93). To Koischwitz, the farmhouse is "fate become visible" (p. 70).

[17] This connection is also drawn by Dietrich (*Das moderne Drama*, p. 209).

[18] The Gelbs, *O'Neill*, p. 568.

(P I 244) on the morning following the reconciliation. The setting is full of useful areas: the gate, the yard, all the rooms. As a general consequence, the scenes need not be as sharply or ironically contrasted with the help of lighting, action, and sound effects as in *The Hairy Ape*. And the house is utilized both with imagination and with due concern for the themes of the play, as it is in *Mourning Becomes Electra*.

The basic solution, a setting revealing several rooms of a house at once, is in *Desire Under the Elms* "not merely spectacular or sensational."[19] The solution leaves an impression of originality, even if a similar house has been "not infrequently" used in Victorian melodramas, as a four-room variant as early as in 1833.[20] *Desire Under the Elms* consists of a rapid series of short scenes placed within an expressive setting; yet the general impression is that of realism. For those worried about a stylistic mixture of this kind there is an answer given by Gassner who approves of "a pragmatic fusion of realistic and theatrical elements," achieved in the 1952 revival of the play, designed by Mordecai Gorelik formalistically, yet without any "mystique of art." "Practical artists arrive at craft-judgments," Gassner continues, "they make decisions based on their analysis of the play and then proceed to carry them out, hoping for the best results."[21] The passage can be applied to O'Neill: he has made his own craft-judgments.

Thematically, *Desire Under the Elms* goes on with the pagan, Nietzschean affirmation of life met in several of O'Neill's plays during the twenties. It does so less hysterically and more convincingly than the pageants through history. An interesting interpretation by Doris V. Falk connects *Desire Under the Elms* with an old acquaintance of O'Neill's rather than with recent background reading. Having referred to O'Neill's habit of scattering literary source materials throughout his plays and to his contempt for the ranting ro-

[19] Cargill *et al.*, p. 471: a reprinting of Downer's article "Eugene O'Neill as Poet of the Theatre," originally published in *Theatre Arts*, Feb. 1951.
[20] Leech, p. 54.
[21] Gassner, *Form and Idea in the Modern Theatre*, pp. 136-37.

manticism in the theatre of his father, Falk finds an old "New England rustic melodrama," *The Old Homestead*, as a basic model behind *Desire Under the Elms*, and uses biographical material to prove that O'Neill must have known the melodrama. She sees the affirmative ending of the tragedy as unconvincing, as a parody of romanticism: "Even when this sin has been compounded with adultery, incest and murder, romantic love 'purties up' everything. . . . Every ideal underlying the last act of *The Old Homestead* is mocked in the last act (Part Three) of *Desire Under the Elms*. There the cradle rocks and the rustics dance but the dance is that of death and the Satyr."[22]

Falk is certainly right in the case of Ephraim's grotesque dance. The prevalent tone is not, however, downright parodic. Rather, we might use the Brechtian term "Gegenentwurf," in English perhaps "counter-sketch." A parody is closely bound to its object and intends to make that object laughable. A counter-sketch is a subject, a new idea full of significance. Both attack a previous work of art, parody by making it look ridiculous, counter-sketch by replacing it with something else. Brecht did not only intend to parody the operetta when writing his *Dreigroschenoper*; he also had something important to put in its place. In the same way O'Neill did not so much parody an artistically deficient and (by now) forgotten New England rustic melodrama as replace it with a more earth-bound and primitive kind of play, under the influence of Nietzsche.

The concept of counter-sketch covers a great portion of modern art, ranging from music to painting. In literature, there is Thomas Mann with his paraphrases of Goethe and the Bible, there is *Ulysses* by James Joyce, there are Eliot and Brecht—and there are the O'Neillian transformations of Greek tragedy, including *Desire Under the Elms, Mourning Becomes Electra*, and *The Iceman Cometh*. Seeing the classical and American parallels, the psychoanalytical and Nietzschean elements, sensing the irony, almost as biting as

[22] Doris V. Falk, "That Paradox, O'Neill," *Modern Drama, 6* (1963), 230-35.

in *The Hairy Ape*, and appreciating the over-all execution and control over scenic means of expression, we may include *Desire Under the Elms*, a play sometimes overestimated,[23] among the major works of O'Neill, even if it is marred by a melodramatizing contrivance and even if the triangle situation is a familiar one. The extra spices of incest and greed, of milieu and characterization almost disguise this basic fact.

Dynamo is a play that does not seem to belong anywhere, least of all to Eugene O'Neill's successful achievements. It is an aftermath of *Desire Under the Elms* in its settings, and an aftermath of *Strange Interlude* in its use of "thought asides." Stylistically, it is a full-fledged melodrama.[24] And as far as evaluations are concerned it is one of those plays which cause fluctuation in the minds of O'Neill critics: one has just decided that the playwright is in control over himself and his medium—and then comes the next play, a flop.

Chronologically, *Dynamo* was preceded by *Strange Interlude*, followed by *Mourning Becomes Electra*. Finished in 1929, five years after *Desire Under the Elms*, it relies fairly heavily on the expressiveness of two settings, one consisting of two dwelling houses with removable walls, the other depicting a Hydro-Electric Power plant, similarly sometimes covered, sometimes partly revealed. This arrangement makes it permissible to deal with the play in this chapter; yet the details of the monologue technique are most advantageously examined after *Strange Interlude* has been discussed.

The houses with removable walls are placed in a small town in contemporary Connecticut. In his description of the home of the Reverend Hutchins Light, O'Neill resorts to

[23] As late as 1952, Brooks Atkinson writes: "When the final accounts are tallied, 'Desire Under the Elms,' may turn out to be the greatest play written by an American" (Miller, p. 131; reprinted from the *New York Times*, Jan. 17, 1952).

[24] O'Neill's friend and critic George Jean Nathan proved the play to be melodramatic by publishing the stage directions of Act I. The impression is engrossing, and so is Nathan's conclusion: *Dynamo* is an "amateurish, strident, and juvenile concoction (Downer [ed.], *American Drama and Its Critics*, p. 114: a reprinting from *The American Mercury*, March 1929).

162

that kind of detailed realism we know from *Beyond the Horizon* and *Diff'rent*. In the sitting room there is a kerosene lamp; as a contrast, "the two rooms in the Fife home, bright with all their electric lights on, are of a glaring newness" (P III 428). Mr. Ramsay Fife, superintendent of a hydroelectric plant, is the town atheist, who enjoys kidding his neighbor, a narrow-minded Puritan.

We are, of course, in the middle of a (melo)dramatic conflict between two views of the world. All O'Neill needed to complete his proposition was a Romeo and a Juliet. They are Reuben Light and Ada Fife; their meeting and Reuben's visit to Ada's home are followed by Mrs. Light in ambush. The situation, with the poor mother behind the bushes in three consecutive scenes, is an example of O'Neill's inclination to go to extremes, this time falling right into the ridiculous.

Unable to decide between using moonlight, which belongs, so to speak, to good O'Neillian tradition, or thunder and lightning, employed in *Lazarus Laughed* two years earlier, O'Neill chose both. The sky is "pale with the light of a quarter-moon. Now and then there is a faint flash of lightning from far off and a low rumble of thunder" (P III 421). What is overemphasized by these lighting and sound effects is a series of schemes and hysterical family quarrels, another example of O'Neill's interest in the theme of betrayal. Deceived by his mother, by Ada, by everyone and everything in this world (as he interprets it), Reuben defies the God of thunder and lightning at the end of Act I. He is not struck. There are two more acts to come.

Fifteen months later Reuben returns from the world, now wise and firm in his new faith in the God of electricity, of modern science.[25] His relation to the seductive Ada is now reversed: the nice boy next door has turned into a cold se-

[25] Both Koischwitz (p. 145) and Blackburn ("Continental Influences," p. 132) connect *Dynamo* with Georg Kaiser's *Gas*, in which modern science is also taken as a god. According to the expressionistic manifesto of Kasimir Edschmid, divine phenomena were to be found in factories (Mann, *Geschichte des deutschen Dramas*, p. 558).

ducer.[26] His mother is dead, and the house is haunted by her memory in a way somewhat reminiscent of *Desire Under the Elms*. There is no lack of mother surrogates; the voluptuous Mrs. Fife, Ada's mother, the dynamo in the plant where Reuben starts to work, and the memory of his deceased mother get somehow confused in his mind. Mrs. Fife and the dynamo hum or purr in the same way; an easy identity is established by this sound effect.

We are now ready to enter the power plant where Reuben electrocutes not the old God as was his intention, but himself. All Reuben gets from his new God, and His reverend representative, the dynamo, is a rigorous demand for sexual purity which leads him to flagellantism—and to murder. Replacing the father's religious Puritanism with the son's scientific Puritanism has changed little. In this play love is so possessive that no sharing is possible in any relationship: Ada or I! the dynamo purrs, while Mrs. Light is so jealous of her only son that she would have made an impossible mother-in-law—as Deborah Harford does later in *More Stately Mansions*. And the playwright can only destroy his Romeo and Juliet, the former in a scenic image intended to be magnificent and deeply symbolic. As Reuben jumps to join with his Mother-God, the dynamo, "there is a flash of bluish light about him and all the lights in the plant dim down until they are almost out and the noise of the dynamo dies until it is the faintest purring hum. Simultaneously Reuben's voice rises in a moan that is a mingling of pain and loving consummation, and this cry dies into a sound that is like the crooning of a baby and merges and is lost in the dynamo's hum" (P III 488). The voices of Beatriz and the nephew fused with the chant of the monks at the end of *The Fountain*,

[26] Raleigh attributes sudden and unmotivated changes of character in O'Neill to the influence of *The Count of Monte Cristo*. Reuben is "a confused, hypersensitive, cowardly young man. He goes away, time passes, and he returns tough, sure, and hard. A few months pass and he becomes a lean, burning ascetic. All these metamorphoses are supposed to be explained by deep-set psychological drives, but they are not: they just happen" ("Eugene O'Neill and the Escape from the Chateau d'If," Gassner [ed.], *O'Neill*, p. 21).

Lazarus laughed himself into pantheism: God is now new, consummation is the same, and so is tragedy.

Lee Simonson, a remarkable American scene designer, tells in an interesting passage of his book *The Stage Is Set* about the preparations for the first production of *Dynamo*. He received from O'Neill a memorandum in which the playwright expressly stated that he did not want "an old melodrama thunderstorm"; instead, "thunder with a menacing, brooding quality as if some Electrical God were on the hills impelling all these people, affecting their thoughts and actions."[27] What this idea and O'Neill's use of the scenic means of expression throughout the play reveal is that there is a vision behind the play—a vision that is not conveyed to the audience. In Act I O'Neill resorted to a worn-out vehicle, "an old melodrama thunderstorm." It is hardly probable that the sound and lighting technicians could turn this act, basically melodramatic in its action and dialogue, into something magnificent, as the playwright expects them to do. The means do not carry the theme; in this play O'Neill is inarticulate in his use of the stage.

O'Neill was certainly inventive in utilizing the dynamo, "huge and black, with something of a massive female idol about it, the exciter set on the main structure like a head with blank, oblong eyes above a gross, rounded torso" (P III 473). In a later scene "the oil switches . . . seem like queer Hindu idols tortured into scientific supplications" (P III 483). Simonson went to the same power plant where O'Neill had seen the model of his creation—and he experienced something similar: "I was touched with a terror and a veneration for the invisible forces controlling modern life that are potentially its salvation and its destruction, its heaven and its hell. I have left many cathedrals less awed and humbled. . . . I had experienced, through a poet's insight, the wonder, the humility and pride, the hunger for power, the ecstasy of calling it forth, in which religions are born."[28]

[27] Cargill *et al.*, pp. 454-55: from *The Stage Is Set* by Lee Simonson (New York: Harcourt, Brace & Co., 1932).
[28] *Ibid.*, p. 457.

Paradoxically enough, Simonson, the scene designer, was able to turn his experience in the power plant more adequately into words than O'Neill, the playwright. The vision, although it romanticizes the dangers of the machine age in a way typical of the twenties, might have had a chance of succeeding in some other context. For Simonson is right in his criticism of *Dynamo*: "The theme of the play was short-circuited before it reached expression."[29] That industrialization or a belief in the power of science should be of necessity combined with monkish restraint is simply an assumption not based on facts; yet the tragic climax of *Dynamo* is built on it. Religious or scientific symbols are not employed in a meaningful way. After these observations, all that remains of the play, contrived as it is in a much more striking way than *Desire Under the Elms*, is a study of a poor neurotic.[30]

If there is (or was to O'Neill) a lesson to be learned from *Dynamo*, it is that no solutions, no matter how successful, can be repeated as such in other works of art. The setting with removable walls, an intricate part of the texture of *Desire Under the Elms*, does not have any inevitable functions here. There are no ironical counterpoints achieved by using it—except the very obvious contrast between the Light and Fife homes. No tensions are built, except superficial curiosity, as more and more of the interior of the power plant is revealed. Nor are the "thought asides" anything more than a mannerism, as we shall see later on; at the beginning of I, iv, they lead to an awkward grouping, when five characters are scattered all over the stage, each in his or her own compartment—and each is soliloquizing. Mysticism is even more personal and less rational here than in its previous forms in the pageant plays; and not much is gained when the clumsy

---

[29] *Ibid.*, p. 457. "I do not for a moment pretend that I succeeded in putting anything of this into my setting," Simonson remarks; yet the production is called by Gassner "visually stunning," "largely thanks to the scenic genius" of Simonson (*Eugene O'Neill*, p. 26).

[30] In her essay "Äventyr med O'Neill" (Adventure with O'Neill) Hagar Olsson calls the play "a sick and bloodless revolt," marked by "hysterical weakness" (*Arbetare i natten*, pp. 117-18). Cf. Doris V. Falk, *Eugene O'Neill and the Tragic Tension*, p. 129.

O'Neillian nature poetry is replaced by Reuben's equally clumsy "electro-poetry" (P III 477). *Dynamo* has been received with enthusiasm only by those who do not think highly of its author; for their purposes, it is a perfect play.[31]

[31] See e.g. a review by Robert Garland: "Nothing crops up that the intelligent schoolboy of eighteen, nineteen or twenty has not figured out for himself" (Miller, p. 63, reprinted from the *New York Telegram*, Feb. 12, 1929).

BEHIND THE MASKS

FROM *THE ANCIENT MARINER* TO *DAYS WITHOUT END*

The use of masks is perhaps the most intriguing single problem in the entire O'Neillian dramaturgy—if it is single. Connecting links can be drawn to theatre history, to O'Neill's view of the world, to his interest in psychology, to his late masterpieces: the masks are focal, no matter which of the above alternatives is our main line of approach. The problem is both central and many-faceted; the difficulties immanent in it are probably the basic reason why it has never been probed in depth. The emphasis in the following discussion is on functional aspects: what are the functions of the masks in a particular play? and how are they fulfilled? As a preliminary distinction, which will be blurred by later complications, we might speak of three different ways in which O'Neill employed masks. He used them for stage crowds; in one play he gave a Congo mask central symbolic significance as a piece of property; and masks were carried by individuals as symptoms of their divided personalities.

In three out of the four plays to be discussed in this chapter the usage is fairly simple. *The Ancient Mariner*, *All God's Chillun Got Wings*, and *Days Without End* each fall into one of the above categories, in the order given. *The Great God Brown* is the play in which different lines of development converge; it might be called O'Neill's "real" masque. In order to understand this play, some background concerning O'Neill's aims and his success or failure is needed. Part of this background involves the previous use of masks; the chapter can thus be opened with *The Ancient Mariner* and *All God's Chillun Got Wings*—and with a summary of still earlier occurrences of this device in O'Neill.

In *Servitude* the word "mask" occurs in the dialogue (LP 80, 123); after that, it was occasionally used in stage directions, usually to convey an impression of lifelessness, of a character who had proceeded beyond emotions, beyond caring. Thus in *Beyond the Horizon*, "Mrs. Mayo's face has lost all character, disintegrated, become a weak mask wearing a helpless, doleful expression of being constantly on the verge of comfortless tears" (P III 112). Mrs. Mayo dies after that act. The emotions of Caleb Williams die in the first act of *Diff'rent*, where his "face sets in its concealment mask of emotionlessness" (P II 518), a description repeated when he makes an appearance thirty years later. These effects were to be achieved with the help of make-up and facial expressions.

The mask is used for the first time as a piece of property in *The Emperor Jones*; it is worn by the medicine man as a traditional part of his costume. In *The Hairy Ape* we have what the Gelbs call a usage "in the symbolic sense of the Greek theatre," in the Fifth Avenue scene. The masks are not specified by O'Neill, but they were employed in the production, and the resulting success was probably another impetus for him to continue experimenting with them.[1]

In fact, the group of masked churchgoers, resembling Frankenstein monsters, represented the crossing of two connotations: those of lifelessness and of anonymity. We have seen how the relations between an individual and a crowd gathered more and more significance in O'Neill's imagination, first in realistic plays like *The Moon of the Caribbees* or *The First Man,* then in all of his pageant plays for the imaginative theatre. His sympathy was, as a rule, on the side of the individual; hence the depreciatory use of masks in *Lazarus Laughed*, where the hero was left unmasked and where "a fantastic proliferation of masks . . . proved happily to be the flood tide of this phase of O'Neill's experimentation,"[2] as Waith puts it. Before that, there was a veiled wom-

---

[1] The Gelbs, *O'Neill*, p. 495. The masks were suggested by Blanche Hays, a costume designer; they were approved of by O'Neill.

[2] Waith, "Eugene O'Neill: An Exercise in Unmasking," p. 184.

an's face in the climax of *The Fountain*; and the mourning over Kukachin's death was solemnized by a masked chorus in *Marco Millions*. *The Ancient Mariner* represents a relatively early phase: the number of masked chorus members is kept within reasonable limits. It was produced, for the first and last time, in the Provincetown Playhouse in 1924, during the opening season of the Jones-Macgowan-O'Neill triumvirate.

"The Ancient Mariner" by Samuel Taylor Coleridge is the only poem O'Neill ever tried to adapt for the stage. What might be called his adaptations of older plays are really re-creations of an ancient theme (*Mourning Becomes Electra*), or "counter-sketches"; they are original plays influenced by more or less distant models. As a contrast, *The Ancient Mariner* is frankly an adaptation; O'Neill's additions (not counting the stage directions) amount "to fewer than a dozen words plus an occasional repetition of a phrase from the poem."[3]

The use of masks is not the only interesting feature in *The Ancient Mariner*, yet the masked chorus has a prominent role in the adaptation. It is composed of six men, who form the crew of the ship, and their pantomime and recitation are used to visualize and accentuate the strange adventures on the far-away seas. The major speaking parts are those of the mariner himself and of the third wedding guest, who acts as a mirror to the mariner by repeating his gestures and reflecting his states of mind. This guest is, significantly enough, without a mask, "naturally alive—a human being," while the other two "have mask-like faces of smug, complacent dullness" and "walk like marionettes" (AM 63).

The drowned seamen who form the chorus and who later wear the masks of holy spirits and of angels belong to the sphere of the supernatural, as Waith remarks. Yet O'Neill was eager to establish another contrast with the masks as well, in line with his previous and later experiments: that

---

[3] O'Neill, *The Ancient Mariner*, dramatic adaptation of Coleridge's poem, edited by Donald Gallup. Preface by the editor: *The Yale University Library Gazette, 35* (1960), 61.

between "the Mariner and the unthinking mass of mankind."[4] This is achieved partly by means of the automaton effect: a glimpse of the bride and groom shows them smiling "like two happy dolls" and kissing "as dolls might" (AM 65); and the shadows of the dancing guests "come & go on the window like shadowgraphs" (AM 63). Not satisfied with these effects, O'Neill apparently felt the temptation to furnish the first and second guests with masks; but this would have resulted in confusion, in identification between the supernatural seamen and the realistic guests. In this dilemma O'Neill resorted to a compromise, to "mask-like faces"; he was later to use a similar solution, in a dilemma of another kind, when writing *Mourning Becomes Electra*. There is an additional compromise: among the apparitions, Death wears the mask of a black skull, but the accompanying Woman has a face "like a white skull—(make up not mask)" (AM 72). Perhaps this is just a whim; perhaps she is intended to stand out among the apparitions, as she is the only female ghost.

The mariner and the third guest, his listener, are thus unmasked, which "makes clear the connection between genuine vitality and spiritual vision."[5] Here we are again, in the Macgowanesque word "spiritual"; Waith is certainly right in saying that "behind life" spirituality was one of O'Neill's basic aims when employing masks. This belief in their expressiveness is echoed by James Light, a stage director associated with the Provincetown group: "We are using masks in *The Ancient Mariner* for this reason," he writes in the playbill, "that we wish to project certain dramatic motifs through that spiritual atmosphere which the mask peculiarly gives. . . . The mask cannot represent life. . . . But it can be used, as we are trying to use it, to show the eyes of tragedy and the face of exaltation."[6] The roots of this assumption will be explored later on; it is enough to state here that we are dealing with a dangerous half-truth: the masks (or lighting) were

4 Waith, p. 184.
5 *Ibid.*, p. 184.
6 AM 61: the playbill is quoted by Gallup.

as such "spiritual." All the artist needed to do was to use them, not necessarily with any clearly definable scenic functions, and he had shown the eyes of tragedy.

When outlining his future role as a member of the Provincetown triumvirate, O'Neill wrote to Macgowan about his theatrical creativeness: "You see, all these ideas of mine are being incorporated into my own plays bit by bit as they fit in, but I can't write plays fast enough to keep up with the production-imagination section of my 'bean.' "[7] Yet, as it turned out, *The Ancient Mariner* and a plan to dramatize the Book of Revelation from John which never materialized were the only visible fruits of that "bean" outside of original plays. Even so, *The Ancient Mariner* is full of scenic means familiar to us; it might be called, with a certain amount of bad will, "O'Neill's Complete Scenic Units."

In addition to masks and the automaton effect, there are examples of the pure spiritual usage of light: "a mystic halo surrounds it [the Albatross] with light" (AM 66). There is moonlight and "fog hiding the sun" (AM 67); there is "blinding sunshine—terrific heat" (AM 70), as in *Thirst* and *Gold*; there are lots of ghosts, of course. And the poem, as such, is a modified monologue; O'Neill did not see any reason to change its nature, fond as he was of soliloquies.

The percentage of scenic units is not as such any indication of failure. The units may be used creatively; in *The Ancient Mariner* they are not. O'Neill took as his tasks to divide the poem into acting roles, to furnish it with a stylized setting, and with equally stylized action. Paradoxically, the flaw in this "dramatic adaptation" is that it did not depart far enough from its source. The whole poem should have been broken into pieces, and a new dramatic form should have been built out of them; O'Neill should have written twelve hundred new words, not fewer than twelve. Instead, he offers a poetry reading with accompanying visual music.

O'Neill was perhaps hampered by the fact that the poem is a classic, and any departure from it might have been taken as an act of sacrilege. A competing explanation is that he relied

[7] The Gelbs, *O'Neill*, p. 526.

too heavily on the masks and other scenic means of expression employed. His basic error was in ignoring the fact that verbal images cannot, without damage, be translated directly into scenic images.[8] When the poem and the mariner on the stage speak of moonlight and a moonlight is, eureka! created by the light technician, nothing is achieved except a naïve demonstration, an "over-pictorialization," disastrous to poetry. "The Ancient Mariner" is a suggestive poem because of its twilight fusion of real and supernatural elements; and the question O'Neill did not ask energetically enough was what happens to the latter if they are introduced as real on the stage. The word "spirit" is more gruesome as a word in its proper context than as a figure rising beside a stage ship, even if it is "all in white planes like a snow crystal" (AM 69). The audiences are hardly unconscious of sitting in the theatre and looking at someone dressed as a spirit and moving, in all probability, somewhat awkwardly around.

O'Neill and the whole Provincetown group presumably believed in the beautifying power of their theatre machinery: it was possible to realize verbal images on the stage, because the masks and lights would "re-spiritualize" them. In *The Ancient Mariner* one sees only a special edition of the poem, with scenic drawings by Eugene O'Neill. And a volume furnished with pictures probably has a better chance of becoming a work of art than a series of scenic images presented simultaneously with the poem itself.[9] The adaptor's creations are on the stage all the time, demanding attention, disturbing and occasionally accentuating the effect of the poem;

[8] "As a rule, too little attention is paid to the fact that images in a play require quite another mode of investigation than, say, images in a lyric poem" (Clemen, *Shakespeare's Imagery*, p. 5). Mutatis mutandis, they need a different kind of treatment from the playwright, too. O'Neill translated the verbal images of the poem into a corresponding string of scenic images—instead of creating a new whole where both verbal and scenic images could have fulfilled their separate functions.

[9] Braem (*Eugene O'Neill*, p. 88) criticizes the adaptation for mixing different scenic forms: the text was partly dramatized, partly read aloud, and partly interpreted through pantomime.

drawings may leave something for the imagination of the receiver to fulfill.[10]

In addition to this basic fault, there is a confusion of the past tense of the poem and the present tense of the stage. In one phase of the action the mariner lies unconscious on the stage and at the same time speaks of his condition as something left behind long ago. As a whole, the early epic stanzas of adventure were more easily staged than the later vertigo of guilt and the resulting reconciliation (the shipmates accuse the mariner over and over again in sequences of slow-motion picture). As a whole, O'Neill chose the easy way out this time.

All God's Chillun Got Wings shares with *The Ancient Mariner* the time of birth: both were written in 1923, produced in the Provincetown Playhouse in 1924. Otherwise, the affinities are not prominent. Both plays use masks (the former only one); and there is a distant similarity in their structure. There are direct lines of development in the first half, then a vertigo of individual guilt and hatred.

All God's Chillun Got Wings is set in contemporary New York society, not on mythical oceans. The settings used in the first three scenes of this two-act play are identical: "Three narrow streets converge. A triangular building in the rear, red brick, four-storied, its ground floor a grocery. Four-story tenements stretch away down the skyline of the two streets. The fire escapes are crowded with people. In the street leading left, the faces are all white; in the street leading right, all black." We are once again in the world of expressionism; hence the typical features, hence the schematization.[11] The contrast between the white and the colored is

[10] George Jean Nathan was right when refuting the adaptation for reasons of exaggerated literalness (Cargill *et al., O'Neill and His Plays*, pp. 166-67, and Downer, *American Drama and Its Critics*, pp. 83-84: reprintings from *The American Mercury*, June 1924).

[11] According to Mann, the expressionists filled the stage "with stylized, simplified elements, often preferring geometric forms, using large surfaces, and strong, meaningful colours" (Friedmann and Mann, *Expressionismus*, p. 232).

further accentuated by songs, laughter, and action. Each street has its own songs in all three scenes, in two its own way of laughing also: "People pass, black and white, the Negroes frankly participants in the spirit of the Spring, the whites laughing constrainedly, awkward in natural emotion" (P II 301). The sounds echo O'Neill's primitivism in a general form, if not the later laughter of Lazarus.[12]

The scenes follow, in a tense and hectic way somewhat reminiscent of *The Hairy Ape*, the development of Jim, a black boy, and Ella, a white girl, from childish attachment to love and marriage. The odds are against them. Other children, adolescents, and adults insult and humiliate Jim, a sensitive, quiet boy who dreams of a career as a lawyer. After an unhappy affair with a white boxer, Ella resorts to chivalrous Jim, "the only white man in the world" (P II 314). These early sequences covering fourteen years would leave a somewhat awkward, over-obvious impression, if they were not combined with the very end of the play, and if they did not build up its fourth scene. This scene, the most obviously expressionistic of all, is placed near the middle of the play. It is the dominant scenic image in Act I. (See Fig. 1.)

Jim and Ella, husband and wife, are leaving a church. No detail in the setting and stylized action is without significance: "The church sets back from the sidewalk in a yard enclosed by a rusty iron railing with a gate at center. On each side of this yard are tenements. The buildings have a stern, forbidding look. All the shades on the windows are drawn down, giving an effect of staring, brutal eyes that pry callously at human beings without acknowledging them. . . . The district is unusually still, as if it were waiting, holding its breath" (P II 318). A Negro voice sings, repeating in the third stanza "with a brooding, earthbound sorrow" the line "Sometimes I wish that I'd never been born." The empty, deserted setting

---

[12] When dramatizing the Irish-Yankee and Negro-white conflict, O'Neill used two old myths: "the captive race, the people in bondage, are really superior, both inwardly and outwardly: they have 'soul' and they have superior physical beauty and vitality . . . while their captors are gross materialists, and usually decadent as well" (Raleigh, *The Plays of Eugene O'Neill*, p. 106).

is suddenly filled with action, following "one startling, metallic clang of the church-bell. As if it were a signal, people—men, women, children—pour from the two tenements, whites from the tenement to the left, blacks from the one to the right. They hurry to form into two racial lines on each side of the gate, rigid and unyielding, staring across at each other with bitter hostile eyes" (P II 319). Ella and Jim, in white and black, "stand in the sunlight, shrinking and confused. All the hostile eyes are now concentrated on them. They become aware of the two lines through which they must pass; they hesitate and tremble; then stand there staring back at the people, as fixed and immovable as they are." The situation freezes while an organ grinder plays. The freeze is sustained until the music ends with "one more single stroke" (P II 320) of the church-bell. Jim then has a fluctuating monologue which fills the rest of the image and gives the theme of the play in a nutshell.

This is a remarkable scenic image, not least because of the economy of the means employed. It is based, no doubt, on sharp expressionistic contrasts within the setting, between the sounds and silences, between the colors, between individuals and groups.[13] Yet the contrasts are utilized with discretion: it is the very silences that make the scene impressive; it is the schematization in the setting, repeated with variation in four scenes, that makes the image gather thematic significance. The silent, hostile crowd is more memorable than all the shouting, dancing, fighting, dying hundreds in *Lazarus Laughed*, no matter how cleverly the latter were spiritualized or depreciated by masks. After having strained (and before straining again) the limits of his medium in search of "behind life" significance, O'Neill suddenly found something in this scenic image, simply by bringing society into it: significance in life, not behind it.

If this scene were hurled at the audience like a single missile, it would not be nearly as effective. The entire act can

---

[13] The apprehensive elements of this scene and setting have been characterized by Koischwitz: they change "mystically into warning, condemnation and hate" (*Eugene O'Neill*, p. 46).

be called an example of how repetitions, unnecessary on the printed page, may in the stream of stage action prove to be assets for the playwright. Every preceding scene is present in this scenic image. Apart from the repetitions, employed in a different way elsewhere, and apart from the monologue, the scene also leaves a singular impression of freshness: it is as if O'Neill had suddenly thrown away a whole cargo of scenic units, some of them used fairly frequently.

The environment, created by the tenements and the iron railing, by action, songs, music, and sound effects, certainly plays a prominent role in *All God's Chillun Got Wings*. The phenomenon can be combined with a line in theatre history drawn by Gassner: "Environment had little, if any, significance to most playwrights before the last quarter of the nineteenth century—that is, before the application to playwriting of the naturalistic idea of environment as a determinative factor." Remembering the determinative settings in *Beyond the Horizon* or *Diff'rent* we can now state that the expressionistic stylization in *All God's Chillun Got Wings* or in *The Hairy Ape* means a departure from realism—but towards emphasizing the importance of the environment even more. In realistic plays the setting "sometimes played the role of destiny,"[14] Gassner says; it certainly does in *All God's Chillun Got Wings*.

O'Neill's first aim was to impress on the minds of his spectators a vision of society as the nemesis of Ella and Jim. After that, he hurried toward the latter half of the play, shaped as a case study in individual psychology. As in *The Hairy Ape*, there are two sections, one on either side of the central scenic image.[15] The setting is still expressive: the living room of the married couple appears to shrink, the furniture and characters to grow, as the atmosphere becomes more oppressive.[16] The thematic emphasis is on a piece of prop-

[14] Gassner, *Form and Idea in the Modern Theatre*, p. 23.

[15] Carpenter has difficulties in approving of the stylistic cleavage; to him, *All God's Chillun* "fails to focus clearly . . . its limited scope and its mixed techniques prevent its full realization" (*Eugene O'Neill*, p. 103). There is a clear focus in the two scenic images of the play.

[16] Raleigh sees in the play a development toward mechanized city

erty, magnified in the last scene by a special lighting effect: a primitive Congolese mask hanging on the wall. The rest of the details in the setting belong to the cultural background, expressing a clash between two civilizations; the mask is something special.

It comes directly from *Masks and Demons* by Macgowan and Rosse, published in 1923. A Congo mask is described in this book: "Out of the Congo . . . [come] the finest masks in the world. An Archipenko in the ashes of voodoo, an Epstein in ebony. The jungle artists have carved in their false faces a beauty they could not find in their own. It is never a natural beauty. . . . [The jungle artist] is not trying to imitate man. He is trying to imitate God. He reproduces emotions instead of people. He is the creative artist, not the fecund animal."[17] And this is how the mask is introduced to Ella and to O'Neill's audiences by Jim's sister Hattie:

HATTIE. . . . It's a Congo mask . . . it's beautifully made, a work of Art by a real artist—as real in his way as your Michael Angelo. (*Forces Ella to take it*) Here. Just notice the workmanship.

ELLA. . . . (*Looking at it with disgust*) Beautiful? Well, some people certainly have queer notions! It looks ugly to me and stupid—like a kid's game—making faces (P II 328-29).

Instead of Archipenko and Epstein, O'Neill uses the better-known "Michael Angelo"; otherwise, these two passages are strikingly similar. In addition to favoring anti-realism, *Masks and Demons* constantly points out the religious origins of the masks: "as the mask goes out of the temple, so religion goes out of the theatre."[18] When writing *All God's Chillun Got Wings* O'Neill was taking his first steps toward bringing religion back into the theatre; he says of this mask in his stage direction that it is "conceived in a true religious spirit."

---

life, as "the rich street life" is replaced by the flat, with its shrinking walls, "suggesting a sense of ever increasing claustrophobia, and the modern city dweller locked in his cell" (*The Plays of Eugene O'Neill*, p. 189; cf. pp. 26-27).

[17] Macgowan and Rosse, *Masks and Demons*, p. 43.

[18] *Ibid.*, p. 141.

It is "a grotesque face, inspiring obscure, dim connotations in one's mind, but beautifully done" (P II 322).

These "obscure, dim connotations" are employed all through Act II. Ella and Jim have come back from France determined to face the situation which forced them into exile.[19] Hattie is used to show that there is something basically wrong in this marriage. Ella's soliloquies are at first disguised as an address to her former friend who is off-stage in the street; later they are not disguised anymore. The mask comes to represent everything she cannot approve of in her husband, in her situation; and she talks frankly to it, revealing her distracted, schizophrenic state of mind: "What have you got against me? I married you, didn't I? Why don't you let Jim alone?" (P II 339). "Dat ole davil, sea," fate, whatever rationalization man can find, is present in these scenes behind the grinning mask.

We see here two scenic units, the mask and the monologue, getting close to one another. The mask is on its way from the stage into the inner consciousness of a character. It is still visible in *All God's Chillun Got Wings*; it is still concrete in *The Great God Brown* and *Days Without End*; yet in *Strange Interlude*, created in the intervening years, the masks were written into the "thought asides" where they interacted with the dialogue. Still later, they were incorporated into the dialogue proper, and expressed by stage directions within the speeches. O'Neill's early inclination to write fluctuating speeches and monologues was confirmed by his interest in the masks. *All God's Chillun Got Wings* represents, in fact, an interesting phase of transition in O'Neill's stage techniques: parallel to his use of the masks for crowds he was developing another, individual and psychological usage. The mask's functions were later taken over by the "thought asides" and, ultimately, by dialogue.

In the last scenic image of the play Ella kills—the mask. She could not stand the idea of Jim's passing his examina-

---

[19] "As with Twain, the point that O'Neill makes in *All God's Chillun*, is that the problem is almost insuperably complex for *any* individual, white or colored, who is involved in it" (Raleigh, p. 112).

tions and becoming a lawyer, and has fled into illness to assure his failure by her helplessness. These final revelations make the image charged with significance. An interpretation based on Adler's "individual psychology" seems to be adequate.[20] The role played by the mask in this triangle drama is described by Ilse Brugger, who ventures to define some of the dim connotations, here and elsewhere: "It is for Ella an unknown and malicious power. . . . Where masks are employed (as pieces of property or as concepts), the stream of life is stopped. . . . The mask belongs to the realm of hate and death, characterized, most markedly, by fear."[21]

At the very end Ella and Jim return to their childhood. The early scenes are needed: the audience has a clear picture of the return, as the childhood was demonstrated on the stage. O'Neill does not contrive or proclaim; the solution is Jim's and Ella's, not the playwright's.[22] And the dialogue of the final pages takes wings and flies toward verbal poetry, a rare occurrence in O'Neill. The poetry is of a harsh and ironic nature, and as such is praised by Waith: "What makes the scene particularly effective is his [Jim's] belief, at the very moment when all his hopes have been frustrated, that he has found happiness—that he too has wings. Utter defeat presents itself to him in the guise of victory."[23] O'Neill's attitude to exaltation is, for a change, critical; so at the end of Act I,

[20] Ella "is compelled to assert her superiority to the Negro. . . . Unable to surpass her Negro husband, she becomes aggressively determined that he shall not surpass her" (Engel, *The Haunted Heroes of Eugene O'Neill*, p. 121).

[21] Ilse Brugger, "Verwendung und Bedeutung der Maske bei O'Neill," *Die neueren Sprachen*, Neue Folge, 6 (1957), 164-65.

[22] Looking for "really tragic significance" and characters of stature, Francis Fergusson sees in the "evasive finale" an "extraordinary failure of Mr. O'Neill's to master his material" (Cargill *et al.*, p. 275: reprinted from *Hound and Horn*, Jan. 1930). Fergusson's Aristotelian view is echoed by Carpenter, p. 104. There is some fluctuation in Nicoll's opinion; having denied that *All God's Chillun* is a tragedy (*World Drama*, p. 887), he is in the last chapter of his book, written later, convinced by Krutch that O'Neill's plays are tragedies (p. 941). Plays by Beckett or Dürrenmatt have, in the intervening years, taught us that admirable characters are not a necessary requirement in modern tragedies.

[23] Waith, "An Exercise in Unmasking," p. 187.

in front of the church, Jim "is maintaining an attitude to support them through the ordeal only by a terrible effort, which manifests itself in the hysteric quality of ecstasy which breaks into his voice" (P II 320). This was exactly the quality of ecstasy that kept breaking into O'Neill's voice in *The Fountain* or in *Lazarus Laughed*.

The Gelbs have found striking similarities between *All God's Chillun Got Wings* and *Long Day's Journey Into Night*. Ella and Jim are the real names of O'Neill's parents; a central theme in both plays is the paradoxical tension between love and hate, another the isolation of the wife, as a result of her socially unequal marriage.[24] Several perceptive writers have, in fact, observed a universality in the play's tension between love and hate. Among them is no less a person than T. S. Eliot;[25] Joseph T. Shipley also notes that the play deals only on the surface with the theme of miscegenation, because both Ella and Jim bring their strictly personal problems into their marriage.[26] These observations add at least a subsidiary layer of meaning to the play.

Taking them as our clue we might have a closer look at the time scheme followed in *All God's Chillun Got Wings*. Act I forms a semicircle from afternoon to morning (as does each of the parts in *Desire Under the Elms*), Act II another from morning to night. There are years or months between the scenes; yet it is feasible to conclude that O'Neill has written here a night's and a day's journey into night, perhaps inspired by *From Morn to Midnight* by Georg Kaiser. In O'Neill's play, where the settings are conspicuously schematized, the time is patterned, too. Another formula O'Neill follows here is an over-all circle: the play both begins and ends in spring, making Ella's and Jim's return to childhood complete.

All God's Chillun Got Wings comes closer to an esteemed

---

[24] The Gelbs, pp. 10, 534-35.
[25] Cargill *et al.*, pp. 168-69: reprinted from *The New Criterion, 4* (1926), 395-96.
[26] Shipley, *The Art of Eugene O'Neill*, p. 16. Cf. Stig Torsslow, *Eugene O'Neill* (1937), p. 38; Raleigh, p. 117; Koischwitz, p. 46.

place in the O'Neill canon than any of his other plays employing masks—and not only by virtue of those details which foreshadowed the late masterpiece. The very use of masks contributes to this estimate. The device is not overburdened; it fulfills it function well. Dim connotations are there, in the presence of the mask; they are not exploited too heavily or explained away. If the (definitely purposeful) schematization of the setting in Act I and the shrinking of the walls in Act II are approved of, the play is without major flaws. Even if it were "not quite so consistently compelling or well-written" as *The Emperor Jones* and *The Hairy Ape*, it has, as Edmund Wilson has remarked, "a certain advantage over either of these other plays in presenting two characters equally strong, in collision with one another, instead of one central character who only contends with himself."[27] The collision was, as later events have proven to us, of central significance to O'Neill; maybe this is part of the reason why the two central images in *All God's Chillun Got Wings* seem to be more effective and thematically significant than many of those we find elsewhere in the O'Neill plays of the twenties.

O'Neill's enthusiasm for masks was shared by several eminent artists both before and after 1920. In his extensive discussion on the sources of *The Great God Brown*, Engel refers to representative figures interested in primitivism, ranging from Thoreau to Nietzsche, from Wagner to Freud. Against this background he places Gordon Craig, whose roots were in the decadents of the 1890's and in symbolists like Verhaeren, Mallarmé, and Maeterlinck. In *The Theatre—Advancing* (1919), Craig laments "the deterioration of Dancing, Pantomime, Marionettes, Masks,"[28] all of which had been esteemed by the ancients. In the fixity of the mask Craig saw a possibility of going beyond reality, beyond the transitory expressions of a human face.

[27] Cargill *et al.*, p. 466: reprinted from *The New Republic*, May 28, 1924. Leech (p. 44) calls *All God's Chillun* "thinner in intellectual content than *The Emperor Jones* or *The Hairy Ape*."
[28] Engel, p. 89.

Craig was responsible for "the first completely non-psychological and formalistic use of masks in theatrical production"[29] in this century—and in a western country—by designing masks for productions of two plays by William Butler Yeats at the Abbey Theatre in Dublin as early as 1911. Yeats is another figure of importance in the present argument: his collection, *Four Plays for Dancers* (1921), includes plays from the preceding years and an introduction in which the author elaborates on the usage, dreaming of future plays written for particular masks, and explains the metamorphosis in a character's personality achieved by changing his mask in the middle of one of the plays.[30] The Irish poet was influenced by the Japanese Noh plays, studied by Ernest Fenollosa and Ezra Pound in their collaborative volume *'Noh' or Accomplishment* (1917). Luigi Pirandello achieved international fame with his play *Six Characters in Search of an Author* in 1921; it was followed by *Henry IV*, a masquerade play, in 1922. Even elsewhere, masks, though not necessarily concretized on the stage, are a central concept in Pirandello's dramaturgy.[31]

On the side of the practical theatre, masks were employed by Max Reinhardt, by Robert Edmond Jones in his production of *Macbeth* in 1921,[32] and in *The Spook Sonata* by Strindberg, produced by the Provincetown triumvirate in 1924. Ilse Brugger provides a connecting link with the

[29] Gassner, *Form and Idea in the Modern Theatre*, p. 167.

[30] William Butler Yeats, *Four Plays for Dancers*, p. vi.

[31] Dietrich devotes a whole chapter to "the theatre of masks and mirrors: Pirandello and Pirandellism" (*Das moderne Drama*, pp. 166-99). As one of the signs of "Pirandellism" she mentions a "renaissance of mask-consciousness" (p. 183). Her discussion is of a wide range, and both forerunners and followers of Pirandello are listed, among them O'Neill, Schnitzler, Benavente, Ionesco, and the Finnish playwright Walentin Chorell. If the mask is taken as a concept, there seems to be no limit to the possible associations; my discussion concentrates only on plays where masks are used as pieces of property. Dietrich also finds several functions for the masks: Pirandello wanted to show "the relativity of truth," O'Neill to "penetrate his figures—as in a Roentgen apparatus" (p. 200). Cf. Koischwitz, p. 42.

[32] Engel, p. 92.

expressionistic playwright in her explanation of why he favored masks: "because he was concerned with the basic situation of man, and because he . . . did not try to present man as a unique individual but in his significance."[33] The influence of our old friend *Masks and Demons* on *The Great God Brown* will be discussed after the play has been analyzed; the influence is marked.

Engel sees in the mask "the symbol of his [O'Neill's] Yea-saying years,"[34] not a stage symbol. In concluding this discussion on the influential background figures it is important to note that most of the enthusiasts for the masks early in this century were not men of the practical theatre. Their interests were literary or historical; even Craig was more of a visionary of the theatre than a scene designer, and Reinhardt was always willing to use any device for spectacular effects. The entire movement for the reintroduction of masks was started *"von oben hinab."* It did not grow out of a social revolution, as the idea of the fourth wall ultimately grew out of industrialization, nor was it a result of improvement in technical facilities, as the renewal in stage lighting was. Even if oriented toward history, the advocates of masks lacked historical perspectives in thinking they could jump over thousands of years of cultural development. And there is an element of aestheticism in the visions of Craig and Macgowan, of Yeats and O'Neill.

So is the total effect left by *The Great God Brown* literary rather than theatrically practical, fanciful rather than imaginative. Masks are symbols of certain portions of the personality, of the social ego. The mask of Dion Anthony, a would-be painter and later architect, is "a fixed forcing of his own face—dark, spiritual, poetic, passionately supersensitive, helplessly unprotected in its childlike, religious faith in life—into the expression of a mocking, reckless, defiant, gayly scoffing and sensual young Pan" (P III 260). Dion al-

[33] Brugger, p. 153.
[34] Engel, p. 94. Raleigh finds the genesis of the masks and other disguises in Fechter's *The Count of Monte Cristo* (Gassner [ed.], *O'Neill*, p. 17); the explanation can hardly be as simple as that.

184

ways wears the mask in company; only when alone or with his mistress-goddess Cybel, will he take it off to reveal his real self. As in *All God's Chillun Got Wings*, masks and monologues go hand in hand; a whole scene (III, ii) consists of a soliloquy addressed to a mask—and when unmasked, Dion hurls a series of questions to the man in the moon,[35] as Yank once did in *The Hairy Ape*: "Why am I afraid to live, I who love life and the beauty of flesh and the living colors of earth and sky and sea? Why am I afraid of love, I who love love? . . . Why was I born without a skin, O God, that I must wear armor in order to touch or to be touched?" (P III 264-65).

In the prologue, staged on a moonlit pier, Dion reveals his real face to Margaret, the girl who loves him and later becomes his wife, thus inheriting the role of Maud from *Bread and Butter*—a role also played against a would-be painter and a failure. She is frightened by that "spiritual, poetic etc." face; and her abhorrence is never motivated from her side, just as Miriam, the wife of Lazarus, was never given a chance. On the other hand, Dion, the self-destroying artist, is given stature even with cheap and over-obvious means: "He kisses his mother, who bows with a strange humility as if she were a servant being saluted by the young master" (P III 261). All through the play Dion is treated as if he were something excellent, yet his stage actions never give any evidence of this excellence. He spends most of his time drinking, pitying himself, and speaking slightly off-key, apparently to show his superiority and misanthropy.

Dion is especially superior to his classmate, Billy Brown, a normal boy who develops into "the Great God Brown," a successful American businessman. He bears resemblance to Edward Brown, John's conventional brother and rival in *Bread and Butter*.

The idealization of Dion reaches the degree of glorifica-

[35] This is one of the few passages which somehow motivate Nathan's estimation: "The dialogue reaches heights of tender profundity that have seldom been equaled in the native drama" (Downer, *American Drama and Its Critics*, p. 89: reprinted from *The American Mercury*, April 1926).

tion as the play progresses. O'Neill decided that he was not, after all, satisfied with the fixity achieved by employing masks. He did not give up the device, however, but made it changeable, as Yeats once did. At the beginning of I, i we read: "His real face has aged greatly. . . . The mask, too, has changed. It is older, more defiant and mocking, its sneer more forced and bitter, its Pan quality becoming Mephistophelean" (P III 269). And in Act II where Dion dies, apparently of self-pity, "his face is that of an ascetic, a martyr, furrowed by pain and self-torture, yet lighted from within by a spiritual calm and human kindliness" (P III 284). His kindliness is oriented toward Cybel, a comforting prostitute, however, rather than toward his wife and children. He has been especially enraged at being compelled to work as an assistant to Billy Brown, now a successful architect. And so he passes away, loved by everyone on the stage.

Yet we are only halfway through the play. Billy, who has never been able to forget his love for Margaret, takes Dion's mask, which has been willed to him for greater safety in Dion's dying speech. Margaret knows nothing of this. Nothing good follows: the poor bourgeois has only taken over the creative self-tortures of an artist. Billy buries Dion's body in his garden and hides the mask in his offices, where part of the action, before and after Dion's death, is placed. Removable walls, though not specified by the playwright, might be a good solution for a scene designer: once only Billy's room is shown (I, ii), once the drafting room (II, ii), and twice both of them (III, i and IV, i). In the prologue and in I, i, O'Neill ordered an arrangement of the benches reminiscent of a courtroom; the idea was dropped in the later scenes, although Western civilization was put on trial. To help the rather laborious shiftings of the scenes (there are thirteen scenes and seven different settings), O'Neill employed a backdrop which, on one occasion, was "painted with the intolerable lifeless realistic detail of . . . stereotyped paintings" (P III 269)—or of O'Neill's plays prior to his conversion to anti-realism.

Margaret is happy for a while with the tender Brown

masked as her husband. But the police are after Dion, suspected of having murdered Brown. In a finale reminiscent of
The Dreamy Kid, the innocent murderer is shot to death by
the police. He is stripped naked except for a loin cloth, the
dress of the Emperor Jones in his dying scene. Cybel is present and recites a paean to eternal recurrence;[36] so is Margaret, who kisses the mask of Dion standing "on the table beneath the light, facing front" (P III 319). After that, there is
only the epilogue, with Margaret, a happy widow, on the pier
in the moonlight. Generations of playgoers pass by, but the
moonlight and the circle structure remain.

After the original production of *The Great God Brown*,
O'Neill sent a letter to several New York newspapers ex-
plaining the symbolic overtones of the play. This letter has
been accepted by later interpreters uncritically, so much so
that it seemed necessary to construct above, for the first time,
a description of the play in which the author's explanation
has been deliberately ignored. As a rule, when artists themselves explain their works, they speak of their intentions,
not of their achievements. Leaving consideration of the
letter until now will give us a chance to see how far the intended themes came across in the finished work of art.

Dion Anthony, so the explanation goes, represents
"Dionysus and St. Anthony—the creative pagan acceptance
of life, fighting eternal war with the masochistic, life-denying
spirit of Christianity as represented by St. Anthony." As a result of this fight, "creative joy in life for life's sake" is frustrated, "distorted by morality from Pan into Satan, into a
Mephistopheles mocking himself in order to feel alive."
Cybel is, of course, the pagan Earth Mother Cybele; Margaret, "the modern direct descendant of the Marguerite [sic!]
of Faust." And William A. Brown, the businessman, is de-

---

[36] "This verbal set-piece is not without its merits, but it goes on
too long, is too consciously and designedly 'lyrical' and 'rhetorical,'
and it is repetitious. Its meaning is of the most general order, saying
simply and only—what it needs no Cybel to tell us—that life repeats
itself" (Raleigh, pp. 217-18).

stroyed by "that creative power made self-destructive by complete frustration."[37]

Turning now back to the play we can see that the theme of Pan and Mephistopheles is carried only by the stage directions and a few references in the dialogue. And the dialogue is so full of references to all kinds of personages, from Thomas à Kempis to John Brown, that these significant passages are drowned. After that, the theme depends on the skill of the mask designer; and it is doubtful whether any mask can suggest a special image like the face of Pan, while at the same time retaining a certain similarity to the face of the actor.[38] Parallels to *Faust* or to Cybele are carried mainly by the names of characters, an easy way of achieving "significance." Cybel is to Leech "especially difficult to endure. She is both the literary stereotype of the good-hearted prostitute and the earth-mother, all-wise."[39]

A practical view of the functions of masks in *The Great God Brown* will reveal the degree of confusion in this play. All drama is based on certain assumptions: in *The Doll's House* we are persuaded to assume that we are looking at Nora's and Helmer's home; in *The Emperor Jones* the presupposition is that we can share the visions and fear of the Emperor. These assumptions do work; both plays offer, within the limits of their different styles, a meaningful experience. In *The Great God Brown* the masks are pieces of property; as there are no conventions regulating their usage in Western civilization, we depend on an agreement with the playwright.

At the beginning of the play the spectators are led to approve of the assumption that the masks are protective walls

---

[37] Quinn, *A History of the American Drama*, II (1927), pp. 192-93: a reprinting of a letter sent by O'Neill to "several New York newspapers" (the Gelbs, p. 580); published also in the *Saturday Evening Post*, Feb. 13, 1926.

[38] Dietrich (p. 229) takes Pan and Mefisto in good faith and sees an echo from Jung in these figures selected from the early history of mankind.

[39] Leech, *Eugene O'Neill*, p. 66.

used in social life.[40] Then in the middle of the play, and for no apparent reason, Dion's mask, this piece of property seen in a certain function for more than two acts, suddenly adopts another function, that of Dion's creative talent. This change is the more difficult to accept since the masks of Cybel and Margaret retain their social function throughout the play. In the scene in which Billy mysteriously inherits Dion's mask, and with it his talent,[41] we are supposed to know of Dion that "it is as Mephistopheles he falls stricken at Brown's feet after having condemned Brown to destruction by willing him his mask, but, this mask falling off as he dies, it is the Saint who kisses Brown's feet in abject contrition."[42] Yet all we see is an actor playing Dion Anthony. Furthermore, the mask of Billy left behind in the office "looks to society like the body of Billy Brown,"[43] as Falk puts it; it is carried as "a body by the legs and shoulders" (P III 318).

Can one approve of these conflicting assumptions? Several interpreters apparently can. As a result, the interpretations are more consistent than the play; *The Great God Brown*, with its literary reminiscences, has been a sure hit among some one-sidedly literary scholars,[44] who apparently forgot even O'Neill's own warning: "It was far from my idea in writing *Brown* that this background pattern of conflicting tides in the soul of Man should ever overshadow and thus

[40] The basic assumption is fairly generally approved of, but the later developments are condemned: "the purpose of the masks in *The Great God Brown* is instantly understandable . . . the difficulty . . . lies in the author's own confusion in regard to the end served by the use of the masks" (John Howard Lawson, *Theory and Technique of Playwriting* [1960], p. 231). Cf. Miller, *Playwright's Progress*, pp. 61, 53, and 169: reprintings of reviews by John Anderson and Brooks Atkinson; and Gassner, *Masters of the Drama*, p. 654.

[41] To Gassner, this is "a provocative idea for which O'Neill unfortunately found an incredibly melodramatic plot" (Gassner, *Eugene O'Neill*, p. 24).

[42] Quinn, p. 193.

[43] Doris V. Falk, *Eugene O'Neill and the Tragic Tension*, p. 105.

[44] Engel (p. 155) and Blackburn ("Continental Influences," p. 122) find the conflict between Dion's Christian and pagan selves to be central in the play. Cf. references 38, 43, 49, and 50 of this chapter, and Engel, p. 166.

189

throw out of proportion the living drama of the recognizable human beings." To a reader who approaches the play with the idea of penetrating the fog of previous interpretations, it seems to symbolize, in the first place, that "the mystery any one man or woman can feel but not understand as the meaning of any event"[45] is essentially that everyone is jealous of everyone else.[46] Why else these conspicuous triangles, three in number (Dion—Margaret—Billy, Dion—Cybel—Billy, Dion—Margaret—their sons)? And if there is, in the second place, a social implication, it can be summarized as follows: an American businessman takes over the creative genius of a dead artist and is shot to death by the police. What is the pattern in society that corresponds to this plot? The action is "symbolic," of course, but not in a meaningful way.[47]

The plot of *The Great God Brown* makes just as little sense as that of *Dynamo*. It seems probable that O'Neill got so carried away with the terrible thought of the poor artist in the middle of this world of materialism that he had no time to demonstrate it on the stage. Perhaps he was not even conscious of the difficulties immanent in the theme: an artist's creative work happens inside his mind; how can it be externalized for the stage? There is, it is true, quite a lot of talk about Dion's last creation, a cathedral so ingeniously blasphemous that only Dion himself realizes it; yet the theme never rises above the level of sentimental discussions on the subject. And the use of the masks is far too confused with other issues to carry the full implications of this difficult theme.

Doris V. Falk has presented an explanation of the play based on psychoanalysis. For her the mask corresponds to the Jungian "persona," and Dion and Billy are ultimately

---

[45] Quinn, pp. 193-94.

[46] "In this play no one ever really knows who or what the other person is" (Raleigh, p. 134, on *The Great God Brown*).

[47] Stig Ahlgren regrets that O'Neill's cultural criticism is pushed into the background by his scenic whims ("Eugene O'Neills författarskap," *Ord och bild, 46*, 1937, 178). Lawson works his way toward a similar conclusion: "There is no *additional* meaning, no 'background pattern' which conforms to the author's intention" (p. 134).

halves of one and the same personality,[48] recognized as such by Cybel: "You are Dion Brown!" (P III 320). Here we have another theme—again, not properly handled by O'Neill. If O'Neill wanted to imply that Dion and Brown were elements of one personality, why did he establish their separate characters so firmly in the prologue by introducing two pairs of solidly bourgeois parents?[49] Perhaps O'Neill got this idea only after he had finished the prologue? Possibly so; yet as late as in his dying scene Dion explicitly reminds Billy of their meeting in childhood; the passage sounds like another ingredient in the theme of artist versus unsympathetic surroundings rather than a preparation for a Jekyll-Hyde theme. This is one of the loose ends in the play; another is the sudden twist toward realism, when Margaret asks Dion to stop "at the butchers' and have them send two pounds of pork chops" (P III 273). The symbolism of the pork chops has not yet been explained by anyone. O'Neill apparently had so many aims in his mind that the total effect he produced is that of aimlessness.

In short, quite a lot of sympathy and understanding has been wasted on *The Great God Brown*. Literary themes not well managed by the playwright have been readily accepted by some critics. It is an essential task for a dramatist to make abstract themes concrete in terms of the stage; and yet, when some critics meet a play where nothing is successfully concretized, they are happy with the abstractions they can pick out of the dialogue.

Dionysus and Pan, Mephistopheles and St. Anthony, Faust

[48] Doris V. Falk, *Eugene O'Neill and the Tragic Tension*, p. 105.

[49] Dion and Billy "are, in one sense, two separate and opposing characters; in another, they are the conflicting aspects of the single character, 'Man.' Both the complexity and the confusion of the play lies in its uncertainty concerning these two alternatives" (Carpenter, p. 111). The same scholar presents a matter-of-fact analysis of O'Neill's entanglement with the masks; yet he is ready to make admissions: "And this grotesque mixture of incongruous metaphors suggests the confusion of the modern world" (p. 112). This is a commonplace in criticism; if it is taken to be generally valid, why praise works of art with a marked order? Apparently, only confusion of genius should be applauded—which leaves *The Great God Brown* out of count.

and Margarete, Cybele and Satan, George W. Babbitt and John Brown—O'Neill gathered quite a congregation to do service to his great god Brown.[50] All of these are old friends; yet the feeling of moving in good company should not prevent a critic from asking an awkward question. Can the play stand by itself? Even in this century of parodies and "counter-sketches" a certain observation is valid: only if the new work of art is at least in some respect comparable to the classic used as its source, only if it is the creation of a remarkable artist, can it stand the burden of classical parallels without falling into pathos and pretentiousness. The re-creations of Thomas Mann, James Joyce, or Bertolt Brecht stand solidly; *The Great God Brown* does not. It is a heap of literary reminiscences, unorganized, undigested. A different conclusion is possible in the case of some other O'Neill plays; *Desire Under the Elms* has already been treated with due respect. One more point of comparison: it is hardly possible to defend the vagueness of *The Great God Brown* by saying that the play is mysterious because of its very subject matter;[51] Franz Kafka turned his vision of the mysteries of life into forms as clear as crystal.

O'Neill had succumbed to a temptation to defend himself against the charge that he was not "literary" enough. In the case of the pageant plays, most notably *Lazarus Laughed*, he was lured in the wrong direction, toward mass spectacles; this time he was tempted to use easy paraphrases. And he fell into an indiscriminate overuse of masks, recommended by Macgowan.

It has been noted above that *Masks and Demons* had a

---

[50] Dietrich adds two writers to this company: "Strindberg's consciousness of mysteries and Tolstoi's Christianity" are there, too; yet the idea of mask play is dramaturgically and scenically "clearly shaped" (*Das moderne Drama*, p. 211).

[51] Raleigh connects the confusion and "total anarchy of values" of *The Great God Brown* on one hand with modern city life (p. 190), on the other with modern (p. 242) or American literature (p. 258). Seeing *Bread and Butter* (certainly an autobiographical play) in the background, one might speculate that O'Neill created mystery too much out of his personal preoccupations, too little out of a sense of doom or of modern life.

direct influence on certain details in *Marco Millions* and *All God's Chillun Got Wings*. The volume as a whole seems to be in the background of *The Great God Brown*. The aim of the text is propagandistic: "The task of the artist of the theatre may be to seek out new symbols—the symbols, perhaps, of beauty and pain, of exaltation and pathos—and to make us feel them in one of the greatest of symbols, the ancient and mysterious mask."[52] Furthermore: "All masks have some curious and oppressive sense of the dead made living, the spirit given flesh, the god or demon brought into physical contact. . . . The mask is symbol per se."[53] Here we have it, the dangerous belief in the expressive power of the mask as such, without any scenic functions: "For the end of the mask is Drama."[54]

Macgowan does not try to explain the mystery of the mask; he cultivates it. And he does so in an uncritical manner, without real knowledge; he is an aesthete, in love with his own fantasy picture of the wonderful world of primitive people. "Spiritualism flourishes very like a sport in West Africa," he informs us. "It takes the place of baseball among the young bucks."[55] This comparison with the highly organized modern society, admitting that it is journalistically striking on purpose, shows that Macgowan did not understand the holistic world of primitive people, analyzed by later psychology. He was a romantic, mostly nostalgic, not quite imperceptive to horror romanticism.

The question neither Macgowan nor O'Neill as his pupil asked was this: psychoanalysis has revealed the dependence of our minds on fundamental impulses which completely govern the minds of primitive people—so then what? Masks were employed in early forms of drama around the world—so then? Where is the connecting link with modern drama, with the twentieth century?[56] In *All God's Chillun Got Wings*, we

[52] Macgowan and Rosse, *Masks and Demons*, p. 161.
[53] *Ibid.*, p. 45.   [54] *Ibid.*, p. xii.   [55] *Ibid.*, p. 41.
[56] Stephen Ullmann, *Semantics*: An Introduction to the Science of Meaning, includes a remark applicable to the semantics of the stage. Ullmann does not approve of what he calls "etymological reduction" which can be "a veritable obsession with some writers and thinkers."

might answer that, connected to a specific theme and used with discretion, the device was effective. It was not in *The Great God Brown*, where "the dependence on the mask is far too great,"[57] as Waith remarks. The play is, as it were, written for people who have read *Masks and Demons* and who share Macgowan's enthusiasm, conveyed so suggestively by his text and by the pictures.

Even more specifically, the parallels between *Masks and Demons* and O'Neill's masque are remarkable. "When a man puts on a mask he experiences a kind of release from his inhibited and bashful and circumscribed soul. He can say and do strange and terrible things, and he likes it." Dion certainly does. "Legend is theatre. And the greatest legend of all, the legend of death and resurrection, carries man into the greatest drama, Greek tragedy."[58] This is a crucial point: when O'Neill wrote *The Great God Brown*, he was, in fact, doing "big work," writing a "legend of death and resurrection."

First of all, the name of the play—"The Great God Brown"—sounds somewhat over-obvious in its satire; we know that O'Neill was capable of both over-obviousness and satire. Yet he also had a fancy for double meanings: witness *The First Man, Mourning Becomes Electra, Days Without End, The Iceman Cometh*. In *The Great God Brown* we have Dionysus, a god, "brought into physical contact"; perhaps there is an ambiguity in the name. Brown is both the God of American materialism and a reincarnation of Dionysus. "The peculiar and dramatic thing about Dionysus was his story of death and rebirth. His body has been rent apart and scattered like leaves in the fall, and he has been reborn as the earth is reborn each spring,"[59] Mac-

---

"Some philosophers . . . believe that they can grasp the essential significance of words by uncovering their derivation" (p. 100). O'Neill and Macgowan tried to grasp the essential significance of drama by returning to the time and place where drama originated: to ancient Greece, with its masks and rituals.

[57] Waith, "An Exercise in Unmasking," p. 188.

[58] Macgowan and Rosse, p. xii.

[59] *Ibid.*, p. 107.

gowan writes. Dion is reborn as Billy, and the time is specified as spring. Moreover, his body is buried in the garden,
and Billy addresses the grave: "Now I am drinking your
strength, Dion—strength to love in this world and die and
sleep and become fertile earth, as you are becoming now in
my garden" (P III 307). Another reference to eternal recurrence is sung by Cybel in the climax of the play. "Now it was
the custom of early man not only to deify his priestly chiefs
after death, but to see that they were in a proper state for
deification by murdering them before their vigor failed. . . .
The chief's murder was often described more pleasantly as
a 'going away.' "[60] Billy Brown plans "going away" together
with Margaret: "We must hustle off to Europe now—and
murder him there!" (P III 307). The only possible explanation for the criminal melodrama at the end of the play is that
it is intended as a criticism against an American society which
does not approve of ritual murders. Poor us, O'Neill says,
we cannot even murder our deified chiefs in a delightful
pagan way; Old Mama Christianity is always in our way,
turning all into a tragedy. And a businessman is not fit to
assume the personality of Dionysus. *The Great God Brown*
is a tragedy about the impossibility of real Greek tragedy in
modern times.

One more point: "The mask is as full of mysteries and
terrors as fetishism itself. The greatest, the simplest, and the
grimmest is the grip of fear in which the mask holds even the
most enlightened of men. George W. Babbitt, master of
phonograph and radio, looks with a certain disquietude upon
a mask."[61] Now it happens to be so that the only character in
the entire O'Neill canon furnished with the initial of a middle
name is William A. Brown—as a paraphrasis of George W.
Babbitt? Or to satirize the habit of using the initial at all?
Brown has inherited Babbitt's role; why not the form of the
name as well? One of the ideas behind *The Great God
Brown*, behind O'Neill's total output, in fact, was to arouse
disquietude in the Babbitts, the masters of business.

[60] *Ibid.*, p. 51.
[61] *Ibid.*, p. 55.

There is Dionysus in *The Great God Brown*, there is the death of Dion and his rebirth as Dion Brown—and there is Cybele, the Earth Mother, bringing a consoling message of eternal rebirth. On the level of scenic means of expression, there were the masks, supposed to bring the audiences directly into Athens. Certainly O'Neill must have read of the Dionysus cult and George W. Babbitt elsewhere; yet the parallels between *Masks and Demons* and O'Neill's play are too numerous to be merely coincidental.[62]

The purpose of the above discussion has not for a moment been to imply that these meanings come through in the play; the aim has been only to show why the play is what it is. The play was born broken; no amount of grace from an interpreter can glue it together. The stage is a place where there is a continuous discrepancy between what the playwright thinks he is expressing, what the director and actors think they are conveying—and what the audience thinks it is receiving. It is no wonder that these tensions result in a few corpses now and then; it is no wonder that the more enterprising playwrights sometimes deliver still-born babies, a severe disappointment to the creator's high-flown hopes. *The Great God Brown* is such a baby. It meant much more to O'Neill (and to Macgowan, the concealed godfather) than to anyone not initiated. The playwright apparently decided not to relate his explanation directly to *Masks and Demons*, in order to avoid suspicions of plagiarism. This is also why he emphasized his own creative work, "the living drama of recognizable human beings," at the end of his interpretation.

To conclude: *The Great God Brown* is a "Greek" play, even more pronouncedly so than has been assumed so far; and it is a focal play. When O'Neill grasped the theme of the *Oresteia*, he already had three adaptations of Greek tragedy behind him—one of them successful (*Desire Under the Elms*), the other two (*Lazarus Laughed* and *The Great God*

---

[62] Cf. Brustein on the early plays: " . . . one is never convinced that O'Neill has read very deeply in those philosophies that he affirms or rejects; his works display the intellectual attitudinizing of the self-conscious autodidact" (*The Theatre of Revolt*, p. 333).

Brown) failures on a grand scale. Remarkably enough, the road to his successes was paved with the corpses of earlier plays.

Even if a corpse, *The Great God Brown* is a focal play, a window to the theatre of the twenties. It shows us what was behind the masks employed by O'Neill—in a word, primitivism. Whether the masks were employed by stage crowds, or seen as an object of terror by Ella, far advanced in her retrogressive flight toward the safe world of childhood, whether tossed around by the cast of O'Neill's real masque, celebrating the rebirth of Dion Anthony, god and artist—in all of these cases O'Neill was straining his medium toward primitive, mysterious processes of nature. He was trying to "belong."[63] And he was trying to realize the programme of Kenneth Macgowan, a visionary of the theatre of tomorrow: "But whatever the form of the play, the content will have a spiritual quality that gives us this subliminal sense of mysterious age-old processes alive in us today."[64]

There is an interval of eight years between the opening nights of *The Great God Brown* and *Days Without End*, O'Neill's last mask play (1926-34). That his enthusiasm did not vanish in the intervening years is evidenced by a series of three articles written by him and published in *The American Spectator* in November and December of 1932 and January of 1933. "Memoranda on Masks" was the original title of the first article.

The articles show that O'Neill believed in masks as such:

[63] O'Neill and Macgowan were reflecting the primitivism of the Cambridge school of comparative anthropology influenced by Nietzsche. Michael Anderson writes: "Drama as ritual is an aesthetic theory, thinly disguised as scientific doctrine. . . . What, finally, links *The Birth of Tragedy*, the work of the Cambridge school and (in part) the later writings of Jung, is a sense that drama-as-ritual restores the possibility of religious experience in a world that has abandoned faith" ("Dionysus and the Cultured Policeman," T36, pp. 102-03). According to Nietzsche, the Greeks experienced "an exultant feeling of one-ness with nature" (*ibid.*, p. 101); parallels with O'Neill are obvious.

[64] Macgowan, *The Theatre of Tomorrow*, p. 265.

"Looked at from even the most practical standpoint of the practicing playwright, the mask *is* dramatic in itself, *has always* been dramatic in itself, *is* a proven weapon of attack. At its best, it is more subtly, imaginatively, suggestively dramatic than any actor's face can ever be" [original in italics].[65] For the doubting Thomas he recommends studies in Japanese, Chinese, or African masks (but fails to mention a certain book in which photographs of these might be seen). Secondly, he repents for not having used the masks even more widely. The apparitions in *The Emperor Jones*, Yank's fellow seamen from the opening of Scene iv in *The Hairy Ape*, secondary figures in *All God's Chillun Got Wings*, and the people of the East in *Marco Millions*—all these should have been masked to fulfill different functions. Why not? we may answer; yet the themes of these plays come through clearly enough even without the special device, and O'Neill's second thoughts might have led only to over-obviousness, a constant risk in his case.

O'Neill's enthusiasm has now turned toward a purely psychological use of masks: "For I hold more and more surely to the conviction that the use of masks will be discovered eventually to be the freest solution of the modern dramatist's problem as to how—with the greatest possible dramatic clarity and economy of means—he can express those profound hidden conflicts of the mind which the probings of psychology continue to disclose to us. He must find some method to present this inner drama in his work, or confess himself incapable of portraying one of the most characteristic preoccupations and uniquely significant, spiritual impulses of his time."[66]

O'Neill still believes in psychoanalysis and in "spirituality." What he has more or less lost is his faith in Nietzsche, in paganism. The German is "the hero in such plays as *The Great God Brown* and *Dynamo* but the villain in *Days With-*

[65] Cargill *et al.*, p. 117. "Memoranda on Masks" is used as an over-all title for the three articles.
[66] *Ibid.*, p. 116.

198

out End," Broussard remarks.[67] As far as the philosophical implications are concerned, the finished version of *Days Without End* is, in a curious way, the antipode of *The Great God Brown*. "But, on the other hand," the wicked half of its hero reasons, not without nostalgia, "I'll grant you the pseudo-Nietzschean savior I just evoked out of my past is an equally futile ghost. Even if he came, we'd only send him to the insane asylum for teaching that we should have a nobler aim for our lives than getting all four feet in a trough of swill" (P III 543). But in the final scene we meet the victorious better half of the hero in a church, in front of a Cross with a life-size Christ.[68] This is now the place and the situation where Lazarus laughs: "Life laughs with God's love again! Life laughs with love!" (P III 567).

In *The Great God Brown* we met confusion—in the structure, in the functions of the masks, in almost every aspect of the play. *Days Without End* is a play interesting and controversial primarily from the viewpoint of O'Neill's "*Weltanschauung.*"[69] Technically, it is smooth, though its use of the stage is not particularly imaginative or inventive: a few

[67] Broussard, *American Drama*, p. 11. To Brustein, *Days Without End* "exposes the author's growing doubts about his own capacities as a modern Evangelist . . . for O'Neill, as for Strindberg, organized religion is only a way station on a continuing journey" (pp. 331-32).

[68] Having mentioned a number of various deities in O'Neill, Raleigh remarks: "Only at the end of *Days Without End* does He exist in a meaningful and complete sense for the total dramatic world created" (p. 9).

[69] Doris V. Falk has described O'Neill's progress through eight versions of manuscript toward a solution that has been taken mostly as overt Catholicism: "Follow these and you will see him at every turn rejecting the supernatural for the natural, while each step only brings him closer to his final reluctant and skeptical capitulation" (*Eugene O'Neill and the Tragic Tension*, p. 149: reprinted in Cargill *et al.*, p. 419). O'Neill's fluctuating opinions on the finale are described in detail by the Gelbs (pp. 763-65). Waith takes a sensible view of the matter: "Which solution to the philosophical problems O'Neill himself might have chosen at this period of his life I would not presume to guess. He was obviously capable of imagining several"—out of which he chose a dramatic one, Waith says ("An Exercise in Unmasking," p. 186).

scenic units are employed in a purposeful way. John Anderson was right in his contemporary observation that "O'Neill returns to a mixture of the *Strange Interlude* technique and the mask business of *The Great God Brown*."[70] The latter is now handled properly; yet O'Neill hardly expresses any "profound hidden conflicts," which he set as the task of modern dramatists in his "Memoranda." Rather, the schematic conflict between John, the erring searcher, and Loving, his tempter to nihilism, strikes one as a repetition of the age-old controversy between heroes and villains.[71] The play can also be taken as "O'Neill's version of the Faust legend";[72] the phrase is used by Doris V. Falk together with a reference to a passage in the "Memoranda."

This time the playwright's agreement with the audience about the masks is carefully ratified and remains unbroken throughout the play. The opening of the very first scene is obviously the decisive phase. The lights are concentrated on the figures of John and Loving, then spread imperceptibly to penetrate the whole office. John is the hero, Loving his surname and shadow: "He is the same age, of the same height and figure, is dressed in every detail exactly the same. His hair is the same. . . . Loving's face is a mask whose features reproduce exactly the features of John's face—the death mask of a John who has died with a sneer of scornful mockery on his lips" (P III 493-94). Loving corresponds to the mask of Dion, John to what was behind it. After the controversy between these two has been established in the first speeches, O'Neill was ready with the last article of the agreement. A third character makes his entrance to indicate how

[70] Cargill *et al.*, p. 201: reprinted from the *New York Evening Journal*, Jan. 9, 1934.

[71] When *Days Without End* was produced in Sweden as a radio play in 1958, John and Loving were played by the same actor. Gierow calls O'Neill's technique "unnecessarily demonstrative": it meant discharging the tension, not charging it (*Introduktioner till Eugene O'Neills dramatik*, p. 34). Cf. Gunnar Hallingberg, *Radiodramat*, p. 243. Blackburn ("Continental Influences," p. 133) and Koischwitz (p. 145) compare the play with *Der Spiegelmensch* (*Mirror-Man*) by Franz Werfel.

[72] Doris V. Falk, *Eugene O'Neill and the Tragic Tension*, p. 147.

John and Loving are taken by the rest of the cast: "His eyes pass over Loving without seeing him. He does not see him now or later. He sees and hears only John, even when Loving speaks. And it will be so with all the characters" (P III 496).

O'Neill employs this new modification of the masks so that he can write externalized fluctuating monologues in those scenes where John and Loving are tête-à-tête. In the other scenes he adds another facet in order to guarantee even there the emphatic position of monologues: John is planning to write a novel, and under the slight guise of telling its plot, he has, in fact, free hands to follow his inner compulsion and reveal his dilemma.[73] Again, fluctuation is furnished by sardonic remarks from Loving. These two special innovations, the masked Loving and the novel, make it possible for O'Neill to indulge in modified monologues in their typical form.

"Plot for a novel" also plays an important role in the plot of this play. It is used as a subtitle for three out of four acts; in these John gradually discloses his adultery to his wife who has high ideals of their marriage. The hero of the novel wishes his wife dead. Elsa Loving senses the obvious parallel between the novel and reality; she goes walking in the rain while convalescing from a chill and gets pneumonia. After that John is caught between two fires: the faith of his youth is personalized by Father Baird, his uncle and former guardian, who is little more than another sector of his personality, a counterweight to Loving. The task of the Father is to listen to John's confessional and to ejaculate "Jack!" whenever Loving has made an exceptionally blasphemous remark; all gradations of reproof in his voice are tried.

In one scene O'Neill falls again into the "thought-aside" technique proper. At the end of IV, i, shortly before John's final resolution to go to church and pray, the conflict within his (or their) mind has become so intense and personal that O'Neill could no longer make it known to the other characters on the stage in the form of intertwined speeches from John and Loving. Instead, he freezes the doctor and the

[73] Braem (*Eugene O'Neill*, p. 108) sees in the novel a kind of mask.

nurse: "There is a pause of silent immobility in the room" (P III 561)—as there was in the original production of *Strange Interlude* whenever anyone spoke his thoughts. Elsa takes part in the controversy with a few exclamations, but the doctor and the nurse remain frozen.

Idealization of central characters was a youthful feature in O'Neill, markedly so near the end of his career. In *The Great God Brown* the victim of glorification was Dion; this time it is Elsa. She is a bit of a bore—so very sweet and understanding in her scene with her guilty friend Lucy. As a contrast, the Earth Mother has fared rather badly: she has turned into a middle-aged adulteress. "She is still an extremely attractive woman but, in contrast to Elsa, her age shows, in spite of a heavy make-up. There are wrinkles about her eyes" (P III 515). Such is the price of sin.

The unit of the living room is employed in the setting, as well as a removable wall in IV, i. When Father Baird speaks of an apparition he had in front of the crucifix, he uses an expression we know from *Lazarus Laughed*: "His face seemed alive as a living man's would be, but radiant with eternal life, too, especially the sad, pitying eyes" (P III 507). In his search for strange gods O'Neill has now turned away from the dynamo and Dionysus, from Cybele and Buddha; what remains as before are his scenic means of expression. In the church scene we meet a familiar arrangement: "A side wall runs diagonally back from left, front, two-thirds of the width of the stage, where it meets an end wall that extends back from right, front" (P III 564). There is a door in the end wall. This is not an imprisoning arrangement, but relieving, encouraging, even in its proportions. If the right wall covered two-thirds of the width, we should be in a prison. And the effect is, of course, accentuated by "spiritual" lighting: Loving has hardly fallen dead in front of Christ (and John), when the sun also rises, and "the light of the dawn on the stained glass windows swiftly rises to a brilliant intensity of crimson and green and gold" (P III 566). All the figures in this scenic image, Christ, John, and Loving, form a cross.

It is not altogether impossible that O'Neill may have been influenced, perhaps on the level of unconscious memories, by a clever little play by Alice Gerstenberg called *Overtones*. It was copyrighted in 1913, first produced by the Washington Square Players in 1915, and published in 1921. In this one-act play the lady playwright uses expert knowledge to sketch two pictures of ladies, both with their social and private egos. As in *Days Without End*, the roles are played by separate actors: so we have Harriet and her counterpart or overtone Hetty; Margaret and her primitive self Maggie. Hetty and Maggie are scarfed or veiled when they play their roles in public. As in O'Neill's play, the temporary convention is carefully created in the beginning of the play. Only Harriet is shown:

HETTY: Harriet. (*There is no answer*). Harriet, my other self. (*There is no answer*). My trained self.

HARRIET (*listens intently*): Yes? (*From behind Harriet's chair Hetty rises slowly.*)[74]

Gerstenberg uses her overtones mainly for ironical effect. Since she has two pairs of actresses, she can apply the technique with more variation than O'Neill. Communication is possible on three levels: between the parts of the same personality, between Harriet and Margaret, and between the lower halves—who speak the naked truth. The play proceeds cautiously toward a more complicated usage. *Overtones* is an amusing, sophisticated, and poignant playlet, a kind of five-finger exercise, as far as possible from the mental atmosphere of *Days Without End*; whether its technique had any effect on O'Neill is a matter of conjecture.

Loving's participation in the dialogue has been described above; his positions on the stage are of interest, too. Since Loving is not seen by the others, his gestures and actions can have no effect on them. He acts only by using his voice: he is the opposite of a pantomime artist. Yet in one scene O'Neill employs him as a personification of evil, suggestive because

[74] Alice Gerstenberg, *Ten One-Act Plays* (1934), pp. 37-38.

of its very presence. Loving's evil intentions are concentrated in his eyes. After John has told about the death of the wife in his "novel," he and Father Baird leave the stage, but "Loving remains, his gaze concentrated on the back of Elsa's head with a cruel, implacable intensity. She is still staring before her with the same strange fascinated dread. Then, as if in obedience to his will, she rises slowly to her feet and walks slowly and woodenly back past him and disappears in the hall . . ." (P III 541). She goes out into the rain. This is a new way of employing ghosts even for O'Neill. Elsewhere, too, O'Neill is as careful with Loving's positions as he was with those of the entire cast in *Mourning Becomes Electra*. He usually places Loving behind John, in ambush, his sneering mask easily visible to the audience. This is the strongest position, as on the stairs of the Mannon house. It is an indication of Loving's final defeat that he is compelled to relinquish this advantageous position in the church scene, where he enters "first, retreating backward before John whom he desperately, but always without touching him, endeavors to keep from entering the church. But John is stronger now and, the same look of obsessed resolution in his eyes, he forces Loving back" (P III 564).

In some aspects *Days Without End* points toward *The Iceman Cometh*. Loving sometimes forecasts Larry's grandstand in the later play: "human life is unimportant and meaningless" (P III 535). And the relation between Elsa and John resembles Hickey's marriage.[75] On the whole, however, the play represents an aftermath rather than a new start, especially in its clear but somehow dry and obvious use of the masked shadow. The message takes so focal a place that *Days Without End* is one of the most conspicuous exponents of a general feature. O'Neill was always trying to define his own relation to life in its entirety, and this relation was just as constantly full of tensions, on many occasions colored by a violent love-hate. *Problemstellung* along these lines,

[75] Martin Lamm has remarked that the husband is already here both moved and annoyed by his wife's firm belief in her ability to improve him (*Det moderna dramat*, p. 336).

generalized to the point of vagueness, led him both to valiant deeds and to embarrassing errors.[76] This time it led him into dull mediocrity. Despite the mask, *Days Without End* might have been written by a believing Catholic with half O'Neill's knowledge of the workings of the stage.

In two out of his four mask plays O'Neill tried to achieve a high style in his dialogue. He did not succeed. *All God's Chillun Got Wings*, also well controlled in its use of the stage, is the best play in this group, partly because in it a too-personal involvement was replaced by an interest in the parents of the playwright, partly because it employed that kind of "underdog" language of which O'Neill was a master. *The Great God Brown* is especially unsuccessful in its highly poetic pretensions, while the dialogue in *Days Without End* is mainly edgeless, especially in those scenes where Loving is not present (at least he furnished the dialogue with ironic twists).[77] "The Ancient Mariner," on the other hand, did not receive from O'Neill the treatment that would have given it a scenic language to match the poetry of Coleridge.

We can, in fact, find in these four plays some of the most personal (and therefore sentimental) writing in the whole canon.[78] There is more engagement than distance, there is more raw feeling than self-criticism in O'Neill's relations both to his themes and to the stage. Perhaps this is partly due to the fact that O'Neill saw the mask not only as a stage symbol, with all its tempting and unrealizable possibilities, but also as a personal emblem, concretizing something of his view

[76] "O'Neill, like Strindberg and the German expressionistic dramatists, is concerned with eternal issues" (Blackburn, "Continental Influences," p. 133).

[77] "A mystery play presupposes faith and a poetic language. Paul Claudel, the Frenchman, has both; O'Neill has neither" (Koischwitz, p. 131).

[78] According to Raleigh, *Welded* and *Days Without End* are "both, significantly, dreadful plays, two of O'Neill's worst in banality, stale rhetoric, inconclusive characterization, and a kind of embarrassing, even at this date, outpouring of the author's own thoughts and desires" (p. 132).

of the world.[79] "One's outer life passes in a solitude haunted by the masks of others; one's inner life passes in a solitude hounded by the masks of oneself,"[80] he wrote in his "Memoranda." These four plays are not only a branch of O'Neill's interest in the Macgowanesque imaginative theatre; they are also a milestone in his journey toward the inner circles of his personality.

And O'Neill had, again in a typical way, a love-hate relation toward the masks. When they were worn by the characters they usually had a pejorative connotation. Only in *The Great God Brown* was the mask something forced upon the hero by society; here O'Neill exaggerated his pitying admiration, as he exaggerated his disgust elsewhere. Perhaps he would not have been such a powerful dramatist with a strong focus in almost every play, if he had not been carried away by strong sympathies and antipathies in his least successful efforts. For the discouraged readers of his mask plays there is another consolation too: experimenting with this device was probably a necessary phase in O'Neill's development toward dynamic realism, where the masks were incorporated into dialogue.

[79] Olsson sees in the masks something central to all of O'Neill: he is a master in removing them (*Arbetare i natten*, p. 103).
[80] Cargill *et al.*, p. 117.

❦ 11 ❦

ASIDES AROUND WOMEN

WELDED, STRANGE INTERLUDE

This is primarily a chapter in the development of O'Neill's dialogue, a theme which has already been touched on. *Welded*, finished in 1923, produced in 1924, is a much less important play than *Strange Interlude* (written in 1927, produced in 1928), a somewhat outdated yet impressive achievement. Both plays show how interested O'Neill was in evolving new variations of the modified monologue, a familiar scenic unit. Both deal with problems of love and marriage. *Welded*, a play that has sometimes been called its author's very worst,[1] discusses little else: its elements are bare, its style high melodrama spiced with the mustard of expressionism.

The latter ingredient is literally visible as soon as the curtain rises. "The room is in darkness. Then a circle of light reveals Eleanor lying back on a chaise longue. . . . A door . . . is noiselessly opened and Michael comes in. (A circle of light appears with him, follows him into the room. These two circles of light, like auras of egoism, emphasize and intensify Eleanor and Michael throughout the play. There is no other lighting)" (P II 443). Preoccupied with this lighting idea, O'Neill omitted his usual careful description of the setting, specifying only a studio apartment with a stairway as the main place of action. At the very end of the play, when the Capes have reached at least a tentative exaltation, and reached it together on the top of the stairs, their arms and bodies "form together one cross" (P II 489). This scenic image is the second anti-realistic visual effect in that apartment; it might be called expressionistic with better reason

---

[1] Raleigh finds O'Neill's "worst plays" among those dealing with contemporary life: *The First Man, Welded*, and *Days Without End* (*The Plays of Eugene O'Neill*, p. 34).

than the most interesting and more independent stylistic feature in the play, the introduction of inner monologues, or, as O'Neill himself chose to call them, "thought asides."

The special arrangement demanded by this innovation is described in the stage directions: "Their [Eleanor's and Michael's] chairs are side by side, each facing front, so near that by a slight movement each could touch the other, but during the following scene they stare straight ahead and remain motionless. They speak, ostensibly to the other, but showing by their tone it is a thinking aloud to oneself, and neither appears to hear what the other has said" (P II 452). In these intertwined modified monologues Michael complains that his wife has let the outer world disturb their all-consuming love; Eleanor feels crushed because of Michael's possessiveness. After an opening act of wild fluctuations between love and hate, they both decide to kill their love by trying to love someone else. Eleanor turns to her old admirer John, Michael to a prostitute called simply "Woman."[2] Yet both discover that they cannot get rid of their love; and the play ends with a reconciliation.

Several critics have noticed that the scene which employs thought asides foreshadows *Strange Interlude*.[3] Yet (for obvious reasons) neither this scene nor the later variation in Act III have been connected with the recently published *More Stately Mansions*, in which there is a parallel arrangement: in II, iii, all the members of the triangle—mother, son, and daughter-in-law—are placed side by side like Eleanor and Michael; they fall into thought asides and steal side glances at one another: "She [the daughter-in-law] turns to stare at him with a revengeful hostility. As they meet each other's eyes, each turns away guiltily" (MSM 121). This is repeated until all possible pairs have been exhausted, like turns in an old dance.

Anticipating details are, in fact, almost all we can find of interest in *Welded*; some are twenty years ahead of their

---

[2] Omitting the names of characters was fairly common in expressionism (Mann, *Geschichte des deutschen Dramas*, p. 566).

[3] E.g. Biese, *Aspects of Expression I*, pp. 60-61.

later occurrence. There is repetition in the way the setting is combined with action. In each of the three acts (including II, i) there is a stairway, which is used as a threshold for Eleanor: she is about to ascend it with Michael when their marital peace is disturbed by the outer world; she cannot pass the first step with John; she goes all the way up in the finale to form a cross with her husband. Thematic significance gathers around the stairs as it does around the tenements in *All God's Chillun Got Wings*—or around the stairs of the Mannon house in *Mourning Becomes Electra* or the Tyrone house in *Long Day's Journey Into Night*. Doris V. Falk calls the cross a "traditionally connotative blending of sexual and religious imagery," as the passion on it "unites within itself the pain and sacrifice demanded by love."[4] It is a link to *Days Without End*, and not the only one.[5]

"I can only stutter like an idiot!" Michael exclaims, reminding one of the famous self-confession in *Long Day's Journey Into Night*. The different tones used to express the same idea are indicative of O'Neill's development. Edmund is wryly self-ironic—"I just stammered. That is the best I'll ever do" (LDJ 154)—Michael speaks "half-sobbing as the intensity of his passion breaks the spell of his exultation" (P II 488). When O'Neill matured, as a man and as an artist, he depended less and less on violent outbursts and exclamation marks;[6] instead of the former staccato tempo he developed a more quiet, flowing rhythm, fit for reminiscences. His exclamation marks were smuggled into characterization, and into his non-verbal means of expression.

The hectic, melodramatic speeches in *Welded* are a major

---

[4] Doris V. Falk, *Eugene O'Neill and the Tragic Tension*, p. 87.

[5] There are verbal parallels between *Welded* and *Days Without End*: both plays speak of marriage as "a true sacrament" (the Gelbs, *O'Neill*, p. 765). The mask is used as an indication of dead emotions in Act II, repeatedly.

[6] Carpenter speaks of emotion "so overstrained that it seldom falls below the level of hysteria," and of "the exaggerated intensity" of the dialogue (*Eugene O'Neill*, pp. 46-47). Series of exclamation marks belonged to the marks of expressionism (Sokel, *Der literarische Expressionismus*, p. 10); they are condemned as an O'Neillian means of expression by Nicoll (*World Drama*, pp. 881, 891).

reason for the failure of this play. Its closest predecessors are *Servitude*, *The First Man*, and the last act of *Bread and Butter*; and the melodrama is not transformed into anything else by using a special lighting arrangement or a few thought asides, or by contriving toward a feeling of sexual-religious exaltation.[7]

The third act does have some merit in it. But the preceding two acts of melodrama have probably so numbed the spectators' emotional sensitivity that they cannot respond to its successful aspects. Even so, it is worth mentioning here as an example of O'Neill's unevenness within a play. "We communicate in code—when neither has the other's key!" (P III 270) Dion Anthony sighs to his Margaret in *The Great God Brown*; and so it is in this scene between Eleanor and Michael, "separated by a barrier of language" (P II 480). Momentary harmonies and recurrent misunderstandings fluctuate in a way not entirely void of subtlety. The effect is spoiled toward the end of the act when a revelation, important to an understanding of the characters, is given only in a stage direction and a few ejaculations, inadequate to convey the meaning.

This is the proper place for paying attention to a friend who has been with us for a long time: August Strindberg. *Welded*, which George Jean Nathan called "very third-rate Strindberg,"[8] certainly bears the marks of O'Neill's Swedish teacher. Fleisher locates the period of strongest influence between 1918 and 1923; affinities "in their philosophy and methods of expression are clear enough to support the conclusion that Strindberg was undoubtedly a factor of impor-

[7] Leech is right: "the play veers awkwardly between realism and expressionism. We cannot accept Eleanor and Michael as convincing human beings: they posture and declaim too grotesquely for that. And they have too much personal background to achieve the elemental quality of Jones or Yank, or even of Jim Harris and Ella Downey" (*Eugene O'Neill*, p. 45).

[8] Cargill *et al.*, p. 52: from *The Intimate Notebooks of George Jean Nathan* (New York: Alfred A. Knopf, 1932). Cf. Nathan in Downer, *American Drama and Its Critics*, p. 82. *Welded* is also connected with Strindberg by Brustein (*The Theatre of Revolt*, p. 327), and Torsslow (*Eugene O'Neill*, p. 37).

tance, though he did not play as much of a role as Nietzsche.
. . . It is therefore probable that O'Neill overemphasized his
debt to Strindberg in his speech in acceptance of the Nobel
Prize in literature."[9] Even if O'Neill's words (Strindberg is
"still our leader"[10]) were a polite exaggeration, the master
did lead O'Neill to a few solutions in his use of the stage,
mentioned above, and guided him toward the mental atmosphere of *Welded*, this play of love and hatred in a marriage, centered around a woman.

The asides, woven equally around Eleanor and Michael,
come from O'Neill's own past works. He had shown an interest in the monologue from the first (*A Wife for a Life,
Bound East for Cardiff*); he had written plays consisting
merely or mostly of monologues (*Before Breakfast, Shell
Shock*); and he had ventured into monologues on special
occasions even in full-length plays, providing his soliloquizing hero with an abundance of visual and aural expression
as well (*The Emperor Jones, The Hairy Ape, The Fountain*). Two occurrences, in *'Anna Christie'* and *Diff'rent*,
mentioned (and criticized) by Kaucher,[11] come closest to
the conventional asides of the "well-made play": they are
dictated by the plot and little else.

Around 1920, fluctuations in a character's state of mind,
originally typical of emotional climaxes, were transferred to
modified monologues. By 1923 O'Neill was ready to make a
tentative effort toward a monologue that was assisted only by
the actor's individual expression; furthermore, the usage in
Welded depended entirely upon an agreement between the
playwright and his audience. Soliloquies addressed to a mask
or to a character off-stage (in *All God's Chillun Got Wings*
and *The Great God Brown*) were to follow; so was the
ironical, realistically motivated usage in *Desire Under the
Elms*. Through all of these steps he arrived at *Strange Interlude*, where thought asides are a major stylistic feature with
multiple scenic functions.

[9] Fleisher, "Strindberg and O'Neill," p. 93.
[10] The Gelbs, *O'Neill*, p. 814.
[11] Kaucher, *Modern Dramatic Structure*, p. 138.

This is how the development of O'Neill's use of the interior monologue can be seen by us with our historical perspective.[12] Credit must be given to Macgowan for his prediction in *The Theatre of Tomorrow*, two years before *Welded*, that the soliloquy and even the aside would return "as a deliberate piece of theatricalism."[13] It is also noteworthy that he mentions Gerstenberg's *Overtones*, a play that might have exercised some influence not only on *Days Without End* but also on *Strange Interlude*.[14]

A year after the original production of the latter play Macgowan published a study on "The O'Neill Soliloquy"; most of the lines of development after *Bound East for Cardiff* are gathered here. O'Neill's preoccupation with revealing inner states of mind is duly emphasized, and a connection with the masks in *The Great God Brown* is made. Macgowan also mentions previous occurrences of the monologue in stage practice and in recent plays by H. L. Mencken, Zoe Akins, and, more significantly, in Elmer Rice's expressionistic *The Adding Machine*. He concludes: "None of these attempts comes so close as O'Neill's to the consistent and illusive illumination of realism by the light of the inner mind. O'Neill's device is his own because he has worked long and painfully over it and brought it to a complete development."[15] The stage of "complete development" includes such facets as purposefulness, intricate connections with the themes of the play, and several scenic functions.

One might speak of six different functions of the interior monologue in *Strange Interlude*. They are not always clearly distinguishable, of course; sometimes they overlap, one and the same speech or sentence being appropriate to several

---

[12] In 1962, Miller was still under the influence of the astounded critical reaction. According to his summary, O'Neill's "monologue-soliloquy style exploded the bomb," "without previous warning"; yet Miller himself catalogues several earlier occurrences of monologues (*Eugene O'Neill and the American Critic*, p. 41).

[13] Macgowan, *The Theatre of Tomorrow*, p. 243.

[14] *Ibid.*, p. 249.

[15] Cargill *et al.*, pp. 452-53: from the *Theatre Guild Magazine*, Feb. 1929.

categories.[16] As in *Days Without End* O'Neill exercises great
care in establishing his new convention: the play opens with
a long monologue by Charles Marsden, starting with a few
remarks to a maid off-stage. Both layers of the dialogue are
thus employed before ten words are uttered. Marsden, an
effeminate writer of popular fiction, is in the study of his
friend Henry Leeds, a New England professor. His interior
monologue serves, first of all, what might be called function
number one: exposition materials are placed into a character's stream of consciousness.[17]

(1) We learn that Nina Leeds, the professor's only child,
has lost her fiancé Gordon two days before the armistice at
the end of World War I. The theme of Nina's obsessive love
for Gordon, a primary motive for her mental troubles, is thus
introduced right in this expository monologue.[18] The same
function is preserved in seven out of nine acts, as Engel has
remarked;[19] once, in Act III, there is a variation, as Nina
reads a letter she has just finished writing. In the last two acts
an opening monologue is unnecessary: in Act VIII the attention is at once concentrated on the exciting boat race and
there is no room for a tranquil introduction, while Act IX
begins with Nina's son Gordon, Jr., and his fiancée Madeleine, neither of whom are greatly disposed to practice introspection. Otherwise, the expository monologues are an

[16] Biese (p. 16n) quotes a classification from *Das sprachliche
Kunstwerk* by Wolfgang Kayser (p. 198): there are 1) technical, 2)
epic, 3) lyrical monologues, 4) monologues of reflection, and 5) dramatic monologues. Biese finds several of these types in *Strange Interlude* (p. 28); his viewpoint is linguistic (p. 31), his main interest in
the verbalization of "the fleeting images flowing through the mind
of the character" (p. 72). My classification has grown from the
material of this study; preferring it to that of Kayser is thus purposeful (cf. above, Chapter 2, n. 13).

[17] The dramatic functions (1), (2), and (4) characterized in this
study are mentioned by Biese, pp. 29, 65.

[18] Lawson (*Theory and Technique of Playwriting*, p. 237) has
paid attention to the opening soliloquy and the following scene between Marsden and Professor Leeds: "All the causes, the sexual
relationships and emotions, which O'Neill regards as basic, are com-
pactly presented in this scene, and lead directly to the conclusion."

[19] Engel, *The Haunted Heroes of Eugene O'Neill*, p. 225.

economic means of handling the rather complicated machinery. This is a "plotty" play; the action is full of twists, and the spectators are, naturally enough, always anxious for news of the heroine.

(2) The very same opening monologue is an introduction not only to the plot but also to the character of the speaker. In a manner embarrassing in its straightforwardness O'Neill lets his novelist fall into reminiscing about a painful childhood experience in a brothel (P I 6). A key to one of the central characters is thus given, engaging the attention of the spectators right away. This is how some of the elements that might be called epic are utilized throughout the play: by telling about themselves and others the characters keep defining their own character.[20]

(3) A major purpose of this special technique is, of course, to show the conflict between a character's thoughts and his spoken words; it might be called the social or "mask" function of the asides.[21] Ironic contrasts are constantly built, especially around the credulous figure of Sam Evans, Nina's husband. Marsden and Ned Darrell, Nina's lover, play truthful friends to him, at the same time calling him a simpleton in their minds. Inner thoughts reveal a character's real feelings—of love, hatred, or disgust—not "censored by decorum."[22]

(4) With the help of this device O'Neill had his hands free to indulge in continuous fluctuations in the minds of his characters. This is one of the strongest links to the previous usage in O'Neill: his thought asides are only a variation, stylized

[20] Olsson speaks of O'Neill as "a hunter of secret motives" and of the erotic problem treated in *Strange Interlude* "with cold-blooded, harsh, clinical matter-of-factness" (*Arbetare i natten*, p. 110).

[21] The masks and asides are connected by Engel (p. 224), Koischwitz (p. 42), and Robert E. Spiller (*The Third Dimension*, p. 184). John Anderson calls the asides and the accompanying halt of all motion "a cumbersome, and sometimes a ridiculously awkward procedure," yet "splendid for comedy, since the blurting out of hidden feelings provides an edge of rudeness that is inescapably funny in the theatre" (Miller, *Playwright's Progress*, p. 58: reprinted from the *New York Evening Journal*, Jan. 31, 1928).

[22] Engel, p. 225.

to the extreme, of his modified monologues. They arise mainly out of inner compulsion; or, they are a meeting place of outer impetus and inner quality of character, more honestly so than ordinary dialogue. Instead of relieving the inhibitions of his characters by fear or drunkenness, O'Neill was able to resort to his self-created theatre convention. In the case of Marsden, who has the greatest inclination to self-analysis and who plays a kind of raisonneur in the play, the fluctuations frequently take the form of an inner dialogue: "but he [Sam] might be good for Nina . . . if she were married to this simpleton would she be faithful? . . . and then I? . . . what a vile thought! . . . I don't mean that! . . ." (P I 33). Marsden has a censor even for his silent thoughts. And although the entire play was for O'Neill an opportunity to write monologues not heard by anyone else on the stage, he could not resist the temptation of writing a "traditional" modified monologue, emphasizing the solitude of Marsden even more strongly. When the poor novelist, this time actually drunk, proposes to Nina in a speech that is more courageous than his earlier thoughts, "Nina pays no attention to him" (P I 177).

(5) As a result of this fluctuation, the relations between the characters are paradoxically inconsistent. Basically, *Strange Interlude* is a play about a constellation of characters; it is thus important to see what the relations between the members of this group are like. No one can ever be certain of the feelings of his neighbors: he or she can only silently ask, doubt, and suffer.[23] The thought asides are a primary means of expressing the typically O'Neillian theme of *"odi et amo."* What was expressed by violent, melodramatic outer action in *Welded* is here turned into a flow of incessant questioning. The only person who has no doubts is Sam Evans, a potential psychopath: he is certain of everyone's love, yet he has

[23] Feelings of alienation and lack of contact are mentioned as a motivation for the thought asides by Braem (*Eugene O'Neill*, p. 47) and Peter Szondi (*Theorie des modernen Dramas*, p. 117). Arnold Goldman has explored the fluctuation in O'Neill's dialogue, its causes and effects in *Strange Interlude* and elsewhere (John Russell Brown and Bernard Harris [eds.], *American Theatre*, pp. 29-39).

only their pity. This touch of irony is not apt to make the life of self-sacrificing Nina and Ned more convenient. Young Gordon, even if he later develops into a healthy, lovable college boy, has his share of suffering in his dilemma between Sam, his official father, and Ned, his real father and his mother's lover: "I wish Darrell'd get out of here! . . . what's he always hanging 'round for?" (P I 138).

(6) The fifth task helped us to make a connecting link with a major theme in the play; the last but not least function can be combined with the total structure of *Strange Interlude*. Thoughts heard by the audience but not by other characters on the stage help to create an atmosphere of secrecy. When will this mystery be revealed? Or will it remain secret? O'Neill proceeds in this play as if he were constructing a mine field. In early halves of Acts I–IV he lays minor mines, one in each act; they are then allowed to explode in the latter halves. They are: the interference of Professor Leeds with the love affair between Nina and Gordon; Nina's promiscuity in the hospital; the hereditary madness in Sam's family; Nina's plan to use Ned as an ersatz father in order to have the child Sam and Nina needed. The last of these mines explodes when Sam is off-stage; his ignorance means that the biggest mine is laid. It is never allowed to explode, but it charges the atmosphere of the remaining five acts with tension.[24] In Act VI little Gordon almost guesses part of the truth; in Act IX it is revealed to him, but he misunderstands it. Marsden is clever enough to suspect that there is a skeleton in the cupboard; its exact location is disclosed to him in Act VIII.

Seeing this as the basic formula of the entire play, we can now have a closer look at the positions given to thought asides within the acts. The expository function of the asides explains why seven acts are opened with a monologue. Moreover, when a character has made his entrance, he is usually granted an opportunity to reveal his present state of mind;

[24] "There is enough in the air to cause an explosion in any moment; yet there is no explosion. . . . It is a walk along the edge of dangerous, enticing precipices" (Koischwitz, pp. 121-22).

each has a minor exposition scene. Another principle followed is that as the characters get closer to the mines, and thus as the tension increases, so does the frequency and length of the inner monologues. After the explosion or repression of the secret, there is a calming down and a tendency toward ordinary dialogue; if the acts are closed with thought asides, their tone is not as anxiously questioning as before the climaxes.

The thought asides are on the stage for a large part of the playing time of *Strange Interlude*, fulfilling these six functions: they help expositions and characterization; they serve as the unmasked face, as modified monologues, and as a means to express conflicts between love and hate; they create secrets. In so doing they interact with ordinary dialogue, with movements of the characters, with the setting; their position is so prominent that Edmond M. Gagey has reason to remark that "O'Neill employed the regular dialogue to supplement the asides, rather than vice versa."[25] Their form is, not surprisingly, rhapsodic; these incomplete sentences, following one another in disjointed sequences according to the principle of more or less free association, grow quite naturally out of O'Neill's previous dialogue.[26] Whatever their percentage—the novelty of the technique tends to underline their role—they are an integral part of the play.

There are three acts in *Strange Interlude* in which the setting acquires an important function. In Act III the ghastly atmosphere of the Evans homestead is created by references in the dialogue and by the setting: "The wall paper, a repulsive brown, is stained at the ceiling line with damp blotches of mildew, and here and there has started to peel back where the strips join . . . the light from the window . . . is cheerless

[25] Edmond M. Gagey, *Revolution in American Drama*, p. 56.
[26] "The sentences are often of a rather incoherent nature, being made up of loosely connected word-groups. Nominal clauses occur very often . . . the loose syntax employed is often admirably suited to the presentation of the rapid succession of images that come and pass through a person's mind, one image and thought leading to another" (Biese, p. 21).

217

and sickly" (P I 48). This is another of O'Neill's old family houses, inhabited by the ghosts of the past—like the Cabot farm or the Mannon house.[27]

In all of the other acts the furniture is arranged according to a certain formula. There is a table with two chairs at center, toward left, a chair at the back, and a bench at right; despite variations in the details, the relation between these pieces of furniture remains constant. Through this arrangement O'Neill guarantees to each of his leading characters a certain area of action, typical of him or her. Or of his heir: after Professor Leeds's death his chair and role are inherited by Marsden in two key scenes with Ned and Nina (P I 34, 39), anticipating the final solution of the play. When Sam has insured his position as master of the house, he is given this place at the table; and even if there is, naturally enough, some elasticity in the positions, the basic areas are utilized so frequently that they gather thematic significance. The attention of the audience is concentrated on these areas in the first of the two memorable scenic images in the entire play: at the end of Act VI O'Neill gathers all of Nina's men into a family portrait, as it were.[28]

This is the scenic image in which the cast of *Strange Interlude* is shown in a state of equilibrium,[29] in the embrace of fate; each of the men is sitting on his chair, while "Nina remains standing, dominating them," and having triumphant thoughts: "My three men! . . . I feel their desires converge in

[27] To Carpenter, the plot of *Strange Interlude* is "artificially contrived" at the point of Sam's hereditary illness: "And this device of insanity is truly arbitrary and romantic, resembling *Jane Eyre* and the old Gothic novels rather than modern realistic fiction" (p. 73).

[28] The emphasis of the play is on "the whole group" of characters (Alan D. Mickle, *Six Plays of Eugene O'Neill* [1929], p. 159). The famous group scene is praised e.g. by Carpenter (p. 126) and Howard Taubman who calls it "a triumph of theatre magic" (Miller, p. 174: reprinted from the *New York Times*, March 1, 1964). Koischwitz compares it with the end of *Erdgeist* by Frank Wedekind and concludes that Nina is a version of Lulu made commonplace (p. 140).

[29] Peacock sees in a constellation of characters a typical feature in all drama (*The Art of Drama*, p. 160).

me! . . . to form one complete beautiful male desire which I absorb . . . and am whole . . ." (P I 133, 135). It is an exceptional scene, in this play full of disharmonies: here Nina is for a passing moment whole,[30] with her husband, lover, father substitute, and little Gordon, growing in her body. All essential elements from the preceding acts are present. It is also a scene in which the thought asides play an active role: each of the men is given a chance to express his innermost thoughts, which, even in the case of Ned, are to a certain extent conciliatory. And it is a scene which has a strong focusing effect, ultimately on our total impression of the play: "A whole woman somehow emerges from the different elements of this chronicle of fixations and frustrations,"[31] Gassner writes. It does, in this scenic image.

As a contrast, Act VIII is full of dissatisfaction and conflicts. It is interesting to note that O'Neill harked all the way back to *Abortion* (1913-14) when constructing this effective act. There is a connection even in the subject matter: both the early one-act play and this decisive act deal with sports as a feature of college life, and do so in an ironical vein. The cast of *Strange Interlude* is gathered on board Sam's motor cruiser to watch young Gordon row his team to victory. In building a scenic image at the end of the act O'Neill resorts to a repetitive sound effect which increases in intensity, as he did in *Abortion* and in *The Emperor Jones*: "The whistles and sirens from the yachts up the river begin to be heard. This grows momentarily louder as one after another other yachts join in the chorus as the crews approach nearer and nearer until toward the close of the scene there is a perfect pandemonium of sound" (P I 176).

The tension of the race corresponds to the tensions of the characters present; the effects carry the themes. Nina especially is in a state of nervous excitement, as she is about

---

[30] "But since one of the themes of the play is the instability of human relations, Nina's felicity cannot last, and if she is always the magnet for the males, the steel filings are always, kaleidoscope-like, rearranging themselves." (Raleigh, *The Plays of Eugene O'Neill*, p. 136).

[31] Gassner, *Masters of the Drama*, p. 656.

to lose Gordon, her only consolation after Ned left. The whole act is based on a series of contrasts and tensions: between the members of the familiar quadrangle, Nina—Marsden—Sam—Ned; between Nina and Madeleine whose situation is similar to that of Nina's at the beginning of the play; between old Gordon and young Gordon, a loser and a winner; and between what Marsden has written all his life and what he plans to write now, encouraged by his proposal to Nina and by several drinks. The discussion moves closer than ever to the major concealed mine; yet there is no explosion. Nina reveals the family secret only to Marsden, and everyone's attention is caught by the sudden death of Sam who, ironically enough, had only the tension of the race to endure. This is the final double irony in his story, the tale of a weakling who governed his surroundings by his very weakness.[32]

Death is present throughout this act, represented by Marsden's mourning costume. Engel is undoubtedly right in his interpretation of this detail in Act IX: in marrying Marsden Nina "shall be wedded to her father, to death."[33] Moreover, as the same scholar has pointed out, the black costume worn by Marsden was already associated in Act V with death and father: "Black . . . in the midst of happiness . . . black comes . . . again . . . death . . . my father . . . comes between me and happiness! . . ." (P I 98). Nina's addresses to God the Father or God the Mother are not, as a rule, well integrated with the rest of the play; they add to it a conspicuous literary layer. Yet in this particular case the symbolism "belongs"; Act VIII is the decisive phase, where the solution is already present, Act IX only a necessary epilogue, with its reconciliation to death.

O'Neill is a careful and patient builder of drama in *Strange Interlude.* "Part I gives us the gradual establishment of a

[32] ". . . it is the ironies of time that are exhibited by the plot of *Strange Interlude.* . . . For nothing ever turns out as expected, and the future, as it unfolds, often turns out to be a kind of grim joke on the past" (Raleigh, p. 188).
[33] Engel, p. 209. Cf. Koischwitz, p. 96.

stable situation," Leech remarks, "Part II shows us the tolerable anguish that the passing years bring to it."[34] The extreme duration demanded by this building project compels us to face, for the first time, a dilemma that might be called the paradox of O'Neillian length.[35] One has an awkward feeling that the script needs cutting down—and at the same time an opposite suspicion that considerable cutting would lead from bad to worse: the play would lose its individual qualities, which have been achieved through a careful piling up of details. Where to draw the border line? A drastically shortened radio version of *Strange Interlude* certainly lost its flavor; there was nothing left but a mediocre triangle or quadrangle melodrama.

Yet *Strange Interlude* is not the most troublesome case in the O'Neill canon; one might shorten it. Its basic fault is that conventional elements are used in characterization.[36] The melodrama is there, albeit disguised by the resourceful aside technique and elements of real value. Nina has been called both "one of the great tragic figures in world literature"[37] and "in some ways a classic example of the soap-opera heroine."[38] The Gelbs, responsible for the latter definition, come closer to the truth; nor is Ned much more than a truthful romantic admirer, just as comfortable a solution to the playwright as John in *Welded*.[39] Without meaning it,

[34] Leech, p. 79.

[35] "The art of the theater, in every age, is the art of preparations; and the art of the epic . . . is as well" (Stoll, *Shakespeare and Other Masters*, p. 393). *Long Day's Journey* shows O'Neill's ability to handle his themes as if they were motives in a composition, and *Strange Interlude* is a step in this direction.

[36] To Taubman, writing about the 1964 revival of *Strange Interlude*, the play "is fatally flawed by the incredibility of its central character"; its asides are "pretentious and archaic" (Miller, p. 173). Brustein complains that the soliloquies, "instead of going deeper into the unconscious mind, merely compound the verbalized trivialities of the characters with their trivial unspoken thoughts" (p. 327).

[37] Gustav Kirchner, "Eugene Gladstone O'Neill (1888-1953)," *Zeitschrift für Anglistik und Amerikanistik*, 2 (1954), 157.

[38] The Gelbs, p. 628.

[39] Alexander, calling *Strange Interlude* "a play that consistently reflects Schopenhauer's ideas," criticizes an omission: "At no time

O'Neill wrote popular successes, both in *The Great God Brown* and in *Strange Interlude*: imagine a woman being married to a stranger under the mask of her husband! What an altruistic motive Nina has for her adultery!

The valuable elements are partly bound to the use of thought asides, analyzed above, partly to the two scenic images, likewise described, and to Nina's characterization. It was probably a surprise to O'Neill's contemporaries that the technique of thought asides was not adopted by other playwrights and that O'Neill himself employed it only twice thereafter; even in the case of *More Stately Mansions* it is doubtful whether he would have kept the thought asides in the finished version.[40] A twofold explanation is possible: after O'Neill's major success with asides, other playwrights may have avoided using them for fear of being accused of plagiarism; or perhaps they were simply not as interested as O'Neill in compulsive modified monologues. O'Neill himself came to understand, after the failure of *Dynamo*, that the scenic functions of the asides were so intimately bound together with the themes of *Strange Interlude* that a repetition of the procedure would be, if not downright impossible, at least difficult.

In *Dynamo* O'Neill employed thought asides in ways familiar to us. There are examples of fluctuation and self-analysis in Reuben's thoughts: "I'm glad she's dead! . . . (*Then immediately remorseful*) No! . . . I don't mean that, Mother . . ." (P III 471). Exposition materials are conveyed with this device, and there are occasional contrasts between verbal expression and hidden thoughts. Yet the general impression is one of looseness, created especially by scenes in

---

does O'Neill present Darrell in a genuine conflict between love and work" ("*Strange Interlude* and Schopenhauer," pp. 220, 218). Cf. Chapter 9, n. 11.

[40] According to Gierow, the asides are fit for a radio performance rather than for the stage. What there is between the words should not be spoken; what is only dimly visible, should not be pointed out (*Introduktioner*, p. 19). Biese thinks that O'Neill might have found the new technique "more or less unsatisfactory from the point of view of actual production on the stage" (p. 68).

which characters continue soliloquizing by themselves.[41] There are sequences of several consecutive thought asides by characters in different parts of the setting in I, ii-iv; in these cases the thought asides have lost contact with ordinary dialogue and have changed into asides proper. It is no wonder that O'Neill wrote in his working diary, published after the opening of *Mourning Becomes Electra*: "Warning! —always hereafter regard with suspicion hangover inclination to use 'Interlude' technique regardless—that was what principally hurt 'Dynamo,' being forced into thought-asides method which was quite alien to essential psychological form of its characters—did not ring true—"[42] This may be taken as a qualified epitaph to the thought asides, written by their inventor himself. It is worth noticing, however, that this technique, with all its flexibility, was more appropriate to his needs than the awkward, mechanical masks which did not allow for any gradations.[43] In *Strange Interlude* O'Neill took several steps toward his late dialogue.

As to the real elements in Nina's characterization, it seems probable that there are closer parallels between *Strange Interlude* and *Long Day's Journey Into Night* than has heretofore been assumed. The tragic and believable elements in Nina's fate have affinities with the tragedy experienced by Mary. Both Nina and Mary married men who were economic successes but did not make their wives happy; there is a family curse involved; Nina is apt to flee into strange mental states, Mary into her dope dreams; both return to their childhood worlds; and one of Nina's sighs comes strikingly close to Mary's final speech in *Long Day's Journey*

[41] Percy Hammond accuses O'Neill of having overdone the "aside" device in *Dynamo* (Miller, 65: reprinted from the *New York Herald Tribune*, Feb. 12, 1929).

[42] Clark (ed.), *European Theories of the Drama* (1947), p. 534: a reprinting of "Working Notes and Extracts from a Fragmentary Work Diary" by O'Neill, originally published in the *New York Herald Tribune*, Nov. 3, 1931.

[43] Cf. Whitman, "O'Neill's Search," p. 162: "the free use of asides gives the dramatist a flexibility largely lacking in drama tied to externals."

Into Night: "when I was a girl . . . when I was happy . . . before I fell in love with Gordon Shaw and all this tangled mess of love and hate and pain and birth began . . ." (P I 191; LDJ 176). Perhaps some of the obvious contriving in *Strange Interlude*, resulting in the incredible piling up of misfortunes on Nina, comes from the simple fact that in 1927 O'Neill did not yet dare to face his dead squarely and had to invent a plot which had nothing whatsoever to do with the life of his mother. The consequence was realism mixed with melodrama, a by-now familiar combination.

Strange Interlude has been called "a monument of psychoanalytic literature."[44] This may be true; but the play is not a monument of literature. The characters O'Neill dissected with his new tool, invented as a result of his lasting interest in modified monologues, were not deep enough. Still, there are encouraging signs in *Strange Interlude*: O'Neill is now convalescing from his romantic dream of the imaginative theatre, and his relation to psychology is based more soundly than before on a factual basis. Though uneven, the play has both resourcefulness and a kind of dogged impressiveness: it surpasses most of O'Neill's other plays in the twenties.

[44] Sievers, *Freud on Broadway*, p. 118.

12

ELECTRA ENTERS THE HOUSE

MOURNING BECOMES ELECTRA

Desire Under the Elms was O'Neill's synthetic play of the early twenties; *Mourning Becomes Electra* (1931) holds the corresponding position in his next phase, extending to the early thirties. There are familiar solutions in the setting; there are a few soliloquies, a preoccupation with the masks, and an interest in the elemental passions of type characters, mindful of expressionism.[1] Most conspicuously, the trilogy is O'Neill's Greek tragedy. This time he faced the problems of adaptation squarely, confessing his debt to the *Oresteia* even in the title of his play. A question immediately arises: what does a modern playwright do with this age-old plot? In a way, this entire chapter is an effort to answer this question; and the starting point is given by O'Neill himself.

"Working Notes and Extracts from a Fragmentary Work Diary" or "O'Neill's Story of 'Electra' in the Making" is a source of primary interest. In the first entry, spring 1926, O'Neill speculates about the possibility of getting "modern psychological approximation of Greek sense of fate" into a play. In 1928 he calls it a weakness in the preserved ancient drama that "there is no play about Electra's life after the murder of Clytemnestra." Somewhat later he chose the American Civil War as the historical background for his adaptation, because that war possesses "sufficient mask of time and space," and New England as the place of action, because of its "Puritan conviction of man born to sin and punishment." Having finished the first version he wrote, most significantly from our viewpoint, that there was "not enough

---

[1] Friedrich Brie sees, slightly one-sidedly, *Mourning Becomes Electra* as "a typical expressionistic problem play" in which time and location play no role ("Eugene O'Neill als Nachfolger der Griechen," p. 48).

225

of sense of fate hovering over characters, fate of family—living in the house built by Atreus' hatred (Abe Mannon)—a psychological fate . . . in next version I must correct this at all costs . . . use every means to gain added depth and scope. . . ."[2] Not all of the means subsequently employed in the eight manuscript versions were retained in the final one. O'Neill tried and discarded masks, thought asides, and a new modification which he called "stylized soliloquies." Those means which were preserved are, of course, of greater interest to us. To begin with, how was the house employed "to gain added depth and scope"?

"It is a large building of the Greek temple type that was the vogue in the first half of the nineteenth century," we read in the "General Scene of the Trilogy." "A white wooden portico with six tall columns contrasts with the wall of the house proper which is of gray cut stone. . . . Before the doorway a flight of four steps leads from the ground to the portico." The house is stately and isolated;[3] a special curtain shows the house as seen from the street; it is drawn away to reveal "the exterior of the house in the opening act" (P II 2). The house itself is entered in the following acts. At the opening of Part One, "Homecoming," the afternoon sun is used for a preliminary effect: "The white columns cast black bars of shadow on the gray wall behind them. . . . The temple portico is like an incongruous white mask fixed on the house to hide its somber gray ugliness." A big pine tree at the corner of the house is "a black column in striking contrast to the white columns of the portico" (P II 5). To summarize the arrangements: additional depth is achieved by establishing a parallel to one of the traditional performing areas of Greek tragedy, in front of a temple,[4] and by associations to

[2] Clark (ed.), *European Theories*, pp. 534-35.
[3] Gierow calls the house a symbol for the fate of the Mannons: life is outside, both attracting and terrifying them. Indoors, they have what must be kept secret; this results in hypocrisy, self-satisfaction and isolation. The refusal of life conceives its own revenge: there is death up to the third and fourth generation (*Introduktioner*, pp. 27-28).
[4] "Of the three scene-doors likewise the middle opened either into

the prison and to a concealing mask. The isolation and social stature of the Mannons are suggested, and there are tensions between different parts of the setting.

This exterior and several interiors of the house continually
interact with other scenic means of expression. The outdoor
setting is structurally of special importance: Parts Two and
Three are both opened and closed with it, Part One only
opened. The key phases of action occur at the door and on
the stairs: these are the areas which gather thematic significance, while the rest of the setting is a framework, suggestive and variable in different acts. It is noteworthy that both
Christine, O'Neill's Clytemnestra, and Lavinia, his Electra,
enter the stage through that door, and are thus seen by the
audience for the first time at the top of the stairs. Their
entrances are further dramatized by the chorus of townspeople who appear at the beginning of each part to show how the
community at large reacts to the Mannons: "That's her!"
a gossip-monger "whispers excitedly" (P II 8), when Christine is seen. And when Lavinia comes out of the house
through the same door a few minutes later, a parallel and a
contrast between these two women is immediately established.
They are rivals for the favors of Aegisthus, Captain Adam
Brant.

In his descriptions of the outer appearance of mother and
daughter O'Neill hints at several themes developed later on.
Christine "has a fine, voluptuous figure and she moves with
a flowing animal grace. She wears a green satin dress . . .
which brings out the peculiar color of her thick curly hair,
partly a copper brown, partly a bronze gold" (P II 9). La-

---

a palace, grotto, hall, or whatever was of first distinction in the play;
the right-hand door was a retreat for the next in rank; and the
left . . . led to some desolate temple, or had no house" (Pollux in
Onomastikon: Nagler, *A Source Book in Theatrical History* [1959],
p. 8). O'Neill reserved the right and left "scene-doors," likewise, for
the less important exits and entrances: the characters walked around
the corners of the Mannon house. Cf. George Freedley and John A.
Reeves, *A History of the Theatre* (1958), p. 27: "the three doors
were in the back wall and there were steps in front of this terrace-like
playing space which led down into the orchestra where the chorus
remained."

vinia is both unlike and similar; similar by nature, unlike because of a stiffness mindful of her father: "She has a flat dry voice and a habit of snapping out her words like an officer giving orders" (P II 10). Both Christine and her daughter wear the pale mask-like make-up typical of all members of the house of Mannon. Characterization is here expressed in colors and stage action, in distinct ways of moving or speaking. Christine represents the vital rebellious spirit of the flesh, Lavinia the repressive Puritan (and Mannon) death-in-life motif.[5]

The mask-like faces, a vehicle for this theme, are mentioned again and again in the stage directions. O'Neill arrived at this solution after discarding the masks proper, together with his "stylized soliloquies." The latter retarded the action unnecessarily, O'Neill complains in his diary—perhaps echoing his final dissatisfaction with the production of *Strange Interlude*. The half-masks, on the other hand, introduced "an obvious duality-of-character symbolism quite outside" his intent in these plays. Consequently, he pushed the masks into the background by ordering faces which only resembled masks: "what I want from this mask concept is a dramatic arresting visual symbol of the separateness, the fated isolation of this family . . . —I can visualize the death-mask-like expression of characters' faces in repose suddenly being torn open by passion as extraordinarily effective—moreover, its exact visual representation of what I want expressed."[6]

This was O'Neill's intention; not everyone has been happy with the execution. "Since the Mannons are seldom in repose," Downer remarks, "the effect is more potential than actual."[7] O'Neill probably visualized the effect too vividly in

---

[5] To Koischwitz (*Eugene O'Neill*, p. 78), Christine is "an embodiment of all powers of life, inimical to the New England tradition" represented by Ezra. Raleigh finds "the ubiquity of death" underneath all the devices and themes of the play. It is present in the recurring crimson sky, in "the black-white symbolism" where white "means the charnel house," in the songs ("John Brown's Body," "Hanging Johnny")—and in the self-destructive meditations of the Mannons (*The Plays of Eugene O'Neill*, pp. 55-58).

[6] Clark, *European Theories*, pp. 534-35.

[7] Cargill *et al.*, *O'Neill and His Plays*, p. 470. Mennemeier com-

his mind. The pale make-up of the Mannons does not disturb, nor is it a major asset. Fortunately, there are other means which make it perfectly clear that the Mannons are something special.

When the action of Part One begins, Lavinia, the personification of revenge,[8] has just discovered that her mother has committed adultery with Adam. She makes a pointed exit through the door of the house at the end of Act I and of her scene with Adam, after having threatened to reveal everything to her father Ezra: "She turns at the top of the steps . . . and stares at him with such a passion of hatred that he is silenced. Her lips move as if she were going to speak, but she fights back the words, turns stiffly and goes into the house and closes the door behind her" (P II 27). What is here foreshadowed is the very last scenic image in the entire trilogy: Lavinia closes herself into the house, thus punishing herself, the last Mannon.

Indoors, in Act II, the theme of family resemblances is carried by a portrait of Ezra; still later, several portraits of ancestors are introduced, all with mask-like faces. The magic, oppressive atmosphere of the house is accentuated by references in the dialogue and by action (Lavinia or Brant sit in Ezra's chair when they are identified with him).[9] Facing Lavinia's demand that Christine and Adam must not see each other anymore, the lovers decide to kill Ezra on his return home from the war.

When Ezra's homecoming takes place, in Act III, one of O'Neill's favorite lighting effects is employed to invoke fatefulness: "The light of a half moon falls on the house, giving

---

plains that O'Neill killed the motif of the masks "with monumental pedantry" (*Das moderne Drama des Auslandes*, p. 57). The repeated references to the masks occur, however, only in the stage directions: the readers are destined to suffer from them, not the spectators.

[8] Raleigh connects "the revenge motif," "one of the most basic, elemental, and satisfying of dramatic devices" with *The Count of Monte Cristo*, and doubts "if it plays such a seminal role in any other modern playwright as it does in O'Neill" (Gassner [ed.], *O'Neill*, p. 12).

[9] Cf. Koischwitz, p. 127, and Braem, *Eugene O'Neill*, p. 105.

it an unreal, detached, eerie quality" (P II 43). The lighting also makes the most of the blackness of the pine tree and the associations to the prison and the mask.[10] Seth, an old servant of the house, sings, for the second time in the play, "Shenandoah," employed as one of the leitmotifs. Lavinia is seen sitting at the top of the steps to the portico.

We are now dealing with an act in which even the groupings are precisely described by O'Neill. The strongest is behind and above the others—as scheming, sneering Loving was to be behind his weaker self in the early acts of *Days Without End*. Christine's entrance is emphasized by lighting: "She closes the door and comes into the moonlight at the edge of the steps, standing above and a little to the right of Lavinia. The moonlight, falling full on them, accentuates strangely the resemblance between their faces and at the same time the hostile dissimilarity in body and dress" (P II 45). There is quite a lot of fusion of scenic means of expression in this scenic image: no crime has yet been committed, but the air is full of ill omens even before the victim makes his entrance.

Then Ezra comes, a man weary of war, willing to try to defeat the Puritan heritage which has made his marriage a failure. He is a Mannon: "His movements are exact and wooden and he has a mannerism of standing and sitting in stiff, posed attitudes that suggest the statues of military heroes. When he speaks, his deep voice has a hollow repressed quality, as if he were continually withholding emotion from it" (P II 46). He speaks of the death he has seen in abundance on the frontier, of the wall he feels separates him from Christine, of his hopes for a better life; and all the time his wife is sitting behind and above. (See Fig. 2.) Although her eyes close during the latter part of Ezra's modified monologue, his inner compulsion forces him to go on: he speaks "as if he had determined, once started, to go on dog-

---

[10] Koischwitz has described O'Neill's lighting scheme (p. 69). When Christine walks back and forth, between darkness and moonlight, at the beginning of Part Two, Act V, she is "hunted by hellish and celestial powers."

gedly without heeding any interruption" (P II 53). With the feigned tenderness of Christine as his only consolation, Ezra Mannon enters the house and the scene of his death.

Signi Falk sees Ezra's monologue as an example of O'Neill's failure "to write dialogue equal to a situation he had created"; "a rehearsal of so much past history seems very much out of place, artificially holding up action that is imminent."[11] What is overlooked here is the controlled irony of fate built on Ezra's very confession, and its structural motivation. Ezra is not what we have been led to expect; he is a changed man since his homecoming, but he is to die because of what he was before this metamorphosis. There must be a relation between the audience and the stage characters, otherwise the life or death of the latter has no effect at all; and this relation is established when Ezra rehearses past history. His confession is designed to add to the suspense rather than to relieve it.[12]

After the thematically important Act III the last act of Part One presented O'Neill mainly with a problem in the mechanics of the plot. Ezra was to be killed in a way that would not arouse the suspicions of the police, and Lavinia was to be given sufficient proof of the guilt of her mother. O'Neill solved the problem by letting Lavinia witness her father's last accusing words and allowing her to secure the box of poison, which she later places on the dead Ezra's breast in a scene somewhat reminiscent of the re-enactment of the king's murder in *Hamlet*.[13] Both Christine and Orin (O'Neill's Orestes) are present.

[11] Signi Falk, "Dialogue in the Plays of Eugene O'Neill," p. 323.

[12] Stark Young has spoken of O'Neill's adult, classic suspense in this play: "you know that in life you will come to death, but just how the course of all your living will shade and fulfill itself you do not know. . . . Suspense proves thus to be not necessarily a contrivance . . . it is an inner quality" (Gassner [ed.], *O'Neill*, p. 85: reprinted from *Immortal Shadows*, New York: Charles Scribner's Sons, 1948). Braem mentions O'Neill's "technique of delaying" ("Hinhaltetechnik," p. 53), characterized also by Koischwitz (p. 92): O'Neill knew how to delay "long expected, inescapable strikes of fate."

[13] Horst Frenz and Martin Mueller connect O'Neill's "mythological bier test" (Koischwitz, p. 127) with the "Mouse Trap" scene in

The first major repetition takes place in Part Two: this is the play of Orin's homecoming. He arrives on a moonlight night—another soldier weary of death.[14] He sees his mother enter the stage through that fateful door; he goes in as Ezra did; there is a scene full of tension between mother and daughter. Christine remains at the top of the stairs until her fear and suspicions force her to descend to grab Lavinia's arm. The daughter retains the cold poise of a revenger. Christine goes into the house; the first act ends.

The inevitable scene between Lavinia and Orin is postponed in order to sustain the suspense as long as possible. It takes place in Act III. Orin is convinced of his mother's guilt, and we are ready to follow the only portion of the action which is set outside the field of influence of the gloomy Mannon house. Yet the milieu follows the revengers to Adam's ship like the foot of an octopus: it is again a moonlight night, and "Shenandoah" is sung, this time by a drunken chantyman.[15] The scene is not without comic overtones; it reminds one of the grotesque and relieving porter scene in *Macbeth*. The melancholy singing of a ship's crew drifting over the water is used to evoke the atmosphere early in the act—as it was in *The Moon of the Caribbees*. And in the setting there is a solution familiar to us from *Desire Under the Elms*: a section of the ship is removed to reveal part of the interior and to show how Adam is murdered by Orin.[16]

Hamlet when executing a detailed comparison between these two tragedies ("More Shakespeare and Less Aeschylus in O'Neill's *Mourning Becomes Electra*," *American Literature, 38*, 85-100).

[14] Gierow (p. 26) has remarked that Orin has overtaken Iphigeneia's role, too. Ezra took Orin to the front, which fed Christine's hatred for her husband.

[15] Young has analyzed this scenic image "where the mere visual elements convey as much as the words. The chanty with which this scene opens, the song and the singer's drunkenness, the lonely ship in the dusk, establishing as it does the mood of longing, futility, land chains and the sea's invitation and memory, is a fine idea and greatly enriches the texture of the play" (Gassner [ed.], *O'Neill*, p. 84).

[16] Koischwitz (pp. 64-67) calls this setting a typical example of O'Neill's perspective arrangement: the wharf, the ship, and the sea form, in this order, foreground, middle section, and background,

In Act V we are back at home again. In the moonlight finale of Part Two, Orin begins to inherit his father's role: he paces restlessly up and down by the steps, as Ezra had done in the corresponding scene in Part One.[17] The message of Adam's death brings Christine down from her powerful position at the top of the stairs, still anxiously sustained at the beginning of the scene. In the last glimpse we have of Christine "she stands at the top between the two columns of the portico before the front door" (P II 123), then turns and rushes into the house of her death.[18] Lavinia does not prevent her: it is just, she claims, that Christine shoot herself. When this has happened, Lavinia follows Orin into the house, "stiffly erect, her face stern and mask-like" (P II 125). The end of Part Two foreshadows the end of Part Three.

The full pattern of family resemblances is developed in the last part. Lavinia inherits the role of her mother, Orin that of their father.[19] Before the two revengers, now haunted by guilt, return from their escapade to the Blessed Isles of innocence and sexual fulfillment, the chorus of old townspeople gathers in front of the steps. One of them has bet that he is courageous enough to stay overnight in the house with the Mannon ghosts. He comes quickly forward; and the role of

---

open to the far-away distance. A similar solution leaves the right-hand section of the house setting free. In the harbor scene, in fact, we have another example of O'Neill's diagonal settings, found in *The Emperor Jones, The Hairy Ape,* etc. Koischwitz also remarks that the impression of a limitless distance is punctuated by music.

[17] Brant's nervous steps in the harbor scene are connected by Braem (p. 105) with similar sound effects in *Ile* and *Gold*. The last and most effective usage occurs in *Long Day's Journey*: Mary is upstairs, keeping the Tyrone men awake.

[18] ". . . the picture of mother and daughter on the stairs leading to the Mannon house belongs to those that are engraved in one's consciousness forever" (Nils Lüchou, *Teaterstaden Helsingfors* [1960], p. 133; reprinted from *Svenska Pressen*, March 10, 1934).

[19] In a comparison with *Long Day's Journey*, Brustein calls these "physical transformations" "a purely mechanical application of the theme," which is suffering from spiritual and psychological ailments (*The Theatre of Revolt*, p. 350). From his social point of view, Lawson disapproves of the repetitions (*Theory and Technique of Playwriting*, p. 140).

the chorus is finished in a way which renders a comic variation of a major theme in the play, the power of the house over the characters. Different ages and social levels are employed in the three chorus scenes; the youth is, on the other hand, represented by Hazel and Peter Niles, two normal young people who take part in the action throughout the play and form a contrast to Lavinia and Orin.

Situations, costumes, tones of voice, patterns of speech and behavior are employed to drive home the point of inheritance. Orin now has a beard similar to that of his father; he sits in Ezra's chair, forbidden to Adam, and moves in an awkward, soldierly way. Lavinia copies her mother's colors, movements, and hair arrangement. She rebels against the portraits of her ancestors in monologues addressed to them —a variation we remember from *All God's Chillun Got Wings*. Yet the house and the past are stronger than she— and, especially, stronger than Orin, who cannot stand the thought of having caused Christine's suicide. The Mannon death wish has conquered his mind.

Lavinia sends Orin to his suicide, inheriting the role of the mother even as a murderess. There seems to be an escape for Lavinia in Peter, but the hope is destroyed in the final act of the trilogy. It is afternoon, to close the circle.[20] Lavinia sits at the top of the steps listening to Peter with her eyes closed, as Christine had listened to Ezra. By a Freudian slip of the tongue she calls Peter Adam, and the well-kept secret is revealed: she did not kill her mother's lover out of a sense of justice, but out of jealousy. There remains only the grim self-punishment: Lavinia will enter the house, and the shutters will never be opened.[21] "She ascends to the portico—

[20] "Again and again there is the obsessive, binding reiteration: of a word or phrase or of a visual image: the gray stone and the white columns of the Mannon mansion in the crimson sunset" (Raleigh, p. 175).

[21] "With Lavinia Mannon, the pattern begins to change: man's will, and therefore man's responsibility, is given more play in the action. The happiness of belonging is not all, nor is it so poetically conceived in terms of Dionysian ecstasy" (Bogard, in Gassner [ed.], *O'Neill*, p. 71). Bogard's point is that Lavinia does not fight against her fate as the earlier of the O'Neillian protagonists had done: she resigns herself to it.

and then turns and stands for a while, stiff and square-shoul-
dered, staring into the sunlight with frozen eyes. Seth leans
out of the window at the right of the door and pulls the shutters closed with a decisive bang. As if this were a word of
command, Lavinia pivots sharply on her heel and marches
woodenly into the house, closing the door behind her"
(P II 179).

It has been necessary to deal with the exits and entrances
through the front door of the Mannon house and with the
groupings on the steps in some detail. The exterior of the
house is the dominating element in *Mourning Becomes Electra*: it is employed in six out of thirteen acts. (The only case
of a divided act is Part Three, Act I, where an exterior scene
is immediately followed by an interior one.) Moreover, the
acts in front of the façade are placed in the most emphatic
positions, at the beginning and at the end of the parts. The
total number of exits and entrances through the front door
is kept low in order to accentuate each of them; and before
a character goes out of sight, he or she often turns around
and the action is frozen for a moment, as happens when Lavinia enters the house for the last time.

These features are not there by chance: they are all part
of a carefully executed plan. The exterior setting *is* the play,
just as the Cabot farm is *Desire Under the Elms*. The importance of this setting has been emphasized by Leech; Gassner
goes a step further in remarking that O'Neill "assigns a symbolic function to the doors of the house, for example, in the
last scene of the play."[22] The function is not given only in
that particular scene but throughout the play. The steps and
the doors form an area rich in associations; not all of them
can be realized by all the spectators, but they are there. Every
stage director knows about the possibilities of operating in
the unconscious mind of the spectators, by groupings, by
movements, by certain symbolic areas of action; a few playwrights employ these potentialities in their stage directions;

[22] Leech, *Eugene O'Neill,* p. 84; Gassner, *The Theatre in Our
Times,* p. 263.

it is hardly recommendable for the critics to ignore them entirely.

"No stage effect," Doris V. Falk writes about the end of *Mourning Becomes Electra*, "no rhapsodic chant of earth god or goddess, or mystical vision is necessary here."[23] Whether to agree or not depends on the meaning of the term "stage effect." After having seen how Lavinia's entrance into the house has been prepared by a long series of interacting scenic images, some of them outdoors, some within the walls of the house, after having realized the central function of the exterior setting in the entire trilogy, one has full reason to call her decisive action a "stage effect." This scenic image is eagerly admired by those who have seen *Mourning Becomes Electra*: "In the moment when Lavinia, in black, stands framed between the white pillars of the House of Mannon, the sunset dying at her feet, the course of passion run— in that moment, playwright, performer and artist come together in a superb conclusion that belongs as completely and solely to the theatre as Mr. O'Neill himself."[24] Yet the end would be worth nothing, if it had not been prepared for: entering a house is a very ordinary action. O'Neill makes it a significant emotional experience. He is a far-sighted builder of plays in *Mourning Becomes Electra*, even more so than he was in *Strange Interlude*.

O'Neill's methods of constructing his trilogy are described by Gassner in an essay comparing it with another modern play about Electra by Jean Giraudoux. O'Neill uses theatrical means to "punctuate the illusion of reality, not to puncture it"; his play is "a cumulative experience," in which "the things done or stated in the final minutes of climax of scenes or acts are things grown in the womb of each portion of the play like a canker"; by piling detail on detail he does "the slow, methodical work of a day laborer."[25]

[23] Doris V. Falk, *Eugene O'Neill and the Tragic Tension*, p. 143.
[24] Cargill *et al.*, p. 193: a review by John Hutchens on *Mourning Becomes Electra*, reprinted from *Theatre Arts*, Jan. 1932. Cf. reviews by Brooks Atkinson and John Mason Brown, in Miller, pp. 67, 70.
[25] Gassner, *The Theatre in Our Times*, pp. 263-65.

A few notes on the functions of the exterior setting can be added. The house is called "a sepulchre" (P II 17) by Christine, "a tomb" (P II 74) by Orin; psychoanalysts might call it a symbol of the cadaver, or, in this particular context, of mother's womb. Above all, it is an artistic symbol with multiple layers of meaning; it contains references to the Mannon dead, to their repressed way of living in that prison, to Greek tragedy. It is remarkable that this central scenic means of expression is at the same time the most prominent and least artificially contrived Greek element in the plays. The steps in front of the house might perhaps be called an immovable kind of cothurni, used to give stature to the isolated Mannon family.

All in all, the setting is one of the primary means employed "to gain added depth and scope." Among the other means are the whole bundle of details used to express family resemblances: colors of costumes, the peculiar brown-gold hair, personal areas of action, mask-like faces, and ways of speaking and moving, sometimes with the horror of an automaton. Structural patterns are built up with the help of moonlight, with chorus scenes, and with the song "Shenandoah." Leech has stated that a certain amount of remoteness to the characters is achieved and that the trilogy "could have been a mechanical transference of the Greek plot to modern times" or "a mere family case-history from the analyst's note book";[26] it is neither of these. Admitting this, we still have to take a closer look at the amount of success of *Mourning Becomes Electra*.

O'Neill's deviations from the classic plot do not offer any basis for judgment. He omitted Iphigeneia and Chrysothemis as individual stage characters and gave Lavinia a much more prominent part than her brother. "In so doing," Engel writes, "he appears to have followed Euripides' *Electra*, not only diverging from Aeschylus, but also disregarding *The Electra* of Sophocles wherein brother and sister divided the part of

---

[26] Leech, p. 84; to Nicoll, the play is "rather a magnificently presented case-study than a powerful tragic drama" (*World Drama*, p. 891).

237

protagonist."[27] Even if O'Neill made changes in these details and did not go to the extreme of a matricide, it is to be concluded that the Greek parallel furnished him not only with a scheme of action but also with a firm purpose.[28] His tasks were to tell the story, and to find motivations for the characters which would correspond to the Greek sense of fate. This time O'Neill did not leave holes in the motivations, as he did in *The Great God Brown* and *Dynamo*.

To the first of the tasks can be attributed the remarkable vigor with which the action proceeds; the trilogy has been called "O'Neill's masterpiece in dramatic craftsmanship."[29] Not even the bareness of language, considered by many critics to be one of the major flaws of the plays, is capable of destroying them. O'Neill indeed "shows great self-discipline here"[30]—which is even more remarkable when we remember the profusions he had indulged in a few years earlier in plays like *The Great God Brown* and *Dynamo*.[31] The first task is fulfilled with honors.

The crucial point is the second task. It is possible to argue that "modern psychological fate" gave O'Neill a duality of purpose. On one hand, he used an ingenious apparatus, with mask-like faces, Greek parallels, and a house setting, to achieve a distance between the characters and the audience; on the other hand, he asks for our empathy by furnishing his characters with an elaborate system of incestuous family re-

[27] Engel, *The Haunted Heroes of Eugene O'Neill*, p. 247.

[28] Raleigh connects O'Neill's usage of "a Greek myth" with other modern adaptations by Joyce, Eliot, and Jeffers (p. 242). Racey refers to a saying by Eliot: "The use of myth . . . affords the artist both the necessary artistic control to explore his subject and the means of generalization" (Gassner [ed.], *O'Neill*, p. 61).

[29] Eleanor Flexner, *American Playwrights: 1918-1938*, p. 183. Gassner speaks of "the saving grace of purposefulness" (*Masters of the Drama*, p. 658), Young of "clear narrative design" (Gassner [ed.], *O'Neill*, p. 88).

[30] Leech, p. 89.

[31] "This simplicity and directness of language is characteristic of the play as a whole, and while we cannot say that the language of the play is grand or moving or memorable or quotable, at least it cannot be said either that it is strained and hyperbolical, as it often is in *The Fountain* and *Lazarus Laughed*" (Raleigh, p. 216).

lations, modeled directly on Freud.[32] If not case histories, he offers type histories: Lavinia is the typical daughter, in love with her father, full of antipathy toward her mother, etc. As a result, the third part of the trilogy is its slightest. The action is not justified strongly enough by the notion that everything is fatefully repeated. And the characters are somewhere in between: both distant and close to us, both "Greek" and Freudian.

Perhaps the fault is as much in the audiences as in O'Neill. Instead of a crushing fate we want to experience a new facet in human nature; instead of pity and fear we look for knowledge; and when we know, we can discard pity and fear. O'Neill certainly labored valiantly, by saving the decisive piece of knowledge until the very last scene of his lengthy trilogy; and he certainly both strained and controlled his remarkable scenic imagination.[33] Nothing is wrong with it. If only he and his time in general had believed a little less firmly in psychoanalysis as the fate of mankind . . .[34] Yet *Mourning Becomes Electra* is perhaps O'Neill's best play prior to

[32] Several critics have criticized the obvious Freudianism of *Mourning Becomes Electra*. "This 'psychic fate' out-Freuds Freud. . . . The whole significance of the trilogy rests upon psychotic and neurotic impulses," Norman T. Pratt, Jr., writes in "Aeschylus and O'Neill: Two Worlds" (*The Classical Journal, 51*, 4 [Jan. 1956], 166). Cf. Dietrich, *Das moderne Drama*, pp. 230, 401.

[33] J. Chiari criticizes O'Neill's "obsessions with Freudianism," yet calls the characters "terribly human," and the play "an achievement on a grand scale and, of its kind, unsurpassed in twentieth-century drama" (*Landmarks of Contemporary Drama* [1965], pp. 137-38). Koischwitz compares the trilogy with Wagner and his "Gesamtkunst-werk": both Wagner and O'Neill favor too bold symmetrical arrangements, both work energetically on the techniques, both sacrifice true-ness to life to a "too abstract, sublimated conception of the characters" (p. 143).

[34] "Freudianism, like the contributions of Jung, could illuminate some of the hidden motives of the psyche, but it could not possibly answer the existential questions which a playwright like O'Neill raised" (Glicksberg, *The Tragic Vision in Twentieth-Century Literature*, p. 94). This is the core of the problem; there is another formulation by Gassner who says that O'Neill's play leaves "unanswered the larger question O'Neill did *not* ask himself—namely, whether modern dramatic vision needs to be limited, or is actually exhausted, by 'psychological approximation' " (Gassner, *Eugene O'Neill*, p. 34).

World War II. Added scope and the interaction of scenic images are now under control. The play makes competent and impressive reading; and when performed, it must include moments of magnificence—in front of that house, Greek and Puritan at the same time.

We are now approaching the end of O'Neill's experimental period. Out of his prewar plays only one remains to be discussed: *Ah, Wilderness!*, a step toward realism. We have followed his development in terms of several growing points— the setting, the dialogue, the masks, a special device; it is now possible to draw a few conclusions based on this material. In several cases O'Neill overburdened the device or style he had chosen: the masks in *The Great God Brown*, the mass spectacle in *Lazarus Laughed*, Greek elements in both; expressionism in *Welded*, both the thought asides and the skeleton setting in *Dynamo*. In a couple of cases we meet a new creation where the once exaggerated style or device is used with more discretion: the masks in *Days Without End* (even if a poor play in other respects), the Greek parallels in *Mourning Becomes Electra*. And O'Neill's total development up to this point can be seen as a constant effort to enlarge the scope of his drama: toward dynamic expressionism; toward pageantry, with an emphasis still strongly on the individual in the center of the play; toward a stage filled with a significant setting, as if the core had been blown full of air— in *Desire Under the Elms*; toward excavations in the core, with the help of the masks and monologues. His final result before the war is *Mourning Becomes Electra*, a temporary synthesis of the best in these multipurpose experiments.

13

A REALISTIC "DIGRESSION"

AH, WILDERNESS!

With the whole canon in front of us, it is easy to be wise: in all of O'Neill's plays written and produced during the thirties the proportion of realistic elements was growing. *Mourning Becomes Electra* is attached to a particular period in American history and is equipped with psychological motivations; *Days Without End* is less fantastic than its counterpart in the twenties, *The Great God Brown*. O'Neill was writing in an atmosphere that was more prosaic and austere than the roaring twenties, with all kinds of booms, even in the theatre. Yet the depression did not discourage him from writing *Ah, Wilderness!*, a nostalgic comedy of the good old days; in fact, it may even have encouraged him. Whatever the reasons, personal and social, the result was relaxed and realistic.

Ah, Wilderness! is not only realistic; it is a family comedy, limited in scope to the sphere of the familiar. The action is concentrated on the Millers, a middle-class family in a large small-town in Connecticut. The play can be called a counter-sketch of *Bread and Butter*. Nat Miller's son Richard, the hero of the play, is a rebellious boy of seventeen. In addition to a varied crowd of children, the family is furnished with an aunt and an uncle who have been in love with each other for twenty years, yet have never married because Aunt Lily disapproves of Uncle Sid's occasional drinking. What there is of a plot is supplied by a Puritan-minded merchant who finds obscenities in the love poems Richard has quoted in his letters to Muriel, the merchant's daughter. The boy keeps quoting rebellious passages from literature with gusto throughout the play.

There are parallels between *Ah, Wilderness!* and *Long Day's Journey Into Night*, two plays of reminiscence, totally different in tone. The similarities are many and obvious: the living rooms of the two stage families are almost identical,[1] Richard resembles Edmund, Uncle Sid and Richard's brother Arthur have been called two versions of Jamie, Nat Miller is an idealized picture of James Tyrone. The plots, too, have connecting links: both plays begin after breakfast, proceed through a visit to the town center, with the mother anxiously awaiting the return of her favorite son.[2] From our viewpoint it is noteworthy that O'Neill employs many of his familiar scenic units in functions unfamiliar to us; his relation even to his scenic means of expression is relaxed.

Most conspicuously, fluctuations in the dialogue are now used to achieve comic effects. In the middle of Sid's drunken joking, "even Lily suddenly lets out an hysterical giggle and is furious with herself for doing so" (P II 226). Lily and Sid never overcome this fluctuation between attraction and repulsion in their relationship; it is their fate, the most sinister element in this sunny comedy. Richard swings between naïveté and radical opinions, between boyishness and feigned worldliness: "Food!" he "mutters disdainfully," from his "poet's heart"—"But the dish of olives seems to fascinate him and presently he has approached nearer, and stealthily lifts a couple and crams them into his mouth" (P II 217). Nat has two roles to play, those of a strict father and an understanding friend; Mrs. Miller tries hard to disguise her motherly tenderness behind a veil of indignation. The motivations are realistic: Sid's drunkenness, Richard's age, the dilemma of the parents in a situation never before heard of. Contradictory roles were given to Lucy in *Now I Ask You*: now O'Neill laughs again at himself—or at what he once was.[3]

[1] Drew B. Palette, "O'Neill and the Comic Spirit," *Modern Drama*, 3 (1960), 312; the Gelbs, *O'Neill*, pp. 81-86. Cf. Appendix B, p. 354.

[2] John T. Shawcross, "The Road to Ruin: the Beginning of O'Neill's *Long Day's Journey*," *Modern Drama*, 3 (1960), 294-95.

[3] *Ah, Wilderness!* was a surprise to its critics and audiences, as O'Neill had tried to destroy all his previous comedies. Brooks Atkinson writes: "As a writer of comedy Mr. O'Neill has a capacity for tenderness that most of us never suspected" (Miller, *Playwright's Progress*, p. 74: reprinted from the *New York Times*, Oct. 3, 1933).

The use of quotations, a prominent feature both in *Ah, Wilderness!* and in *Long Day's Journey*, is indicative of the difference in the atmosphere. Here the irony is mild and smiling; in the later play it is bitter.[4] Repetitive sound effects, employed most recently at the beginning of *Mourning Becomes Electra*, are now used to remind us of the date of action, the Fourth of July, and "to form a disturbing punctuation to the conversation" (P II 189). Music is used to evoke an idyllic atmosphere,[5] and moonlight is completely devoid of ghastliness: "Halfway down the sky, at rear, left, the crescent of the new moon casts a soft, mysterious, caressing light over everything. The sand of the beach shimmers palely" (P II 275). This is the background for Richard's first meeting with Muriel, in a scene of innocent quarrels and blissful reconciliations that reads like a parody of *Welded*. Suicide is ridiculed, pantheism and Puritanism are smiled at, and, on top of it all, even a ghost is materialized to add to—the comedy: "(Richard comes slowly in from the front parlor . . . walks like one in a trance, his eyes shining with a dreamy happiness, his spirit still too exalted to be conscious of his surroundings, or to remember the threatened punishment . . . [He speaks] dreamily, like a ghost addressing fellow shades) Hello." "It's love, not liquor, this time" (P I 292-93), Nat remarks reassuringly.

In the Greek-Puritan macrocosm of the Mannons there was space enough for a whole series of murders; in the microcosm of the small-town Millers a negligible gesture like Richard's drunkenness assumes enormous importance. With a clever twist of thought, Lionel Trilling has called *Ah, Wilder-*

[4] Raleigh has summarized O'Neill's development in using quotations: from *The First Man* (and *Now I Ask You*, we can add) through *Ah, Wilderness!* to *Long Day's Journey*. Curtis Jayson and *The First Man* are failures: "A much more successful picture of a romantic young imagination wedding life and literature, and living by quotations, so to speak, is that of Richard Miller" (*The Plays of Eugene O'Neill*, p. 230).

[5] The songs belong to the time described in the play, and suggest "a solid, Victorian, family-based culture, all grouped around the piano and singing a song either sentimental or . . . funny" (Raleigh, p. 78).

243

ness! "the satyr-play that follows the tragedy";[6] this is a satyr-play of the more harmless variety, even as far as Richard's rebellion is concerned.[7] When describing the rebel's escapade to a bar O'Neill remains firm in his chivalrous belief in the innocence of prostitutes—as he had been ever since *The Web*. The scene comes closest to melodrama in this otherwise uncontrived play.[8]

The attitude toward *Ah, Wilderness!*, O'Neill's only published full-length comedy, has sometimes been too condescending.[9] It certainly gives evidence of O'Neill's increasing control over scenic means of expression: he is now able to give them new functions, some directly opposite to the previous ones. Fresh potentialities are explored even in this realistic play of a familiar genre. A tragedian uses his means of expression to achieve comic effects: this is the paradox of *Ah, Wilderness!*

Another important indication of O'Neill's development is the three-dimensional characterization of the Millers et consortes. O'Neill is now about to close the circle of his career: from early realism to late dynamic realism.[10] These two styles

[6] Cargill *et al.*, *O'Neill and His Plays*, p. 299: reprinted from *The New Republic*, Sept. 1936.

[7] Koischwitz (p. 140) suspects a connection between *Ah, Wilderness!* and *Frühlings Erwachen* by Wedekind.

[8] Carpenter sees in the bar scene a suggestion of "the dark underworld of alcoholism, prostitution, and spiritual despair" and finds irony everywhere in the play, giving "a biting edge to its humor. . . . The values of conventional middle-class morality remain dominant, but they are seldom described as ideal" (p. 146).

[9] In "The Worth of *Ah, Wilderness!*" Jacob H. Adler (*Modern Drama, 3*, 1960) calls the comedy "a distinguished play" (p. 288) of its own kind. Critical comments on it are "mainly an objection to a genre" (p. 281). The genre, not a major one, is used by O'Neill "successfully for purposes beyond normal," for there are serious elements in the idyll, such as "a recognition of real evil" (p. 282). Cf. Gassner: "It is marred only by an occasional lapse into sentimentality, and it is limited only by that reduction of emotional power that occurs when one writes about sentiment rather than passion" (*Masters of the Drama*, p. 660).

[10] To Brustein, *Ah, Wilderness!* is "a transitional play" (*The Theatre of Revolt*, p. 324). O'Neill "has begun to perceive the hollowness of his messianic pretensions, and to turn towards material which he has pulled out of his being rather than self-consciously adopted;

are far from identical; in between, there are O'Neill's long-lasting efforts to explore the stage. They produced six great or nearly great plays (*The Emperor Jones, The Hairy Ape, Desire Under the Elms, All God's Chillun Got Wings, Strange Interlude* and *Mourning Becomes Electra*); they helped O'Neill to rise to world fame; and they gave a decisive impetus to the entire American drama.

Before turning our glance forward, it is important to note that the whole circle must be kept in mind. Even when O'Neill was farthest away from his starting and finishing points, he learned something that could not but influence him. His skill in *Ah, Wilderness!* is apparent in comparison with the realistic plays on both sides of the year 1920. Exactly what he learned and how he applied his bitterly won competence are questions to be dealt with in the last part of this study. Now it is enough to state that *Ah, Wilderness!* was not a realistic digression, though it might have seemed so to O'Neill's audience at the première, aware of the existence of another mask play. It was *Days Without End* that was a digression—backwards.

---

thematically, he has abandoned myths of incest and romantic love for deeper probes of character; formally, he is learning to combine the solipsistic subjectivity of Strindberg with the more detached, ordered, and indirectly biographical approach of Ibsen" (p. 337).

PART THREE

THE FINAL SYNTHESIS:
DYNAMIC REALISM

"Something? Outside me? No, nothing is there but me. My mind. My life, I suppose you might call it, since I have never lived except in mind. A very frightening prison it becomes at last, full of ghosts and corpses."

Deborah in *More Stately Mansions*, p. 28

❧ 14 ❧

ONE OF THE MISSING LINKS

MORE STATELY MANSIONS

There is an interval of twelve years between the world pre-
mières of *Days Without End* and *The Iceman Cometh* (finished in 1939, produced in 1946). This gap is the more remarkable when we take into consideration that the eighteen
preceding years (Summer 1916 to January 1934) had seen
the production of no less than thirty-six plays by Eugene
O'Neill (if *Exorcism, Chris Christophersen*, and *S. S. Glencairn* are counted)—an average of two plays a year. In spite
of the foreshadowing features in *Ah, Wilderness!* the gap
will never be completely bridged, because most of the plays
drafted or written during these years as parts of an enormous
cycle of eleven chronicle plays were later destroyed by the
playwright. Only two remain, one (*A Touch of the Poet*)
finished by O'Neill himself, the other (*More Stately Mansions*) in an editable shape. What were the steps that brought
O'Neill from his experimental phase to his late dynamic realism? The field is wide open for speculation. *More Stately
Mansions* is only one of the missing links.

The O'Neill of the late thirties and forties is a different
man from the celebrated author of *Mourning Becomes Electra*. Living in seclusion in Georgia and California, O'Neill
fought his lonely battle against an unknown disease which
gradually demolished his ability to coordinate his movements
—most tragically, the movements of his hand. When he had
finished his last play, *A Moon for the Misbegotten*, he still
had before him ten years of tormented isolation within the
sphere of his mind. Against these odds he wrote two un-
doubted masterpieces and a play that comes close to being
one.[1] He did not even have the consolation of seeing them

---

[1] Recent criticism tends to stress the importance of O'Neill's last

successfully produced. Only *The Iceman Cometh* reached Broadway, and in a production that was hardly a success. Its failure was partly due to the fact that O'Neill had to face a new generation of postwar playgoers and critics to whom he had a slightly archaic or anachronistic flavor. The real merits of the play were ignored.

In a way, *More Stately Mansions* belongs to both ends of O'Neill's last creative period, his premature old age. As far as the action of the play is concerned, it follows *A Touch of the Poet*, finished in 1942, the second to last play in the canon. There are still better reasons for dealing with it now: *More Stately Mansions* has definite affinities with O'Neill's experimental period, and it was never finished. There is thus no way of knowing what the shape of the play would have been after a series of more or less realistic plays had shaped O'Neill's late style proper. The published version is based on the third draft, completed in January 1939; even if there were revisions in 1940 and 1941,[2] it is appropriate to discuss the play before *The Iceman Cometh*, finished late in 1939.

The cycle, called finally "A Tale of Possessors Self-Dispossessed," grew continuously in its author's mind—backwards in time. This can be seen from the extant notes and scenarios (eight plays proceeded at least to the first draft

---

phase to the point of depreciating his middle period. "O'Neill will be primarily remembered for his last plays. . . . It was inevitable . . . that the next generation of critics—Francis Fergusson, Lionel Trilling, Eric Bentley—should harp on O'Neill's substantial failings as a thinker, artist, and Broadway hero. . . . During these dark years, ironically, O'Neill's real development began. . . . Maturing in silence . . . he commenced to create plays which were genuine masterpieces of the modern theatre" (Brustein, *The Theatre of Revolt*, pp. 321-23). Agreeing with this, I still find both "artistic" and "historical" (p. 324) interest in the best prewar plays.

[2] The dates and other details pertaining to the fate of the manuscript are mentioned by Gallup, one of the editors, in his foreword for the printed version. The main portion of editing was done by Gierow, who shortened the play for its first production in the Royal Dramatic Theatre, Stockholm, in 1962. When cutting the script into less than half of the original, he omitted, most conspicuously, Act I, Scene i and the Epilogue, which provided connecting links to the preceding and following plays in the cycle (MSM x-xi).

stage). From a trilogy, with its concluding part set in contemporary America, it extended gradually into a series of eleven plays, covering nearly two centuries of American history, from 1757 to 1932. "He had turned inward and backward, driven to examining and evaluating the past," the Gelbs write. In the late thirties, O'Neill "was beginning, more and more, to live with and brood about the ghosts of his past for an answer to the meaning of his own life. He became almost compulsively fascinated with the study of one generation's effect on the next—'The Harford curse,' one of his cycle characters calls it."[3]

"The Harford curse" is certainly a central theme in *More Stately Mansions*, play number six in the series. It describes the tempestuous early married life of Mrs. Sara Harford, the Irish-born heroine of *A Touch of the Poet* who, in fact, was planned to be a central figure even later on, possibly surviving the ninth part.[4] Now, from 1832 to 1841, she is engaged in a life-and-death struggle with her mother-in-law Deborah, who makes a short appearance in the earlier part, over possession of her Yankee husband Simon. The triangle is presented in various constellations throughout the play, and the secondary characters, Simon's brother Joel, the family lawyer Gadsby, and Tenard, a banker, appear only passingly.

Act I, Scene i begins with a monologue by Deborah, who reacts to the Harford curse and to life in general with fear and rejection. This is the first reminder of the central role played by thought asides, modified monologues, and monologues proper in this drama of slow motion and introspection. The setting of the opening scene indicates desolation, as do the settings in all the late plays (in *Long Day's Journey* it is a modest desolation): "A log cabin by a lake in the woods. . . . The cabin gives evidence of having been abandoned for years. The mortar between the stones of the chimney has crumbled and fallen out in spots" (MSM 1). Na-

---

[3] The Gelbs, *O'Neill*, p. 791.

[4] *Ibid.*, p. 792. What is known of the time, place, and action of the cycle plays is summarized by John J. Fitzgerald ("The Bitter Harvest of O'Neill's Projected Cycle," *The New England Qvarterly, 40* [1967], 367-73).

ture is victorious, the forest lives in full autumn colors; man's creations are temporary and worthless.

In *More Stately Mansions* O'Neill is one step short of the inescapable impression left by his later plays in which the action is limited essentially to one setting. In this shortened version, he employs five different stage pictures; a pivotal place is occupied by Deborah's garden, the background of three decisive scenes including the finale. It is in striking contrast to the scene by the lake: "The corner is formed by a brick enclosing wall, eight feet high, at rear and right. At center is an octagonal summer-house, its walls and pointed roof entirely covered by ivy. At left and right of the summer-house are shrubs, with a line of Italian cypresses behind them along the wall. The shrubs, of various sizes, are all clipped into geometrical shapes—cones, cubes, cylinders, spheres, pyramids etc." (MSM 25). The arrangement is asymmetric: the brick wall is at rear and right. The effect aimed at is that of a prison and of "nature distorted and humiliated by a deliberately mocking, petulant arrogance" (MSM 95). Even if victorious, man is still in conflict with nature: he does not fit together with his victim.

The disharmony between man and nature is only a background theme in *More Stately Mansions*. A much more prominent place is occupied by the relations between the characters, grouped around the summer-house. As in the case of the Mannon house, the building has multiple functions; basically, it is the materialization of a compulsion to flee from life into madness. After a futile effort to regain her influence over Simon at the log cabin, we meet Deborah in her seclusion behind the garden wall and in the summer-house: when she steps out of the house, this is a preliminary horror effect. It is of vital importance whether one returns from that house. She is brought news of the catastrophic state of the family company. Henry Harford, Deborah's recently dead "unimaginative" husband, had gambled with land. This is a surprise moment in a vacuum: in the extant version of the cycle Henry never appears on the stage. Deborah swallows her pride and is ready for a reconciliation with Sara and Simon, estranged because of Simon's marriage and his poetical dreams of a social utopia. She closes her former arrogant and seclusive self within the walls of the summer-house and opens herself to love, to communication with Sara and Sara's children. " 'Depart from me, ye cursed!' " she exclaims to her devil, the old Deborah. "There! Now question, and sneer and laugh at your dreams, and sleep with ugliness, and deny yourself, until at last you fall in love with madness" (MSM 40).

A family reunion is achieved. Sara fulfills her primary ambition of gaining possession of the stately Harford mansion; and Deborah receives the longed-for company of Sara's and Simon's children. Yet all efforts to live together fail. Each of them is too possessive to allow any sharing of feelings; in a scene (II, iii) compared above with the corresponding sequence in *Welded*, they speak their suspicions "aloud" in thought asides. This departure from realism extends even into the action: the women "group together in back of him, Deborah at left-rear and Sara at right-rear of his chair. They bend over, each with an arm about the other, until their faces touch the side of his head. Their other arms go around him so that their hands touch on his chest." (See Fig. 7.) At last Simon feels safe and happy, devoured by a mother-mistress: "I cannot keep them separate—they are too strong here in their home— . . . But I feel her arms around me, and she is good now, not evil—she loves me—and so I can surrender and be hers—" (MSM 128-29). The shift in the personal pronoun from "they" to "she" is remarkable: if only Sara and Deborah were a single person Simon would be happy.

They are not; they withdraw from each others touch, and the old jealousies flare up again. In this over-obvious scene the constant quarrels and alliances are repeated, as they are throughout the play. Sara and Simon, wife and husband, join for a while against Deborah; Deborah and Sara against Simon, the naughty little boy; and Simon and Deborah against Sara, who is not a Harford, but a greedy, common slut. There is no break in this continuous fluctuation; there is no possibility of stabilizing the precarious love-hate relations—until the end of the play, when the situation explodes.

O'Neill's plan for the setting of this scene is published as a facsimile, together with four other sketches (see Figs. 4, 5, and 6) and a page from the original manuscript. This particular drawing (MSM 116) reveals three rooms of the Harford mansion: it looks like a conglomerate of the settings for *Desire Under the Elms* and *Mourning Becomes Electra.* Rooms on two floors are shown, as in the former play; the house is a mansion with two pillars at the front door. These sketches show how careful O'Neill was in his planning of the production, and how lively the idea of the stage was in his mind. His sketches for *Desire Under the Elms* have been published before. Yet the plan for II, iii in *More Stately Mansions* must come from an earlier or later stage of composition than the published text, since the verbal description of the setting and the drawing do not coincide; none of the three rooms includes the furniture specified in the stage directions.

One might conjecture that the picture is a late innovation, perhaps eventually discarded. The sketch is far from finished: there is not a single door in any of the three rooms, and the furniture is sparse. None of them looks inhabited. The only sofa, which is mentioned several times in the stage directions, is in the room downstairs at right, which also contains the minimum number of chairs demanded by the action. Another of O'Neill's sketches is the ground plan for this scene; it is published here for the first time (Fig. 6). While giving the placement of furniture in greater detail, it does not quite fit together with the verbal description of the setting (MSM 117): two tables and a chair are missing from the sketch. II, iii is the only scene placed within the walls of the Harford mansion in the abridged version of the play; in the original script there may be several such scenes. Perhaps O'Neill toyed with the idea of removable walls, then drew the ground plans for some of the rooms. As many as seven scenes take place outside the mansion; the skeleton setting could hardly have been made an integral part of the play.

Although the setting with removable walls was discarded,

O'Neill did not hesitate to employ several other scenic units. Monologues are used—in fact, over-used: in addition to the thought asides there are soliloquies proper and lots of modified monologues. From the skeleton of the play one gets the impression that it consists of a series of monologues, occasionally interrupted by scenes between two or three persons. The beginning of I, ii is essentially a monologue by Deborah, with a few ejaculations by Gadsby in between—until he gets his chance and reveals, secondary character as he is, a neat little Napoleon complex. O'Neill needed confidants for his introverted characters and did not choose them too carefully. The inner compulsions are so strong in this play of high-pitched emotions that Simon, an unscrupulous business tycoon, discloses his innermost thoughts to his brother, who cannot see why Simon wishes to discuss such matters with him (MSM 72). Neither can we.

In II, iii O'Neill invents a new modification, a kind of super-monologue. Simon's consciousness determines the thoughts of his women, even though they do not hear his thought aside: "As his thoughts have progressed the expressions on the two women's faces have mirrored his description as though, subconsciously, their mood was created by his mind" (MSM 126). This is a logic continuation of the modified monologues in harmony with a major theme of the play: the characters influence one another so subtly that the means they employ to exert their influence are not demonstrated on the stage.[5] From the point of view of scenic expression these mystical suggestions, as well as the super-monologues, are doubtful.

It is quite possible that these solutions would not have been preserved in the acting version of the play. In two troublesome cases (*Days Without End* and *Mourning Be-*

---

[5] To Raleigh, O'Neill's characters "are not rationally conceived but *felt*, and, as such, are maelstroms of powerful emotions. Their emotions are so strong that these characters are always striving at overleaping the bounds of rationality into an area that suggests—but only suggests—a belief in existence of supersensory perceptions and powers. Intuitions, for example, in both men and women tend to be both powerful and accurate" (*The Plays of Eugene O'Neill*, p. 149).

comes Electra) O'Neill wrote as many as eight versions; and the transformations were radical—witness his own working diary and Doris V. Falk's observations on *Days Without End*.[6] The published version of *More Stately Mansions* is based on a revised third version of the play, from which it would appear that O'Neill had forgotten his own warning against his "hangover inclination" to use thought asides (quoted above, p. 223). Perhaps O'Neill would eventually have changed at least some of the monologues into dialogue proper and written into his working diary something similar to his final evaluation of a discarded technique in *Mourning Becomes Electra*: "in spite of labor on this stylized conception am glad I did it—time not wasted—learned a lot—stylized solil[oquies] uncovered new insights into characters and recurrent themes—job now is to get all this in naturally in straight dialogue."[7] In the case of *More Stately Mansions* that job was never done.

The masks are now written into the stage directions, into O'Neill's descriptions of the outer appearances, actions, or tones of voice of the characters. The inner conflicts implied in these passages are more marked than ever. Deborah plays two roles, youth and old age; these ingredients vary in different proportions throughout the acts. In I, i she is "forty-five but looks much younger" (MSM 2), in the following scene she "seems much older than her forty-nine years. . . . Her figure is still graceful in all its movements, and by contrast with her face, youthful" (MSM 27-28). In II, ii she "has the look of a surprisingly youthful grandmother" (MSM 95), in the final scene "her small, girlish figure has grown so terribly emaciated that she gives the impression of being bodiless, a little, skinny, witch-like, old woman, an evil godmother conjured to life from the pages of a fairy tale." Her face is "a mask of death" (MSM 161), as her persistent efforts to find the Fountain of Youth are now over. The changes, certainly a task for an actress, are assisted by Deborah's cos-

---

[6] Doris V. Falk, *Eugene O'Neill and the Tragic Tension*, pp. 145-55.
[7] Clark (ed.), *European Theories*, pp. 534-35.

tumes: as a rule, she wears white, but in I, iii she wears a black mourning costume.

The masks are changed not only between the scenes and acts; there are frequent shifts from one role to another within the speeches, especially in the monologues. Changes from love to hatred, from anger to apology are abrupt: Sara directs one grateful sentence to Deborah "Moved—impulsively," the next "Abruptly hostile—contemptuously" (MSM 54). Sometimes the roles within a role result in small inner dialogues: "Age? You harp on age as though I were a withered old hag!" (MSM 3). Both "you" and "I" refer to Deborah, soliloquizing at the log cabin. A fourth variation on the use of masks is formed by contrasting ways of speaking: when Sara is angry, she falls into her old Irish brogue, into her former role; when she has lived long enough with Deborah, she begins copying her ladylike, detached manner of speaking. All in all, O'Neill's dynamic late dialogue is about to be conceived; what is lacking is a factual, realistic basis. The masks are already written literally between the lines. At this stage of development the dynamics run wild, shifting romantically and feverishly between extreme opposites.

The themes of the play are drawn together in the last scene. As on many previous occasions, O'Neill resorted to moonlight in his attempt to evoke an atmosphere of fatefulness. This time, there are even more ghastly overtones than usual: "There is a full moon, but clouds keep passing across it so that the light is a ghostly grey, in which all objects are indistinct and their outlines merge into one another, with intermittent brief periods of moonlight so clear the geometrical form of each shrub and its black shadow are sharply defined." This repetitive lighting effect gives Deborah's corner of seclusion "more compellingly than ever before the atmosphere of a perversely magnified child's toy garden, distorted and artificial" (MSM 161).

The description is in keeping with the second major function given to the summer-house. Simon has never been able to forget a fairytale told to him by his mother in that garden. An evil and beautiful enchantress, obviously representing Deb-

orah, has banished a young king from his happy land; after
bitter trials he finds a magic door and hears that his kingdom
may be behind it.[8] But he is also made to suspect that the realm
may be changed into a desert—and "so he remained for
the rest of his life standing before the door, and became a
beggar, whining for alms from all who passed by" (MSM
111). In Simon's mind the magic door and the door to the
summer-house have become one. The door built on the stage
became a symbol of both his fear of life and his longing for
the lost world of childhood and motherly love.

In the last scene of the play we find him under the compulsion that he must enter the summer-house with Deborah—
and succumb to madness. Again, the steps of a house are the
area of action where the fate of several characters is decided.
Deborah tries to make Simon enter the house, Sara tries to
hinder him from doing so: as her last desperate gesture Sara
promises to stop fighting. "You know no woman could love
a man more than when she gives him up to save him!" she
says (MSM 188). This is too much for Deborah; she pushes
Simon away and enters the house alone, as full of pride and
disdain for the world as ever, only to return a moment later
clearly out of her mind. Simon is, in a way, saved: he calls
Sara "Mother" like a little boy.[9]

More Stately Mansions must be a disappointment to anyone who expected another posthumous masterpiece[10] like

[8] Braem sees in this detail the influence of *A Dream Play* by
Strindberg (*Eugene O'Neill*, p. 113).

[9] Since the following cycle plays do not exist, we cannot know
for sure how this end is to be interpreted. Braem is inclined to think
that Sara has lost her struggle: he calls Sara "a victim of Simon and
Deborah who at last devote themselves to the dreams, without
reserve" (p. 115). On the other hand, Simon never enters the summer-house; the stage action shows that his solution is different from
Deborah's. To me, the end is an act of exorcism: Sara feels free from
her compulsion to collect material goods, to reach for "more stately
mansions." In the final account, her love proved to be less egoistic
than Deborah's. The bucolic existence planned by Sara (MSM 190-91)
did not, however, give Simon a lasting happiness: he was to die four
years later, making Sara "a widow at thirty-eight" (the Gelbs, p. 792).

[10] "Whatever the favorable impression of the Swedish production,

Long Day's Journey Into Night, or even a play actable and worth acting like *A Touch of the Poet*. Gierow and Gallup, the editors, have evidently done what men and doctors can; the play, as a whole, could not be salvaged. Gierow, in his comments about the unevenness of the manuscript, found among the unshaped scenes some of "savage dramatic power."[11] This description is, indeed, applicable to the final scenic image: a kind of overpowering awe emerges in it, mainly as a result of the strongly concentrated means of expression employed. Deborah's seclusion is there, represented by the garden wall; so is the whole complex relationship between mother and son, between fear of life and daring to face it, symbolized by that fateful door with the dimension of time behind it—it opens into Simon's childhood.

Yet one cannot help noticing blemishes even in this scene. One of the most amazing circles O'Neill ever closed is that this unfinished play echoes his very first effort, the crude melodrama *A Wife for a Life*. Sara's decisive speech is a transformation of the absolving quotation at the end of young O'Neill's sketch for the vaudeville: " 'Greater love hath no man than this that he giveth his wife for his friend' " (LP 156). And the atmosphere reminds us, of all plays, of *Where the Cross Is Made*: a parent, this time a mother, is about to drive her son to madness in a moonlight scene where irrational compulsions and the past are powerfully present.

Proceeding to more fundamental faults we can note that *More Stately Mansions* veers awkwardly between realism and something else, which can perhaps be called expressionism, perhaps an effort toward a Greek sense of fate. The central characters cannot be taken as representatives of different sectors within a psyche, full of conflicting tensions. There are too many realistic ingredients to allow for this interpretation: Sara is bound to her Irish-American background;

---

the published play may well strike a reader as decidedly scattered in effect" (Gassner, *Eugene O'Neill*, p. 42).

[11] Cargill *et al.*, p. 379: a reprinting of "Eugene O'Neill's Posthumous Plays" by Gierow, originally published in *World Theatre*, Spring 1958.

Deborah has her garden, Simon his office. On the other hand, as a picture of the life of a businessman the play is just as illuminating as *The Great God Brown* was in its efforts to depict an artist. O'Neill never seems to have developed beyond the level of certain stock opinions in his social thinking: materialism is bad; power leads its possessors into corruption.[12] These "discoveries" are demonstrated pretentiously and melodramatically. Moreover, Simon's (and Deborah's) view of reality is precariously romantic, of the horror romanticism variety: "You will have to learn to be shameless here. You will have to deal daily with the greedy fact of life as it really lives. You will have to strip life naked, and face it" (MSM 91), he lectures to Sara. His sudden transformation from a young idealist into a business tycoon completely void of conscience is unconvincing; both his roles are those of old melodrama, if not those of *The Count of Monte Cristo* itself.[13] And he preaches too much, even for a recently disappointed idealist turned cynic.

Eric Bentley, a critic from the forties, has spoken of the "over life-size" characters in *Mourning Becomes Electra*: "Unhappily this is not because of the size of their bones but, as it were, by inflation with gas, cultural and psychological."[14] The remark is better justified in the case of *More Stately Mansions*. The proper reaction to a tragedy is not to feel a temptation to pat the characters on the shoulder: Relax! Take it easy! It cannot be as terrible as that to have both a wife and a mother, can it? Yet O'Neill is not wholly irresponsible for that reaction. *More Stately Mansions* is a play in

[12] Carpenter connects *More Stately Mansions* with O'Neill's dissatisfaction with his own homes, and sees in the name of the play a suggestion of "all the early American idealism which O'Neill and his modern pessimism were now rejecting" (*Eugene O'Neill*, p. 58).

[13] Raleigh makes a comparison: "Now as *Monte Cristo* was fake history attached to real history through the evocation of Napoleon, O'Neill's cycle was intended to be imaginary (although 'real,' psychologically, socially, and morally) history, but attached to actual history through the recreation of the American past. And Napoleon was to have played an important role too" (p. 62).

[14] Cargill *et al.*, p. 342: a reprinting of "Trying to Like O'Neill," first published in the *Kenyon Review, 14* (1952), 476-92, republished in *In Search of the Theatre* (New York: Alfred A. Knopf, 1953).

which an implausible triangle theme is demonstrated with O'Neill's furious thoroughness.

In general, a story of isolation is not easily told in terms of the stage. Drama is a form of art where people come into contact with one another: Deborah's dilemma, an irresistible temptation to flee from all forms of contact with life, is not a natural subject for a playwright. It is not concretized in a treatment like this. Deborah's speeches and her suffering have an abstract flavor—indeed, because there is more verbal analysis of the suffering than exploration of its causes.

More Stately Mansions was published after *Long Day's Journey Into Night*, and it is impossible to ignore its many autobiographical elements. They are still more prominent because the play lacks artistic distance: it is, in many passages, embarrassingly frank. Deborah is another Nina Leeds and another Mary Tyrone, and the entire play is an elaborate circumlocution by O'Neill who did not yet dare to face his dead.[15] Substitute drug addiction for a compulsion to withdraw from the wicked world into a garden and you have a better motivation for Deborah's behavior than any of those presented in the play. Take the hyphen from the word "summer-house" and you have a "summer house," the scene of *Long Day's Journey*; biographies tell us that it was located in New London, Connecticut. Listen to Simon and compare his speech with Edmund's anxiety when he learns about his mother's drug addiction (LDJ 118): "I have never forgotten the anguished sense of being suddenly betrayed, of being wounded and deserted and left alone in a life in which there was no security or faith or love but only danger and suspicion and devouring greed! By God, I hated you then! I wished you dead! I wished I had never been born!" (MSM 184). Simon's brother Joel is only scorned by him; Joel's capabilities are limited, and in one scene (III, i) he is, rather unnecessarily, shown full of lascivious intentions typical of

[15] ". . . the basis for plot and character is rooted in O'Neill's love-hate battle with his own brother, his childhood hostility toward his father and his subsequent neurotic relationship with women" (Arthur Gelb, "Onstage He Played the Novelist," *New York Times Book Review*, Aug. 30, 1964).

261

Jamie Tyrone. Or take the banker Tenard, a full-chested man like so many of O'Neill's father-images in his plays; his scene is motivated, to be sure, by an intention to show the ruthless methods used by Simon and Sara in their business dealings. Yet the scene is exaggerated, in an unpleasant and needless way, until the banker "seems to collapse inside" (MSM 155)—as a minor revenge on all full-chested fathers afraid of poverty. *More Stately Mansions* is, however, first and foremost a revenge on Ella Quinlan O'Neill, without the pity and compassion of *Long Day's Journey Into Night*— perhaps because O'Neill's family chronicle, opus six, was intended to be better disguised by distance in time and plot. Nor is *A Touch of the Poet*, a play about a deep-chested actor and poser, as cruel or as devoid of conciliatory tones as *More Stately Mansions*, this play about a mother who proudly flees from her duty to love and from the outer reality which crushes her into dreams and into madness.

The theme of a play may be terrifying and yet the play itself have a victorious harmony of its own; it proves an artist's mastery over his material. What gives *More Stately Mansions* a kind of ghastly aura is that O'Neill is not in control over his theme; yet he has, by and large, control over his means of expression. Except for the overuse of monologues, modified and proper, the scenic means are used in a meaningful way. It is the situations that are driven into absurdity; it is the feelings that are swollen, artificial, hollow.[16] In this unfinished play O'Neill's scenic imagination is like an enormous machine, forever working, forever grinding, with the precision of a machine, going empty, without a meaning, like one of his own horror effects, the automaton. If there is a general harkening back—to history, to childhood and early

---

[16] Richard Gilman has paid attention to the verbal deficiencies of *More Stately Mansions*: "the moral and metaphysical critique and vision exist mostly as a series of statements and isolated confrontations which lack an organic base and a coherent impulse. As elsewhere in O'Neill there is a strenuous attempt to compensate for this condition through an atmosphere of portentousness, a heavy air of 'high' poetry, apocalypse, fervid declamations and mysterious psychological irruptions" ("Mr. O'Neill's very last curtain call," *New York Herald Tribune*, Book Week, May 31, 1964).

adolescence—to be seen in O'Neill's last phase, there is also this faithfulness, perhaps appropriately called symbolic, to the art he first learned something about, to the art of the theatre.

A suspicion also arises, when we remember O'Neill's compulsion to deal with his own family, in the disguise of "the Harford curse." If the cycle had been completed perhaps we would only have received nine more plays about Mary and James Tyrone? All presumably less successful, because less frank, compassionate, and understanding than *Long Day's Journey Into Night*? What helps to make *More Stately Mansions* deficient as a work of art is also its unsatisfactory compromise between realism and "super-naturalism"; O'Neill was only on his way toward his late realism, toward his carefully motivated confession. This is not to say that realism, as such, would be preferred to all other styles: it is only to say that it was the school of writing most appropriate for the play about his parents, brother, and himself which O'Neill had been trying to write throughout his career. In between, there is still another play, another step from the experimental period toward dynamic realism: *The Iceman Cometh*.

15

COMPOSITION FOR SOLOS

AND A CHORUS

THE ICEMAN COMETH

The Iceman Cometh fits the picture of O'Neill's development in many respects. On his way toward his adolescence, toward the summer house in New London, O'Neill stopped for a while in a New York saloon to visit a group of friends he had known in the early nineteen-tens.[1] On his way toward three-dimensional characterization in serious plays, he left the triangle of *More Stately Mansions*, with its abstract Freudian elements, behind. The derelicts in Harry Hope's "hotel" "call for a compassion and sympathetic understanding that is seldom aroused by Reuben Light or even the Mannons."[2] And on his way toward dynamic realism O'Neill has now both the dynamics and the realism under control: behind the surface of realism there is a purposeful patterning of the material, and the result might be called a composition for the theatre.

Evidences of realism are apparent from the first, in the description of the setting; the pendulum of the dynamics is put into motion in the characterization of the cast. "The back room is crammed with round tables and chairs placed so close together that it is a difficult squeeze to pass between them. . . . The walls and ceiling once were white, but it was a long time ago, and they are now so splotched, peeled, stained and dusty that their color can best be described as dirty" (IC 3). At the tables there is a motley crowd of roomers,

---

[1] Raleigh has explored the social background of the play: Tammany Hall, the protector of Harry Hope and others, was both "richly, unashamedly corrupt" (*The Plays of Eugene O'Neill*, p. 67) and had "a sense of humor about itself" (p. 74); popular songs were employed in the play to evoke memories of the good old days (p. 73).

[2] Pallette, "O'Neill's *A Touch of the Poet* and His Other Last Plays," *Arizona Quarterly, 13*, 4 (1957), 313.

slumbering in the early morning hours. Nine of them are furnished with the epithet "one-time" in the list of characters; Willie Oban is, even more ironically, "a Harvard Law School alumnus" (IC v). Thus the characters are given two roles, two masks right away: a contrast is immediately established between what they are now and what they once were—and still believe they might be tomorrow.[3]

The tension is further emphasized by what might be called a "yet," "but," or "still" quality, so common in O'Neill's descriptions of the outer appearance of his characters: "Still, he manages to preserve an atmosphere of nattiness and there is nothing dirty about his appearance"—Joe Mott, a Negro. "But despite his blubbery mouth and sodden bloodshot blue eyes, there is still a suggestion of old authority lurking in him like a memory of the drowned"—Piet Wetjoen, the Boer "General." "But his forehead is fine, his eyes are intelligent and there once was a competent ability in him" (IC 5-6)— James Cameron, one-time war correspondent, now "Jimmy Tomorrow." These and other contrasts are demonstrated in stage action and speeches from the moment the play opens, and its dialogue starts swinging.

Larry Slade, a pivotal character, sits at the table at left front in a prominent position. Larry's first role is that of a "Spielleiter"; he introduces the cast to Don Parritt, a newcomer. His second function is begun at the same time: he is to play unwilling confidant and finally executioner to Parritt, a tense eighteen-year-old boy, perhaps Larry's son, who has betrayed a group of anarchists to the police, among them his mother Rose. Why this happened is a carefully guarded secret, not to be revealed before the main action of the play reaches its climax—and this cannot even begin until Hickey,

[3] Raleigh speaks of the importance of names in the play: "Like the blind, or like primitive man, the characters can only perceive something by attaching a name to it, but the name, like its object, is often shifting and ambiguous in meaning." Is Rocky a pimp or a bartender? Is Joe black or white? "The point is . . . that no one is quite sure who or what he or she is" (p. 167)—or what mask he or she is wearing, we might say.

a jocular and profuse salesman, enters the scene to celebrate Harry Hope's birthday as he has always done.

He is eagerly expected all through Act I.[4] While the characters are being introduced, they are also being organized into pairs and small groups. Within the total field of tension minor areas of local contact and conflict emerge. Larry, "the old Foolosopher" on his grandstand, pretends to have lost all faith and interest in life, especially in the Anarchist Movement to which he once belonged; he sits at the same table with Hugo Kalmar, a foreign-born anarchist, who periodically wakes up from his drunken stupor to denounce capitalism or sing snatches from a battle song. It is the year 1912: "General" Wetjoen, obviously of Dutch origin, is still fighting the Boer War against "Captain" Lewis, an obvious Englishman; they have a connecting link with Jimmy Tomorrow, correspondent in the same war. By gathering different nationalities into his cast O'Neill apparently aimed at a miniature of the American melting pot. Harry Hope, the benevolent proprietor of the saloon, is surrounded by two parasitic relatives, both "retired": Ed Mosher, a circus man, and Pat McCloin, a police lieutenant ousted from his job. The latter has a point of connection with Willie Oban, the law student, most advanced in his alcoholism. Joe Mott, the Negro, is most often alone among a white cast; he helps the bartenders, who have their private sources of income—Rocky keeps two street walkers, Chuck plans to marry his Cora.

These groups are played against one another and in parallel directions.[5] Controlling a cast of twenty characters, among them a uniform group of ten roomers, would have been a difficult task if O'Neill had not employed these minor circles within the large one. The greatest common denominator between all characters is their belief in a delusion, a "pipe

---

[4] ". . . Hickey's entrance is delayed so long that—like another long-awaited figure, Beckett's Godot—he begins to accumulate supernatural qualities" (Brustein, *The Theatre of Revolt*, p. 343).

[5] After O'Neill had given up his God-mongering and universe-mongering, the "only generalization that remained was the principle of polarity, for he could never see human experience except in terms of antinomies, alternations, and repetitions" (Raleigh, p. 17).

dream." Cora, Pearl, and Margie are just tarts, not whores; Rocky and Chuck are bartenders, not pimps; the roomers are firm in their belief in getting their old jobs back. There is thus a state of happy equilibrium in this "No Chance Saloon . . . , The End of the line Café, The Bottom of the Sea Rathskeller" (IC 25)—until Hickey arrives.

He is a changed Hickey. He has given up drinking, and starts selling his new message with all the persuasiveness of an efficient salesman. It hits everyone on the stage where he is weakest. Away with the pipe dreams! cries Hickey. Why not face life as it is, without any delusions? Hickey has done so, and is now full of peace and contentment. He succeeds in spoiling Harry's birthday party beyond repair by telling them that his wife Evelyn is dead. Feelings of uneasiness and aggression start coming to the surface in Act III, after Hickey has spent all night convincing the others that it is necessary to realize one's pipe dreams in order to kill them.

The roomers come down and go out—in pairs, in small groups. The door of the bar is treated as the doors of the Mannon house and of the Harford summer-house were; there is thematic significance gathering around it. Only this time the intention is tragi-comic. Indoors the characters have found refuge; they are forced by Hickey to empty their stock of excuses and finally to enter the oppressing world outside. Last of all, to gain full advantage of the preceding repetitions, O'Neill lets Harry Hope cross the fateful threshold: he has not been outside since his beloved (and nagging) wife died twenty years ago. He is not outside long when an automobile, a novelty to him, nearly runs him over. At least this is how he tells it—not very convincingly. As in *Ah, Wilderness!* O'Neill employs a scenic unit used previously with tragic connotations to create comedy, here as an interlude in a tragedy.

All the time, the characters and events encountered by Hickey and Parritt bring these two closer to the final confession. At the end of Act III Hickey tells his audience that Evelyn was murdered. Rocky and Larry have their misgivings; together with them we begin to suspect Hickey. Through these means O'Neill deliberately directs our attention to a specific question: why? In a straightforward thriller the problem would be: who? All obstacles, half-truths, abruptly interrupted sentences, and the illusion of final peace and contentment are swept aside in Hickey's long modified monologue, face to face with those he wanted to save. He did not kill Evelyn because he wanted to spare her from further suffering as the wife of a hopeless victim to periodical drinking bouts; he killed her because he could not stand being forgiven any longer.[6] In a sudden twist, where the voltage between love and hate is at its highest, Hickey reveals that he cursed his dead wife and her illusions of his amendment: "Well, you know what you can do with your pipe dream now, you damned bitch!" (IC 241). (See Fig. 8.) The confession, told "obliviously," is immediately followed by unconvincing persuasions of love; and Hickey's self-defensive remark that he must have been out of his mind is eagerly accepted by the roomers. (See Fig. 9.) If they can believe that Hickey has been insane from the beginning, they can safely return to their old dreams.[7] So they do; all except Parritt, who is forced by Hickey's example into a parallel confession. He commits suicide, the only relief granted to him by Larry. His body hits the ground on the backyard shortly

---

[6] Jamie Tyrone comes with a variation of "The Ballad of Reading Gaol" by Wilde (LDJ 166)—and so does Chiari, by calling *The Iceman Cometh* "a kind of Dance of death," in which guilty men "end in killing the thing they love because they are all too aware that they cannot love enough" (*Landmarks of Contemporary Drama*, p. 139).

[7] Bentley misinterprets Hickey as a real maniac (Cargill *et al.*, *O'Neill and His Plays*, p. 340: reprinted from *In Search of Theater*). He is corrected by Brustein: Hickey "only claims to have been insane at the time of the murder, but even this is a self-deception which he adopts so as not to face his real feelings towards his wife." The crowd is willing to let Hickey have his illusion, if he lets them have theirs: "Hickey hesitates because he knows he told them the truth, but for the sake of his own peace, he must agree to the trade. Thus, he enters their community at last: mutual toleration through mutual silence" (pp. 346-47). A similar conclusion is drawn by Carpenter (*Eugene O'Neill*, p. 156).

before the roomers, as a final touch of irony,[8] begin singing in a drunken chorus, each a different song. O'Neill's composition closes with a cacophony, out of which a French Revolutionary song sung by Parritt's fellow anarchist, Hugo Kalmar, emerges victorious.

The Iceman Cometh is essentially a series of modified monologues. They are intertwined and counterpointed, until the final impression is far from static; and their material is richer than in *More Stately Mansions*. There are numerous stage directions in which O'Neill remarks that his characters speak out of inner compulsions and that the listeners are inattentive. Parritt goes on "as if Larry hadn't spoken" (IC 125); Hickey speaks "staring ahead of him now as if he were talking aloud to himself as much as to them" (IC 81). These are the two characters in whom the inner compulsions are too strong to be subdued by any amount of resistance, not even that furnished by a stage full of antagonistic listeners. Willie Oban and Hugo Kalmar, on the other hand, have the minimum amount of restraint: they emerge from their drunken stupor to shout their thoughts and pass away again. The others are in between; yet all are given an opportunity to reveal their characteristic fluctuation between two different masks.

The dynamics within the speeches are part of the reason why O'Neill was now capable of relying on his dialogue more than ever. The speeches are written in his native tongue— the American vernacular.[9] The changes in the visual stage picture are kept to a minimum: there are three settings, all

[8] "Ours is preeminently an age of tragic irony. The irony is implicit in the dominant mode of metaphysical interrogation and defiance that pervades the work of such writers as Kafka, Malraux, Camus, Gide, Eugene O'Neill, and Samuel Beckett" (Glicksberg, *The Tragic Vision in Twentieth-Century Literature*, p. 152).

[9] To Raleigh, *The Iceman Cometh* is the "greatest and most comprehensive linguistic symphony that O'Neill composed. . . . Of this collection of accents O'Neill is in complete control, especially the resources for humor" (pp. 226-27). Raleigh also calls the play a return to the "melting pot" cast of O'Neill's early plays (p. 253).

depicting the same bar with minor variations in the angle. It is worth noticing that even here O'Neill remained truthful to his circle structure: Acts I and IV have the same setting, with a small but significant change in the placement of the chairs, emphasizing Hickey's lonely position. The impression of immobility is further accentuated by keeping stage action to a minimum; most of the time, all the characters are on stage, sitting solidly in their chairs. All these "demobilizing" factors help to keep the attention of the audience focused on O'Neill's music-like handling of his themes.

On the next level, there is an interaction between different characters and groups of characters. Rosamond Gilder in her review of the original production of *The Iceman Cometh* states: "There is little movement; there is only an antiphonal development of themes. . . . O'Neill's bums . . . spend most of their time in blissful or tormented alcoholic slumber. O'Neill uses this device to bring them in and out of the action without making them leave the stage. As the play progresses, the way the tables are grouped in the backroom and bar and the manner in which actors are grouped around them—slumped over asleep or sitting in a deathly daydream —provides a constant visual comment on the developing theme."[10] Within the realistic framework there is a thematic fluidity which would not be permitted in a tighter play, closer to the formulas of the "well-made play." The coordinating factor is a problem common to all characters—not a plot, in which each should perform his own, highly individual function.[11] The significance of the plot had been diminishing in O'Neill ever since *Ah, Wilderness!*, another indication that *Days Without End* and not the comedy was a digression. *The Iceman Cometh* is, in its orchestral organization of the material, O'Neill's *The Three Sisters*.

The problem of length arises out of necessity. As a matter of fact, it has been actual ever since *Strange Interlude*;

[10] Cargill *et al.*, pp. 206-07: reprinted from *Theatre Arts*, Dec. 1946.

[11] "In a sense all stories in *The Iceman Cometh* are individual variations on one story: the enticements, deceptions, complexities, and ambiguities of 'the pipe dream' " (Raleigh, p. 206).

270

Mourning Becomes Electra, a "plotty" and straightforward play, was not as open to criticism as O'Neill's long postwar plays. There is full reason to refer again to the paradox of the O'Neillian length—a paradox seemingly so easily solved with the help of a blue pencil.[12]

There are circumstances that speak for cautiousness when shortening the mature O'Neill.[13] A certain speech may not carry any theme—but perhaps it helps to create atmosphere. A detail is repeated eighteen times[14]—yet perhaps this kind of piling up is part of the playwright's total plan. What happens to the composition if whole movements are dropped out?[15] It is conceivable that the criterion of those most eager to shorten O'Neill has been a play with a tightly knit plot. *The Iceman Cometh* is a play of another kind. On the other hand, a music-like handling of the themes is not one of the

[12] Bentley shortened *The Iceman Cometh* for his Zürich production, taking away an hour of O'Neillian eloquence or "jelly" from the "iron jar" of the play: "Jelly. Within the tyrannically, mechanically rigid scenes, there is an excessive amount of freedom. The order of speeches can be juggled without loss, and almost any speech can be cut in half." Yet Bentley is led to confess that "the abridgment did call attention rather cruelly to the excessively schematic character of the play" (Cargill *et al.,* p. 337: "Trying to Like O'Neill"). What he does not confess is that he apparently cut away part of the spontaneity of the play.

[13] In principle, repetitions are an essential part of a playwright's *scenic* strategy, as phrased by Clemen: "It is one of the artistic achievements of the great dramatist to prepare in the mind of the audience a whole net of expectations, intuitions and conjectures so that each new act, each new scene, is approached with a definite predisposition. . . . For the climax of the drama does not come suddenly; we ourselves have gone the whole way and have followed the separate threads which led up to the climax" (*The Development of Shakespeare's Imagery,* pp. 6-7).

[14] The Gelbs, *O'Neill,* p. 864.

[15] Brustein calls the play "bulky and unwieldy in the extreme," yet approves of O'Neill's ideas as "totally convincing," and his total plan as a purposeful one: "even the repetitions are an intricate aspect of the total design. O'Neill has multiplied his antagonists in order to illuminate every aspect of his theme. . . ." There are thus different kinds of illusions represented by the characters: political (Hugo), racial (Joe), domestic (Cora and Chuck), status illusions (the prostitutes), psychological (Parritt), intellectual (Oban), philosophical (Larry), and religious (Hickey) (Brustein, pp. 340-42).

first associations an outsider makes when seeing a collection of bums sitting in their "last harbor"; it is possible that someone hears only the words "pipe dream," not the themes persistently carried by them. All in all, I am ready to leave the shortening to the stage directors who know their theatre and their cast and have their own interpretation of the play—hopefully, a profound one. In other words, Gassner is right: some of the repetitiveness "can be removed without injury to the play."[16]

Gassner has also spoken of the "cyclopean" architecture of *The Iceman Cometh*.[17] There is definitely an architecture behind it; even if the action seems to be transferred freely from group to group, from character to character, the play's total structure is carefully planned. It is the director's task to evoke the total atmosphere; it is not his task to call attention to the underlying scheme. There are sudden reversals in the mood of the play: Hickey receives a spirited welcome, then his transformation arouses bafflement; his toast to Harry in the birthday party is greeted by "an enthusiastic chorus," then he mentions the words "pipe dream," and "in an instant the attitude of everyone has reverted to uneasy, suspicious defensiveness" (IC 144-45). One of the pipe dreams that keeps the play swinging from one harbor to another is that insults and revelations are only "kidding." The dynamics are under control; the twists are motivated both psychologically and structurally. Comedy is used to build up tragedy.

Waith has described the whole movement of the play by comparing it to "the advance and retreat of a huge wave." It begins with the characters in a torpor, it ends with their

---

[16] Gassner, *Eugene O'Neill*, p. 38.

[17] Gassner, *Theatre at the Crossroads*, p. 233. Gassner also praises José Quintero's revival of the play for preserving the massiveness of the script: "Quintero submitted to O'Neill instead of trying to tame and refine him" (p. 232). In his article "Postscript to a Journey," Quintero has described the structure of the play in musical terms: "My work was somewhat like that of an orchestra conductor, emphasizing rhythms, being constantly aware of changing tempos" (Raleigh [ed.], *Twentieth Century Interpretations of The Iceman Cometh*, p. 32, reprinted from *Theatre Arts, 41*, Apr. 1957).

"slipping back into drunken stupor; only three of them have been flung free of the wave—Hickey, Parritt, and Larry."[18] The same characters are selected by Tom F. Driver as the core of *The Iceman Cometh*: "The play might be diagrammed with three concentric circles. In orbit on the outer circle are the numerous characters who inhabit Harry Hope's bar, including Harry himself." Larry and Parritt, who do not return to their previous state of existence, are "in a circle within the outer one," while Hickey "occupies the play's innermost circle" and his own story "is virtually a play within the play and . . . the core of the entire business."[19]

After these structural considerations, we are ready to concentrate on the central chorus scenes in *The Iceman Cometh*. It is O'Neill's last group play; as in his previous efforts within the limits of this genre, he is primarily interested in the relations between an individual and a uniformly reacting mass of people. There is interaction, not only within the speeches and within and between minor groups of characters, as indicated above; there is also interaction between Hickey and the roomers, and this tension is partly responsible for the most memorable scenic image in the entire play—the moment of Hickey's confession.

Driver is right: Hickey is the protagonist of *The Iceman Cometh*. Not all critics have drawn this conclusion. Engel writes: "The protagonist, Larry, also serves a choral function as he comments upon the action and interprets the motives of the numerous other characters"; he is echoed by Doris V. Falk.[20] If we say that the protagonist serves a choral func-

[18] Waith, "An Exercise in Unmasking," p. 189.

[19] Tom F. Driver, "On the Last Plays of Eugene O'Neill," *Tulane Drama Review, 3* (1958), 13-14. A slightly different hierarchy is delineated by Raleigh (pp. 162-63). Leonard Chabrowe compares the triangle Hickey—Parritt—Larry with the constellation Lazarus—Tiberius—Caligula, and calls the later play "essentially a transposition of *Lazarus Laughed*" ("Dionysus in *The Iceman Cometh*," *Modern Drama, 4*, 377). His observations on O'Neill's use of the chorus to achieve a ritual effect are remarkable (pp. 385-87).

[20] Engel, *The Haunted Heroes of Eugene O'Neill*, p. 283; in his later study, "O'Neill, 1960," Engel calls Larry "protagonist and chorus" (*Modern Drama, 3*, 1960, 221). Doris V. Falk, *Eugene O'Neill and the Tragic Tension*, p. 159.

tion, the elements of Greek tragedy get confused, and the result is a contradiction in terms. This would not be so harmful, if it were not in this particular case apt to conceal certain central features of the play. For there is a chorus in *The Iceman Cometh*, and there is a protagonist playing against this chorus: Hickey against the roomers.

This is not the first time O'Neill employed one or several choruses. *The Moon of the Caribbees, The Emperor Jones, The Hairy Ape,* and *Marco Millions* included chorus scenes, until the line of development reached its climax in the exuberant arias and "choral odes" of *Lazarus Laughed*. After that, the group of townspeople was utilized with restraint in *Mourning Becomes Electra*, at the beginning of each play. In *The Iceman Cometh* the chorus is still more fully integrated into the fabric of the play: chorus members are simply actors with different roles to perform. They are gathered into a chorus in two key scenes, at the end of Acts II and IV; these scenes are prepared for by the group scene at the close of Act I.

Obviously, this is a dramatic not a lyric chorus. Yet it is possible to draw functional parallels to Greek practice. Lucas writes about the general task of the Athenian chorus: "It provides the poet with a mouthpiece, and the spectator with a counterpart of himself. It forms a living foreground of common humanity above which the heroes tower."[21] In their refusal to listen to Hickey's story the roomers express the natural abhorrence shared by the audience. Following their temporary chorus leader, Harry Hope, they denounce the towering hero of the play: "HOPE: Get it over, you longwinded bastard! . . . (*A chorus of dull, resentful protest from all the group. They mumble, like sleepers who curse a person who keeps awakening them, 'What's it to us? We want to pass out in peace!*' . . .)" (IC 234). They are not "wasps, birds, frogs, goats, snakes," nor more fantastically "clouds, dreams, cities, seasons";[22] they are drunkards. Or, if a

[21] Lucas, *Tragedy*, p. 82.

[22] Roy C. Flickinger, *The Greek Theatre and Its Drama* (1926), p. 135.

1. *All God's Chillun Got Wings.* Ella and Jim (Anni Hämäläinen and Kalle Kirjavainen) leaving the church in the scenic image of Act I.

2. *Mourning Becomes Electra.* Christine (Pauline Brunius) sitting above Lavinia (Kerstin Nylander) and Ezra (Axel Slangus) on the steps of the Mannon house.

3. Profile of the young O'Neill. Reprinted by permission of Dr. Donald Gallup, Curator of the Collection of American Literature at Yale University.

4. *More Stately Mansions.* O'Neill's own sketch of the façade of the Harford mansion.

5. Sketch by O'Neill of the sitting room in Sara's house, *More Stately Mansions*, Act I, Scene iii. Cf. Appendix B, p. 355.

6. O'Neill's sketch for the parlor of the Harford mansion, Act II, Scene iii. Cf. Appendix B, p. 355.

These sketches have been reprinted by permission of Carlotta Monterey O'Neill, Dr. Gallup, and Yale University Press from *More Stately Mansions.* Copyright © 1964 by Carlotta Monterey O'Neill.

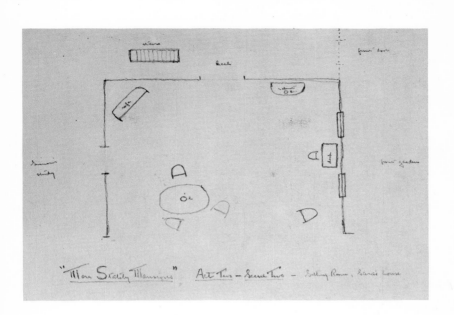

"More Stately Mansions" — Act Two – Scene Two – Sitting Room, Simon's house

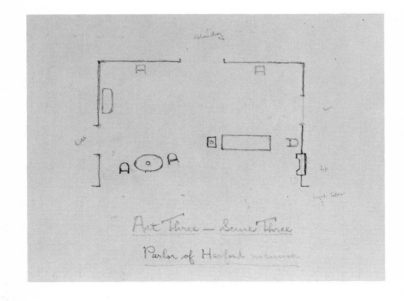

Act Three – Scene Three

Parlor of Harford mansion

7. *More Stately Mansions*. Deborah (Ingrid Bergman) and
Sara (Colleen Dewhurst) trying to devour Simon (Arthur Hill)
in the New York production of *More Stately Mansions*.
Photograph by Tony Esparza.

more fantastic interpretation is allowed within the realistic framework of the play, we come close to one of the roles listed above: they are pipe dreams.

More specifically, O'Neill seems to be closest to the functions given to the chorus by Sophocles. In a well-known passage of his *Poetics* Aristotle recommends the dramatic function: "The chorus should be treated as one of the actors, should be an integral part of the whole, and should participate in the action, not as in the plays of Euripides but as in those of Sophocles."[23] Most specifically, O'Neill moves close to the functions given in the *Antigone* and the *Oedipus Tyrannus*: "When Creon, in the *Tyrannus*, enters in indignation, the chorus is there to receive him, but the scene gains enormously in effectiveness from the fact that it thus begins on a level of neutrality, from which it can gradually work up to its violent close."[24] In *The Iceman Cometh* the role of the chorus begins on a level of friendship and eager acceptance, from which it can gradually work up to the level of antagonism and hatred—until the final, ironical twist brings back the friendly atmosphere. O'Neill was not satisfied with one swing of the pendulum: he made it turn back again, to add to the dynamics of the play.

It is important to emphasize both the functional parallels and the formal discrepancies. O'Neill employs the chorus of the roomers much less literally than the several choruses in the pretentious sequences in *Lazarus Laughed* located in antique Greece and Rome. Hickey has sixteen listeners in both of the chorus scenes, in the latter only after the arrival of the two policemen; this is one more than the prescribed fifteen—if Larry is not interpreted as "the second actor." Whether this conjecture is correct or not has no bearing on the effectiveness of the chorus scenes. Any of the choreutae can be made to leave this function and carry with his individuality a fragment of one of the themes. The movements are mainly mental; the reactions are described with precision (even

[23] Allan H. Gilbert (ed.), *Literary Criticism: Plato to Dryden* (1940), p. 97.
[24] H. D. F. Kitto, *Greek Tragedy* (1954), p. 168.

the silences are recorded). The role of the choryphaeus is alternately occupied by several characters, occasionally by Larry or even Chuck, most consistently by Harry Hope. The first of the chorus scenes is more fluid and less intense than the finale; short interruptions in the conversation between Hickey and the chorus are possible in both—in Act II Willie even sings his song. When Hickey approaches his final confession, the intensity of the scene increases and the interpolations become shorter: the protagonist eats, as it were, the role of the chorus, in spite of its collective efforts.

O'Neill mentions the word "chorus" several times in his stage directions; yet its decisive function in the total dynamics of *The Iceman Cometh* has hardly been recognized emphatically enough. This time O'Neill did not seek for added scope by employing literary parallels; he employed devices of the theatre. Everything in the play is made to concern a whole group of characters, and this group is drawn together into a chorus which forms a background for the soloists. Hickey's sudden reversal from pretended love to real hatred reverberates much more strongly than any of the fluctuations in *More Stately Mansions* simply because his modified monologue is addressed to a stageful of characters, all reacting to the speech, if not otherwise, at least by keeping silent.[25] They are a continuous visual and aural commentary on the monologue; this is the scene in which the illustrating function of the secondary characters, mentioned by Gilder, has its greatest impetus. Nor is O'Neill alone among the modern dramatists to employ various modifications of the antique chorus; T. S. Eliot, Jean Giraudoux, Sean O'Casey, Bertolt Brecht, and Friedrich Dürrenmatt share his company, the last in *The Visit*, where the chorus scenes proceed toward greater tightness and intensity, as they do in *The Iceman Cometh*. What is even more important than distinguished company is that the chorus is made an intricate part of O'Neill's play, of its

[25] Hickey's "fifteen minute harangue" is mentioned by Gassner as "the most memorable episode in O'Neill's play, which is never more genuinely tragic than at that point" (*Theatre at the Crossroads*, p. 62).

dynamics.[26] It does not imitate the outer form of the Greek chorus; it repeats its accentuating function. The solos and the chorus sing the same melody.

The acute observations on the structure of *The Iceman Cometh* put forth by Driver have been quoted above; they are supported by scenic evidence, by the grouping of the characters in Act IV. Driver also mentions the function of the secondary characters as a chorus. Later on in his study, he drifts to rather doubtful conclusions via *A Touch of the Poet*. He senses in that play a kind of distrust in art, in the creations of human imagination. According to this line of thought, O'Neill was interested in art only as a formula for philosophical quest: "he was not concerned with art as form, or if he was so, only negatively, as a matter of pure necessity. . . . His vocation of writing plays was not followed for the purpose of achieving the best possible plays, the right forms incarnating the right conceptions, but rather for the purpose of using the writing to wrestle with life itself. . . . [His work] is weak at almost every point where we care to ask an aesthetic question."[27]

Driver's aesthetics apparently do not include the art of the theatre, for this is where O'Neill's plays are strong at almost every point. A man who is "not concerned with art as form" does not write masterpieces; after *The Iceman Cometh* O'Neill completed another, *Long Day's Journey Into Night*. Nor did he renounce every aspect of his past in *The Iceman Cometh*, as Engel assumes: "he repudiated not only love, faith and truth but also, by implication, that to which he had dedicated his life: the theatre itself depending as it is upon the willing acceptance of illusion."[28] O'Neill's dedication to the theatre is written on every page of his canon, not by any means excluding the late climax; the speculations of Driver

[26] According to Clemen, "the young Shakespeare employs [verbal] images as superfluous adornment," while "the mature Shakespeare—in contrast—employs them as a direct form of expression, as the vehicle of his thoughts" (*Shakespeare's Imagery*, pp. 33-34). The chorus, an adornment in *Marco Millions*, is employed by the mature O'Neill "as a direct form of expression."

[27] Driver, p. 17.

[28] Engel, p. 295.

and Engel are unnecessary. O'Neill might have been separated from the theatre of the late thirties and forties, but
he was not estranged from his personal means of expression,
tried and conquered during thirty years of restless and vigorous experimentation. Now, approaching the end of his career,
he masters them.[29]

A fallacy of another kind is to deny all development in
O'Neill's last plays. A primary exponent for this opinion was
Miller, who said in 1962: "There was really nothing new.
Only two plays had previously been unseen, and they showed
nothing beyond extreme length (this was old hat) and heavy-
handed 'realism' (an early O'Neill trademark)."[30] It is remarkable that the word "realism" is furnished with apostrophes, as an indication of uncertainty. It *is* a vague word:
it means hardly anything because it means almost anything.
It is a concept in the history of literature, denoting a phase
in the development of the novel after Flaubert; Gassner calls
it "Modern Classicism"[31] in drama, and any recent best-selling novel is acclaimed for its "harsh realism." In the middle
of this confusion all one can do is to furnish this vague word
with some additional epithet; that is why I have termed
O'Neill's late style "dynamic realism." The point to be made
is that there *is* something new in his postwar plays, that it
would have been utterly impossible for the young O'Neill
to write *The Iceman Cometh, Long Day's Journey Into
Night, A Moon for the Misbegotten,* or even *A Touch of
the Poet,* closest of these to conventional realism.

How much inner movement there is in the "heavy-handed

[29] "And having learned all 'the tricks of the trade,' he will not, in
these days of his mastership, discard from his store a single one of
them. The Chorus, the Presenters, the Dumb Show, a Prologue or
an Epilogue—devices not to be depended on, but there may be
fitness and utility in them still." This is Granville-Barker on Shakespeare (*Prefaces,* II, 140); and this Raleigh on O'Neill: "Practically
all of O'Neill's characteristic methods and devices appear in the late
plays, only in a simple and elemental, and hence unobtrusive, form"
(p. 175).
[30] Miller, *Eugene O'Neill and the American Critic,* p. 30.
[31] Gassner, *Form and Idea in the Modern Theatre*: the name of a
chapter in which this idea is elaborated, pp. 79-96.

278

realism" of *The Iceman Cometh* has, hopefully, been shown above. The speeches would be static without the special device of modified monologue, combined with masks; the masks of past and present open up the dimension of time;[32] the drama would not proceed without its courageous music-like handling of the themes and of groups of characters; and the play would lack dynamics without the chorus, a scenic unit O'Neill learned to utilize during his excursions into Greek tragedy. *The Iceman Cometh* is based on the results of O'Neill's experimental period; these are now presented in new modifications.[33]

Robert F. Whitman has noticed a connection between fluctuation in the states of mind and the liberal use of spirits in O'Neill's postwar plays: "Liquor . . . serves two functions: it permits the dramatist to show the contrast between a man sober, with his defenses up, and drunk, when his subconscious drives become overt, and allows the rapid juxtaposition of contradictory moods and impulses once a person *is* drunk. It is a device which O'Neill uses for much the same purposes as the more radical innovations, to reveal the conflicts which tear his characters apart and frustrate their potentialities as complete human beings, without appearing arbitrary or mechanical."[34]

These observations are ingenious, especially because Whit-

[32] Hugo von Hofmannsthal has described a dichotomy between static and active elements, in his article on O'Neill (Cargill *et al.*, p. 252). Raleigh applies the idea to O'Neill's late plays, finding "that the static element is action in the present and the dynamic element is the unfolding of the past" (p. 200).

[33] Stamm and Waith have seen both the differences and affinities between O'Neill's middle and final periods. Stamm points out O'Neill's successful solution of his language problem, his epic ambitions to create in terms of lengthy cycles (" 'Faithful realism,' " pp. 242-43), and speaks of his visual symbolism and theatre images in passages quoted in the introduction to this study (p. 9). Waith has stressed the importance of the masks; his primary concern is their function as parts of the total mental movement of an O'Neill play. There is also "preoccupation with concealment and discovery" (p. 182) in plays without concrete masks; a primary vehicle for these disguises and revelations are the masks written into the stage directions within the speeches, we might add. Cf. Dorn, *Erlösungsthematik*, p. 87.

[34] Whitman, "O'Neill's Search," pp. 167-68.

man recognizes the connection between O'Neill's earlier "radical inventions" and the more cautious, yet dynamic later style. A play in which a similar method is used is *Mr. Puntila and His Hired Man, Matti* (Herr Puntila und sein Knecht Matti) by Brecht and Hella Wuolijoki. The above quotation has full validity in the case of *Long Day's Journey Into Night*; elsewhere, it is perhaps pushed a little too far. There is no drinking at all in *More Stately Mansions*, a play Whitman was not familiar with; and it is not so much liquor as the lack of it, combined with Hickey's dogged preaching, that makes the derelicts of *The Iceman Cometh* reveal themselves. In *A Touch of the Poet* Nora and Sara disclose their innermost thoughts when under mental pressure; it can be said that pressure of some kind is the primary reason for fluctuation. Liquor (and morphine) are, to be sure, used in several cases as a realistic motivation and as an additional impetus. Modified monologues, with their inner compulsions, hark far back in O'Neill.

More Stately Mansions helps to reveal the central theme and a central weakness in *The Iceman Cometh* more clearly than before. In a way, the later play can be called a direct continuation of the cycle play. *More Stately Mansions* ends with a choice: Simon decides to kill one of his pipe dreams, to escape the intolerable conflict between two vectors within his personality by regressing into childhood. When *The Iceman Cometh* begins, Hickey has made his choice; the play shows what follows—death. It is as if O'Neill had left only two alternatives to man, one tragic, the other dishonest.[35] Relieve the tension and die; try to deal with it in the best possible way by ignoring it, and go on living and dreaming. There is powerful irony in the last minutes of the play, when Hickey is taken away and the roomers return to their pipe dreams. The choice is precisely described

[35] "In *The Wild Duck*, it is morally wrong to rob people of their life-lies; in *The Iceman Cometh*, it is *tragic*. . . . But the whole world is inadequate to Hickey's demands, for the truth he offers is a naked, blinding light which kills. Thus, *The Wild Duck* is a savage indictment of some men; *The Iceman Cometh* is a compassionate insight into all" (Brustein, p. 340).

by the Finnish poet Uuno Kailas in his lapidary lines from 1931: *"Vain kaks on ovea mulla, / kaks: uneen ja kuolemaan"* ("I have but two doors, / but two: to the dream and to death").[36]

Yet O'Neill is not so much concerned about the pipe dreams as such as about their influence on our neighbors. He does not condemn the roomers; he pities them. His judgment of those who impose their dreams on people they love is harsher. Sara's dream of more stately mansions spurs Simon forward along the wrong road; Deborah needs her little boy Simon to fulfill her dreams. Evelyn's stubborn belief in Hickey's ability to "stay on the wagon" is presented as the basic reason for his tragedy; and things only went from bad to worse when Hickey started to preach his new message.[37]

[36] Uuno Kailas, *Runoja* (1946), p. 179. Kailas is "a writer in extremis," like O'Neill: "Hickey would destroy the past of the individuals in the play. . . . But man needs his past and his future, no matter how illusory, for he is incurably lonely" (Raleigh, p. 168). "To O'Neill, an air castle is not a possible alternative to despair; it is the only one" (Braem, p. 119). Braem (p. 36) refers to the influence of a Nietzschean thesis on O'Neill: life is possible only in lie. Cf. Chabrowe, p. 380.

[37] Cyrus Day has found "several tantalizing resemblances" between *The Iceman Cometh* and the New Testament. O'Neill agreed with Freud, Day reasons, that religion is an illusion, yet he did not believe that man could live without it. In *The Iceman Cometh*, "he equates the drunken Hickey with the secular savior Freud and the Christian Savior Christ, and at the same time rejects the gospels preached by both." As this certainly interesting interpretation has been widely quoted, it is worth while seeing how far it is supported by scenic evidence.

"Hickey as savior has twelve disciples. They drink wine at Hope's supper party, and their grouping on the stage, according to O'Neill's directions, is reminiscent of Leonardo da Vinci's painting of the Last Supper. Hickey leaves the party, as Christ does, aware that he is about to be executed. The three whores correspond in number to the three Marys, and sympathize with Hickey as the three Marys sympathize with Christ . . ."

"One of the derelicts, Parritt, resembles Judas Iscariot in several ways. He is the twelfth in the list of dramatis personae; Judas is twelfth in the New Testament of the Disciples. He has betrayed his anarchist mother for a paltry $200; Judas betrayed Christ for thirty pieces of silver. He is from the far-away Pacific Coast; Judas was from far-away Judaea. Hickey reads his mind and motives; Christ reads Judas's. Parritt compares himself to Iscariot when he says that his mother would regard anyone who quit the 'Movement' as a Judas

281

Selling all kinds of ideologies, including the ideology of complete disillusionment, leads only to aggression and to death, as the happy equilibrium is destroyed. O'Neill had recently recovered from the disturbing effects of the ideology of

---

who ought to be boiled in oil. He commits suicide by jumping off a fire escape; Judas fell from a high place (Acts I:18) or 'hanged himself' (Matthew 27:5)" (Day, "The Iceman and the Bridegroom," *Modern Drama, 1,* 1958, 6-7).

Let us proceed point by point. Hugo is not a roomer; there are twelve male roomers at Harry Hope's; Day has not explained how he arrived at the figure twelve. Has he not counted Larry as a disciple? Are not the two bartenders, Chuck and Rocky, rather of a different lot? O'Neill has not chosen a clear-cut twelve, as his group of disciples. Cf. O'Neill's sketch in Dorn (facing p. 32).

There are seventeen characters present at O'Neill's "Last Supper," among them three women. They drink, more specifically, champagne. Hickey sits at the left end of the table (IC 142), not in the middle as Christ does in Leonardo's painting. It is impossible to avoid all similarity with this painting, since there is a crowd present and the reactions of all characters are of importance. From the scenic point of view, a long table across the stage is the natural solution—as it is from the practical point of view, too: in a party, the guests cannot sit at separate tables. The deviations from Leonardo are too great and numerous to allow for a theory of a conscious parallel. The painting has a harmonious composition, the scene a dynamic one.

Hickey does not leave the *party* to be executed; he leaves the saloon in Act IV. The three Marys go through the same process as the other characters: from original sympathy through antagonism and aggression to a renewed sympathy.

The parallel to Judas is possible; yet it is fairly far from the focus of the play. Hickey reads Parritt's mind, because their situation is similar; this is what is hinted at by employing this detail. The parallel can also be interpreted as a continuation of the theme of betrayal, so central in all of O'Neill.

Day refers to "the unnecessarily large number of derelicts" (p. 7) to support his idea of the twelve disciples. Competing interpretations can be based on autobiographical and structural considerations. Each roomer has at least one candidate mentioned in the biographies as his probable model in reality (the Gelbs, pp. 170, 186, 285-87, 297-98; Cargill *et al.,* pp. 42, 59-60). The structural interpretation can be backed by the observation that the play is organized around certain groups of characters. These two theories are not incompatible: perhaps O'Neill picked the characters from memory, keeping an eye on their compatibility and interaction.

To me, Day is right when he calls Hickey a savior. Yet O'Neill did not construct his parable along the lines drawn by Day. Luckily so; the play or Hickey's role as a secular savior does not need such obvious and distracting parallels.

Nietzscheism on his art;[38] perhaps the Anarchist Movement is referred to so many times only as "the Movement" in order to give it a kind of general validity. *The Iceman Cometh* is a counter-sketch of O'Neill's own *Lazarus Laughed*.

Seclusion, Deborah's private hell in *More Stately Mansions*, is now seen as the only comfortable form of existence. The themes of isolation and non-communication are even given a comic treatment in the role of Harry Hope, who pretends to be half-blind and half-deaf: "Can't hear a word you're saying. You're a God-damned liar, anyway!" (IC 195). The reconciliatory tones are devoted to the roomers who do not disturb anyone with their dreams. Hickey is a tragic hero:[39] he neither asks nor receives any reconciliation after his self-recognition.

This is how the basic relation between the protagonist and the chorus, between an individual and the common mass of mankind can be seen in *The Iceman Cometh*. The tragic figure is placed in the middle of this world of ours, not quite without its comedy; it is his task to choose between the absolutes, between love and hatred, life and death. Leech calls the play "a comedy with tragic overtones";[40] rather, it is a tragedy with comic overtones. Hickey even fits in with the Aristotelian formula, if this is given a fairly wide application: he is given stature by the chorus, by great expectations, by his function as a savior. His social position is high in comparison with the other characters on the stage. This is all that any playwright gives us: relative stature in a microcosm. Hickey is the one-eyed king in the country of the blind.

[38] ". . . O'Neill rejects the heroic teachings of Nietzsche, repudiating superhuman salvation while affirming humanity, pity, and love. . . . Larry's facile pessimism, his cynicism, and his fascination with death are all qualities found in O'Neill's earlier 'sardonic' heroes, but these are now exposed as mere attitudinizing" (Brustein, p. 343).

[39] To Brustein, Hickey "has some of the dimension of a tragic protagonist, and is brought right up to the brink of a tragic perception; if he does not look over, then Larry Slade does, and what he sees is the bottomless abyss of a totally divested reality. . . . Like O'Neill's, his tragic posturing has developed finally into a deeply experienced tragic sense of life" (pp. 347-48).

[40] Leech, p. 105.

The weak spot of the play is Larry. He is a descendant of Simon who does too much preaching and attitudinizing; his role may lead to an overpowering temptation to abridge. Fortunately, he was not made the protagonist of *The Iceman Cometh*. It is as if Larry's problem—to pity or not to pity?—had been too closely personal to O'Neill: the playwright himself had recently decided to pity, but could not help continuing to dispute the point in the play, somewhat aside from its center. This state of mind was fruitful for writing a tragedy, however, with its combination of two necessary ingredients, pity and grimness.[41] A tragedian, not reconciled to existence as it is, sees grimly and pityingly disharmonies and conflicts between human absolutes, such as life and death, love and hatred, guilt and innocence, then exaggerates and stylizes them for the good of his play. Part of the controversies among critics start at the point when the permissible degree of exaggeration and stylization are to be judged: shall there be people of eminent social stature involved? Can there be human dignity in Harry Hope's saloon? There can; and a katharsis is achieved, perhaps through the purgation of pity and fear, whatever this means, more probably through a comprehension of the playwright's vision. In *The Iceman Cometh* O'Neill is a much better tragedian than in *More Stately Mansions*, left to us as a torso. In the finished play his vision is more generally valid, his form less contrived, his mastery over the scenic means of expression more complete.

[41] Dietrich finds two poetic potences at work in *The Iceman Cometh*: the dramatic power "to see life in its inescapable contrasts," and the lyrical one "to express the lamentation of the human being" (*Das moderne Drama*, p. 222).

16

THROUGH THE FOG INTO
THE MONOLOGUE

LONG DAY'S JOURNEY INTO NIGHT

In *Long Day's Journey Into Night* O'Neill's reliance on the expressive power of his dialogue is still greater than in *The Iceman Cometh*. He has only five characters in his cast; there is no chorus, nor are there any changes in the setting; there is a most effective return to the repetitive sound effect. In spite of these dissimilarities the dynamics of these two plays work in a similar manner. Instead of transferring from one group of characters to another, O'Neill now goes from one theme to another. There is more variety of theme, less of character; all the four Tyrones stand out as fully individualized human beings, bound together by a common fate, by an inescapable love-hate relationship. This tragedy has four protagonists. When working his way toward the final revelations, toward four magnificent modified monologues, O'Neill employed in his dialogue several solutions we know from *The Iceman Cometh*.

There are, first of all, the masks. Mary Tyrone has two masks in Act I, those of relaxed self-confidence and of nervousness. She is back at home after a cure in a sanatorium for drug addicts; the three Tyrone men have confidence in her ability to resist the temptation this time. Her gradual return to the old habit is the decisive change in the family situation during this long day's journey. It releases unexpected reactions in the others, in the famous actor James Tyrone, in his thirty-three-year-old actor son Jamie, a failure and an alcoholic, and in Edmund, a journalist ten years younger than his brother who is about to be sent to a tuberculosis sanatorium.[1]

[1] It is understandable that those who approach O'Neill from a

In Act I there is still hope: the inner struggle is still going on in Mary. Hence the masks, given in the initial description of Mary and in the stage directions between and within the speeches: "What strikes one immediately is her extreme nervousness. Her hands are never still" (LDJ 12). Another fixing point for this mask is her hair: "(*She stops abruptly, catching Jamie's eyes regarding her with an uneasy, probing look. Her smile vanishes and her manner becomes self-conscious*) Why are you staring, Jamie? (*Her hands flutter up to her hair*)" (LDJ 20). The mask is made visible through these means, and there is interaction with changes in the tone of voice, with facial expressions, with the gestures and groupings.

The opening act closes with a pantomime by Mary. She makes the apprehensive men leave her alone, and the tension between her two roles is shown: "Her first reaction is one of relief. She appears to relax. . . . But suddenly she grows terribly tense again. Her eyes open and she strains forward, seized by a fit of nervous panic. She begins a desperate battle with herself. Her long fingers, warped and knotted by rheumatism, drum on the arms of the chair, driven by an insistent life of their own, without her consent" (LDJ 49).

The battle is lost. In the following acts Mary progresses deeper and deeper into the secluded world of a drug addict, swinging all the time between two roles, wearing alternately two masks. When she has her defenses up, no petitions from the others, no events on the stage, can reach her. She is as strangely detached as Deborah. And when she has not yet totally escaped, she feels guilty—of her irrational flight, of

---

biographical point of view have found it a matter of interest to compare *Long Day's Journey* with the facts of his life. There are detailed discussions by the Gelbs (*O'Neill*, pp. 3-8, *et passim*), by Carpenter (*Eugene O'Neill*, pp. 20-24), and by Raleigh (*The Plays of Eugene O'Neill*, pp. 87-95). What should not be forgotten, however, is that the "truthfulness" or "distortion" of the facts does not matter finally: "the O'Neills have all gone to their graves, while the play remains" (Raleigh, p. 91). Or, to agree with Gierow, the first theatre person to read the script: *Long Day's Journey* is a self-dependent work of art, its autobiographical nature does not mean very much (*Introduktioner*, p. 38).

the death of one of her sons, called Eugene in the play, of
Edmund having been born at all, of life in general. She may
confess her concern for Edmund or her fear of consumption,
she may speak of her own guilt—only to turn abruptly away
again: "Then, catching herself, with an instant change to
stubborn denial" (LDJ 88). It is foolish to worry; it is reas-
suring to cling to the pipe dream that Edmund has only a
bad summer cold.

The further Mary recedes from the living room of the
Tyrones, the clearer it becomes that her two roles are played
behind the masks of her two different ages. "Her most appealing quality is the simple, unaffected charm of a shy con-
vent-girl youthfulness she has never lost—an innate un-
worldly innocence" (LDJ 13). When she has escaped, when
she wears the mask of detachment, she lives in her convent
days again, far from James Tyrone and the shabby hotel
rooms that have been her surroundings throughout her married life. This movement in the dimension of time resembles
the dynamics in *More Stately Mansions* and *The Iceman
Cometh*: Mary is a "one-time" convent girl.[2] The masks,
written into the stage directions, are given three different
functions in the case of Mary Tyrone; they show the conflict
between temptation and resistance, between her drugged
and normal states, and between her adolescence and old
age.

Mary is the best example of the application made of the
masks in *Long Day's Journey Into Night*, yet she is not the
only one. The continuous vacillation between attachment and
repulsion has been observed by several critics.[3] In fact,

[2] Carpenter compares *Long Day's Journey* with *The Emperor
Jones*: "The dramatic progression of the action in present time
counterpoints the dramatic regression of the memory into time past,
which in turn develops a progressive understanding of the psychological motivation within the mind" (p. 93).

[3] "The family, in brief, is chained together by resentment, guilt,
recrimination; yet, the chains that hold it are those of love as well
as hate" (Brustein, *The Theatre of Revolt*, p. 351). Gascoigne speaks
of the changes of masks "properly buried here in the language," and
of the entanglement of the characters "by a network of recrimina-
tions" (*Twentieth-Century Drama*, p. 118). Cf. Whitman, "O'Neill's

each of the characters wears two masks in his relations to the other members of the family: those of love and hatred. The play is a chain of small circles, all touching the areas of mutual sympathy and antagonism, all obeying the mechanics of defenses, accusations, and counter-accusations. On the stage, the circles are drawn by the actors: their positions, gestures, vocal and facial expressions.

Temporary harmonies are possible, even between Tyrone and Jamie, two archenemies: "His son looks at him, for the first time with an understanding sympathy. It is as if suddenly a deep bond of common feeling existed between them in which their antagonisms could be forgotten" (LDJ 36). Yet in the next moment the pendulum swings toward bitter enmity; another circle is started. A primary vehicle for this incessant movement, in addition to the sudden, paradoxical change of masks, is the clipped quality of the dialogue. When Hickey was coming close to dangerous areas, to the mine fields of *The Iceman Cometh*, he interrupted his sentences, giving his listeners only a hint, letting only an uneasy suspicion form in their minds.[4] It is so also in *Long Day's Journey Into Night*.

We might speak of five different uses made of the interrupted sentences. Three of them are closely associated with the total dynamics of the play. (1) It is certainly not O'Neill's invention that the adversaries interrupt one another in emotionally tense scenes out of mere excitement; there are such cases in *Long Day's Journey*. (2) Especially in Act I the Tyrones guard one another, preventing the speakers from approaching dangerous subjects of discussion—Edmund's illness, or Mary's newly aroused inclination, revealed by her

Search," p. 167; Gassner, *Theatre at the Crossroads*, p. 72; Stamm, " 'Faithful Realism,' " p. 244; Waith, "An Exercise in Unmasking," p. 189; Åke Janzon, *Bonniers Litterära Magasin*, 25, 3 (March 1956), 238; and Dorn, *Erlösungsthematik*, pp. 17-27.

⁴ "It is precisely the fact that these intimations are not fully understood at the moment of their use which is important from the point of view of the dramatist: the audience has as yet no clear conception of the meaning, a residue of doubt remains, at once disturbing and a source of enhanced concentration" (Clemen on *The Merchant of Venice: The Development of Shakespeare's Imagery*, p. 83).

movements the previous night. It is a family taboo even to suspect that Mary is not completely healed—and another that Edmund might be in real danger. Mary has barely hinted at her feeling that the men are keeping an eye on her when Edmund interrupts, "too vehemently": "I didn't think anything!" (LDJ 47). Or, Jamie has hardly interpreted a remark by Tyrone as an indication that the father is thinking of Edmund's death when he is checked by Tyrone, in a "guiltily explosive" speech (LDJ 34).

(3) They are checked not only by one another but also by themselves. Examples of sentences interrupted by the speaker himself are numerous: the Tyrones often stop themselves right on the threshold of a terrible accusation or self-accusation. They need another drink or shot in the arm to come out with the truth—as they finally do. Before they reach the stage of modified monologues, they exercise introspection by leaving something unsaid. "Please stop staring!" Mary exclaims. "One would think you were accusing me—" (LDJ 68)—of having taken morphine again, she is about to say, but does not dare. Both this and the second usage have two functions: they add to the tension of the play by creating secrets, and they leave an impression that all of the characters know what is about to be revealed. This is not the first time these circles are run through. They are parts of an incessant discussion, parts of a relentless family fate, realized from year to year, from day to day—and into night.

(4) A modification of this, not as dynamic, is the interruption as a result of an overpowering feeling. There is nothing more to be added by the speaker; the sentence is complete in its context, even if deficient in its form. Tyrone speaks "shakenly" to Mary after one of her outpourings of accusations against doctors, in spite of Edmund's presence and the delicacy of the theme of death: "Yes, Mary, it's no time—" (LDJ 74).

(5) The last usage, again closely bound to the total dynamics, occurs when one of the four interrupts a speaker, not so much because these two were getting into an argument, as to give a helping hand to a third. "James, do be quiet"

(LDJ 22), Mary says to her husband who is reproaching Jamie. As in *More Stately Mansions* there is no end of new frontiers being formed. The boys react against Tyrone (LDJ 77), the parents against their sons, all the men against Mary; the mother defends her sons, each of them at different times. *The Iceman Cometh,* with its massive dynamics, operated with a few emphatic frontiers: the chorus for or against Hickey. *Long Day's Journey Into Night,* with its fewer characters, is a more fluid and labile play.

If we start looking for the roots of this kind of dialogue, it is possible to go back as far as to the first fluctuating monologues in O'Neill. The small circles drawn by Yank in *The Hairy Ape* in his efforts to overcome the difficulties of communication have an affinity with the way the Tyrones proceed. The circles are now drawn by several characters in their attempts to understand. The last act of *Welded,* with its precarious harmony and violent accusations, *Strange Interlude,* with its vacillation, and all of the mask plays were important later developments. Essentially, this kind of dialogue has dramatic rather than literary merits: it speaks not with striking verbal images, but with its incessant movement. It has hardly been fully analyzed or appreciated by the literary critics of drama.[5]

It is an abstraction to say that the small circles in *Long Day's Journey Into Night* are formed by alternating love and hatred. The concrete elements in a play are its themes: the circles are built out of bits of discussion, mostly reminiscences. Instead of groups of characters, this play has groups of speeches, each around a theme. The topics discussed include Mary's hatred of doctors, her convent days, her in-

---

[5] Raleigh admits that Edmund is "capable, sporadically, of a certain eloquence" (p. 235) and says that O'Neill learned "three things: the necessity for restraint, the tonic value of irony, and, the *sine qua non* for the drama, propriety of speech to speaker" (pp. 237-38). Yet the scenic merits of the dialogue are not duly considered; to Raleigh, "the plays are but words on pages, as is all literature finally, and the words themselves very often have little about them that can be called distinctive" (p. 236).

8. *The Iceman Cometh*. Hickey (Sasu Haapanen) at the moment of his final self-revelation.

9. A drunken chorus of roomers, from the same production. Photographs by Pentti Unho.

10. *Long Day's Journey Into Night.*
Mary (Kirsti Ortola) and Edmund (Ismo Kallio) in a Helsinki
production, directed by Timo Tiusanen.

11. The Tyrone family falling apart—Risto Mäkelä, Kirsti Ortola, Ismo Kallio and Hannes Häyrinen. Photographs by Pentti Auer.

12. *A Touch of the Poet*. Major Cornelius Melody (Tauno Palo), having abandoned his social pretensions, is ministered to by Nora (Ruth Snellman), Sara (Leena Häkinen), and Cregan (Jalmari Rinne).

13. *A Moon for the Misbegotten*. Josie (Salome Jens)
and Jamie (Mitchell Ryan), virgin and son in the moonlight.
Photograph by Max Waldman.

tolerable life in shabby hotels; Tyrone's stinginess, his hard childhood, his drinking habits; Jamie's failure, in all its varied aspects; Edmund's illness, his rebellious opinions on politics and literature, his experiences on the sea. None of these themes is given a conclusive treatment in the first three acts of the play: again, O'Neill is a careful builder of drama.

One theme is taken up and developed to an emotional climax, then there is a standstill until a new theme is picked up, to be treated in a similar way.[6] This is a picture of O'Neill's total development, too: he picked up a certain scenic means of expression, developed it (often to an over-use), and then began working with another. Near the end of his career, he drew his means of expression together—as he did the themes of *Long Day's Journey*.

Even if the emphasis is on the dialogue, it is necessary to pay attention to the interaction of several scenic means of expression. The autobiographical character of the setting is of lesser interest to us than its functional aspects. One of the bookshelves may include most of the books young O'Neill read and admired; this is not, however, of great significance because their names and authors can hardly be made visible to the audience. The relation between Mary and the setting is, on the other hand, interesting: the house is inescapable to her, more so than to the others.[7] We never see Mary leave the house; we know that when she goes out it is only to fetch more morphine. As a contrast, the departures of the men are demonstrated on the stage. Tyrone and Jamie go out to cut the hedge; Edmund takes a walk in the fog, escaping into his poetic vision; all three go downtown, have company, and come home drunk. They do come home—to carry the burden of their family fate.

    [6] Clemen remarks that independent parts can be separated from the novels or epic poems, while the "texture of the drama is of a much closer web, and the necessity of an inner continuity, of a mutual cooperation and connection of all parts is greater in drama. . . . In a truly great drama nothing is left disconnected, everything is carried on" (p. 6).
    [7] Cf. Brustein on the existential drama: "But even when the setting is relatively realistic—as in the plays of Pirandello, Brecht, and O'Neill—the claustrophobic atmosphere is just as oppressive" (p. 32).

Mary is deserted by the men: this is the impression conveyed by leaving her alone on the stage at the end of two scenes. Act I is closed with Mary's pantomime, quoted above. She is left even more emphatically alone at the close of II, ii, when Edmund leaves her in the living room, Tyrone and Jamie shout their "Goodbye, Mary" and "Goodbye, Mama" from the hall. She sighs of relief—only to go to the other extreme and give her curtain line: "Then Mother of God, why do I feel so lonely?" (LDJ 95). Whether to call this desertion symbolic or not is a pure conjecture; one might say that it is both completely realistic and deeply symbolic, at the same time. In fact, this is the way all scenic means of expression are employed in *Long Day's Journey Into Night*: they have a multiple motivation, both realistic and symbolic.[8]

All the outer world means to Mary is a place from which she can obtain drugs. James is the only one of the four who has contacts with the "respectable" people in the town: he can go on talking with them, even forgetting his family and the waiting meal in doing so. The specific place of action, between back and front parlors, is interpreted by Doris V. Falk: "The family 'lives' in that mid-region between the bright formality of the exterior front parlor—the mask— and the little-known dark of the rear-room."[9] In addition to these symbolic overtones belonging to the setting as a whole, there is a significance attached to the rooms upstairs, where Mary is known or suspected to be drugging herself. Her character is firmly established in the first three acts, where she leaves the stage only to go into the two parlors and through the front parlor upstairs—so firmly established, in fact, that it is more suggestive to keep her off-stage through most of Act IV. All that reminds us of her are references in the dialogue and the noise of her steps. Mary lives in the imagina-

[8] Clemen has spoken of the "deeply organic nature" of Shakespeare's verbal images in the balcony scene of *Romeo and Juliet*: "So everything in this image has a double function: the clouds and the heavenly messengers may be reality, and at the same time they are symbols" (p. 67).

[9] Doris V. Falk, *Eugene O'Neill and the Tragic Tension*, p. 181.

tion of the audience—to come and make her shocking entrance at the end of the play.

There is an interaction between the setting, the foghorn, and Mary's modified monologue in Act III, in a scenic image that might be called a preliminary synthesis of Mary's role. She is again alone, right in the focus of interest; she has reached the stage of frankly confessional monologues earlier than the men; and then the foghorn comes, with its gloomy message of hopelessness. She has used Cathleen, the "second girl," as an excuse for her modified monologue, indicating how little choice she has in her search for human contacts.[10] Now she is without company and relaxes, her fingers calm. Even the pause is recorded, as elsewhere in the play: "It is growing dark in the room. There is a pause of dead quiet. Then from the world outside comes the melancholy moan of the foghorn, followed by a chorus of bells, muffled by the fog, from the anchored craft in the harbor. Mary's face gives no sign she has heard, but her hands jerk and the fingers automatically play for a moment on the air. . . . She suddenly loses all the girlish quality and is an aging, cynically sad, embittered woman" (LDJ 107). Mary's shift from one role to another is given an emphatic treatment here by using the movements of her fingers and reminding us, once again, of one of her dreams: to become a concert pianist. In her monologue she expresses her disillusionment: not even the Blessed Virgin, whose consolation is her dearest pipe dream, cares to help a dope fiend. She has just decided to go and get some more morphine when the men come in, to end the scenic image, to relieve her from the joy and burden of loneliness, and to start the circular movement again.

The presence of the fog is conveyed to the audience through the foghorn and through references in the dialogue. Mary's attitude is typically ambivalent: the fog is both a disguise from the world and a symbol of her guilty escape.[11] "It

[10] Cf. Raleigh, p. 104.

[11] As Raleigh remarks, the fog both forms "a profound, brooding, and steadily deepening, natural backdrop for the various tragedies of the Tyrones," and represents "that blessed loss of identity for which all the main characters, the father excepted, are seeking" (p. 24).

hides you from the world and the world from you," she explains to Cathleen. "You feel that everything has changed, and nothing is what it seemed to be. No one can find or touch you any more. . . . It's the foghorn I hate. It won't let you alone. It keeps reminding you, and warning you, and calling you back" (LDJ 98-99). Edmund has experienced the same fascination of escape during his walk in the fog: "Everything looked and sounded unreal. Nothing was what it is. That's what I wanted—to be alone with myself in another world where truth is untrue and life can hide from itself. . . . Who wants to see life as it is, if they can help it?" (LDJ 131). Yet Edmund comes back from the fog to describe his experience, to give it a verbal form, to turn it into art.[12]

O'Neill specifies the use of the foghorn, with its connotations of fascination and dread, of fate and unreality, at three phases during the play. One of them is discussed above; one is an introductory usage at the beginning of Act III; the third will be discussed in this paragraph. Elsewhere, the foghorn is utilized as a kind of repetitive sound coulisse, to be resorted to according to the judgment of the stage director. In a scene between Mary and Edmund we have a beautiful example of O'Neill's sense of drama, in his transference from human expression into the foghorn. Edmund has voiced his bitterest accusation ("It's pretty hard to take at times, having a dope fiend for a mother!"), and immediately asks for forgiveness after seeing his mother's reaction—all life seems "to drain from her face, leaving it with the appearance of a plaster cast." There is a standstill, the emotion cannot be developed further; and this is where the foghorn is employed: "(*There is a pause in which the foghorn and the ships' bells are heard.*) MARY (*Goes slowly to the windows at right like an automaton—looking out, a blank far-off quality in her voice.*) Just listen to that awful foghorn. And the

___

[12] "For the playwright has discovered another escape besides alcohol, Nirvana, or death from the terrible chaos of life: the escape of art where chaos is ordered and the meaningless made meaningful. The play itself is an act of forgiveness and reconciliation, the artist's lifelong resentment disintegrated through complete understanding of the past and total self-honesty" (Brustein, pp. 355-56).

294

bells. Why is it fog makes everything sound so sad and lost, I wonder?" (LDJ 120-21). Another familiar scenic unit employed is the automaton effect, also met occasionally in *Long Day's Journey Into Night*. As to this scenic image as a whole, we might speak of the old principle of *"pars pro toto"*: O'Neill needed a sense of the total tragedy between mother and son, and evoked it by giving a concrete part of it—the noise of the foghorn.

The theme of the fog is given even a comic treatment in Jamie's homecoming. "The fron [sic] steps tried to trample on me," he complains in the beginning of his drunken and grotesquely comic appearance. "Took advantage of fog to waylay me. Ought to be a lighthouse out there" (LDJ 155). It is worth emphasizing that *Long Day's Journey Into Night* is not void of comedy.[13] One of the functions of Cathleen is to provide comic relief. She also plays confidante to Mary and has a choral function: "He's a fine gentleman," she says of Tyrone, "and you're a lucky woman" (LDJ 106). This is how the Tyrones must look in the eyes of outsiders; yet the opinion has an ironical effect in its context. So has her innocent remark somewhat earlier in the scene: "You've taken some of the medicine? It made you act funny, Ma'am" (LDJ 104). One of the excuses, here, as well as in *The Iceman Cometh*, is an unconvincing effort to be jocular—afterwards. Insults are "only teasing" or "only kidding" (LDJ 42, 90).

Tyrone and Edmund begin to play cards early in Act IV. But the compulsions to confess, to find sympathy, are stronger than the merely mechanical act of handling the cards. Tyrone begins to speak about the play he bought, and how he guaranteed his economic success and artistic failure with it: no one wanted to see him in any other role. Then he "glances vaguely at his cards" and asks: "My play, isn't it?" (LDJ 150). The intention is bitterly ironic: this is what is left of Tyrone's play, of his life—a handful of cards.

[13] " 'Comic relief' has a crude sound; but, to some degree and in some form or other, the thing it suggests is a necessity" (Granville-Barker, *Prefaces*, I, 310). On the "comic relief" in *Long Day's Journey* cf. Brustein, p. 351, Carpenter, p. 152.

Stage action and groupings also interact with dialogue elsewhere. When Mary has taken her first dose of drug, everyone avoids looking at her. She herself goes behind Edmund, the most innocent and least suspicious of her men, to save him from the observation as long as possible (LDJ 58). (See Fig. 10.) Two situations are repeated with variation, to show how Mary's position is changed by her fall. Tyrone, the closest person to her, enters together with her in Act I—and follows behind her in II, ii, in a similar entrance after a meal. He keeps beside Mary in their exit at the end of II, i—and remains on the stage in Act III after her exit "as if not knowing what to do. He is a sad, bewildered, broken old man. He walks wearily off" (LDJ 123). These changes occur in emphatic phases of the play; they are important indications of development in the relations between the characters. So is the scattered grouping at the beginning of II, ii. Tyrone and Jamie look out of the door and the window; Edmund sits so that he does not have to watch his mother (LDJ 71). The family is falling apart. (See Fig. 11.)

A special feature in *Long Day's Journey Into Night* is its plentiful quotations,[14] most of which appear in Act IV. They prepare the way for the confessions, they accentuate the tragic feeling created by the modified monologues. Leech is worried about O'Neill's taste when choosing the poems: "it appears they are quoted *con amore*, with the implication that they represent what poetry exclusively is."[15] On the other hand, they are quoted both seriously and parodically. O'Neill is on his guard against sentimentality in this late play: before he reaches pathos, he turns around by using a sudden ironic twist. And there is no doubt that the quotations fulfill their

[14] Raleigh says that O'Neill uses quotations "both to create a cultural continuum" and to characterize the Tyrones (p. 230). To James Tyrone, Shakespeare is an "optimistic moralizer," while his sons are steeped in "degenerate" European writers, distasteful to their father. Jamie uses Shakespeare "as one of his many weapons in his endless verbal war with his father"; and "there is a design to his literary quotations: hate is Shakespeare; boisterousness is Kipling; elegy is Wilde, Rossetti, and, above all, Swinburne" (p. 232).

[15] Leech, *Eugene O'Neill*, p. 57.

basic function, described by Sigvard Mårtensson: they make it possible for the playwright to "express the elevated emotion, the strong tension otherwise not easily articulated by the realistic dialogue. The technique is employed with distinction and never breaks the frame."[16] It is quite natural to quote poetry in a family of two actors and a would-be author.

The central problem of guilt is touched on once by employing a Shakespearean quotation. "The fault, dear Brutus, is not in our stars, but in ourselves that we are underlings" (LDJ 152), James Tyrone sighs—not, however, recognizing his own fault. His quotations are ridiculed by his sons; as Raleigh has remarked, in O'Neill's last plays we "are asked to take nothing on faith."[17] Tyrone's confidential disclosure of his failure is accepted as truth by Edmund and by the audience; yet its impact is lessened by the sneering Jamie a few minutes later: "He's been putting on the old sob act for you, eh?" (LDJ 157). And the ultimate question of guilt is left unsolved in this relativistic play: "Nothing is to blame except everybody."[18] Fate, fog, life itself, all of us may be guilty—yet finding a scapegoat does not change at all our unredeemable situation.

Act IV in *Long Day's Journey Into Night* is magnificent;[19] and the quotations help to make it so. Each of the four Tyrones is driven to his final confession in a modified monologue. Everything said or done in the play contributes to these revelation scenes,[20] following one another in a series of

[16] Sigvard Mårtensson, *Eugene O'Neills dramatik* (1957), pp. 118-19.

[17] Raleigh, p. 204.

[18] Raleigh, p. 95: a quotation from his own earlier study, "O'Neill's *Long Day's Journey Into Night* and New England Irish-Catholicism," Gassner (ed.), *O'Neill*, p. 125. To Gassner, *Long Day's Journey* is "perhaps the modern theater's outstanding dramatization of the ambivalences omnipresent in the human species" (*Eugene O'Neill*, p. 40).

[19] ". . . the fourth act is among the most powerful scenes in all dramatic literature" (Brustein, p. 350).

[20] "Dramatic exposition . . . finally became in effect the entire substance of the play itself," Raleigh concludes (p. 195). At the end of "the backward journey into the past," there are "the ultimate disclosures," "either confessionals or justifications" or a combination of these two modes (p. 197).

scenic images. The first of these is analyzed in the introduction (pp. 17-18). Tyrone speaks of the ambitions of a young Shakespearean actor; and we realize, as Waith has acutely observed, "that his longing for his youth is no less poignant than his wife's."[21] If ever the life of a human being has been weighed on the stage, in a manner both honest and warm, if ever deep tragedy is in the next moment followed by tragicomedy, this is the case.[22]

Edmund describes his experience of freedom and belonging on the sea. The passage is written in the same vein as the vision of Stephen Daedalus at the end of *A Portrait of the Artist as a Young Man.* "For a second you see—and seeing the secret, are the secret. For a second there is meaning!"— is not this what so many creative artists have experienced?[23] The epiphany is presented as momentary, it is a part of a tragedy that certainly does not sing in rapture for the ecstasy of living; and it is followed, as many of Edmund's and Jamie's speeches are, by a self-ironic afterthought. "It was a great mistake," Edmund grins wryly, "my being born a man, I would have been much more successful as a sea gull or a fish" (LDJ 153). And he agrees with his father that he has perhaps only the makings of a poet: "I just stammered. That's the best I'll ever do. I mean, if I live. Well, it will be faithful realism, at least. Stammering is the native eloquence of us fog people" (LDJ 154).

This is only the second climax in the act: Jamie is still to be revealed, and the final synthesis of the family situation is still to be achieved by letting Mary join the others. So is a

[21] Waith, "An Exercise in Unmasking," p. 190.

[22] The universality of the characters is indicated by several critics: "these people become larger than their own small lives; they become humanity, looking for something but not knowing exactly what it is looking for" (John Chapman, in Miller's *Playwright's Progress*, p. 134: reprinted from the *New York Daily News*, Nov. 8, 1956). Cf. Chiari, *Landmarks of Contemporary Drama*, p. 139, and Braem, *Eugene O'Neill*, p. 120.

[23] Raleigh calls Edmund's modified monologue a "fumbling expression to what, so far, has been the climactic experience in American literature, what can only be called the American metaphysical ecstasy: man alone confronting a gigantic, looming feature of Nature" (p. 283).

focusing synthesis of several scenic means of expression to come. Behind the mask of the brother and best friend who has "put Edmund wise" on women and the world in general there has been jealousy and resentment in Jamie: he hates and loves his brother—and his mother. His "love" meeting with Fat Violet in the town brothel is a grotesque revenge on Mary; he brought Violet upstairs—where Mary is in the Tyrone house. When remembering Mary's first fall, he identifies his mother with the whores: "Christ, I'd never dreamed before that any women but whores took dope!" (LDJ 163). Jamie is partly dead—he is destructive and poisonous— while Edmund feels that he belongs to Life itself. This time there is a contrast, not an equation, as between Mary and Tyrone: Edmund is called by Waith a "creator."[24] Yet there is also love, of a helpless and moving kind, in Jamie: "Greater love hath no man than this, that he saveth his brother from himself" (LDJ 167).[25]

The long day's journey into four monologues is completed, and everything is revealed, when Mary comes down and plays the piano "with a forgetful, stiff-fingered groping, as if an awkward schoolgirl were practicing . . . for the first time" (LDJ 169-70). Then she enters the final scenic image in the play, likewise described in the introduction of this study (p. 18). It looks for a while as if Edmund may break through her defenses; but only for a while. She soon returns into her fog, listens but does not hear Jamie quoting Swinburne (perfectly appropriately in this context), and says her curtain line from far away in her past.[26]

[24] Waith, p. 191.

[25] Carpenter finds in the scene between Edmund and Jamie "the true climax of the play. It provides the final moment of illumination, and of tragic catharsis," because there is a conflict implied between Jamie's "mephistophelian cynicism and Edmund's genuine tragic idealism" (pp. 161-62).

[26] To Raleigh, this scenic image is "the soul-chilling climax of the greatest tragedy in the history of the American theater and one of the greatest tragedies of the Western theater" (p. 238); to Brustein, Mary's final speech means O'Neill's emergence from the night into the daylight—"into a perception of his true role as a man and an artist" (p. 358).

According to certain formulas of critical thought, *Long Day's Journey Into Night* should be a poor play. It is "undoubtedly too long—one long scene seems almost irrelevant; there is too much quoting of classic poetry; and the deliberate formlessness of it all is enervating. Still, it is a dramatic achievement of the first order," "a masterpiece."[27] A euphemistic way of putting it is to say that the play is great "in spite of"[28]—and then let the merits remain largely unanalyzed.

If a play is a masterpiece "in spite of" several critical presuppositions, it is high time to start asking whether there is anything wrong—with the presuppositions. If we have not given up the hope of finding rational explanations to art, we should be busy looking for reasons *why Long Day's Journey Into Night* is a masterpiece—instead of weighing down the other end of the scale with our inapplicable criteria. One thing is certain: emotional power does not come through on the stage without some kind of technique; only physical power might. And *Long Day's Journey Into Night* does not shout; it speaks through its form.

Admitting that the play is void of outer action, there is good reason to emphasize that it is full of inner action. It is within the speeches that a major part of the drama is acted; it is within the utterances that the masks are changed. O'Neill let himself be bound by the tradition of realism because he knew that he could utilize the amount of freedom granted to him by the shortish chain of this style. He was convinced of his ability to dance in these chains. He knew that he could write in a style infiltrated by the results of his experimental period; he knew how to achieve porousness by making every detail both realistic and symbolic. "His contrapuntal arrangement of events that are seen in the theatre and reported events, which become real in the threatre of the mind only, makes his realism a free and spacious style,"[29] Stamm writes,

---

[27] Bowen, *The Curse of the Misbegotten*, pp. 273, 366.

[28] In *O'Neill and the American Critic*, Miller goes as far as to say that O'Neill's late plays will survive "in spite of, and not because of, the technical contributions of these or any other of his plays" (p. 30).

[29] Stamm, " 'Faithful Realism,' " p. 249.

recognizing clearly an important aspect of O'Neill's dynamic realism. Yet the reminiscent speeches of *Long Day's Journey Into Night* would be static if O'Neill had not employed his small circles, drawn to touch love and hatred, sympathy and antagonism, guilt and accusations. O'Neill does not only move backwards in time, he also makes the past present. The past is an actual phenomenon, not asking but demanding reactions from the agonized characters. The wild fluctuation in the mind of Caligula or Ponce de Leon was attached only to the stage situation; now O'Neill has also the rich orchestra of human memories to play with.

"The past is the present, isn't it? It's the future, too. We all try to lie out of that but life won't let us" (LDJ 87), Mary complains in one of her most lucid moments.[30] If the first sentence could be taken as the motto for O'Neill's technique, the second reveals the core of his tragic vision. In fact, this is a statement in which O'Neill's method of constructing his play and his vision meet one another. The circle had been his favorite structural formula ever since his early efforts: yet as late as in this confessional play we see how deeply it was rooted in his personal attitude toward life. Fate is in the circles, in the inescapable repetitions, in the power of the past over the present and over the future.[31] It may shout with the foghorn, too—but the sound has a meaning only to those who are living through the long chain of small, inescapable circles. This is O'Neill's modern artistic approximation to Fate, more personal than his psychological one in *Mourning Becomes Electra*.

The basic motivation for the numerous repetitions in *Long Day's Journey Into Night* is given above. Facing the paradox of length once again, we might formulate a question: how

[30] "Hating the present, fearing the future, he withdraws into the past, and writes his plays on the theme of time and memory," Brustein writes about all existential tragedians (p. 30).

[31] "The vicious circle becomes obsessive. The action lasts for one day, but it might have lasted for a century: it lasts in fact as long as the torments of hell" (Nicola Chiaromonte, "Eugene O'Neill," *Sewanee Review, 68*, 1960, 496). Raleigh remarks that O'Neill, Joyce, and Proust all based their major works "on their own memories," thus exercising a kind of "self-directed psychoanalysis" (p. 83).

many links can one take out of a chain and still make it reach? The more links that are added to a chain, the longer and weightier it becomes; and to those who prefer chains of a smaller calibre, all that can be said is that these are the shackles given to his characters by a tragedian. Some of the repetitions are further motivated by an urge to render ironically conflicting versions of familiar stories at different points of the action and by different characters: Tyrone's picture of Mary's father deviates from that cherished by Mary herself; Mary speaks of her falling in love in contrasting ways.[32] If after these considerations there is still a temptation to abridge, let it happen in small bits, mostly somewhere in the first three acts. It certainly will not do to say in an offhand manner that "there is too much quoting of classic poetry" or that a whole scene is irrelevant.

Long Day's Journey Into Night is seen by Mottram as a synthesis of O'Neill's playwriting career. His "earliest one-acters melt into Edmund's sea-voyaging region of dream reality"; there is material from the saloons, utilized even in a group of other plays; *The Straw* is represented by Edmund's tuberculosis; "the Strindbergian elemental family is at last achieved without bogus classicism or pop-Freudianism"; and "the calm of *The Iceman Cometh* comes through again in this last harbour."[33] It is possible to speak of a synthesis from another point of view as well: O'Neill applies here several scenic means of expression he knows thoroughly from previous usages. There is the idea of the fog, expressed mainly through a repetitive sound effect; there are modified monologues, again as the climaxes of the play; there is a continuous circular movement in the dialogue; symbolic significance gradually gathers around one portion of the setting; there are quotations rendering an additional layer of meaning. In a way, the quotations are still another modification of masks:

[32] "One of the great sources of power of *Long Day's Journey* arises from the fact that four passionate but disparate imaginations are all focused on essentially the same set of past facts. But how differently this identical past comes out of each of the four wells of memory!" (Raleigh, p. 204).

[33] Mottram, "Men and Gods," p. 43.

by reciting a poem it is possible for the characters to express }
feelings not otherwise revealed.

All these means of expression are used in a purposeful way and executed flawlessly within the limits of the style chosen by the playwright: dynamic realism. Even in a play with little or no plot there can be quite a lot of interaction between the scenic images. Besides, *Long Day's Journey Into Night* has a plot of an unconventional kind: its action proceeds through the fog into the monologues. Agreeing with Gassner in that "a continuing tension between naturalism and a variety of alternatives of dramatic stylization has characterized the century's theatre,"[34] we might call *Long Day's Journey Into Night* one of O'Neill's major answers to the challenge created by this tension. It is more than a major answer: it is a masterful one.

[34] Gassner, *Theatre at the Crossroads*, p. xiv.

17

VIRGIN AND SON IN THE
MOONLIGHT

A MOON FOR THE MISBEGOTTEN

Dialogue and a central scenic image are focal in *A Moon for the Misbegotten*, a sequel to *Long Day's Journey Into Night*. Here we meet Jamie Tyrone after eleven years have elapsed: he has proceeded on his lonesome road toward self-destruction, toward death as a hopeless alcoholic. O'Neill, for his part, has proceeded toward elimination. Instead of a cast of twenty, he has only five characters; instead of intricate relations between all of them, he concentrates mainly on two characters and their unconventional relationship. They are placed on the stairs of a farmhouse in the memorable scenic image that means the crystallization of the themes of the play. (See Fig. 13.) Their meeting, two acts long, is developed with the help of a dialogue as paradoxically vacillating as that of *Long Day's Journey Into Night*.

The action is placed in and around the house of an Irish-born tenant farmer, Phil Hogan. His landlord is Jamie Tyrone, who has by now lost both his parents. Themes of desolation and alienation from nature are introduced in the description of the farmhouse setting: "The house is not, to speak mildly, a fine example of New England architecture, placed so perfectly in its setting that it appears a harmonious part of the landscape, rooted in the earth. It has been moved to its present site, and looks it." The Cabot farm was bound to its surroundings by the elms and by the gateway; now there are layers of timber between the house, "an old box-like, clapboarded affair," and the ground. Windowpanes are missing, the paint is splotched and weathered, and "to make matters worse, a one-story, one-room addition has been tacked on at right"[1]—Josie's bedroom. Jamie has an outer appearance that makes him an appropriate person to figure against this background—he is another example of nature spoiled by man: "His naturally fine physique has become soft and soggy from dissipation, but his face is still good-looking despite its unhealthy puffiness and the bags under the eyes" (AMM 37). Both of Jamie's masks are given in that description: his youthful, irresponsible charm; his middle-aged self-destructiveness.[2]

While the tension between the contrasting elements in the setting seems to run parallel to the central conflict in Jamie, there is a detail that might be taken as a symbol of Josie, Hogan's oversize daughter who boasts about her promiscuity. Close to the house, not far from her bedroom, there is a big boulder with a flat top. It is planted on stage, as firm and inexplicable as the power of nature—or as Josie, personified love. Another interpretation is presented by Mennemeier who sees in the setting "a model of the landscape of the last times, typical of the modern drama." His main point, interestingly enough, is to connect O'Neill with the theatre of the absurd; to him the farm is an "end of the line station," as Harry Hope's saloon was, while the boulder is "a symbolic reference to the hardness and bareness of the life lived by the Hogans, and to the irreconcilableness of a malevolent fate; at the same time, the stone is simply a terrible strange block, an absurd immobile thing, to be explained as you wish."[3] A functional aspect is applied here: the boulder is seen against the background of the entire play. Perhaps these two interpretations are not incompatible: as a whole, the setting is a picture of Jamie's situation, yet there are overtones in the boulder that attach it to Josie's character and function.

The first act of *A Moon for the Misbegotten* reads like a

[1] *A Moon for the Misbegotten*, "Scene of the Play" at the beginning of the volume; there is no page number.

[2] In O'Neill's late plays, the final disclosures are "hinted at, almost from the beginning of the play. . . . As a result there is set up almost immediately a continuous tension between the present and the past" (Raleigh, *The Plays of Eugene O'Neill*, p. 199).

[3] Mennemeier, *Das moderne Drama des Auslandes*, p. 72.

counter-sketch of *Desire Under the Elms* as far as the plot is concerned, too.[4] Josie's brother Mike leaves the farm, as the older brothers did in the earlier play. Only the misbegotten stay. The exposition is slightly awkward, as Josie and Mike tell each other things both of them must know well enough; yet it also begins important themes. Josie treats those she loves roughly: she slaps Mike, revealing that her feelings toward him are maternal. Both of these features forecast her relationship with Jamie in a more fundamental way than the spectators can guess at this point of the action.

Josie is a paradoxical mixture of roughness and tenderness. These masks, her private pieces of property, are carefully hidden in the speeches and stage directions, as in all of O'Neill's late plays. The only unmasked character, T. Stedman Harder, a millionaire, is a mercilessly satirical portrait. Even Mike, definitely a secondary and unsympathetic character, shows an inclination to clever scheming behind his façade of pious self-righteousness. His plan is that Josie should trick Jamie into marrying her; it is eagerly adopted and skillfully developed by Hogan. What is behind Hogan's apparent calculation is not revealed until the last scene of the play.

For a major portion of the play, there is communication only between the masks. The central problem concerns whether Josie and Jamie can reach a deep level of understanding, assisted by their mutual love. In the early acts this seems to be impossible, because both use "*kidding* and raillery as a defense mechanism,"[5] as Sievers puts it. Josie speaks coarsely of her lovers in order to conceal that she is a virgin —in this last harbor innocence is something to be ashamed of. Yet Jamie has seen through her pretenses: "Just be yourself" (AMM 105), he warns her at the beginning of their long meeting in the moonlight. Up to this encounter, which fills the end of Act II and all of Act III, Josie has revealed

---

[4] *A Moon for the Misbegotten* and *Desire Under the Elms* are compared by Raleigh (p. 32): "the picture is comic, practically a parody. . . . Thus if farming and farm life are a tragedy in O'Neill's first major play, they finally become a farce in his last major play."

[5] Sievers, *Freud on Broadway*, p. 129.

her feelings only by her fluctuating way of speaking and by
being angry at illogical points.

Jamie's speeches have also been full of abrupt changes
of mood, expressing the conflict in his attitudes. He needs
Josie and her love, not to respond to it, but in order that he
may confess and be absolved. His dilemma is expressed in a
most emphatic way by interrupting the action for the interval
between the acts: Jamie is alone on the stage, striking "a
match which lights up his face, on which there is now an expression of miserable guilt." His self-damnation is short and
pointed: "You rotten bastard!" (AMM 107). And the curtain falls—only to rise again and reveal Jamie in his previous preoccupation.

Once again the stairs and the door of a house are the area
of action where all the decisive events are staged. Before
starting to light his cigarette, Jamie has been sitting on the
stairs; he must stand either on one of the steps or close to
them during that emphatic phase of action. This is not the
first time he is placed there: when the meeting of Josie and
Jamie begins in Act I, she steps out through that door and
stands above and behind Jamie. Later on their grouping in
the night scene is prepared by letting Josie sit on the top step,
Jamie on a lower one. She is the stronger of the two, and she
has minor reactions which the audience is supposed to see,
but not Jamie. They never enter the house through that door
together: when they do go in at the end of Act I, O'Neill is
careful to make them use the front door. The bedroom is
not, however, a sacred area to Jamie, who is guided in by
Josie to watch the Hogans ridicule T. Stedman Harder.
Jamie has permission to go in, but he does not.

Furthermore, when Josie is waiting for Jamie early in Act
II, she sits on the front steps. The bedroom steps are reserved
for another usage: the long meeting of the "lovers." After
every movement they return to the same basic grouping:
Josie behind and above, not so much in ambush as ready to
protect and console Jamie. The thematic significance gathered around the steps is used both in the central scenic image
of the play, to be analyzed below, and in its very last image.

307

When Josie enters the house, through that very door, her exit has a poignancy comparable to the impression left by Lavinia's grim withdrawal from the outer world at the end of *Mourning Becomes Electra*. Lavinia, a Greek-Freudian heroine, entered a mansion; Josie, her realistic counterpart, enters a misbegotten part of a farmhouse.

O'Neill's plays for the imaginative theatre, with their wide variety of settings, did not allow for gradual piling up of significance around certain parts of the setting. Yet he experimented along these lines at the same time, using schematic repetitions in plays like *The Hairy Ape* and *All God's Chillun Got Wings*, and resorting to an unchanged, yet expressive basic setting in *Desire Under the Elms*. A removable wall is employed again in *A Moon for the Misbegotten*, in Act II where the interior of the sitting room is revealed; the solution is practical rather than symbolic. The interior of the characters is disclosed as late as Act III, where the wall is back in its place. As a whole, O'Neill's settings have not been over-obviously symbolic ever since the thirties: they certainly help to create an atmosphere, and they interact with the groupings and movements, but not in too conspicuous a way. The roles of the settings are implicit rather than explicit. Instead of writing scenic journalism, the mature O'Neill designed scenic art.[6]

When Jamie has succeeded in lighting his cigarette, he "starts pacing back and forth a few steps," as the guilty Mannon men did. He does so "as if in a cell of his own thought" (AMM 111), then sings two lines of an old sob song, used as a leitmotif leading to his final confession. What is at stake from his point of view in the following vacillating scene between two sensitive individuals is his ability to break down the thick protective wall of that cell and meet some-

---

[6] "And in general a profound relationship will be the mark of true poetic imagery, in which the subject illuminates the theme, while a precise, neat and consciously effective linking of theme and subject will be the mark of a more purely intellectual or logical process in which the purpose is to illustrate or almost to define." All I should like to add to this statement of Ellis-Fermor's is the adjective "scenic" before the word "imagery" (*Some Recent Research in Shakespeare's Imagery*, p. 10).

one, anyone who would be able to forgive and send him to peace.[7] What is at stake from Josie's point of view is her love, the love of a proud and unconquered woman who is over-conscious of her exceptional size and inclined to self-depreciation, yet knows very well her own worth. They are at cross purposes; they do not communicate.

As they drift slowly toward the mine fields of the play, toward the basic reason for Jamie's overpowering feeling of guilt, their dialogue has the same clipped and fluctuating quality we know from O'Neill's previous plays.[8] "Her face betrays the confused conflict within her of fright, passion, happiness, and bitter resentment" (AMM 114), we read of Josie; her speeches betray the same. The tension between love and hate reaches its highest point and is discharged when Jamie refutes Josie, after discovering innocence and interpreting her love to be only lust. Josie's tenderness is great enough to stand even this insult; yet their relation is basically changed. She gives up her hope and starts playing mother-substitute. Jamie can confess only under these circumstances, only to a woman representing his mother. He has found a consoling and forgiving listener to his modified monologue.[9]

[7] Raleigh calls *A Moon* "the play devoted to understanding and forgiving Jamie" who is, like Mary in *Long Day's Journey*, "one of the walking wounded, lost, lonely, afraid, and separated irrevocably from what he should have become." Jamie's quotations are this time, "by and large, romantic and elegiac" (p. 233).

[8] To Chiaromonte, this is "one of the most awkward and clumsy, and at the same time most extraordinarily touching scenes in modern drama . . . nowhere else is the almost insurmountable difficulty preventing two human creatures from communicating as such, expressed with like violence, with like torment, with a like rough, wordy and disorderly confusion, but with like moving authenticity. . . . We are present not at a dialogue but at a struggle in the dark" ("Eugene O'Neill," pp. 498-99).

[9] Bentley's opinions of O'Neill are strangely ambivalent; on one hand, he is perceptive, on the other, disparaging. He writes under the influence of his own private O'Neill complex—or under a more general disturbance, to be called national masochism, which becomes manifest in a great many judgments passed on American writers in the United States. To him, *A Moon* has "a happy middle" in Jamie's confession, in the "'inner' climax which O'Neill substitutes for the

The self-control exercised by the Tyrones in *Long Day's Journey Into Night* is now turned into self-hatred. With grim satisfaction Jamie speaks of the absolute demand of honesty shared by these two misbegotten: "We can kid the world but we can't fool ourselves . . . no matter where we run away" (AMM 135). In another speech he warns Josie: "And don't let me get away with pretending I'm so soused I don't know what I'm doing. I always know. Or part of me does" (AMM 126). His personality is divided; in a key passage his monologue is stylized into inner dialogue, as also happened in the case of Deborah. Jamie acts out a scene at his mother's coffin when he pretended sorrow, stricken by guilt because of his drinking: "I flopped on my knees and hid my face in my hands and faked some sobs and cried, 'Mama! Mama! My dear mother!' But all the time I kept saying to myself, 'You lousy ham! You God-damned lousy ham! . . .' " (AMM 148). And the whole complex relationship between mother and son, consisting of feelings of guilt, of relief because Mary need not suffer anymore, and of sorrow, affected and real, leads to a grotesque and terrifying revenge.[10] When bringing the coffin across the continent, he had a whore with him every night, while an old sentimental song kept going through his brain, like a compulsion turned into words and melody:

> And baby's cries can't waken her
> In the baggage coach ahead (AMM 150).

This is the sin Jamie Tyrone wants to be absolved of; and this is the core of the modified monologue that leads to one

---

expected melodramatic climax" (*The Dramatic Event*, 1954, pp. 30-31). Yet Bentley finds in the play and in "its central image" only "neurotic fantasy unorganized into art" (p. 33), not grandeur or poetry. After *Long Day's Journey*, our relation to Jamie must be different: in his case, neurotic fantasy happens to be both true to life and relevant to us.

[10] Raleigh finds suffering behind Hickey's and Jamie's "Rabelaisian wordplay," "for to them prostitutes are not only bought flesh but are also instruments by which these sinners torture themselves, piling guilt upon guilt. . . . Both men go from these desecrations to their death, in a sense to their suicides: Hickey to the electric chair . . . and Jamie to the slow and prolonged suicide of alcoholism" (pp. 121-22).

of the most memorable scenic images in all of O'Neill. Josie does forgive, Jamie has communicated; yet there remains the basic irony that she was bound to be disappointed, that Jamie was beyond her love, beyond anyone's help. So they sit, all night long, with his head on her lap, a combined figure radiating strange, grotesque beauty: a virgin and her dead child in the moonlight.

If Eugene O'Neill ever was a poet of the theatre, he is in that scenic image.[11] It is noteworthy how many of his favorite means of expression he employed when creating it or when preparing a way for it. This image is constructed by an expert, by an artist who has mastered his material because he has explored its possibilities.[12]

The moon is present; the couple sits on the stairs of a house with a removable wall, in front of a symbolic setting; Jamie's modified monologue, with its merciless self-revelation, lingers in the air. A song and a poem have been quoted; Jamie's "haggard, dissipated face" has looked "like a pale mask in the moonlight—at peace as a death mask is at peace" (AMM 142), and it looks so again, when he falls asleep. He has been able to tell his story only by speaking like an automaton: "His voice becomes impersonal and objective, as though what he told concerned some man he had known, but had nothing to do with him" (AMM 146). The ghost of Mary is there, called forth by Josie in her modified monologue: "*She* hears. I feel her in the moonlight, her soul wrapped in it like a silver mantle, and I know she understands and forgives me, too, and her blessing lies on me" (AMM 152-53). And Mary is present in the grouping itself: Josie and Jamie form a picture of his past, of his complicated relationship with his mother. He is now relieved from its tensions

11 "In the final act of this last play, all the contradictions of O'Neill's contradictory life and dramatic art combine to produce a single unforgettable image" (Carpenter, *Eugene O'Neill*, p. 167).

12 "Night, fog, ghosts, sleep, the past, dreams, elegy, loneliness: this is how O'Neill's world ends in *Long Day's Journey*. In the coda and epilogue to his dramatic career, *A Moon for the Misbegotten*, the same pattern evolves" (Raleigh, p. 152).

in this image of forgiveness and peace. It has been his most important, if not his only important relationship with a fellow human being; it is now revived, without the burden of guilt. O'Neill certainly knew what resting against his dead mother's breast meant to Jamie; yet he was on his guard against sentimentality, and closed the act with a dryly self-ironic remark by Josie, reminding one of a similar twist at the end of Edmund's sea monologue: "(. . . *She forces a defensive, self-derisive smile.*) God forgive me, it's a fine end to all my scheming, to sit here with the dead hugged to my breast, and the silly mug of the moon grinning down, enjoying the joke!" (AMM 153).

The image is again emphasized by sustaining it over the interval between Acts III and IV. Both the mental and physical lighting is changed, when we meet the couple early the next morning: Josie is tired now. "The two make a strangely tragic picture in the wan dawn light—this big sorrowful woman hugging a haggard-faced, middle-aged drunkard against her breast, as if he were a sick child" (AMM 157). All that remains to be explored in their relationship is whether Jamie remembers that he has been absolved, that this night has been different from all the rest.[13] He finally does; and he is sent away by Josie's curtain line: "May you have your wish and die in your sleep soon, Jim, darling. May you rest for ever in forgiveness and peace" (AMM 176).

Josie returns to the company of her father; and they go on treating one another with the same mixture of roughness and raillery that has always made them feel safe. There was, after all, a trick behind Hogan's trick; he had tried to scheme Josie into seducing Jamie, not out of any economic calculations but because he saw that these two were in love. In fact, everything in this play has double bottoms: there is real love behind the schemes of love-making, there is a play within the play—the scene with Harder, watched by Jamie in his hide-out, there is real beauty in the moonlight, though

[13] Cf. Dietrich, *Das moderne Drama*, p. 224; and Braem, *Eugene O'Neill*, pp. 126-27.

it is sneered at.[14] It is possible to see religious overtones in the image of a virgin and a son; yet O'Neill blasphemy is not, after all, blasphemy, because there is a rare kind of beauty in that very image. This time, O'Neill does not take any short cuts to poetry, as he did in plays like *The Fountain* or *Lazarus Laughed* in a desperate and hysterical manner. He goes the long way round: he achieves a personal kind of poetry, through elements of grotesqueness and irony. Early morning lighting, employed in *Beyond the Horizon, All God's Chillun Got Wings,* and *Days Without End,* is now presented as both truly admirable and despicable because of its very beauty: "God seems to be putting on quite a display. I like Belasco better. Rise of curtain, Act-Four stuff" (AMM 172). O'Neill is full of love and hatred toward his former aesthetic ideals, and he expresses both of these feelings.[15]

O'Neill's paradoxical attitude toward the language, a parallel phenomenon, has been observed by Mennemeier: "Where the 'high' expression of tragedy is not applicable any more, as in the case of O'Neill, there seems to appear a necessity to save the contents of tragedy by concessions to 'lower' expression." Jamie has hardly finished quoting poetry when he discards its effect with an ironical remark; his analysis of the sunrise, cited above, is preceded by this stage direction: "He is profoundly moved but immediately becomes self-conscious and tries to sneer it off—cynically" (AMM 172). Jamie's reaction to his own situation corresponds to O'Neill's attitude toward his task as a writer of modern tragedy, Mennemeier goes on. "On one hand, there still exists un-adulterated, real suffering because of the state of the world,

---

[14] "Each of the three characters tries to trick the others, and none is ever quite sure what the true intentions of the others are. For that matter, none is ever quite sure what his own intentions are" (Carpenter, p. 164).

[15] "The most spectacular and effective 'truth-telling' dawn occurs in *A Moon for the Misbegotten.*" After Jamie's confession in the moonlight, the sun "provides the background for his absolution and also for the return to reality: the knowledge on the part of both characters that theirs is an impossible love and that Jamie has one last reality to face and undergo: death" (Raleigh, pp. 18-19).

and because God is concealed or lost; on the other hand, it does not seem to be relevant to speak of this suffering in the language we still have for this suffering. The play and especially its language bear the impression of a painful compromise . . . between the positions of traditional tragedy and modern comedy or satire, free of all pathos. There seems to be only a short step to the theatre of the 'absurd,' in several scenes."[16] Yet O'Neill does not take that step, the German critic concludes; in dealing with the theme of difficulties in communication he keeps within the limits of realism.

In addition to Mennemeier, a few critics have paid due attention to the central image in the play and to its other merits.[17] On the other hand, it has been treated in a manner undeservedly harsh.[18] Even if the hero of *A Moon for the Misbegotten* is tired, the play is not—it has vigor and grotesque beauty; even if Jamie's role is not full of outer activity, there are certainly elements of inner drama in his characterization. In fact, this play has a sharper focus than *Long Day's Journey Into Night*, and its central scenic image, right in that focus, is only slightly affected by the weakest point in the play.

The crudely comic ingredients are probably given an overemphatic treatment by the playwright. The satyr play, with masks on, is about to prevent us from seeing the subtle vacillation in the relationship between Josie and Jamie, when the masks are off or about to be taken away. "The rustic and drastic elements in the dialogue are quite monotonous and

---

[16] Mennemeier, p. 70. Anouilh, Beckett, Dürrenmatt, and Pinter can be called writers of modern tragicomedy. Ironical and grotesque elements in late O'Neill are described by Dorn (pp. 109-13).

[17] Mottram, "Men and Gods," p. 44; Sievers, p. 131; Gassner, *Theatre at the Crossroads*, pp. 234-35; Cargill *et al.*, pp. 209-11: a reprinting of Mary McCarthy's review from the *New York Times Book Review*, Aug. 31, 1952.

[18] Miller says that *A Moon* is "generally accepted as a 'tired' work" (*Eugene O'Neill and the American Critic*, p. 72). Doris V. Falk calls its outward situation "the theatrical cliché of clichés," Jamie Tyrone "probably the least dramatic of any of O'Neill's protagonists" (*Eugene O'Neill and the Tragic Tension*, pp. 172, 175).

play against the finer shades in the psychology of the play,"[19] Mårtensson says. It is possible to see how O'Neill came to run a risk of this kind: his interest was in the total atmosphere and in the scenic images, not in the plot. Consequently, he made a series of schemes out of his plot and treated these schemes as one of his themes: the Hogans cheat subtly, and are subtly cheated by life. This very process led to an overdue emphasis on the comic elements. The exposition is awkward, as has been remarked above, and O'Neill plays quite a while with Hogan's secret in Act II: what had happened in the inn? It is all a part of Hogan's role within a role, of his trick behind the trick; yet the crude surface grows so thick that it must be a red herring to the actors or readers.

In spite of these reservations *A Moon for the Misbegotten* ranks high in the canon. A less ambitious play than *The Iceman Cometh*, it nevertheless comes close to the level of that collective masterpiece. Its themes are strongly concentrated in a single scenic image, striking, personal, and fresh, though fusing several of O'Neill's scenic units together. More than any other of his late plays, this drama of two misbegotten, sensitive human beings, both behind a thick mask of protection, seems to presuppose a theatre production. Their precarious, paradoxical relationship, with all of its shades of meaning, is made to be experienced in the audience; the poetic image of virgin and son in the moonlight, called by Mennemeier "urtümliche Pietà,"[20] is composed for the stage.

[19] Mårtensson, *Eugene O'Neills dramatik*, p. 114.
[20] Mennemeier, p. 77.

18

GHOSTS OF THE PAST

HUGHIE, A TOUCH OF THE POET

Hughie, a posthumously published one-act play, is woven around a familiar theme: difficulties in communication. It was completed in 1941, two years before *A Moon for the Misbegotten*. In its shorter form this theme is even more prominent. The needs of its two characters are modest: "Erie" Smith, a teller of tales, and a night clerk in a third-class hotel do not expect absolution or love; they would be happy with just a little excitement and comradeship, with a share in something still alive. But not even such a small amount of mutual understanding is easily found on O'Neill's stage. It is made to matter, whether it is found or not.

The play consists of two modified monologues. When they cut across each other, when contact is established for the first time and monologues are turned into a dialogue, the action reaches its quiet climax. *Hughie* is the only remnant of a cycle of eight one-act plays planned by O'Neill during his last years; what is known of the project seems to indicate that monologues would also have figured in the rest.[1] The over-all title of the cycle was "By Way of Obit": Hughie is the name of a dead night clerk, to be resurrected at the end of the playlet.

"Erie" Smith, "a Broadway sport and a Wise Guy" (H 9), has come to a seedy New York hotel to reminisce about his late friend, Hughie. Dead a week now, he was a favorite "sucker" (H 20) of Mr. Smith's, "a small fry gambler and horse player"(H 9) who used to tell the clerk about important events in the chronicles of crime and racing as if he had taken part in them. The above samples from the vocabulary of the play are sufficient to show that colloquialisms

---

[1] The Gelbs, *O'Neill*, p. 843; *Hughie*, front lap.

from the twenties and from Broadway are plentifully used in the dialogue and in the stage directions. As in *The Iceman Cometh*, set in a similar milieu, O'Neill is again writing in American slang.[2]

The new night clerk, Erie's unwilling listener, has no identity. "His nose is large and without character. So is his mouth. So are his ears. So is his thinning brown hair, powdered with dandruff. Behind horn-rimmed spectacles, his blank brown eyes contain no discernible expression" (H 8). And he is beyond caring, in a state of emptiness, of nothingness: "There is nothing to do. He is not thinking. He is not sleepy. He simply droops and stares acquiescently at nothing" (H 7). The namelessness of this living corpse is confirmed when it turns out that his name is Hughes, too.

Yet there are aggressions behind his blank mask. He listens to the noises of the night, to banging garbage cans, to a rattling El train, to a cruising taxi, to the footfalls of a cop, to cars and ambulances, to the siren of a fire engine. A key to his character is given by Henry Hewes: he has never dared to do anything more ambitious than waiting for time to pass as a night clerk.[3] "He daydreams about his suppressed hostility against a world he never made, and his vicarious desire to join, without risk, the more reckless doers of deeds."[4] So it is; he imagines a discussion with a fireman, ending in resignation: he had hoped the fire would destroy everything, yet it was not "big enough to burn down the whole damn city" (H 27).

[2] To Gassner, O'Neill's "marvelously vivid and rhythmic dialogue" seems here "utterly authentic in its colloquialism and slang" (*Eugene O'Neill*, p. 42). Raleigh calls Erie's monologue "the real O'Neill tour de force in the use of American slang" (*The Plays of Eugene O'Neill*, p. 228). "Broadway lingo" is "the language of hope and courage" in *Hughie*; in *Long Day's Journey* and *A Moon*, it is "the language of hatred, cynicism and nihilism" (p. 229). The nickname "Erie" is a clue to his small-town background (H 14); it is furnished with quotes in the list of characters, but not elsewhere in the play.

[3] Both Erie and Hughes are nostalgic; yet Erie is active (he still plays poker and gambles), the night clerk just exists (Braem, *Eugene O'Neill*, p. 125).

[4] Cargill *et al.*, p. 224: reprinted from the *Saturday Review*, Oct. 4, 1958.

Listening to the noises and thinking his own private thoughts is one of the clerk's masks—or rather his unmasked face. His consciousness fluctuates between two levels; the alternative is furnished by Erie and his story. Whenever the Wise Guy voices a question or expects a gesture of participation from his listener, there follows a crisis. The clerk's mind is in the street. The play proceeds through a series of small circles, as did *Long Day's Journey Into Night*; one phase constantly repeated is a silence, expressing a complete break in the lines of communication. It is followed by a biting remark from Erie or by his threatening to leave the stage. Yet his inner compulsion is too strong; he has to go on with his story about Hughie. Erie and his new Hughie vacillate between an increase and decrease in their distance, as Josie and Jamie do in *A Moon for the Misbegotten*.

The growing significance of off-stage characters and events is characteristic of O'Neill's last phase. Rosa and Evelyn, the two most important woman characters in *The Iceman Cometh* are never brought on stage; Simon is not shown in *A Touch of the Poet*, nor Henry Harford in *More Stately Mansions; Long Day's Journey Into Night* is full of reported events; the core of Jamie's confession in *A Moon for the Misbegotten* is the story of his crime, which has been committed in the past. Paradoxically enough, the most complete character portrait in *Hughie* is the original Hughie himself, likewise never shown to the audience. There emerges a full picture of the life of a very ordinary man: youth in a small town, adolescence as a night clerk, coming to the city, meeting a girl in the underground, marriage, middle-age, death. Modest dreams, a more modest reality.[5] Hughie is an off-stage Yank, a re-creation from *Bound East for Cardiff*.

No wonder that Hughie was dependent on Erie and his tales. But the play also makes another point: Erie has been

---

[5] "*Hughie* is Night and the City, one of the most powerful brief evocations of the loneliness, boredom, and despair of the bottom-dog in the modern city in the language. Only Melville's *Bartleby* is comparable" (Raleigh, p. 28). Goldman finds "the whole pattern of *The Iceman* and *Hughie*" in *Bound East* (Brown and Harris, *American Theatre*, p. 45).

just as dependent on his listener. Boasting to Hughie, showing off his good luck with women and money, and playing dice with his "sucker" have given Erie added self-reliance, even if they have been using only "chicken food," taking a cent to be a dollar. Hughie has been the soft spot in this hard guy. There is that familiar "yet" quality in Erie, expressed in the description of his outer appearance: "Yet there is something phoney about his characterization of himself, some sentimental softness behind it which doesn't belong in the hard-boiled picture" (H 9). The relation of Erie to his "sucker" is crystallized in a scenic image which occurs offstage, so to speak: he brought a big horseshoe of red roses to the funeral. His desperate efforts to establish a corresponding relation with the new clerk make Erie lose his mask: "He pauses, his false poker face as nakedly forlorn as an organ grinder's monkey's" (H 31).

Then the twist comes. Erie happens to call life a "goddamned racket," and the clerk agrees eagerly: "But we might as well make the best of it, because—Well, you can't burn it all down, can you? There's too much steel and stone" (H 33). He is ready to fill his vacuum with the role formerly occupied by Hughie, and O'Neill is ready once more to sign his modified acceptance of pipe dreams: "But what the hell, Hughie loved it, and it didn't cost nobody nothin' . . ." (H 29). Why not, if dreaming causes no harm to anyone else?[6] And the decisive test is an off-hand question by Erie: "Want to give these dice the once-over before we start?" (H 37). The clerk does not; he is Hughie.

It is a difficult task to judge *Hughie* for several reasons. A play in which the most violent action is throwing dice is radically different from O'Neill's early one-act plays, often marred by melodramatic contrasts. *Hughie* definitely belongs to the late plays; yet seeing connections to these does

---

[6] To Raleigh, Erie is O'Neill's "only affirmative male in the late plays"; negatively, he is less intelligent and sensitive than the Tyrones, positively, he is endowed with "a genuine and unambiguous feeling for other people, and with 'gallantry,' the courage to carry one" (p. 155).

not help, because O'Neill has left a central problem unsolved in his use of the scenic means of expression. An important section of the play is written into its stage directions: it is simply impossible for any actor to draw a picture of the clerk's unmasked face with the help of silent acting alone.[7] These stage directions contain imagined speeches and fragments of thought that are essential for the understanding of the play; indeed, they are another modification of O'Neill's "thought-asides" technique, reminding one of the fact that he was working on *More Stately Mansions* at the same time. He thought of some new kind of technique, "possibly utilizing a filmed background and sound track," yet "shrugged off the problem," as the Gelbs report, saying: " 'It would require tremendous imagination. Let whoever does it figure it out. I wouldn't want to be around to see it.' "[8]

Not all of those who have done it have figured it out.[9] A possible solution is an adaptation for the radio: part of the important stage directions could be read by a speaker, while the clerk could voice his own speeches placed in the directions. The noises from the street, a role played against the clerk, could be given an emphatic treatment. On the other hand, radio plays apparently have no great future in the United States, where *Hughie* is closely bound due to its use of colloquialisms. As a rule, O'Neill proceeded further toward the solution of staging problems than most playwrights; this time, he created a problem instead. If *Hughie* is taken as it is written, it is closer to a short story than to an actable drama in the miniature.

Mottram has applied a sociological approach to *Hughie*. He calls Erie and the clerk "underdeveloped men in an idealistically over-developed society"; they "partake of society only at the elemental level."[10] Indeed, the physically

[7] Cf. Raleigh, p. 212.

[8] The Gelbs, p. 844. Cf. Doris Alexander, "The Missing Half of *Hughie*," *Tulane Drama Review*, *11*, 4 (Summer 1967), pp. 125-26.

[9] Cargill *et al.*, p. 226: Hewes's review; Mottram, "Men and Gods," p. 27.

[10] Mottram, "Men and Gods," p. 28.

crippled or handicapped characters in the plays of Samuel Beckett are not far off; yet O'Neill did not transgress the limits of his late dynamic realism, in this case as little as in *A Moon for the Misbegotten*. His way of constructing paradoxical characters works too easily in the case of Erie: there is something "phoney" and mechanical in the way this portrait is drawn. Both of the Hughies are better managed; they are one with the play's total atmosphere. Even if melancholy, the play is not without O'Neill's late relaxed humor. As a matter of fact, several central elements of O'Neill are present in that shabby hotel, and they are treated in a way that is void of his frequent overemphases.

The new clerk became a ghost of the past in *Hughie*; Major Cornelius Melody, the protagonist of *A Touch of the Poet*, gets rid of a ghost by killing it. The full-length play, fifth in O'Neill's cycle and the only play completed by the playwright himself, takes place in a tavern close to Boston during a day in 1828. The past has predilection over the present even in the setting: "The tavern is over a hundred years old. It had once been prosperous . . . but . . . for some years now . . . has fallen upon neglected days" (TP 7). Like the Hogan farmhouse, this "one-time" building is made only worse by a slight effort to improve it by installing a flimsy partition between the dining room and barroom.

Major Melody lives in the past tense. He is given stature by stories about his heroic deeds as an officer in the Wellington army, as a Don Juan, as a gambler: "There nivir was a madder divil" (TP 13), his cousin Jamie Cregan remarks with admiration. A scandalous duel forced Melody to resign: he sold his stately Irish castle, earned by his father, a "self-made" gentleman, and immigrated to America, where he was swindled into buying this tavern, destined to decay. Now he is deeply in debt, yet keeps up his stature by loathing both the prosperous Yankees and the Irish-born, his potential customers. His attitude is demonstrated by making him every now and then assume a self-admiring pose in front of a mirror[11] and quote Lord Byron: ". . . in the crowd / They could not deem me one of such—I stood / Among them, but not of them . . ." (TP 43).

During this performance Con Melody obviously wears a mask, with comic overtones. A sharp contrast is made between what he thinks of himself and what his surroundings do. His pipe dream is not harmless: it is imposed upon his wife Nora and his daughter Sara, both tired and humiliated from trying to keep up a way of living appropriate for the master of the house and his thoroughbred mare.[12] Nora humbly withstands the insults showered on her by Melody in anger, drunkenness, or both: she is a peasant girl who has tricked him into marrying her. Nora has repressed her hatred, Sara her love. There are continual tensions between father and daughter, who scolds him for living in a pipe dream, yet cannot help admiring the hero of the battle of Talavera.

The crisis in these family relations is accentuated by Simon Harford, a Yankee idealist in love with Sara. He is upstairs convalescing from an illness and is kept off-stage throughout the play.[13] Con and Simon, both with a touch of the poet in them, live upstairs, above the tough realities of this world and the domain of the women. A specific area of action is

[11] "In two of O'Neill's last plays, *A Touch of the Poet* and *The Iceman Cometh*, two ambiguous characters, Con Melody and Theodore Hickman, have a preoccupation with mirrors. . . . When they look into a mirror they are, of course, searching for themselves, looking to see if they can see what they are" (Raleigh, p. 99).

[12] "Among the characters there are two cravings: one for beauty and the other for reconciliation, with themselves and with their mates or fellows. . . . Jamie Tyrone, Erie Smith, and Con Melody have at the root of their imagination the image of the sleekness and symmetry of a horse as representing some kind of physical beauty that human life cannot approximate." It is also implied "that the highest act of human charity is simply to try to understand, although this is not always to be understood as equivalent to forgiving" (Raleigh, 207-08).

[13] Carpenter divides the play, perhaps too sharply, into two plots, one dealing with the Harfords, the other with the Melodys. O'Neill's imagination hardly worked in terms of abstract "isms" (romanticism, realism, materialism), as Carpenter suggests (*Eugene O'Neill*, pp. 147-50).

in front of the mirror, which is attached to Melody's role as a gentleman and a hero. Still more conspicuously, this mask of his is created with the help of his old uniform, taken from the attic to celebrate the anniversary of Talavera. As the Gelbs have remarked, it can be compared with Mary Tyrone's wedding gown in *Long Day's Journey Into Night*. Both of these beloved costumes help their owners to leave the unhappy present and nonexistent future and revive their glorious past.[14] According to Con's own words, the uniform makes him "feel at least the ghost of the man" he was then (TP 39). Melody's uniform is a pipe dream that has become a costume.

Both the dream and the costume are scratched before the play is over. The concept of family honor, totally inapt in Con's situation, demands him to take a revenge on the Harfords who make an effort to pay Sara off in order to prevent a mesalliance. Living in his private world of dreams he believes that duels are still possible; they are not, and he returns home after a fight with the servants of Harford and the police. When he enters the stage, after Nora's anxious hours of waiting have built up tension, he moves woodenly, and his outer appearance is not far from the shape of another O'Neill hero—the Emperor Jones: "His scarlet uniform is filthy and torn and pulled awry. The pallor of his face is ghastly. He has a cut over his left eye, a blue swelling on his left cheekbone, and his lips are cut and bloody. . . . His eyes are empty and lifeless" (TP 152). The mental shock is of equal importance: he is now ready to kill the ghost of the Major—by shooting his mare, one of the few remaining symbols of his social pretensions. After that, he descends to the company of the drunken Irish carousing in the bar downstairs, not as a squire, but as a truthful son of his trickster father, a shebeen keeper back home in Ireland.[15] His life circle is completed. (See Fig. 12.)

[14] The Gelbs, p. 800.

[15] Both Braem (p. 118) and Raleigh find elements of tragedy in Con's fate, Raleigh in Con's third mask, that of "nothingness" (pp. 148-49). He also remarks that Con's basic ambiguities are never "finally and neatly resolved. . . . His glorious past was not all illusory, as Cregan attests" (pp. 197-98).

What is left of O'Neill's enormous cycle project belongs, basically, to an earlier phase of development than his more frankly autobiographical plays. An indication of this is the amount of emphasis put on the plot in both of the Harford chronicles. *A Touch of the Poet* cannot be discussed without giving the outlines of its plot, in which the two roles or masks of Con have a key position. The mask is not the only scenic unit employed, nor is this function given only to Con's uniform and his recitation number.

The fluctuating dialogue of the play proceeds through a series of masked and unmasked states of mind. "For a second his eyes waver and he looks guilty," we read of Con. "Then his face becomes expressionless" (TP 33). Mary Tyrone flew into her drugged state; Con escapes into drunkenness or behind the mask of "gentlemanly urbanity" (TP 44). Confusion of the feelings, a recurring phenomenon in *A Touch of the Poet*, once makes Con "ashamed of being ashamed" (TP 37). Sara has her share of emotional conflicts, too; she resorts to an Irish brogue when she wants to tease her father: this is an audible mask given to her.[16] On the visual side, "there is a curious blending in her of what are commonly considered aristocratic and peasant characteristics" (TP 15). Among the central characters, Nora is the soundest in mind, due to her unshakeable feelings; yet even she fluctuates in her modified monologue, designed as a part of the central scenic image in the play.

There are elements of old melodrama in *A Touch of the Poet*, as well as of a "plotty," well-made play. Con is compelled into a decisive action, as according to the formulas he should be. This solution is counterbalanced by keeping Con's fight off-stage; the young O'Neill, author of '*Anna Christie*', would hardly have neglected an opportunity like this of indulging in a violent, melodramatic climax. Furthermore, Sara and Nora follow the formula of typically O'Neillian drama-

---

[16] Cf. Raleigh, pp. 222-24. O'Neill turned to the novels of Charles Lever for Irish touches of language and for historical background, e.g. in the hunting description partly quoted below (Alexander, "Eugene O'Neill and Charles Lever," *Modern Drama, 5*, 415-20).

turgy: they are not compelled to actions, but to decisive monologues—or, more accurately, Sara both acts and speaks.

Four scenic images are employed, all interacting, all carrying important themes. Con in front of the mirror; Sara serving her father and his drunken companions during the dinner party; Con's return from the battle, described above; Sara and Nora keeping vigil, in the scene to be analyzed below. The first of these images gains significance from repetitions: at the end of the play, the poem is given even a parodical treatment. When Con makes Sara act as a waitress, we have an image full of social conflict between his imagined importance and his real standing, and full of love-hate tension between father and daughter. Con uses the plates on the table to demonstrate the movements of troops on the battlefield; this, with its ironic overtones, is one of the details evidencing the "rich histrionic opportunities"[17] O'Neill always gave to his actors. Melody's role, with its posing and power, with its comedy and tragedy, is certainly a major exponent of this feature in O'Neill. In the background of this scene, there are three Irishmen sitting at a side table: they represent the chorus heard from off-stage throughout Act IV. Though the role of the chorus is far less important than in *The Iceman Cometh*, it is noteworthy that the question of an individual's belonging or not belonging to a social group is still of primary interest to O'Neill. Con finally joins the chorus: this play is a comedy with tragic overtones.

On the other hand, there are poetic overtones in the scene between Sara and Nora early in Act IV.[18] Sara comes from Simon's room, as the audience knows, and "there is a change in her. All the bitterness and defiance have disappeared from her face. It looks gentle and calm and at the same time dreamily happy and exultant. She is much prettier than she has ever been before" (TP 136). Her mere presence forms a counterpart to Nora's long and anxious modified mono-

[17] Gassner, *Theatre at the Crossroads*, p. 240, on *A Touch of the Poet*.

[18] This scene is chosen by Brooks Atkinson for special praise (Miller, *Playwright's Progress*, p. 167: reprinted from the *New York Times*, Oct. 3, 1958).

logue; a similar solution was utilized as early as in *Before Breakfast*. Nora's first speech after Sara's entrance is furnished with seventeen stage directions, written between her sentences: in this and in the following fluctuating speeches there emerges a full picture of her character and of her relation to Con. She reveals that she sees through the pretenses of her husband, "then is horrified at herself as if she had blasphemed" (TP 138); she rebels and loves. She is about to leave the tavern and go to the priest to confess, yet cannot because of Con: "He'd feel I'd betrayed him and my word and my love for him—and for all his scorn, he knows my love is all he has in the world to comfort him" (TP 139). The possibility of betrayal, central in all of O'Neill's plays, is here refuted: to O'Neill this is a final proof of Nora's love.[19]

When Sara starts describing her love scene with Simon, the counterpoint between mother and daughter is further developed. There is, first of all, the parallel between their situation: Nora married Con under circumstances similar to those now seen or heard on the stage. There is the dimension of time behind the constellation of characters—as there was in the meeting of Josie and Jamie, between a son and a mother-substitute. The concept of a family fate is worked out in these late plays in a way far less artificial than in *Mourning Becomes Electra*: it is merely an overtone in this scenic image. We cannot, of course, know how conspicuously O'Neill might have dealt with this central idea in the rest of the cycle; the Melodys are aside from the Harfords who were right in the core of O'Neill's genealogical interests.

Against this background of parallel situations O'Neill builds a scene of intertwined monologues. They comment on one another: Sara speaks of Simon, Nora of Con, both of love. What the girl says of her future husband is confirmed by her middle-aged mother; there is a touch of the poet in their men, and their attitude to this dreamer is the same.

[19] " . . . indeed all the late, great plays are in great part about feminine suffering: Nora Melody, Hickey's wife, Parritt's mother, Hughie's wife, Mary Tyrone, and Josie Hogan, who is the final and, literally, the largest, dramatization of feminine frustration, sorrow, and humiliation" (Raleigh, p. 142).

SARA: . . . So I kissed him and told him he was too a poet, and always would be, and it was what I loved most about him.

NORA: The police! Let one av thim lay his dirty hand on Con Melody, and he'll knock him senseless with one blow (TP 145).

In its combination of comic and serious tones, in its quiet inner dynamism, in the warmth felt by the playwright toward his three-dimensional character portraits, this scene is typical of O'Neill's late style. The scenic means of expression employed are not striking, yet the total impression left by this image can aptly be described only with word "poetic."

Nora and Sara are led, by and by, toward the point where Nora suddenly realizes what her daughter is talking about and what has happened. There is a twist from the modified monologues, spoken in deep personal preoccupation, into dialogue. This was the climax of *Hughie*, but it is not the climax of this scene. The emphasis here is not on the moment of communication, but on the relation between the characters. The surprise moment has been eliminated: the audience knows or guesses where Sara has come from. The theme of difficulties in communications is not as central as it was in *Hughie*; yet this theme is again given a comic treatment in the scene between Con and Nicolas Gadsby, the family lawyer of the Harfords. They deal at cross-purposes, as the word "settlement" is misunderstood by Con; his error is used to heighten his anger, which leads to the only fight on the stage. This grotesque phase may be said to represent Con's and Cregan's off-stage action—why not even to function as a parody of the glorious battle of Talavera.

Apparently, there are autobiographical elements in *A Touch of the Poet*, most conspicuously in the characterization of Con Melody, another father-image, as the Gelbs have remarked.[20] Five descriptive words are used both in *Long Day's Journey Into Night* and in *A Touch of the Poet*: James Tyrone and Con Melody are "broad-shouldered, deep-chested, soldierly and handsome," with something of a

[20] The Gelbs, p. 800.

"peasant" in their outer appearance (TP 33; LDJ 13).
The Gelbs have also found similar incidents in *A Moon for
the Misbegotten* and in the cycle play dealing with Irish immi-
grants. In both, there is a daughter who tries to be calculating in seducing the man she loves, yet falls captive to her own
feelings; in both a Yankee intruder is defeated in a verbal or
bodily skirmish.[21] In addition, Edmund's lyrical outburst when
reminiscing about the sea can be compared with Con's more
aristocratic and misanthropic description of hunting: "Melody Castle in the days that's gone! A wind from the south,
and a sky gray with clouds—good weather for the hounds.
A true Irish hunter under me that knows and loves me and
would raise to a jump over hell if I gave the word! To hell
with men, I say!—and women, too!—with their cowardly
hearts rotten and stinking with lies and greed and treach-
ery! Give me a horse to love and I'll cry quits to men! And
then away, with the hounds in full cry, and after them!"
(TP 102).

O'Neill's late plays are really of a piece. Not only because
they can all be classified under the heading "dynamic realism" but also because there are thematic cross-references.
In a differentiated picture both the similarities and the individual features should be considered. The emphasis is on
possessive love in *More Stately Mansions*, on pipe dreams
in *The Iceman Cometh*, on inescapable love-hate relations in
Long Day's Journey Into Night, on guilty self-destruction
and need of absolution in *A Moon for the Misbegotten*, on
difficulties in communication in *Hughie*, and on a conflict between false pride and genuine love in *A Touch of the Poet*.
Yet what is a focal theme in one of the plays frequently occurs as a secondary theme in one or several others: pipe
dreams figure in every play; love-hate relations between the
central characters are customary. It has been shown in detail
above that these and other themes are expressed with the help
of scenic means of expression conquered by O'Neill during
several decades of restless experimentation.

[21] The Gelbs, pp. 92, 800.

328

At the end of *A Touch of the Poet* Sara is on her way toward her final unselfish solution in *More Stately Mansions*; yet there is a discrepancy in the role of Deborah. She makes a puzzling appearance in the tavern, and one gets the impression that she tries to warn Sara against marrying Simon, not out of possessive love, but because she knows that marriage with a Harford is nothing to envy. Perhaps this lack of continuity can be connected with O'Neill's complaint that the total vision behind his cycle was falling to pieces in the years of the war. Be that as it might, it is safe to state that the cycle plays are not on the same level with O'Neill's late autobiographical confessions. His late style, his dynamic realism, depends rather heavily on the modified monologues: and these seem to fit better with autobiography than with history. The resistance of the material was greater when O'Neill tried to penetrate his paradoxical characters through a distance of a century instead of studying those closest to him in time and in family fate. Besides, the awkwardness of exposition and the melodramatic elements in *A Touch of the Poet* have been justly remarked upon;[22] a surprise moment is worn out by letting other characters interrupt Con in an inapt moment, not once or twice but five times. The closest point of comparison to *A Touch of the Poet* is *A Moon for the Misbegotten*: the cycle play has both graver faults and fewer merits. None of its scenic images has the striking and unconventional quality of the image with a virgin and son in the moonlight. At best, in the scene between Sara and Nora the play achieves the level of quietly insistent poetry for the theatre; and the best one can say of the play as a whole is that it "has substance, a point of view, human principle and theatre."[23]

In *More Stately Mansions,* in that uncompleted link of his uncompleted cycle, Eugene O'Neill quoted "The Chambered Nautilus" by Oliver Wendell Holmes. The quotation is interrupted; so was O'Neill's cycle. It is as if he had found an

[22] Leech, *Eugene O'Neill*, p. 115; Doris V. Falk, *Eugene O'Neill and the Tragic Tension*, pp. 170-71; Mottram, p. 42.

[23] Atkinson, in Miller, *Eugene O'Neill and the American Critics*, p. 167.

epitaph not only for the unfinished cycle but also for his entire career. Yet let us not, when reading this epitaph, forget that Eugene O'Neill did build an impressive series of temples, with noble domes for us to admire, before he was set free from this life of ours:

> Build thee more stately mansions, O my soul,
>> As the swift seasons roll!
>> Leave thy low-vaulted past!
> Let each new temple, nobler than the last,
> Shut thee from heaven with a dome more vast,
>> Till thou at length art free,
>> Leaving thine outgrown shell
>>> —(MSM 148)

CONCLUSION

O'NEILL'S SCENIC IMAGES

Eugene O'Neill's scenic images have been seen in their primary connections in the above discussion: they are particles of individual works of art. Each play has been viewed in terms of a circle, to be approached through the scenic sector (cf. "Introduction," pp. 19-20 above). In a few cases, most markedly when dealing with O'Neill's three lost and refound manuscripts, other sectors seemed to open broader routes to the core of the plays; these opportunities have been taken advantage of. The existence of all four sectors has not been forgotten, at least not intentionally. The resulting observations have been related to those attained through the other sectors, that is, by using literary, psychological, or sociological approaches to drama.

Connecting links still remain to be drawn—to O'Neill's total artistic development, to his personality, to his time. The characteristic features of these scenic images will now be described, and their constituents compared with one another. The central problem of dialogue versus other scenic means of expression needs further probing. And an effort must be made to evaluate the method applied in this study.

Our widest circle, a picture of O'Neill's total output, can be approached by considering his settings. This is, in fact, how most analyses of the individual plays were begun. Around the year 1920 O'Neill faced a specific problem. It was his ambition to write full-length plays, with several stage pictures and with several interacting scenic images. At the same time he was eager to make his settings symbolic; he was after "behind life" significance, even in his use of the settings. This had been easy enough in one-act plays: the

331

settings of *Thirst* or *Bound East for Cardiff* combined realism with symbolic overtones. It was not as easy in longer plays. The settings of *Bread and Butter* were obviously satirical, those of *Beyond the Horizon* both symbolic and realistic, contrasted in a sharp, even clumsy way; in *Diff'rent*, there were two realistic stage pictures. *The Emperor Jones* was a special case, an outgrowth of unicellular plays; a fusion of several means of expression was employed to achieve a cumulative effect in front of a forest setting.

In *The Hairy Ape*, a tension between two trends becomes manifest. On one hand, O'Neill had a strong inclination to concentrate, to write plays with the focus on a particular scenic image. On the other hand, there was the need to create variety, to build antitheses between different milieus, different social strata. In this dilemma O'Neill constructed a few plays with multiple settings, yet with one detail repeated in each of the stage pictures: thus the central scenes of *The Hairy Ape* modified the idea of modern surroundings as prison cells. In the middle of variety there was a constant.

The tension between diversity and concentration led to other solutions in *All God's Chillun Got Wings*. There are contrasts between the white and the colored in their behavior, in the setting, in the groupings of statists, and in the songs throughout Act I. The time of year and the age of the central characters were subject to change; the racial contrast remained. The setting also stood solidly in the scenes of Act II, except that the room appeared to shrink; thematic significance was gathered around the ominous Congo mask.

From our point of view, *All God's Chillun* is a focal play. Two typically O'Neillian methods of achieving concentration and strong dynamics were employed in its two acts. In Act I there is a contrast immanent in the setting, and the tension between contrasting elements is further accentuated by using other scenic means of expression. In Act II a certain detail of the setting—or a piece of property—is singled out as a point of attachment for a memorable scenic image. The action of the play heightens the effect of the Congo mask; later plays show that the detail chosen to gather thematic significance may be perfectly commonplace. If someone goes through a door several times in situations repeated with variation, every repetition adds something to the whole. There is, as it were, a new dimension of significance opening behind the door. The setting need not be conspicuously (and, perhaps, artificially) symbolic; it may be made symbolic by letting it interact with other scenic means of expression. Within the limits of a short scene, this had happened with the signpost in *The Straw*. The procedure is an elaboration of a typical feature in O'Neill, characterized by Michel Zeraffa. The obsessions of his characters find their fixing points in details of the settings or in pieces of property, witness the organ in *Ile*, the weighing scales in *The Straw*, or things made of steel in *The Hairy Ape*.[1]

The two solutions of *All God's Chillun* were resorted to, in various modifications, throughout the rest of the canon, often within one and the same setting. They were an asset in constructing plays with one basic setting. Tensions were hidden within a certain stage picture rather than built between several. This is a practice in line with O'Neill's early inclination, mentioned by Koischwitz, to divide the stage into back, middle, and foreground areas, and to use "sound coulisses" to accentuate the illusion of depth.[2] O'Neill was eager to grasp not only what was behind life but also what was behind the stage.

Compared with this basic line of development, O'Neill's three pageant plays constitute a digression. In these centrifugal and incoherent plays the repetitions employed lead to over-obviousness. The procedure is modeled on that of *The Hairy Ape* rather than *All God's Chillun Got Wings*. A few details are kept constant in the midst of an abundance of variable expression. The fountain is patiently carried from Europe to the New World on the heels of Juan Ponce de Leon; the schematic groupings of eastern figures are an easy solution in the early scenes of *Marco Millions*; and neither the proliferation of the masks nor the energetically

[1] Michel Zeraffa, *O'Neill dramaturge*, pp. 113-14.
[2] Koischwitz, *Eugene O'Neill*, pp. 64-65, 104-05.

repeated arias and chorus songs in *Lazarus Laughed* were able to bring this hysterical play together. O'Neill was not a playwright to create for the Imaginative Theatre. The problem of combining variety with a sharp focus was not to be solved in this way. It may well be that this is a central problem in all playwriting. Most great plays are a combination of richness and compactness.

We are now concerned with O'Neill's total development rather than with the estimation of his individual plays. The idea of a detail repeated in several stage pictures did work in *The Hairy Ape*; it did not in *The Fountain*. The solutions of *All God's Chillun* proved to be more fruitful in that they were more widely applicable. During the rest of his experimental period O'Neill seems to have found out that it was possible to create interacting scenic images even if the amount of changes in the setting was limited to a minimum. It was possible to gain variety by employing other scenic means of expression: the setting was the most natural element to remain constant. As a whole, it was to be used as an active visual element, with hidden tensions. And a part of it was to be disconnected from the rest, as it were, to be made a functional element in the action.

The next steps are thus *Desire Under the Elms* and *Strange Interlude*. In the former, the framework of the farmhouse is a constant commentary on the action of the play. It both unites and separates the characters. Thematic significance is gathered around the gate and in Maw's parlor. In the latter play, the repeated arrangement of furniture is a formalistic element; the emphasis is on a constellation of characters, and the focal scenic images are built on it, rather than on the setting. As a rule, the formalistic elements are becoming less conspicuous: *Welded*, with its two stairways and a grouping resembling a cross, represents an early phase of development. The synthesis of O'Neill's prewar experiments, in this as well as in other respects, is *Mourning Becomes Electra*, in which several definitely integrated functions were given to the exterior setting and to the stairs in front of the Mannon house.

The idea of a basically unchanged setting, with a special

functional mission given to part of it, was incorporated into the O'Neillian play as a regular element. The playwright was able to concentrate on creating dynamic scenic images against this unchangeable background. There was one less obstacle on his way toward writing plays with one striking image directly in the center of interest. An additional asset was a dialogue full of inner movement, interacting with the immobile setting. This is where we meet him in all of his late plays. The summer-house is not the only stage picture in *More Stately Mansions*, yet it is clearly the emphatic one. The audience never leaves Harry Hope's saloon in *The Iceman Cometh*, nor the living room of the Tyrones, nor the Hogan farm, nor the inn owned by Cornelius Melody. The settings are inescapable.

Since particular significance is attached to one part of the setting, a brief description of these important areas of action seems justified. *Welded* is the first play in which stairways have specific functions; it is followed by *Mourning Becomes Electra, More Stately Mansions*, and *A Moon for the Misbegotten*. The stairs are, as such, a locality full of dramatic potentialities: the actors can be placed on several levels and behind one another. Yet this is not the only function of the stairs; another feature is disclosed, if we add to this list of symbolic areas the gate in *Desire Under the Elms*, the doors in *The Iceman Cometh* and *A Touch of the Poet*. In each of these cases the specific area is a meeting place of private and public worlds. This is where the characters act out the decisive crises of their lives. Is it possible to achieve true communication with a fellow human being? How is the threshold between one's mind and the outer world to be trespassed? Or is it true that "life is for each man a solitary cell whose walls are mirrors" (P I 309)? One of O'Neill's major themes[3]—difficulties in communication—is carried by these solutions in the settings of his plays.

[3] To Gassner, O'Neill's plays reveal "a keen sense of loss of connection—of connection with God, nature, society, family, father" (Gassner [ed.], *O'Neill*, "A Summary and Appraisal," p. 168). Raleigh speaks of Melville's and O'Neill's characters existing "in a kind of cosmic aloneness": "When these characters do enter into

Diagonal arrangements of the settings were employed in *Beyond the Horizon*, in *Days Without End*, and in several plays in between. Oblique lines across the stage either stop the characters in the middle of their attempt to reach for others—or open the door to true communion. In *Beyond the Horizon*, the wide vistas are, at long last, an ironical denial of Robert Mayo's dreams. In one particular case, symbolic significance is attached to an area where a man living in his solitary cell looks at his reflection in the mirror: Cornelius Melody in *A Touch of The Poet*. Another special character is Mary Tyrone, drugging herself upstairs. The entire setting is a picture of her isolation, her room the place of her fall.

As a whole, scenic evidence speaks strongly in favor of an observation presented by Sievers: "O'Neill, perhaps more than any other dramatist, illustrates the subtle interplay between external influences and the inner experiences, conscious and unconscious, which compel his material to assume certain forms."[4] One of these forms is created by making the settings, or parts of them, interact with the dialogue of the play.

It is evident that a certain area on the stage does not miraculously gather significance. The playwright has to work methodically toward this end. An essential feature in O'Neill is that he was a careful builder of plays.[5] His building materials are actions and situations, described in the stage directions and immanent in the dialogue; his tools are his scenic means of expression. In the above sketch of O'Neill's total artistic development, the emphasis was on the setting. It is time now to turn to the dialogue, another scenic means of expression on stage all the time.

One of the functions of O'Neill's dialogue is to develop

human contact, the relationship is never stable but fluctuates constantly between withdrawal into a solitary state and the equally real, if less powerful, desire to enter into communion and love with another human being" (*The Plays of Eugene O'Neill*, pp. 255-56).

[4] Sievers, *Freud on Broadway*, p. 133.

[5] O'Neill's ability to control his plays as rhythmic wholes is emphasized by Koischwitz, p. 86.

thematic repetitions, needed to make the focal scenic images pregnant with meaning. A medium appropriate for this purpose was not conceived along with his earliest plays. There is a long distance from the jerky dialogue of *Thirst* and from the mechanical repetitions of a phrase or two in *'Anna Christie'* to the reminiscent speeches full of quiet agony in the late plays. *The Hairy Ape*, with its incessant movement back and forth, toward and through a thick wall of inarticulateness in Yank's monologue, is an important link in O'Neill's development toward a dialogue resembling a chain of small circles. So is *Desire Under the Elms*, in its reliance on gestures to convey what words cannot. Between the early realism and the late dynamic speeches there is a phase of Dionysian ejaculations, quasi-poetry, and vague, general phrasing: "Death is dead! . . . There is only life!" (P I 280). "Be brave enough to be possessed!" (P I 352) Lazarus exhorted. The name of the cycle planned by the aging O'Neill is different: "A Tale of Possessors Self-Dispossessed." Calmer tones and more critical attitudes are signs of maturing in O'Neill.

During this process of change O'Neill came to rely more and more heavily on modified monologues, as such an appropriate medium for exercising criticism. Like the doors, gates or stairways in the settings, these monologues are places where private worlds and outer circumstances meet in a more straightforward way than in ordinary dialogue. They are doors leading to privacy. It has been shown in detail how these fluctuating confessions, arising out of inner compulsions and leading toward self-revelations, achieved central functions in front of immobile settings. In the "thought-asides" technique of *Strange Interlude* they are more conspicuous than ever. Outer action was, to a great extent, replaced by inner action in the mature O'Neill—so much so that several American critics, accustomed to a native drama in which rash, even violent outer action is a stock feature, have found it difficult to appreciate fully O'Neill's late dialogue, or his Chekhovian way of constructing a play.

O'Neill's road led toward elimination in other respects as well. Ghosts, materialized in his early plays, begin to appear only as references in the dialogue and as overtones of images. Focal characters are kept off-stage. Masks are turned from pieces of property into stage directions. Two scenic units are used during thirty years of playwriting: the moonlight and repetitive sound effects; the moon is even mentioned in the names of two plays. The idea of fog haunted O'Neill's imagination just as long. As a rule, the use of special devices is less conspicuous in the late plays. Elements are fused together, innovations are infiltrated into dynamic realism— and, more specifically, into dialogue.

In *The Emperor Jones*, his early masterpiece, O'Neill was able to create a striking series of scenic images with the help of pantomime and dance, tom-tom and reports, a costume and a crocodile, moonlight and forest scenery. These means were nothing extraneous; they belonged. Choruses and crowds, haloes and apparitions, masks and mask-like make-ups were employed en masse later on; they either belonged or did not, they led either to striking effects or to over-emphases, to hollow scenes not sustained by themes significant enough. Some of these and other scenic units were preserved through the subsequent process of elimination in one form or another. They were utilized as constituents in memorable scenic images, in which they interacted with a dialogue more expressive, extensive, and purposeful than before. The fact that the setting was left unchanged did not create O'Neill's characteristic scenic images; it only created circumstances favorable for constructing them. These opportunities were utilized with distinction: O'Neill took care in finishing his modified monologues at the right moment, close to the thematic climaxes of the plays. And he gave further emphasis to these culmination scenes by using moonlight and a chorus, a wedding gown and a uniform, by stopping the action for the interval between the acts, and by repeating situations known to the audience from his characters' past. No matter how much variety there has been in the action of the play, every line of development is drawn together in the central scenic image, written for a whole orchestra of scenic means of expression. There is both variety and coherence. An image is the focusing element.

There is a fusion of the means again, as there was in *The Emperor Jones*. It is fusion within the limits of a different style. Dialogue plays the leading role: it subdues other means of expression, as the tom-tom once controlled the chanting of the Negro slaves. Scenic image is a concept that does not presuppose any particular style or school of playwriting; it assumes only a purposeful and imaginative use of the potentialities of the stage.

At his best, Eugene O'Neill was doubtless capable of this. Compared with this basic fact, it is a question of minor importance that he did not write smooth or effortless literary prose. Those critics who have been most eager to complain about his language have hardly analyzed the dramatic qualities of O'Neill's dialogue thoroughly enough.[6] If not rich in striking and original verbal images, his prose has movement; if not fit for the parlor, it is appropriate as the speech of the playwright's down-and-outers, as Lionel Abel has remarked;[7]

[6] It is difficult to agree with Richard Hayes in his claim that O'Neill's insensibility to words "expands into the larger indifference to anything like selection," or that the actor is bound to experience "the despair of realizing that he can make this world 'work' only by the marshaling of personal obsession: varieties of realism, however individually effective, will bring him but to chaos" (Gassner [ed.], *O'Neill*, pp. 54, 56: reprinted from *Theatre Arts*, Oct. 1963). My experience when working as a stage director on a Finnish translation of *Long Day's Journey* is quite the contrary: the highly competent cast took voicing these speeches as a privilege.

[7] Lionel Abel, "O'Neill and His Critics," *The New Leader*, Jan. 6, 1958. Three German scholars have praised O'Neill's language: Braem, *Eugene O'Neill*, p. 50, Koischwitz, p. 57, and Galinsky, "Eugene O'Neill: Die Wendung des modernen amerikanischen Theaters zur Tragödie," p. 236. Are their foreign ears just insensitive? Or do American literary scholars have a prejudice against their own slang? There is a balanced discussion on O'Neill's language in Raleigh, *The Plays of Eugene O'Neill*, pp. 208-38. The playwright "did not write in one mode of speech but in several, and in this, as in all other matters, he was constantly experimenting" (pp. 214-15). Raleigh remarks against the excesses of O'Neill's romantic style and concludes: "He detached dramatic dialogue from the stilted conventionality of the average American play of the early twentieth century and attached it to the living, spoken language" (p. 220).

339

if not epigrammatic, it is rhythmic and speakable, as Gassner has stated.[8] And taking "poetry" in the larger sense of the word, as it should be taken in dramatic criticism,[9] we can call Eugene O'Neill a poet of the theatre, agreeing with Dudley Nichols that "he was a gifted poet, who put his poetry into perception and architecture rather than into words—satisfied to let his words be as exact and expressive as he could make them. Poetry is simply a 'making' power; it is the creative spirit of all the arts—not just an arrangement of words as so many unpoetical people imagine."[10] Eugene O'Neill's scenic images are the creations of his "making" power.

We can clarify the characteristic features of the houses built by this architect if we construct an imaginary model of their constant elements.[11] The most typical O'Neillian scenic image would consist of a dynamically fluctuating modified monologue by a tense, self-contradictory character who stands in front of a house with removable walls on a moonlit night, while there is a repetitious sound effect from off-stage. In the modified monologue he speaks of the sea and of being lost in fog, in a way both pleasant and oppres-

[8] Gassner, *Masters of the Drama*, p. 642.

[9] "Besides being a dramatist, he was necessarily a writer—but how good a writer was he?" (Carpenter, *Eugene O'Neill*, p. 169). Is it not more essential to know how good a *dramatist* O'Neill was? "No words of rich import and beauty wing themselves from his pages; we remember his scenes but not the language in which they are couched" (Nicoll, *World Drama*, p. 881). Is it not enough to remember a playwright's scenic images?

[10] Gassner, *Theatre at the Crossroads*, p. 241. The quotation is from a letter sent by Dudley Nichols to Gassner; no date is mentioned. Cf. Granville-Barker, *Prefaces to Shakespeare*, I, 29: "For dramatic poetry is not primarily a matter of words, but of the poetic conception of character and action."

[11] Raleigh makes a suggestion toward "O'Neill's figure in the carpet" (p. 172): "Men drinking, not very happily; women waiting or weeping: this is the primordial O'Neill situation. Throughout his writing career his imagination carried him and his dramatic world over vast reaches of space and time . . . but the home and the bar were like Hardy's stones or Dostoevski's houses or Vermeer's tables and carpets, the quintessential and emblematic background for his most powerful dramatic creations" (p. 173).

sing. O'Neill never created a scene exactly like this; yet the above conglomerate of his favorite scenic units comes close to the situation of two late O'Neillian heroes: Edmund in *Long Day's Journey*, Jamie Tyrone in *A Moon for the Misbegotten*.

There is an ambivalence immanent in the scenic units themselves. On one hand, they are apt to lead to mannerisms, to easy solutions: the removable walls in *Dynamo*, the plentiful modified monologues in *More Stately Mansions*. On the other hand, they are a playwright's dearest property: he resorts to them, when he is under the greatest pressure, when he is about to create a scenic image to function as the core of an entire play. If a playwright's most valuable goods are easily displayed, then he is arranging a sale. Eugene O'Neill, an energetic salesman, cannot plead not guilty when accused of the crime of dumping. Yet during his long journey into self-revelation as an artist, he learned to employ his means with discrimination.

It is easy to find tensions hidden in our model construction or in O'Neill's scenic images at large.[12] There are contrasts in the settings, in sound and lighting effects, and between individuals and crowds. In the dialogue, there is an incessant movement between the antipodes of love and hatred, of guilt and self-defense, of past and present, of comedy and tragedy; there are beautiful and disgusting elements in a grotesque mixture. The characters are masked or otherwise split into halves. O'Neill's development led him from elementary melodramas into masterpieces of dynamic realism—and from simple scenic images into intricate and stratified ones. These complex images interacted with other images: the result was a play with rich dramatic texture. There was a parallel development in characterization. Raleigh finds "an enormous difference . . . between the sticklike bundles of clichés that pass for representations of human character in some of the

[12] Contrast and repetition are chosen by Raleigh as O'Neill's basic artistic devices (p. 173; cf. p. 3). Koischwitz mentions polar tensions as a common feature in the minds of all O'Neill characters (p. 80).

early plays . . . and the excruciatingly 'real' people of *Long Day's Journey* and *A Moon for the Misbegotten*."[13]

Gassner calls O'Neill "a characteristically modern dramatist" in *Long Day's Journey*, "a divided man who was acutely aware of the division not only in himself but in his fellow men. Like his favorite modern playwright Strindberg, O'Neill made the division itself the subject of his plays. In them he tried to master the division he found in human nature and in the human condition, and because this was no easy enterprise he was doomed to repeat the effort constantly."[14] And he was doomed to create scenic images in which his basic gloomy vision is crystallized into art. His images are full of disharmonies. If it was beyond his powers to change the human situation, he could at least do what the artists have always been able to do: describe it, master it in the world of their creation.[15]

The focal themes of division and alienation are carried by O'Neill's scenic means of expression. An effort to see the typical position of his scenic images as functional parts of his plays leads us to the word "massive": "Whenever there is truth or depth of experience in the plays it is futile to wish that he had composed them less repetitively and insistently. Their emotional power is bound up with their massiveness."[16] There are certainly paradoxes in the psyche of a man who writes a farce about his attempted suicide; among the paradoxes of Eugene O'Neill the artist there is the fact that he is a combination of clumsiness and explosive energy. From the jerky dialogue of *Thirst* to the awkward exposition of *A Touch of the Poet* there are indications of overgrowth; on the other hand, the plays are full of incommensurate energy. One of O'Neill's scenic units is an automaton, moving me-

[13] Raleigh, p. 202.

[14] Gassner, *Theatre at the Crossroads*, p. 72. Cf. Gassner (ed.), *O'Neill*, "A Summary and Appraisal," pp. 169, 171.

[15] Brustein has drawn a type picture of the rebel dramatist, vacillating between "negation and affirmation, between rebellion and reality": "Unable to master his contradictions, he dramatizes them in his plays, grateful for a form in which tensions do not have to be resolved" (*The Theatre of Revolt*, p. 13).

[16] Gassner, *Theatre at the Crossroads*, p. 70. Cf. Gassner, *Eugene O'Neill*, p. 43.

chanically; on the other hand, it cannot be said that his late
dialogue was void of subtlety. We can object to O'Neill's
stiffness, we can remark upon it; yet we cannot deny that
this vice is a result of his virtues. Without the repetitions,
without constant interaction, the central scenic images would
not work; there would not be any play at all. It is as if both
O'Neill and his Yank in *The Hairy Ape* had been compelled
to give their clumsiness its say before they were able
to explode.

And the basic paradox in Eugene O'Neill: he was a divided monomaniac. He experienced and expressed, with all
of his furious energy, a sense of being out of harmony. This
is the point where his matter and manner meet. It can be seen
from his scenic units and images; both are essential parts of
a playwright's world.

O'Neill's world cannot be separated from the time of its
birth.[17] Young O'Neill was heralded as a revolutionary; his
career coincides with an age of drama in which change has
been the rule rather than the exception. Two central vectors
in it are seen by Gassner: "A continuing tension between
naturalism and a variety of alternatives of dramatic stylization has characterized the century's theatre."[18] Taking some
playwrights mentioned by Gassner and adding a few remarkable colleagues from several countries to their company, one
might say that this tension has been felt almost universally.
It is the fate of modern dramatists.

Since the 1860's, realism has been killed and resurrected
half a dozen times. One of the most paradoxical features in
this circular movement is that exactly those major playwrights who once killed this "out-dated" style have returned
to it—and, vice versa, the very masters of realism have in
one phase of their career or another given up realistic drama

[17] "No fine work can be fully appreciated apart from the tradition
to which it belongs—apart from its language (in the literal sense or
the figurative), its medium and technique" (Stoll, *Shakespeare and
Other Masters*, p. 60).

[18] Gassner, *Theatre at the Crossroads*, p. xiv.

in favor of a more imaginative, more poetic theatre. Ibsen, of course, is a case in point; so is Strindberg. There is a long distance from the Shaw of *Mrs. Warren's Profession* to the author of *Back to Methuselah*—as long as from the Hauptmann of *Die Weber* to the poet of *Die versunkene Glocke*. On the other hand two young playwrights, Harold Pinter and Edward Albee, have shown a peculiar inclination to glide between the positions of realism and absurdism. Both realistic and theatrical elements have figured in the epic theatre of Bertolt Brecht, and in the grotesque and parodical world of Friedrich Dürrenmatt. Unable to choose between realism and theatricalism, most playwrights have taken both.

O'Neill was furthest away from realism in the twenties. After having escaped from the middle-class living room to the wide seas of his youth and into the sordid surroundings of his young manhood, he turned to stylistic experimentations. It had a marked effect on his later scenic images that he wrote several plays either under the influence of expressionism or as one of the pioneers of this style. The influence was doubtless more fruitful than were O'Neill's contacts with Macgowan's romantic ideals of an Imaginative Theatre. What he learned from his explorations of the European theatre was a liking for strong dynamics. He was encouraged to create sharply contrasting scenic images; Ibsenesque discussion plays were replaced by librettos for the theatre. He was not saved from errors; yet he had developed what might be called a massive belief in the interaction of scenic images when he selected the other road open to modern playwrights, "fluid and poetic drama without breaking the mold of effective realistic dramaturgy."[19] O'Neill's late dynamic realism can be understood only as an outgrowth of his experimental period. Both phases can be connected with the drama created in his surroundings[20]—and with his own person. O'Neill had lived,

[19] Gassner, *Theatre in Our Times*, p. 48.

[20] Several literary connections are drawn by Raleigh, p. 242. Eliot's and Pound's rebellion against Victorian language was led by O'Neill in the domain of drama; Greek myths were employed by O'Neill, Eliot, Jeffers, and others; *The Great God Brown* and *Dynamo* are examples of "the wild, hallucinatory, dreamlike, nightmare-like

in an intensive manner, the rebellious years of an angry young man from the 1910's. Toward the end of his life he lived just as furiously the turning back of an old man, in remembrance of things past. All the time, he lived in his art. He was a true dramatist.

Another facet of O'Neill's relationship to his time is that he was a contemporary of the pioneers of stagecraft in this century. He had a fresh continent before him, even if Adolphe Appia and Gordon Craig were somewhat ahead in time; and he faced a frontier in the field of serious drama. As an actor's son, Eugene O'Neill knew that the written text was not all of the theatre. The ideas of contemporary renewers of the stage confirmed his faith in all kinds of scenic means of expression. He was at his worst when trying to create self-containing poetry; the beginnings of his success were in his interest in "what a modern theatre should be capable of."

O'Neill's masks and "thought asides" are indications of the revolutionary breakthrough of psychoanalysis. He did not only demonstrate Freudian lines of thought on the stage; he also overburdened these ideas, trying to find in them a solution to man's metaphysical dilemma. Yet he is also an exponent of a more sober application of these ideas: complexes, neuroses, or love-hate relations do not solve anything; they just exist. Psychoanalytic elements are, of course, possible building materials for works of art; what is doubtful is whether they can be emphasized as strongly as they were before World War II.[21] *Long Day's Journey Into Night*, O'Neill's posthumous masterpiece, definitely belongs in this and other respects to the postwar era.

Mennemeier has seen O'Neill as a forerunner of absurdism (cf. p. 305 above). One of the themes O'Neill shared with this school of playwriting is that of difficulties in com-

---

quality of human experience" which is characteristic of a great portion of modern literature; on the other hand, O'Neill also followed a trend "toward a kind of classical objectivity."

[21] Dietrich (*Das moderne Drama*, p. 230) presents a similar estimation: the time of exaggerated psychoanalyzing in drama is over. She also stresses the importance of other elements in O'Neill: his heroes seek fulfillment of their lives.

munication. The enjoyment in happy phrasing, experienced by Shakespeare and other Elizabethans,[22] has been replaced by a widespread distrust in the communicative value of language. Enlarging the sphere of discussion outside the theatre we might hint at modern philosophers, careful students of semantics; or at the lesson in the abuse of language taught by Hitler. Though absurdist playwrights were cautious, they kept on creating—for the theatre. Though O'Neill apparently had his misgivings about the possibility of true communication,[23] he kept creating situations in which his characters grope for and occasionally achieve mutual understanding. The problem for O'Neill and the absurdists is the same; the artistic form given to it is different.

Eugene O'Neill's connections with his time emphasize the theatrical quality of his works. When attempting a critical evaluation of the method applied in this study, it is worth remembering that O'Neill is a playwright ideally suited for a scenic approach. He wrote his visions into precise stage directions; he grew up close to the stage; verbal skills were not one of his strong points. Charney, incidentally, mentions O'Neill as an opposite to his own object of study: "It would be much simpler to discuss the presentational imagery of such dramatists as O'Neill or Ibsen, for their stage directions are much fuller than Shakespeare's and the theater for which they wrote much closer to us."[24] In other words, the margin of speculation is bound to be wider when the distance in time and cultural climate grows between a present-day scholar and the object of his interest.

The central concepts employed in this study might be more applicable when dealing with the modern drama than when trying to extend the method to older plays. Yet there is help

[22] "Nor do puns mean to us what they meant to the Elizabethans, delighting in their language for its own sake" (Granville-Barker, *Prefaces to Shakespeare*, I, p. 12).

[23] "In some strange, deep way, and for reasons beyond his lack of a consistent poetic talent, he sometimes did not believe in language, or at least in meaningful language" (Raleigh, p. 209).

[24] Charney, *Shakespeare's Roman Plays*, p. 206.

available from another branch of *Theaterwissenschaft*— from the history of the theatre. It remains to be seen whether mental reconstructions of past conditions in the theatre can offer a solid basis for a research concentrating on the scenic images of, say, a Renaissance playwright.

On the other hand, a portion of the criticism in the field of drama since Ibsen has a slightly anachronistic flavor, because the criteria applied are derived from studies in poetry or in older drama. It is not unusual to read complaints of the definite inferiority of the modern playwrights: why do they not write poetry on the level of Shakespeare? The basic answer is, of course, that they write for a different kind of theatre in which the development of stagecraft has made the functions of dialogue less prominent than before. A critical principle phrased by Peacock has not been acknowledged generally enough: "The intertexture of drama differing so markedly from that of poems, we judge its imaginative quality by different criteria. . . . The poetry of drama is not that of a romantic lyric or symbolist poem."[25] It has been taken as something different in this study. If the central concepts developed will help to make the scenic approach to drama more legitimate, they will have served an essential purpose.

In my introduction the creative process of a playwright was supposed to be more mechanical than it actually is, in order to clarify the argument. It has been so throughout the study. Purely artistic solutions made by Eugene O'Neill have probably been described as having happened too consciously. This procedure has only served as a kind of shorthand. Some part of O'Neill's mind must have relied on the expressive power of his dialogue when he started writing *Long Day's Journey Into Night*: and to that part has been given the name "he." The purpose here has been to show that these solutions were arrived at, not to set forth any theories as to how this happened, somewhere deep in the subconscious mind of a creative artist. This reservation is presented here and now, rather than having been interpolated every time there might have been reason for it.

[25] Peacock, *The Art of Drama*, p. 245.

Nor has it been my intention to write down laws to be followed by all future playwrights. If there are any elements pointing toward a general theory of drama, these are connected with three basic criteria. It seems to be worthwhile to examine whether a playwright uses his scenic means of expression in harmony with the themes of his play, with the style he has chosen, and with his personal qualities. The concepts utilized in this study do not presuppose any absolute standards within any of these dimensions.

The concept of "scenic image" has been used as a surgical knife: it has not been resorted to when it has been possible to characterize a play along more general lines. Admitting that it is questionable whether this instrument is of considerable value for a scholar studying older drama, and admitting that Eugene O'Neill has been an ideal patient, one finds it possible to look toward new vistas in the study of the modern drama. How do new findings along these lines change our total picture of a playwright? What is the relation between Bertolt Brecht's images and the formalistic machinery of his epic theatre? What could one find out about the position of the plays-within-plays on Jean Anouilh's stage? How does Friedrich Dürrenmatt construct his grotesque and parodical scenic images? There are a great many chapters to be written before a study of the relations between the modern playwright and his stage can be complete.

APPENDIX A

LIST OF PLAYS

This chronological list of plays discussed in this study is based on corresponding catalogues published by Cargill, Fagin, and Fisher (*O'Neill and His Plays*, pp. 479-82) and by the Gelbs (*O'Neill*, p. 944), with some obvious errors corrected. The names of three unpublished original plays existing in the Library of Congress have been added.

Title	Year written	First production	First publication
A Wife for a Life	1913	—	1950
The Web	1913	—	1914
Thirst	1913-14	1916	1914
Warnings	1913-14	—	1914
Fog	1913-14	1917	1914
Recklessness	1913-14	—	1914
Servitude	1913-14	—	1950
Abortion	1913-14	1959	1950
Bread and Butter	1914	—	—
Bound East for Cardiff	1914	1916	1916
The Movie Man	1914	1959	1950
The Sniper	1914-15	1917	1950
Before Breakfast	1916	1916	1916
Ile	1916-17	1917	1918
In the Zone	1916-17	1917	1919
The Long Voyage Home	1916-17	1917	1917
The Moon of the Caribbees	1916-17	1918	1918
Now I Ask You	1917	—	—
Beyond the Horizon	1917-18	1920	1920
The Rope	1918	1918	1919
The Dreamy Kid	1918	1919	1920

Title	Year written	First production	First publication
Where the Cross Is Made	1918	1918	1919
Shell Shock	1918	—	—
The Straw	1918-19	1921	1921
'Anna Christie'	1919-20	1921	1922
Gold	1920	1921	1921
The Emperor Jones	1920	1920	1921
Diff'rent	1920	1920	1921
The First Man	1921	1922	1922
The Hairy Ape	1917, 1921	1922	1922
The Fountain	1921-22	1922	1922
Welded	1922-23	1924	1924
All God's Chillun Got Wings	1923	1924	1924
The Ancient Mariner	1923	1924	1960
Desire Under the Elms	1924	1924	1924
Marco Millions	1923-25	1928	1927
The Great God Brown	1925	1926	1926
Lazarus Laughed	1925-26	1928	1927
Strange Interlude	1926-27	1928	1928
Dynamo	1928	1929	1929
Mourning Becomes Electra	1929-31	1931	1931
Ah, Wilderness!	1932	1933	1933
Days Without End	1931-34	1934	1934
More Stately Mansions	1935-41	1962	1964
The Iceman Cometh	1939	1946	1946
Long Day's Journey Into Night	1939-41	1956	1956
Hughie	1941-42	1958	1959
A Touch of the Poet	1935-42	1957	1957
A Moon for the Misbegotten	1943	1947	1952

The dates of composition are approximations; in their review of the sources of information Cargill, Fagin, and Fisher remark (p. 479) that it was O'Neill's habit to revise his scripts during a longer period of time.

APPENDIX B

A SCENIC UNIT IN THE SETTINGS

There are ten settings in all of O'Neill in which one might speak of the influence of a certain scenic unit, manifest in the placement of furniture, doors, and windows. The earliest occurrence is in *Servitude* (or in *Bread and Butter*), the latest in *Long Day's Journey into Night,* covering nearly three decades of playwriting.

The following drawings are not detailed enough to form a basis for executing the settings on the stage. They are intended only to show certain similarities and dissimilarities; only those details which O'Neill mentioned in his stage directions are realized in the drawings.

Bread and Butter, Act IV
Description of the setting: *MS*, p. 47.

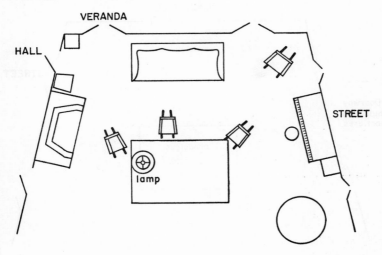

Servitude, Acts I-III
Description: *Lost Plays*, p. 72.

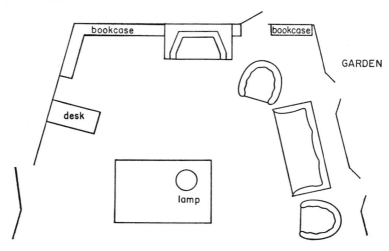

Now I Ask You, Act I
Description: *MS*, p. 5.

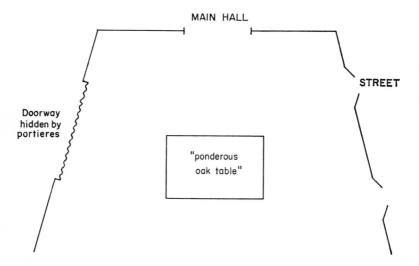

352

The First Man, Acts I and IV
Description: *The Plays II*, p. 553.

HALL

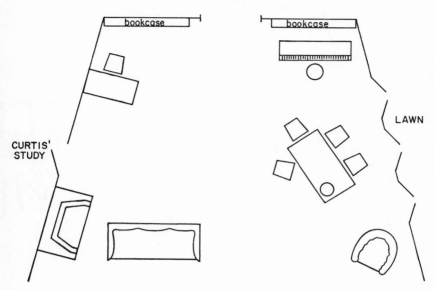

CURTIS'
STUDY

LAWN

Days Without End, Acts II and III, i
Description: *The Plays III*, p. 514.

HALL

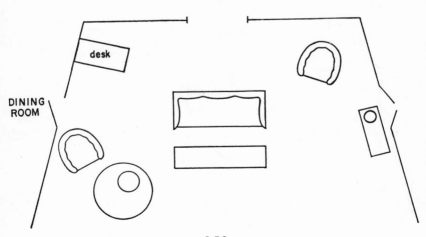

DINING
ROOM

Mourning Becomes Electra: The Hunted, II. The Haunted, I, ii
Description: *The Plays II*, pp. 79, 157.

HALL

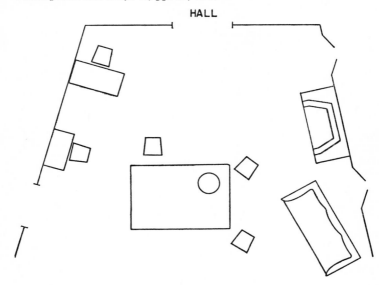

Ah, Wilderness! and *Long Day's Journey Into Night*. (Details belonging *only* to the latter play are marked with 1); a rocker belonging only to the former is marked with 2). Instead of a rocker at left of the table, *Journey* has another wicker chair.)

Descriptions: *The Plays II*, p. 185. *Long Day's Journey Into Night*, pp. 11-12.

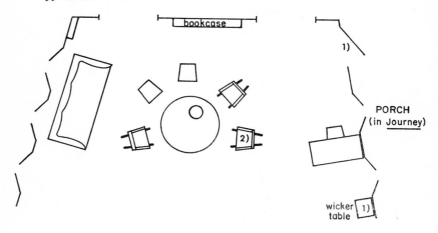

More Stately Mansions, I, iii

An approximate copy of O'Neill's own drawing, published in *More Stately Mansions*, p. 42. (See Fig. 5 for facsimile reproduction.)

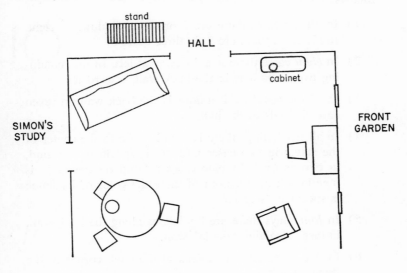

More Stately Mansions, II, iii
Description: *More Stately Mansions*, p. 117. (See Fig. 6.)

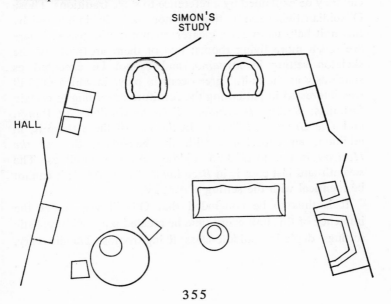

The similarities in these settings can be summarized as follows:

1) In all *ten* cases there are 1 or more windows at right. In six cases there are 2, in three cases 3.

2) In *eight* cases there is a doorway at left. In the remaining two cases it is in the back wall, toward left.

3) In *nine* cases there is a door in the back wall; in seven cases it leads to the hall.

4) In all *ten* settings there is a table close to the center of the stage; in two cases its form is specified as round, in two as oval. In nine cases a lamp on the table is mentioned; in three out of these the color of its shade is specified as green.

5) In *four* plays there are bookcases along the back wall, in three also along the left wall.

6) In *five* cases there is a desk in the back corner of the stage, at left.

These numerous similarities can hardly be coincidental, nor can they be explained by a reference to stage traditions. Those O'Neillian living rooms that are not markedly influenced by this unit help us to get a clearer picture of the usage. There are seven more living rooms; two of them are parts of the skeleton setting in *Dynamo*, and cannot be executed as spaciously as the unit. Three occur in plays in which O'Neill was interested in patterning the furniture according to certain formulas: *Strange Interlude*, *All God's Chillun Got Wings*, and *The Great God Brown*. In the last of these there is, in addition, an experiment with the backdrop. *Beyond the Horizon* is not located in middle class surroundings. The seventh and last case is in *Bread and Butter*, Act I; it cannot be identical with the setting of Act IV.

It is thus to be concluded that O'Neill was under the influence of this unit every time he created plays with realistic settings depicting middle-class living rooms. Details vary, tables and fireplaces are afloat; yet a kind of stem is shared by several plays. The fact that both *Ah, Wilderness!* and *Long Day's Journey* show a strong influence of the unit hints at the autobiographical origin of this scenic pattern.

BIBLIOGRAPHY

Abel, Lionel. "O'Neill and His Critics," *The New Leader, 41*, Jan. 6, 1958.

Adler, Jacob H. "The Worth of *Ah, Wilderness!*," *Modern Drama, 3*, 3 (Dec. 1960).

Ahlgren, Stig. "Eugene O'Neills författarskap," *Ord och bild* (Stockholm), *46*, 3 (March 1937).

Alexander, Doris. "Eugene O'Neill and Charles Lever," *Modern Drama, 5*, 4 (Spring 1963).

————. "Eugene O'Neill and *Light on the Path*," *Modern Drama, 3*, 3 (Dec. 1960).

————. "The Missing Half of *Hughie*," *Tulane Drama Review, 11*, 4 (Summer 1967).

————. "*Strange Interlude* and Schopenhauer," *American Literature, 25*, 2 (May 1953).

————. *The Tempering of Eugene O'Neill*. New York: Harcourt, Brace & World, 1962.

Anderson, Michael. "Dionysus and the Cultured Policeman," *Tulane Drama Review, 11*, 4 (Summer 1967).

Andreach, Robert J. "O'Neill's Use of Dante in *The Fountain* and *The Hairy Ape*," *Modern Drama, 10*, 1 (May 1967).

Atkinson, Brooks. *Broadway Scrapbook*. New York: Theatre Arts, Inc., 1947.

Baum, Bernard. "*The Tempest* and *The Hairy Ape*," *Modern Language Quarterly, 14*, 3 (Sept. 1953).

Bentley, Eric. *The Dramatic Event*. Boston: Beacon Press, 1957 (1954).

————. *The Playwright as Thinker*. New York: Harcourt, Brace & World, 1946.

————. *In Search of Theater*. New York: Alfred A. Knopf, 1953.

Biese, Y. M. *Aspects of Expression I: Eugene O'Neill's*

Strange Interlude *and the Linguistic Presentation of the Interior Monologue*. Helsinki: Annales Academiae Scientiarum Fennicae, B, 118, 3, 1963.

Björk, Lennart A. "The Swedish Critical Reception of O'Neill's Posthumous Plays," *Scandinavian Studies, 38*, 3 (Aug. 1966).

Blackburn, Clara. "Continental Influences on Eugene O'Neill's Expressionistic Dramas," *American Literature, 13*, 2 (May 1941).

Boulton, Agnes. *Part of a Long Story*. New York: Doubleday, 1958.

Bowen, Croswell. *The Curse of the Misbegotten: A Tale of the House of O'Neill*. New York: McGraw-Hill, 1959.

Bradley, A. C. *Shakespearian Tragedy*. London: Macmillan, 1962 (1904).

Braem, Helmut M. *Eugene O'Neill*. Velber bei Hannover: Friedrich Verlag, 1965.

Brie, Friedrich. "Eugene O'Neill als Nachfolger der Griechen," *Germanisch-Romanische Monatschrift, 21*, 1 (Jan.-Feb. 1933).

Broussard, Louis. *American Drama: Contemporary Allegory from Eugene O'Neill to Tennessee Williams*. Norman: University of Oklahoma Press, 1962.

Brown, John Mason. *Dramatis Personae*. New York: The Viking Press, 1963.

Brown, John Russell and Harris, Bernard (eds.). *American Theatre*. Stratford-upon-Avon Studies 10. London: Edward Arnold Ltd., 1967.

Brugger, Ilse. "Verwendung und Bedeutung der Maske bei O'Neill," *Die neueren Sprachen*, Neue Folge, *6*, 4 (Apr. 1957).

Brüning, Eberhard. *Das amerikanische Drama der dreissiger Jahre*. Berlin: Rütten & Loening, 1966.

Brustein, Robert. *The Theatre of Revolt*. London: Methuen & Co., 1965.

Cargill, Oscar; Fagin, N. Bryllion; Fisher, William J. (eds.). *O'Neill and His Plays: Four Decades of Criticism*. Paperback ed.; New York: New York University Press, 1963 (1961).

Carpenter, Frederic I. *Eugene O'Neill.* New York: Twayne Publishers, 1964.

Chabrowe, Leonard. "Dionysos in *The Iceman Cometh*," *Modern Drama, 4,* 4 (Spring 1962).

Chaitin, Norman C. "The Power of Daring," *Modern Drama, 3,* 3 (Dec. 1960).

Chand, Kishen. "Symbolism in Modern Drama," an unpublished doctoral dissertation, University of Punjab, 1940. Yale Drama School Library, New Haven, Conn.

Charney, Maurice. *Shakespeare's Roman Plays.* Cambridge: Harvard University Press, 1961.

Chen, David Y. "Two Chinese Adaptations of Eugene O'Neill's *The Emperor Jones*," *Modern Drama, 9,* 4 (Feb. 1967).

Chiari, J. *Landmarks of Contemporary Drama.* London: Herbert Jenkins, 1965.

Chiaromonte, Nicola. "Eugene O'Neill (1958)," *Sewanee Review, 68,* 3 (July-Sept. 1960).

Clark, Barrett H. *Eugene O'Neill: The Man and His Plays,* 5th rev. ed.; New York: Dover, 1947 (1926).

———— (ed.). *European Theories of the Drama.* Rev. ed.; New York: Crown, 1947 (1918).

Clark, Marden J. "The Tragic Effect in *The Hairy Ape*," *Modern Drama, 10,* 4 (Feb. 1968).

Clay, James H. and Krempel, Daniel. *The Theatrical Image.* New York: McGraw-Hill, 1967.

Clemen, Wolfgang H. *The Development of Shakespeare's Imagery.* Rev. ed. of *Shakespeares Bilder* (Bonn: 1936). Cambridge: Harvard University Press, 1951.

Coghill, Nevill. *Shakespeare's Professional Skills.* Cambridge: Cambridge University Press, 1964.

Coolidge, Olivia. *Eugene O'Neill.* New York: Scribner's, 1966.

Dahlström, Carl E. W. L. "*Dynamo* and *Lazarus Laughed*: Some Limitations," *Modern Drama, 3,* 3 (Dec. 1960).

Day, Cyrus. "*Amor Fati*: O'Neill's Lazarus as Superman and Savior," *Modern Drama, 3,* 3 (Dec. 1960).

Day, Cyrus. "The Iceman and the Bridegroom," *Modern Drama, 1*, 1 (May 1958).

Dietrich, Margret. *Das moderne Drama*. Stuttgart: Alfred Körner Verlag, 1961.

Downer, Alan S. (ed.). *American Drama and Its Critics*. Chicago: The University of Chicago Press, 1965.

———— (ed.). *The American Theater*. Voice of America Forum Lectures, 1967.

————. *Fifty Years of American Drama: 1900-1950*. Chicago: Regnery, 1951.

Driver, Tom F. "On the Last Plays of Eugene O'Neill," *Tulane Drama Review, 3*, 2 (Dec. 1958).

Dusenbury, Winifred L. *The Theme of Loneliness in Modern American Drama*. Gainesville: University of Florida Press, 1960.

Ellis-Fermor, Una. *The Jacobean Drama*. 4th rev. ed.; London: Methuen & Co., University Paperbacks, 1965 (1936).

————. *Shakespeare the Dramatist*. Kenneth Muir (ed.). London: Methuen & Co., 1961.

————. *Some Recent Research in Shakespeare's Imagery*. London: Shakespeare Association, 1937.

Engel, Edwin A. *The Haunted Heroes of Eugene O'Neill*. Cambridge: Harvard University Press, 1953.

————. "O'Neill, 1960," *Modern Drama, 3*, 3 (Dec. 1960).

Falk, Doris V. *Eugene O'Neill and the Tragic Tension: An Interpretative Study of the Plays*. New Brunswick, N.J.: Rutgers University Press, 1958.

————. "That Paradox, O'Neill," *Modern Drama, 6*, 3 (Feb. 1963).

Falk, Signi. "Dialogue in the Plays of Eugene O'Neill," *Modern Drama, 3*, 3 (Dec. 1960).

Fitzgerald, John J. "The Bitter Harvest of O'Neill's Projected Cycle," *The New England Qvarterly, 40*, 3 (Sept. 1967).

Fleisher, Frederic. "Strindberg and O'Neill," *Symposium* (Syracuse University, N.Y.), *10* (Spring 1956).

Flexner, Eleanor. *American Playwrights: 1918-1938: The Theatre Retreats from Reality*. New York: Simon and Schuster, 1938.

Flickinger, Roy C. *The Greek Theatre and Its Drama.* 3rd ed.; Chicago: Chicago University Press, 1926 (1918).

Freedley, George, and Reeves, John A. *A History of the Theatre.* Rev. ed.; New York: Crown, 1958 (1941).

Frenz, Horst. *Eugene O'Neill.* Berlin: Colloquium Verlag, 1965.

————. "Eugene O'Neill in Deutschland," *Euphorion* (Heidelberg: Carl Winter, Universitätsverlag), *50*, 3 (Summer 1956).

———— and Fleisher, Frederic. "Eugene O'Neill and the Royal Dramatic Theatre of Stockholm," *Modern Drama, 10*, 3 (Dec. 1967).

———— and Mueller, Martin. "More Shakespeare and Less Aeschylus in Eugene O'Neill's *Mourning Becomes Electra,*" *American Literature, 38*, 1 (March 1966).

Freud, Sigmund. *Selbstdarstellung.* 2d rev. ed.; 1936 (1925). Reissued in *Gesammelte Werke,* XIV. London: Imago, 1948.

Friedmann, Hermann, and Mann, Otto (eds.). *Expressionismus.* Heidelberg: Wolfgang Rother Verlag, 1956.

Gagey, Edmond M. *Revolution in American Drama.* New York: Columbia University Press, 1947.

Galinsky, Hans. "Eugene O'Neill: Die Wendung des modernen amerikanischen Theaters zur Tragödie," *Die neueren Sprachen,* Neue Folge, *2*, 6 (June 1953).

Gascoigne, Bamber. *Twentieth-Century Drama.* London: Hutchinson & Co., 1962.

Gassner, John (ed.). *Best American Plays, 1945-1951.* New York: Crown, 1952.

————. *Eugene O'Neill.* Minneapolis: University of Minnesota Press, 1965.

————. *Form and Idea in the Modern Theatre.* New York: Holt, Rinehart & Winston, 1956.

———— (ed.). *Ideas in the Drama.* New York: Columbia University Press, 1964.

————. *Masters of the Drama.* 3rd rev. ed.; New York: Dover, 1954 (Random House, 1940).

Gassner, John (ed.). *O'Neill: A Collection of Critical Essays.* Englewood Cliffs, N.J.: Prentice-Hall, 1964.

————. *Theatre at the Crossroads.* New York: Holt, Rinehart & Winston, 1960.

————. *The Theatre in Our Times.* New York: Crown, 1954.

Geddes, Virgil. *The Melodramadness of Eugene O'Neill.* Brookfield, Conn.: The Brookfield Players, 1934.

Gelb, Arthur. "Onstage He Played the Novelist," *New York Times Book Review,* Aug. 30, 1964.

Gelb, Arthur and Barbara. *O'Neill.* 2d ed.; New York: Harper & Row, 1962 (1960).

Gerstenberg, Alice. *Ten One-Act Plays.* New York: Longmans, Green & Co., 1934 (Brentano's, 1921).

Gierow, Karl Ragnar. *Introduktioner till Eugene O'Neills dramatik.* Stockholm: Sveriges radio, 1958.

Gilbert, Allan H. (ed.). *Literary Criticism: Plato to Dryden.* New York: Wayne, 1940.

Gilman, Richard. "Mr. O'Neill's very last curtain call," *New York Herald Tribune,* Book Week, May 31, 1964.

Glicksberg, Charles I. *The Tragic Vision in Twentieth-Century Literature.* Carbondale, Ill.: Southern Illinois University Press, 1963.

Goldberg, Isaac. *The Theatre of George Jean Nathan.* New York: Simon and Schuster, 1926.

Gould, Jean. *Modern American Playwrights.* New York: Dodd, Mead & Co., 1966.

Granger, Bruce I. "Illusion and Reality in Eugene O'Neill," *Modern Language Notes, 73,* 3 (March 1958).

Granville-Barker, Harley. *Prefaces to Shakespeare.* 2 vols. London: B. T. Batsford Ltd., 1958 (1927-30).

Gump, Margaret. "From Ape to Man and from Man to Ape," *Kentucky Foreign Language Quarterly, 4,* 4 (Fall 1957).

Hallingberg, Gunnar. *Radiodramat.* Stockholm: Sveriges Radios förlag, 1967.

Janzon, Åke. "Lång dags färd mot natt," *Bonniers Litterära Magasin, 25,* 3 (March 1956).

Kailas, Uuno. *Runoja.* Porvoo: WSOY, 1946 (1932).

Kaucher, Dorothy J. *Modern Dramatic Structure*. The University of Missouri Studies, *3*, 4 (Oct. 1928).

Kerr, Alfred. *Die Welt im Drama*. Gerhard F. Hering (ed.). Köln-Berlin: Kiepenheuer & Witsch, 1964 (1954).

Kirchner, Gustav. "Eugene Gladstone O'Neill (1888-1953). Ein Rückblick," *Zeitschrift für Anglistik und Amerikanistik, 2*, 2 (March 1954).

Kitto, H. D. F. *Greek Tragedy: A Literary Study*. 3rd ed.; New York: Doubleday, 1954 (1939).

Klavsons, Janis. "O'Neill's Dreamer: Success and Failure," *Modern Drama, 3*, 3 (Dec. 1960).

Koischwitz, Otto. *O'Neill*. Berlin: Junker und Dünnhaupt, 1938.

Krutch, Joseph Wood. *The American Drama Since 1918*. Rev. ed.; New York: Braziller, 1957 (Random House, 1939).

————. *"Modernism" in Modern Drama*. Ithaca, N.Y.: Cornell University Press, 1953.

Krämer, Edgar. "Freiheit und Notwendigkeit als tragisches Problem bei O'Neill," an unpublished doctoral dissertation, Christian-Albrechts-Universität zu Kiel, 1953.

Kutscher, Artur. *Grundriss der Theaterwissenschaft I-II*. Part One: *Die Elemente des Theaters*; Part Two: *Stilkunde des Theaters*. Düsseldorf: Pflugschar Verlag, Klein Vater u. Sohn, 1932, 1936.

Lamm, Martin. *Det moderna dramat*. Stockholm: Albert Bonniers förlag, 1948.

Langner, Lawrence. *The Play's the Thing*. Ithaca, N.Y.: Cornell University Press, 1960.

Lawson, John Howard. *Theory and Technique of Playwriting*. With a new introduction. New York: Hill and Wang, 1960 (1936).

Lee, Hyo Young. "Eugene O'Neill's Struggle for Self-Realization Reflected in His Works," an unpublished M.A. thesis, Yale University, 1961. Yale Drama School Library, New Haven, Conn.

Lee, Robert C. "The Lonely Dream," *Modern Drama, 9*, 2 (Sept. 1966).

Leech, Clifford. *Eugene O'Neill.* New York: Grove Press, 1963 (Edinburgh, Scotland: Oliver and Boyd, 1963).

Lewis, Allan. *American Plays and Playwrights of the Contemporary Theatre.* New York: Crown, 1965.

Lindberg, Per. *Kring ridån.* Stockholm: Albert Bonniers förlag, 1932.

Link, Franz H. *Eugene O'Neill und die Wiedergeburt der Tragödie aus dem Unbewussten.* Frankfurt am Main: Athenäum Verlag, 1967.

Long, Chester Clayton. *The Role of Nemesis in the Structure of Selected Plays by Eugene O'Neill.* The Hague: Mouton & Co., 1968.

Lucas, F. L. *Tragedy.* 2d ed.; London: The Hogarth Press, 1958 (1927).

Lumley, Frederick. *Trends in 20th Century Drama.* London: Rockliff, 1956.

Lüchou, Nils. *Teaterstaden Helsingfors.* Marianne Lüchou (ed.). Tampere: Söderström & Co, 1960.

McAleer, John J. "Christ Symbolism in '*Anna Christie*'," *Modern Drama, 4,* 4 (Spring 1962).

McCarthy, Mary. *The Humanist in the Bathtub.* New York: The New American Library, 1964.

Macgowan, Kenneth. *The Theatre of Tomorrow.* New York: Boni and Liveright, 1921.

———— and Rosse, Herman. *Masks and Demons.* New York: Harcourt, Brace & Co., 1923.

Mann, Otto. *Geschichte des deutschen Dramas.* Stuttgart: Alfred Kröner Verlag, 1960.

Mårtensson, Sigvard. *Eugene O'Neills dramatik.* Stockholm: Radiotjänst, 1957.

Melchinger, Siegfried. *Drama zwischen Shaw und Brecht.* 4th rev. ed.; Bremen: Carl Schünemann Verlag, 1961 (1957).

Mennemeier, Franz Norbert. *Das moderne Drama des Auslandes.* Düsseldorf: August Bagel Verlag, 1961.

Metzger, Deena P. "Variations on a Theme: A Study of *Exiles* by James Joyce and *The Great God Brown* by Eugene O'Neill," *Modern Drama, 8,* 2 (Sept. 1965).

Mickle, Alan D. *Six Plays of Eugene O'Neill.* New York: Horace Liveright, 1929 (London: Jonathan Cape, 1929).

Miller, Jordan Y. *Eugene O'Neill and the American Critic: A Summary and Bibliographical Checklist.* Hamden, Conn.: Shoe String, 1962.

―――. *Playwright's Progress: O'Neill and the Critics.* Chicago: Scott, Foresman and Company, 1965.

Mottram, Eric. "Men and Gods: A Study of Eugene O'Neill," *Encore, 10,* 5 (Sept.-Oct. 1963).

Nagler, A. M. *A Source Book in Theatrical History.* New York: Dover Publications, 1959 (*Sources of Theatrical History*, 1952).

Nathan, George Jean. "Eugene O'Neill after Twelve Years," *The American Mercury, 63,* 274 (Oct. 1946).

Nethercot, Arthur H. "The Psychoanalyzing of Eugene O'Neill," *Modern Drama, 3,* 3-4 (Dec. 1960, Feb. 1961).

―――. "The Psychoanalyzing of Eugene O'Neill: Postscript," *Modern Drama, 8,* 2 (Sept. 1965).

Nicoll, Allardyce. *World Drama.* London: George G. Harrap & Co., 1964 (1949).

O'Hara, Frank Hurburt. *Today in American Drama.* Chicago: Chicago University Press, 1939.

Olsoni, Eric. *Från Strindberg till Anouilh.* Porvoo: Söderström & Co, 1964.

Olsson, Hagar. *Arbetare i natten.* Helsinki: Holger Schildts förlag, 1935.

O'Neill, Eugene. *The Ancient Mariner.* Dramatic adaptation of Coleridge's poem, Donald Gallup (ed.). *The Yale University Library Gazette* (New Haven, Conn.), *35,* 2 (Oct. 1960).

―――. *Bread and Butter.* An unpublished manuscript. Library of Congress: D 36911 (May 2, 1914).

―――. *The Emperor Jones. The Straw.* New York: The Modern Library, 1928.

―――. *Hughie.* New Haven: Yale University Press, 1959.

―――. *The Iceman Cometh.* New York: Random House, 1946.

O'Neill, Eugene. *Long Day's Journey Into Night*. New Haven: Yale University Press, 1956.

————. *Lost Plays of Eugene O'Neill*. New York: Citadel Press, 1958 (New Fathoms, 1950).

————. *A Moon for the Misbegotten*. New York: Random House, 1952.

————. *More Stately Mansions*. Shortened from the author's partly revised script by Karl Ragnar Gierow. Donald Gallup (ed.). New Haven: Yale University Press, 1964.

————. *Nine Plays by Eugene O'Neill*. With an introduction by Joseph Wood Krutch. New York: Horace Liveright, 1932.

————. *Now I Ask You*. An unpublished manuscript. O'Neill Collection, Yale University Library. 1917.

————. *The Plays of Eugene O'Neill*, I-III. New York: Random House, 1941.

————. *Shell Shock*. An unpublished manuscript. Library of Congress: D 50100 (Aug. 5, 1918).

————. *Thirst And Other One Act Plays*. Boston: The Gorham Press, 1914.

————. *A Touch of the Poet*. New Haven: Yale University Press, 1957.

O'Neill, Joseph P., S.J. "The Tragic Theory of Eugene O'Neill," *Texas Studies in Literature and Language, 4*, 4 (Winter 1963).

Pallette, Drew B. "O'Neill and the Comic Spirit," *Modern Drama, 3*, 3 (Dec. 1960).

————. "O'Neill's *A Touch of the Poet* and His Other Last Plays," *Arizona Quarterly, 13*, 4 (Winter 1957).

Peacock, Ronald. *The Art of Drama*. New York: Macmillan, 1957 (London: Routledge & Kegan Paul, 1957).

Pommer, Henry F. "The Mysticism of Eugene O'Neill," *Modern Drama, 9*, 1 (May 1966).

Pratt, Norman T., Jr. "Aeschylus and O'Neill: Two Worlds," *The Classical Journal, 51*, 4 (Jan. 1956).

Quinn, Arthur Hobson. *A History of the American Drama*, II: *From William Vaughan Moody to the Present Day*. New York: Harper & Brothers, 1927.

Raleigh, John Henry. "O'Neill's *Long Day's Journey Into Night* and New England Irish-Catholicism," *Partisan Review, 26*, 4 (Fall 1959).

————. *The Plays of Eugene O'Neill.* Carbondale and Edwardsville, Ill.: Southern Illinois University Press, 1965.

———— (ed.). *Twentieth Century Interpretations of The Iceman Cometh.* Englewood Cliffs, N.J.: Prentice-Hall, 1968.

Reardon, William R. "O'Neill since World War II: Critical Reception in New York," *Modern Drama, 10*, 3 (Dec. 1967).

Rust, R. Dilworth. "The Unity of O'Neill's *S.S. Glencairn*," *American Literature, 37*, 3 (Nov. 1965).

Schücking, Levin L. *Character Problems in Shakespeare's Plays.* London: George G. Harrap & Co., 1922.

————. *Essays.* Wiesbaden: Dieterich'sche Verlagsbuchhandlung, 1948.

————. *The Meaning of Hamlet.* Revised translation of *Der Sinn des Hamlet* (Leipzig: Quelle und Meyer, 1935). London: Oxford University Press, 1937.

————. *Shakespeare und der Tragödienstil seiner Zeit.* Bern: A. Francke Verlag, 1947.

Shaw, George Bernard. *Plays Pleasant.* London: Penguin Books, 1955 (1898).

Shawcross, John T. "The Road to Ruin: The Beginning of O'Neill's *Long Day's Journey*," *Modern Drama, 3*, 3 (Dec. 1960).

Shipley, Joseph T. *The Art of Eugene O'Neill.* Seattle: University of Washington Chapbooks, 1928.

Sievers, W. David. *Freud on Broadway.* New York: Hermitage House, 1955.

Skinner, Richard Dana. *Eugene O'Neill: A Poet's Quest.* New York: Longmans, Green & Co., 1935.

Sokel, Walter H. *Der literarische Expressionismus (The Writer in Extremis).* München: Albert Langen—Georg Müller Verlag, 1959.

Spiller, Robert E. *The Third Dimension: Studies in Literary History.* New York: Macmillan, 1965 (London: Collier-Macmillan Ltd.).

Spiller, Robert E. (ed.). *A Time of Harvest: American Literature 1910-1960*. New York: Hill and Wang, 1963.

Stamm, Rudolf. " 'Faithful Realism': Eugene O'Neill and the Problem of Style," *English Studies, 40*, 4 (Aug. 1959).

———. "Das Spätwerk Eugene O'Neills," *Deutsche Vierteljahrschrift für Literaturwissenschaft und Geistesgeschichte, 34*, 1 (May 1960).

Stoll, E. E. *Art and Artifice in Shakespeare*. New York: Barnes & Noble, 1951 (Cambridge: Cambridge University Press, 1933).

———. *Shakespeare and Other Masters*. Cambridge: Harvard University Press, 1940.

Straumann, Heinrich. *American Literature in the Twentieth Century*. Rev. ed.; London: Arrow Books, 1962 (1951).

Szondi, Peter. *Theorie des modernen Dramas*. Frankfurt am Main: Suhrkamp Verlag, 1959.

Thorpe, Willard. *American Writing in the Twentieth Century*. Cambridge: Harvard University Press, 1963 (1960).

Törnqvist, Egil. "Ibsen and O'Neill: A Study in Influence," *Scandinavian Studies, 37*, 3 (Aug. 1965).

———. "Personal Nomenclature in the Plays of Eugene O'Neill," *Modern Drama, 8*, 4 (Feb. 1966).

Torsslow, Stig. *Eugene O'Neill*. Stockholm: Albert Bonniers förlag, 1937.

Ullmann, Stephen. *Semantics: An Introduction to the Science of Meaning*. Oxford: Basil Blackwell, 1964 (1962).

Valgemae, Mardi. "O'Neill and German Expressionism," *Modern Drama, 10*, 2 (Sept. 1967).

Verho, Urho. *Uuden teatterin tiennäyttäjiä*. Turku: Tajo, 1963.

Viljanen, Lauri. *Taisteleva humanismi*. Rev. ed.; Hämeenlinna: Arvi A. Karisto Oy, 1950 (1936).

Waith, Eugene M. "Eugene O'Neill: an Exercise in Unmasking," *Educational Theatre Journal, 13*, 3 (Oct. 1961).

Weales, Gerald. *American Drama Since World War II*. New York: Harcourt, Brace & World, 1962.

Weissman, Philip. "*Mourning Becomes Electra* and *The*

Prodigal: Electra and Orestes," *Modern Drama, 3,* 3 (Dec. 1960).

Whicher, Stephen. "O'Neill's Long Journey," *The Commonweal, 63,* 24 (March 16, 1956).

Whitman, Robert F. "O'Neill's Search for a 'Language of the Theatre,' " *The Quarterly Journal of Speech, 46,* 2 (April 1960).

Williams, Raymond. *Modern Tragedy.* London: Chatto and Windus, 1966.

Wilson, J. Dover. *The Essential Shakespeare.* Cambridge: Cambridge University Press, 1935 (1932).

Winther, Sophus Keith. "*Desire Under the Elms*: A Modern Tragedy," *Modern Drama, 3,* 3 (Dec. 1960).

————. *Eugene O'Neill: A Critical Study.* 2d ed.; New York: Random House, 1961 (1934).

————. "O'Neill's Tragic Themes: *Long Day's Journey Into Night,*" *Arizona Quarterly, 13,* 4 (Winter (1957).

Wright, Robert C. "O'Neill's Universalizing Technique in *The Iceman Cometh,*" *Modern Drama, 8,* 1 (May 1965).

Yeats, William Butler. *Four Plays for Dancers.* New York: Macmillan, 1921.

Zeraffa, Michel. *O'Neill dramaturge.* Paris: L'Arche, Editeur, 1956.

ADDENDUM

Dorn, Knut. *Die Erlösungsthematik bei Eugene O'Neill: Eine Analyse der Strukturen im Spätwerk.* Heidelberg: Carl Winter, Universitätsverlag, 1968.

INDEX

Abbey Theatre (Dublin), 183
Abel, Lionel, 339n
Abortion, *44-45*, 47, 54f, 66, 71, 156, 219, 349
abstraction, 100, 148, 191
absurdism, 157, 305, 314, 344ff
Adamov, Arthur, 167
adaptation, 170ff, 225, 320
Adler, Alfred, 180
Adler, Jacob H., 244n
Aeschylus, 237
aestheticism, 149, 184, 193, 197n
aesthetics, 147, 277
Ahlgren, Stig, 190n
Ah, Wilderness!: compared with MS. plays, 61, 65n, 66, 72, 83, 240, *241-45*, 249, 267, 270, 350; scenic unit in the setting, 354, 357
Akins, Zoe, 212
Albee, Edward, 344
Alexander, Doris, 26; "Eugene O'Neill and Charles Lever," 324n; "Eugene O'Neill and *Light on the Path*," 133n; "The Missing Half of *Hughie*," 320n; "*Strange Interlude* and Schopenhauer," 156n, 221-22n; *The Tempering of Eugene O'Neill*, 26n, 33n
alienation, 49-50, 120, 304, 342
All God's Chillun Got Wings, 27n, 74n; and expressionism, 90, 99, 168, *174-82*, 205, 245, 313, 350; masks and monologues, 185, 193, 198, 211, 234; settings, 209, 308, 332-34, 356
ambiguity, 194. *See also* ambivalence
ambivalence: between fear and joy of life, 43f, 88, 259, 293-94; between love and hate, 34f, 40,

158, 181, 204ff, 208, 211, 215ff, 254, 268, 276, 285, 287-90, 297n, 309, 325, 328; in scenic units, 341
American drama and theatre, 31-34, 49, 67-70, 72ff, 76, 98-101, 130, 245
anarchism, 122, 265f, 269, 281n
Ancient Mariner, The, 17, 52, 168, *170-74*, 205, 350
Anderson, John, 189n, 200, 214n
Anderson, Maxwell, 41n
Anderson, Michael, 108n, 197n
Andreach, Robert J., 118n
'Anna Christie', 27n, 43, 82, *86-89*, 92, 126, 156, 211, 324, 337, 350
Anouilh, Jean, 314n, 348
anthropology, Cambridge school of, 136, 197n
Apollo, 146
apparition, *see* ghosts
appearance of characters, 53, 227-29, 327-28; with a conflict, 51-52, 89-90, 256, 265, 305, 319
Appia, Adolphe, 32, 345
Archipenko, Alexander, 176
Arden, John, 24
Aristotle, *Poetics*, 4, 8, 180n, 275, 283
assumptions in drama, 188-89, 200-201, 203, 211ff
Atkinson, Brooks, 162n, 236n, 242n, 325n, 329n; *Broadway Scrapbook*, 189n
Atrocity, 57n
autobiography, *see* O'Neill, Eugene
automaton effect: in early plays, 42, 54, 90; in experimental plays, 104, 121, 145, 171f, 230,

237; in late plays, 262, 294-95, 311, 323, 342-43

Babbitt, George W., 192, 195-96
backdrop, 186, 356
Baker, George Pierce, 30
Beckett, Samuel, 24, 58, 157, 180n, 266n, 269n, 314n, 321
Before Breakfast, 50, 53, 62, 72, 79, 211, 326, 349
"behind life," 132, 176, 331, 333
Belasco, David, 32, 142, 313
Bellows, George, 61
"belonging," 69, 120ff, 125, 197, 220, 234n, 298, 325, 338
Belshazzar, 57n
Benavente, Jacinto, 183n
Bentley, Eric, 250n; *The Dramatic Event*, 34n, 309n; *The Playwright as Thinker*, 154n; "Trying to Like O'Neill," 260n, 268n, 271n
betrayal, theme of, 156-57, 163, 261, 265, 282n, 271n
Beyond the Horizon, 42n, 63, 73-81, 82, 84, 156, 169, 313, 349; setting, 134, 153, 163, 332, 336, 356
Biese, Y. M., *Aspects of Expression I*, 5n, 39n, 107n-108n, 208n, 213n, 217n, 222n
Blackburn, Clara, 99n, 114n, 115n, 118n, 121n, 122n, 142n, 163n, 189n, 200n, 205n
Bogard, Travis, 88n, 234n
Boulton, Agnes, 40n, 64n, 65
Bound East for Cardiff, 43-44, 45-49, 50, 54f, 90, 126, 318, 349; monologues in, 78-79, 211f; setting, 115, 332
Bowen, Croswell, 26n, 300n
Bradley, A. C., 6
Braem, Helmut M., *Eugene O'Neill*, 33n, 79n, 116n, 173n, 201n, 215n, 229n, 231n, 233n, 258n, 281n, 298n, 312n, 317n, 323n, 339n
Bread and Butter, 57-63, 64n, 65, 72, 74, 78, 91n, 100, 156, 210, 241, 349; compared with *The*

Great God Brown, 185, 192n; setting, 332, 351, 356
Brecht, Bertolt, 8, 24, 161, 192, 270, 291n, 344, 348; *Dreigroschenoper*, 161; *Herr Puntila und sein Knecht Matti*, 280
Brie, Friedrich, 225n
Broussard, Louis, 98-101, 199
Brown, John Mason, 138, 236n
Brown, John Russell (and Harris, Bernard, eds.), *American Theatre*, 215n, 318n
Brugger, Ilse, 180, 183, 184n
Brustein, Robert, *The Theatre of Revolt*, in notes: 33, 99, 123, 132, 145, 156, 196, 199, 210, 221, 233, 244f, 250, 266, 268, 271, 280, 283, 287, 291, 294, 295, 297, 299, 301, 342
Bryant, Louise, 65n
Buddha, 137f, 202
Byron, George Gordon, 322

Camus, Albert, 269n
Čapek, Karel, 99, 118
Cargill, Oscar (and Fagin, N. Bryllion; Fisher, William J., eds.), *O'Neill and His Plays*, 29, 36, 349f; in notes: 3, 7, 15, 22, 32, 41, 46, 47, 49, 73, 86, 89, 100, 108, 113, 125, 126, 132, 136, 138, 143, 155, 160, 165, 174, 180, 181, 182, 198, 199, 200, 206, 210, 212, 228, 236, 244, 259, 260, 268, 270, 271, 279, 282, 314, 317, 320
Carlin, Terry, 88
Carpenter, Frederic I., *Eugene O'Neill*, in notes: 78, 86, 107, 135, 137, 144, 147, 177, 180, 191, 209, 218, 244, 260, 268, 286, 287, 295, 299, 311, 313, 322, 340
catharsis, *see* katharsis
centrifugal plays, 129, 147-48, 333
Chabrowe, Leonard, 273n, 281n
Chambers, Sir E. K., 5
Chaplin, Charles, 118
Chapman, John, 298n
characterization: in early plays,

Day, Cyrus, 33n, 146, 281n-82n
Days Without End, 194, 197, *199-205*, 207n, 209, 212f, 230, 241, 249, 255, 270, 313, 350; masks, 168, 179, 240, 245; setting, 336, 353
Dear Doctor, The, 57n
delusion: in early plays, 55, 90; in *The Emperor Jones*, 104; in *The Iceman Cometh*, 35, 266-68, 272, 275, 280-83, 328; in *Long Day's Journey*, 287, 293; in *Hughie*, 319; influence on other people, 281-83, 322-23
DeMille, Cecil B., 145n
Desire Under the Elms: 51, *151-62*, 181, 211, 225, 245, 306, 337, 350; setting, 49, 76, 164, 166, 232, 235, 240, 254, 308, 334f; Greek elements, 149, 192, 196
determinism, 75ff, 177
dialect, *see* slang
dialectics, 147
dialogue: as a scenic means of expression, 11, 331, 347; in early plays, 42f, 53-54, 69, 72, 78-80; development in O'Neill, 79-80, 336-40; in expressionism, 110, 115-17, 122; in *Strange Interlude*, 217; inner movement in, 257, 278-79, 300-301, 304, 309-11, 318, 335, 341
Dietrich, Margret, *Das moderne Drama*, 33n, 159n, 183n, 188n, 192n, 239n, 284n, 312n, 345n
Diff'rent, 34, 53n, *89-92*, 107, 156, 169, 211, 350; and realism, 75, 111, 163, 332
Dionysus, 145, 187, 191, 194ff, 202; Dionysian, 146, 158, 234n, 337
Dorn, Knut, 26n, 61n, 279n, 282n, 288n, 314n
Dostoevski, Fedor, 86, 340n
Downer, Alan S., 31, 69, 75, 160n, 228; *American Drama and Its Critics* (ed.), 162n, 174n, 185n, 210n; *Fifty Years*

of American Drama, 31n, 75n; "The Revolt from Broadway," 31n, 33n, 34n, 70n, 94n
"Dramatist's Notebook, A," 143
Dreamy Kid, The, 52, 54f, 63, 66, 72, 151, 187, 349
Driscoll, 100, 148
Driver, Tom F., 273n, 277n
"duality of the theatre," 126-27
Dumas, Alexandre (*fils*), 86; *The Count of Monte Cristo*, 33n, 47n, 93n, 132, 164n, 184n, 229n, 260
Dürrenmatt, Friedrich, 24, 180n, 314n, 344, 348; *The Visit*, 276
Dusenbury, Winifred, 124n
dynamic realism, *see* realism
dynamics, 332, 344; in *The Emperor Jones*, 107; in *The Iceman Cometh*, 269, 275; in *Long Day's Journey*, 285ff, 288-90; in *A Touch of the Poet*, 327
Dynamo, *162-67*, 190, 199, 222-23, 238, 240, 341, 344n, 350, 356

Earth Mother, 187, 196, 202
Eaton, Walter Prichard, 98n, 113n, 125n, 126n
Eberle, Oskar, 5
Edschmid, Kasimir, 163n
Eliot, T. S., 161, 181, 238n, 276, 344n
Ellis-Fermor, Una, 6; *The Jacobean Drama*, 6n; *Shakespeare the Dramatist*, 6n, 15n; *Some Recent Research in Shakespeare's Imagery*, 6n, 308n
Emperor Jones, The, 27n, 42, *97-112*, 148, 169, 182, 211, 274, 287n, 338f, 350; and expressionism, 12, 75, 92, 129, 159; sound effects, 44, 47, 71, 219; compared with *The Dreamy Kid*, 52, 151, 187; apparitions, 52, 188, 198; setting, 83f, 115, 134, 233n, 332; compared with *The Hairy Ape*, 113f, 119, 124ff, 127-28, 245